MW00637300

AGENTS OF EMPIRE

Agents of Empire

The First Oregon Cavalry and the
Opening of the Interior Pacific
Northwest during the Civil War

JAMES ROBBINS JEWELL

University of Nebraska Press

LINCOLN

The University of Nebraska Press is part of a land-grant institution with campuses and programs on the past, present, and future homelands of the Pawnee, Ponca, Otoe-Missouria, Omaha, Dakota, Lakota, Kaw, Cheyenne, and Arapaho Peoples, as well as those of the relocated Ho-Chunk, Sac and Fox, and Iowa Peoples.

Library of Congress Cataloging-in-Publication Data

Names: Jewell, James Robbins, author.
Title: Agents of empire: the First Oregon Cavalry and the opening of the interior Pacific Northwest during the Civil War / James Robbins Jewell.
Other titles: First Oregon Cavalry and the opening of the interior Pacific Northwest during the Civil War
Description: Lincoln: University of Nebraska Press, 2023.
Includes bibliographical references and index.
Identifiers: LCCN 2022043610
ISBN 9781496233035 (hardback)
ISBN 9781496236401 (epub)
ISBN 9781496236418 (pdf)
Subjects: LCSH: United States. Army. Oregon Cavalry Regiment, 1st (1861–1866)—History. | Northwest, Pacific—History, Military—19th century. | Indians of North America—Wars—Northwest, Pacific. | United States—History—Civil War, 1861–1865—Cavalry operations. | United States—History—Civil War, 1861–1865—Regimental histories. | Frontier and pioneer life—Northwest, Pacific. | BISAC: HISTORY / United States / Civil War Period (1850–1877) | HISTORY / United States / State & Local / Pacific Northwest (OR, WA)
Classification: LCC E526.6 1st .J49 2023 | DDC 973.7/495—dc23/eng/20220923
LC record available at https://lccn.loc.gov/2022043610

Set in Minion Pro by Scribe Inc.

For my parents,
the late (Charles) Lee
and
Susan E. (Robbins) Jewell,
who instilled in me the family tradition
of a love of history and encouraged
an endless curiosity

CONTENTS

ILLUSTRATIONS

Photographs

Figures

Maps

ACKNOWLEDGMENTS

My association with the First Oregon Volunteer Cavalry Regiment began more than twenty years ago as a doctoral student at West Virginia University. Since that first seminar paper on the Union military's command in the Far West, I have written a dissertation, several articles, and one previous book in part or entirely focused on the Oregon Cavalry. As I bring that active association nearly to an end, I will do my best to acknowledge those who have assisted me on this specific project over the past four years. Should I unintentionally omit someone, I apologize.

Like every historian, I owe a tremendous debt to the interlibrary loan magicians who procured obscure works from skeptical staffs at other libraries. For the past four years, it has been a great boon to me that my friend Patty Torok-Pierce has handled that job at North Idaho College (NIC). I thank her most sincerely, not just for all the work she did to track down hard-to-find sources, but for the many conversations we had on history, education, and life. I am happy for you, but I will enjoy my trips to the library much less now that you are retiring.

Though I finished most of my work at the Oregon Historical Society (OHS) when working on my previous book, there were still a few collections I needed to investigate for this book. Unfortunately, a remodeling project at the OHS and then COVID-19 closed the doors to the public. Luckily, Scott Daniels in the Research Library scanned many letters and one entire diary for me, thereby allowing me to overcome the COVID-19 obstacle. For that extra effort,

I thank him specifically and the OHS in general, both of which continue to impress me.

While Patty and Scott provided tremendous research assistance, two others made the final product infinitely better than the original draft. All errors are my own and were included despite the incredible assistance of Chris Rein and Larry Briggs. Chris, who read the original draft twice, once at my request and once at the request of the press, gave much-needed encouragement and macro-level suggestions. I needed the former to keep going and took a new look because of the latter. Thank you for both. Dr. Larry Briggs, a somewhat lapsed historian and my former dean, employed his considerable wordsmithing talents to great effect. The finished work is exponentially better because of the micro-level attention he gave each of the chapters he read. To say thank you to Chris and Larry seems a terribly insufficient expression of my appreciation.

If Chris and Larry made the book better through their valuable and helpful suggestions and critiques, three others made it better by keeping me sane. Both of our sons continue to remind their mother and me what really matters in life. Though busy with his own collegiate pursuits, Jacob continues to be immensely enjoyable, if just a little too certain of his knowledge about everything, including fantasy football. Cullen has become my alpine hiking partner. As such, he spent many summer and early fall days hiking with me to the mountain lakes in northeast Washington, the Idaho panhandle, and western Montana. His eagerness to try anything is inspiring even when we "go somewhere we might stumble and have an accident."

Of course, none of us would stay on track if it were not for my wife, Elizabeth. She has endured more random comments about the Oregon Cavalry as I work through ideas out loud than she could have imagined when she signed on for this crazy journey over thirty years ago. She has always encouraged my various historical pursuits, regardless of how odd they seem, and has not complained about the slow consumption of the lower floor of the house by my library. For all that she does, as well as for what she endures, I thank her and am amazed by her patience and tolerance.

Lastly, I must thank two groups of people who made this work much easier to see through to successful publication. First, I owe a debt of gratitude to my colleagues on the sabbatical selection committee at North Idaho College, who selected my proposal for a sabbatical for fall semester 2020. I would also like to thank all those who wrote letters of support, Dean Larry Briggs (NIC, retired); Dr. Brad Codr (NIC), my friend and co-chair of the Social and Behavioral Sciences Division; Drs. Adam Arenson (Manhattan College) and Andy Graybill (Southern Methodist University), who years ago, as co-editors, selected my submission to lead off an essay collection written by amazingly talented historians; and Dr. Eugene Van Sickle (University of North Georgia), my brother from the other side of the country and my co-editor of a recent article as well as the next book project. Lastly, I thank Dr. Lita Burns, vice president of instruction at NIC (retired), for approving my sabbatical and the NIC Board of Trustees for confirming it. Before I wrap this up, I also need to thank Dan Dolezal, proprietor of Camera Corral in Coeur d'Alene, for working his magic at the eleventh hour on some of the images included in this work. Finally, I wish to thank Clark Whitehorn at Bison Press and Brianna Blackburn and the team at Scribe. At a critical moment, Clark expressed enthusiasm for this project and has since guided me (not always an easy task—I really do read the emails, Clark) through the process with more patience than I probably earned. He and the team at Bison / University of Nebraska Press have been incredibly supportive, for which I am very thankful. Though it was at times a humbling experience, the work done by Brianna and the team at Scribe is greatly appreciated.

One final thought: I wish my dad was still here to spend a summer traveling into the regions ridden through by the Oregon Cavalry. It was the sort of thing that he was still ready to do into his late seventies. I would have enjoyed one more season wandering around the wilderness with him, when he always taught me something new.

Sitting here on my back deck and thinking about the next topic to investigate, I realize some things that I could not have anticipated in life became like oxygen, for better and worse.

INTRODUCTION

John Drake did not like this change in plans at all. He felt it was a mistake, "the very worst thing that could have been done," even. The idea itself was not entirely new. When he led his roughly 150 troopers out of Fort Dalles three weeks earlier, on April 20, 1864, he knew he would never find it "advisable," as the district commander Brig. Gen. Benjamin Alvord had weakly suggested "at some juncture for your command and Captain Currey's to unite." Drake instead focused on the portion of the orders that informed him, "The selection of the route of travel and site of your wagon depot, is left entirely to your judgment."[1] Alvord soon realized that merely suggesting a merger of the two large expeditions would never suffice. So on May 6 he ordered both Capts. George B. Currey and Drake to join their commands somewhere near Harney Lake in southeastern Oregon.[2] Drake's feared loss of independence had been realized.

On May 11, the day after receiving that unwanted order, Drake began moving toward the lake, venting his frustration into his journal: "Why could the Gen. not have left each free to govern himself. . . . What a blunder?"[3] Drake, who possessed a keen mind for frontier service, was right to question the wisdom of concentrating the two large commands. His sentiments also reflected an acute desire to lead his own expedition, with full responsibility for the decisions he made—and the successes his actions might bring. Drake knew that as a senior captain, Currey would assume command during their joint operations and therefore get the largest share of any credit their operations might garner. Of course, should they fail, criticism would fall hardest on Currey's shoulders.

Capt. George B. Currey, the most experienced of the First Oregon Volunteer Cavalry Regiment's officers, never recorded his thoughts on Gen. Benjamin Alvord's changes. Even if he had, it is doubtful he would have been as critical as Drake. Alvord made his trust in Currey clear when he issued him broad orders for the next six months that sounded very similar to those given to Captain Drake. There was one important exception: if Drake and Currey's commands ever met, Alvord told Currey, "You must of course command."[4] John Drake was educated, with a sharp, often biting wit, whereas Currey, who was also educated, was pragmatic and no nonsense. They both craved action—or in Currey's case, more of it. By the third year of their service, both understood they would never be sent east to fight in the great battles of the Civil War and instead would battle the Indians that whites simply called Snakes (an appellation that included Northern Paiutes, Bannocks, and Northern Shoshones). Rather than worry about the wisdom of Alvord's changes, Currey saw the 1864 campaign in simple terms. The "Snake Indians being [his] objective point," he determined to find and engage the Northern Paiutes of eastern Oregon.[5] He did not care if he led the two-plus companies of his own expedition or one combined with Drake's force; the goal was the same. Despite chaffing at the idea of losing his independence, Drake, who harbored no ill will toward Currey, agreed with his colleague about the objective of their operations.

Their joint operations lasted only a month, after which Drake and Currey resumed their separate expeditions in August. By the end of the campaigning season, both had failed to bring on the defining clash with the Paiute raiders they sought. The third prong of the 1864 campaign, commanded by Lt. Col. Charles Drew, also failed in its primary objective. That does not, however, mean that the 1864 summer campaigns had been entirely unsuccessful. Each explored over a thousand miles of largely frontier lands, recording what they saw in official reports and, in Drew's case, publishing it in a local newspaper. At the same time, the

troopers wrote dozens of anonymous letters for regional newspapers, describing the suitability of those lands for white development. Furthermore, Drew's column protected white travelers
who wedded themselves to his command for protection as his column rode to Fort Boise.

This was their war; making the District of Oregon safe for white
migration and exploring the district's eastern frontier regions was
how the First Oregon Volunteer Cavalry Regiment contributed to
the Union cause during the Civil War. Unlike service in the East,
where cavalry regiments generally functioned as part of mounted
brigades and even divisions, that was not possible for the Oregon
Cavalry; no other mounted forces were stationed in the entire District of Oregon during the war. There would be no national coverage of romanticized raids as there was for Confederates like Jeb
Stuart or Union leaders like Benjamin Grierson. Serving in the
Pacific Northwest was different than service elsewhere during
the Civil War. Structurally, the Oregon Cavalry functioned much
more like the antebellum forces stationed in the West. The regiment
never concentrated in one place. Like the prewar army forces on
the western frontier, the Oregon Cavalry's companies were split up
and stationed throughout a vast district at forts and camps from
north-central Oregon and southeastern Washington Territory down
to southern Idaho Territory. Such a distribution meant the company was the most important administrative and tactical level of
command. Therefore, the story of the Oregon Cavalry's contribution to the Union cause must be told primarily from the perspective of its company-level officers and the cavalrymen in the ranks.

The Oregon Cavalry never reached the agreed-upon minimum
strength of ten full companies—by comparison, the First California Cavalry Regiment had thirteen companies, the second had
twelve. It was, however, allowed to claim regimental status with
just six companies—the seventh was recruited in 1863. With those
commands spread throughout the district, junior officers had an
unusual level of autonomy. Therefore, it is through their thoughts,
decisions, and actions that the history of the regiment unfolds. The
most important of those men were the ones who did not just serve

the longest but were most active during the regiment's life span. While most company officers joined during the initial recruiting period in late 1861 or early 1862, two men stand out above the others, Captains Currey and Drake. Both were there at the regiment's organization, and both led their companies on weeks or, more often, monthslong expeditions across thousands of miles of mostly underexplored lands between 1862 and 1864. In recognition of their abilities, the two were transferred out of the First Oregon Volunteer Cavalry Regiment and assigned to serve as regimental officers in command of the new First Oregon Volunteer Infantry Regiment at the end of 1864. Most of the time, Currey and Drake operated independently, leading not just their own companies but sometimes others' as well, which was the case in 1864. They exercised more independence and made more command decisions than many cavalry brigade commanders fighting the Confederacy.

As important as Currey and Drake are to properly understand the service of the Oregon Cavalry, they did not serve alone. Ten others also served as company commanders at some time during the regiment's service. Similarly, a number of subalterns played important roles in the regiment between 1861 and 1866. Capts. William Kelly, Richard S. Caldwell, and William V. Rinehart were among the former, while Lts. James Waymire, William Hand, John F. Noble, and John T. Apperson represent the latter group. The reality was that District of Oregon commanders, especially Brig. Gen. Benjamin Alvord, who held that post from July 1862 to March 1865, crafted the operational goals and general strategy prior to the start of each campaigning season. Then the two men who served as regimental commanders of the Oregon Cavalry sometimes led, but more often ordered, their subordinates into the field to achieve the goals. Finally, it was the company-level officers and the troopers who put the plans into action in the field, riding all over Oregon as well as parts of Idaho Territory, even into Nevada, sometimes through mountain snow and at other times across parched and desolate scrublands under the inescapable sun.

Like soldiers throughout history, military service forged a close camaraderie among the Oregon cavalrymen. Surviving information,

including correspondence and diaries, indicates this was particularly true for junior officers, even though some of them interacted
only intermittently with each other. Despite Oregon's small population, it appears only a few of them knew each other prior to their
service. Thus, the friendships formed during the war originated
through their shared experiences and hardships and, it must be
said of many, their shared desire to eliminate what they saw as
the Indian obstacle to development and opportunity—theirs and
other whites'.

During the early years of their service, a number of the junior
officers had something else in common. Several became smit-
ten with the Gaines sisters, Amanda (twenty-one) and Jennie
(eighteen), who arrived in Oregon with their family in 1845. The
Gaines family lived in Oregon City in early 1862, where some of
the recruiting took place. During those dreary winter and early
spring months, the sisters first met some of the junior officers.
Two years later, when the sisters married William V. Rinehart
(October 1864) and George B. Currey (December 1864), respectively, it does not seem to have caused any rifts among the cadre
of their cavalry suitors.[6] Through their wives, Currey and Rinehart remained connected. John Drake, who rarely spared anyone
from his sharp criticisms, enjoyed the company of Lts. William
Hand and James Waymire. Lt. John Apperson, more than anyone
else, bound the officer corps together during the war, even more
so than the Gaines sisters. The scattered collections of Apperson's
letters at repositories around the Pacific Northwest show that he
maintained frequent and friendly correspondence with many of
his fellow officers. Apperson, John M. McCall, Rinehart, Waymire,
and others shared gossip about their friends and poked fun at their
efforts to win Amanda's and Jennie's affection. He even served as
his friend William V. Rinehart's proxy while Rinehart was in the
field in 1864, attesting to his friend's character, as Rinehart tried
to win the hand of Amanda Gaines, the younger of the two popular sisters, via their correspondence.[7]

The Oregon cavalrymen were not the only ones whose decisions
and actions influenced the regiment's experience. Whites eager
to open eastern Oregon for development worried most about the

omnipresent Snake Indians. They generally felt they were the most dangerous and hostile Indians living within the military's District of Oregon. Currey, using descriptors common among whites, felt those particular Indians were "formidable as assassins and troublesome as thieves."[8] The Snake Indians were a white creation; there was no such tribe. Both civilians and the military applied the term rather indiscriminately. In 1863 the Oregon superintendent of Indian Affairs expressed his rather broad view that the "various bands of Snakes" were composed of "Klamaths, Modocs, Shoshones, Bannocks, Winnas, and probably other tribes," which numbered four to five thousand.[9] More commonly, whites applied the term to bands from three tribes: Northern Paiutes, Bannocks, and Northern Shoshones. The combined ancestral homelands of those three tribes, each broken down into many bands, covered most of central and eastern Oregon, down into Nevada and California (Northern Paiutes), southwestern Idaho (Bannocks and Shoshones), and across to the area near Fort Hall (mostly Shoshones but some Bannocks).

Following the 1878 Bannock "War," the few remaining Bannock people, whose name is Panati, moved onto the Fort Hall Indian Reservation in southeastern Idaho. Today, they have mostly been incorporated with the Northern Shoshone people into the federally recognized Shoshone–Bannocks, living on the Fort Hall Reservation. However, they were originally members of the Northern Paiute tribe. Living in south-central and southeastern Idaho, in close proximity to the Northern Shoshones, led to the Shoshonean influence. Like many of the Shoshone bands, the Bannocks shared some traits with the Great Plains people due to their acquisition of horses. By 1861 there were few Bannocks left; victims of disease and white encroachment onto their lands and the devastation to plants, such as the foundational food camas wrought by the white migrants' livestock, it is estimated they numbered between five hundred and six hundred. Fighting for their existence, the mobile bands attacked both emigrant trains and miners entering their homelands. When the Oregon Cavalry rode from Fort Walla Walla to the outskirts of Fort Hall in 1863, their primary objective was protecting those emigrant trains from both the Bannocks and Shoshones. Lt. Col. Reuben Maury did not distinguish between the two tribes, simply calling them all Snakes during his operations that extended to southeastern Idaho Territory. As much as the Bannocks had aggressively attacked the growing number of whites entering their lands, they factored very little into Oregon Cavalry activities after 1863.[10] This was the result of the cavalry contracting its operational areas.

There were four large divisions of Shoshonean people (Eastern, Western, Northern, and Southern), whose lands stretched from Idaho south into Utah and east to the western edge of Wyoming. As the Northern Shoshones lived primarily within the boundaries of the military District of Oregon, they were the focus of the Oregon Cavalry's 1863 operations. Whites recognized four subgroups of the Northern Shoshone people: Western, Mountain, Northwestern, and Pohogwe. During its 1863 operations, the Oregon Cavalry either encountered or anticipated contacting Western, Northwestern, and possibly Pohogwe bands. Boise and Bruneau groups of the Western band lived in the Boise basin, while bands of Pohogwes lived on the extreme eastern fringe of the cavalry's 1863 operational area, around Fort Hall. After California volunteers massacred between two hundred and three hundred Northwestern Shoshones at Bear River in Idaho on January 29, 1863, bands in Utah and southern Idaho signed a series of treaties. By then, the Oregon Cavalry had contracted its area of operations so that Fort Boise was at the eastern edge of its responsibility. From that point on they had less interaction with Shoshone groups for the remainder of the regiment's existence. Though some bands had attacked the steadily increasing numbers of white migrants over the years, the attacks, as one official noted, were due to "the scarcity of game in these Territories, and the occupation of the most fertile portions thereof by our settlements, have reduced these Indians to a state of extreme destitution," which had "literally compelled [them] to resort to plunder in order to obtain the necessities of life."[11] While the Shoshones and Bannocks were spared some white hostility, whites showed no sense of understanding about the precarious existence facing the other group they called Snakes, the Northern Paiutes.

While the Bannocks and Northern Shoshones had long been referred to as Snakes by whites, the Oregon Cavalry used the name more often on Northern Paiutes. There were over twenty bands of Northern Paiutes living in Oregon east of the Cascade Range. Their lands stretched from the headwaters of the John Day River, south across the Nevada border, and east to the southwestern corner of Idaho Territory. The bands were often named after their primary food source, such as Koaagaitokas (salmon eaters) and Moakoka-dos (wild onion eaters).[12] Among those bands were the Wadateka'a (or Wada-Tika), the seed eaters, who lived in southeastern Oregon between Harney and Malheur Lakes, a region they called Heweh Ma Be Neen.[13] The Walpapi lived to the north of the Wadateka'a in the region that stretched from the Crooked River valley to the headwaters of the John Day River. This band had a number of violent encounters with the Oregon Cavalry during the war years. They were led by Panaina, the most despised and feared Indian leader in the District of Oregon; whites called him Chief Paulina or sometimes Polini.[14] The Tagotokas band of Northern Paiutes lived along the southeastern Oregon–southwestern Idaho Territory border.[15] Many, but not all, Northern Paiute bands raided emigrant trains and stole livestock from ranchers and express depots before and during the war years. Attacks were often motivated by starvation as much as a hopeless effort to defend their lands from encroachment. The most aggressive were the Walpapi, who were blamed for attacks on travelers and miners along Canyon City Road and near the Owyhee mines.

Even though the three tribes that whites called Snakes greatly influenced the experience and history of the First Oregon Volunteer Cavalry Regiment, Chief Paulina was the most important individual Indian person in the regiment's history. His prominence even exceeded the regiment's first commander, Col. Thomas R. Cornelius, a well-known Oregon pioneer. Chief Paulina frightened eastern Oregon civilians in the dark corners of their stereotyping imaginations. The Oregon troops' failure to force a confrontation with his band exacerbated their sense of frustration. The press, which gave his band credit for more attacks against white miners, farmers, and travelers in eastern Oregon than any other single Paiute leader, enhanced the legend of the Northern Paiute leader. Scared settlers put pressure on politicians, who in turn pressed for a military solution, creating the Oregon Cavalry's archnemesis as a result. Lacking any Confederates against which to demonstrate their patriotism, the Paiute leader became the military district's Robert E. Lee, without the respect Lee engendered among his enemies. As such, Chief Paulina is a key figure in the history of the First Oregon Volunteer Cavalry Regiment. In truth, though denigrated by whites, he achieved more permanent (if largely mysterious) recognition than any of the Oregon cavalrymen who pursued him during the mid-1860s.[16] Today, his name is attached to several geographic locations and waterways.

The land and the climate influenced the experiences and the work done by the Oregon Cavalry just as much as the Indian people with whom they came in contact. This was clear early on when in 1862, the heaviest rains and snowfall in a generation limited recruiting.[17] Each year, weather dictated when the various companies began their operations (midspring) and when those operations ended (midfall). Just as weather influenced the Oregon Cavalry's activity, the terrain presented another challenge.

While the Oregon Cavalry companies did not cross over the summits of the ten-thousand-foot peaks, they did traverse through some narrow mountain passes that exceeded five thousand feet. Doing so left an impression on the Oregon troopers, some of whom wrote about enduring blizzards as early as the start of September and as late as mid-June. They lost riding days to such storms. Days were also lost to the heat. During the summer months, the high plains desert sun was inescapable and dangerous for the men and their mounts—one trooper recorded a temperature of 108 degrees during a summer campaign.[18] Some animals fell to their deaths from steep mountain trails, while others had to be abandoned because they gave out under the broiling sun. As much as Chief Paulina and his Walpapi band frustrated the

Oregon cavalrymen, they had even less control over the weather or the environment.

Efforts to kill Chief Paulina and brutally subdue the Paiutes so whites could colonize their lands captured the public's attention. However, that was just one aspect of how the Oregon Cavalry helped open the Oregon interior to white development while serving the Union cause. Despite appearances, the regiment was initially raised to address fears about the presence of Southern sympathizers among the state's small populace and not to protect whites against what the politicians described as menacing and violent Indians. The Oregon cavalrymen were also deployed to deter any Southern sympathizers from aiding the Confederacy from afar, including attempts to revive the old Pacific Republic scheme or to initiate paramilitary operations. When supposed Southern sympathizers murdered California volunteers and attempted to steal a ship to attack gold shipments out of San Francisco Bay, those concerns gained legitimacy. At the same time, state and federal officials recognized that the Oregon troopers could be used for other purposes on the frontier, starting with providing protection for several years of inbound emigrants. Through exploring, mapping, and assessing the suitability of the lands they traversed for farming and mining possibilities, the Oregon Cavalry provided its most enduring contribution to the development of the interior Pacific Northwest.[19]

By putting the experiences of individual troopers and particularly the decision-making junior officers within the context of the responsibilities placed upon the entire regiment, how they simultaneously contributed to the Union cause and helped open eastern Oregon and western Idaho becomes clear. To achieve that goal, this study is divided into nine chapters. The first chapter reviews the divisions in Oregon Territory, and later the state, over the question of slavery. The contentious 1860 presidential election, in which no candidate won a majority of the Oregon votes, revealed deep divisions among the state's population. A year later those divisions, some governmental officials feared, might be exploited by Southern sympathizers to aid the Confederate cause. That concern was just one of the many threatening the people and military in the District of Oregon as the government withdrew Regular Army commands for service elsewhere. The challenges of recruiting a regiment more than a thousand miles from the seat of war are covered in chapter 2. In chapter 3 the volunteers' demographic and background information is reviewed. The next five chapters cover the Oregon Cavalry's service in the field: 1862 (chapter 4); 1863 (chapter 5), its first full year of service; 1864 (chapters 6 and 7), the last year that all seven companies remained; and finally, the last year and a half of the regiment's service (chapter 8), when few Oregon troopers remained in the ranks due to the expiration of most of their enlistments. Chapter 9 assesses the regiment's service and follows the troopers for the rest of their lives, watching as they contributed to their communities wherever they lived after the war, from the Pacific Northwest to the Deep South.

Almost no studies of the Civil War mention the First Oregon Volunteer Cavalry Regiment, not surprisingly focusing on the units that served from Missouri eastward. Though recruited during the war by the same Union government confronting Confederate forces like the Army of Northern Virginia, the Oregon Cavalry never left the Pacific Northwest and never encountered a Southern enemy. Instead, it acted as a powerful instrument of the federal government's effort to accelerate white expansion into and the economic development of eastern Oregon and the new territory of Idaho. It did so at the expense of the Indian tribes living within its operational area. Historically speaking, the Civil War era in the Pacific Northwest, until being addressed by recent regional studies, has been a historical void. This study seeks to examine the intersection of Civil War, Pacific Northwest, and westward migration history by assessing the important role the First Oregon Volunteer Cavalry Regiment played in opening the Pacific Northwest interior during the Civil War.

A final note about identifying Native peoples and groups: throughout this work, every effort has been made to properly identify the many Indians who shared much of the Oregon Cavalry's experiences. This has been challenging because whites, including the military, rarely attempted to identify the Indian people they encountered in the region, and when they did, they were rarely very specific. The military only made genuine efforts to identify Indian groups during treaty negotiations, when it identified the participants by tribal name and sometimes by band name (particularly noted during negotiations with the Nez Perce people). They almost never identified the small groups they attacked without provocation, or which attacked them. Almost all Indians who engaged the Oregon troopers in prolonged firefights were simply called Snakes, especially if the cavalrymen suffered any casualties, because whites took it as a point of fact that the so-called Snakes were violent and a threat. When writing about the military's perspective, and if unable to confidently identify a tribe, I have used the military's term. Given the difficult challenges of being certain with limited information, I have most often not hypothesized about which band but have used the tribal names as the identifier. This is an imperfect approach that does not always give the Indian people the full identity they deserve, but it is the best method I have found to avoid speculation and the potential resulting misidentification.

AGENTS OF EMPIRE

ONE

Divisions and Dangers

Oregon would never become a slave state because, according to conventional wisdom, its geography and climate were not conducive to the expansion of slavery. In 1859 it joined the Union as a free state. A year later Abraham Lincoln won the state presidential election. Oregon, from a distant view, therefore, appeared to be a solidly Union state as the secession crisis exploded in 1860 and 1861. The region also appeared to have seen the last of the conflicts between whites and the regional Indian tribes. Oregon and the Pacific Northwest did not expect to require a great deal of federal attention as internal strife gripped the nation. That view quickly proved false. Soon federal officials began to worry that forces within Oregon might push for secession. At the same time, increasing white emigration into eastern Oregon and that part of Washington Territory that soon became Idaho Territory created a flashpoint for a return of conflicts with Native people living there. The combined threat of secessionist activity and a resumption of white–Indian conflict led to the decision to recruit a volunteer cavalry regiment to serve in the Pacific Northwest in late 1861.

The role slavery played in the struggle over Oregon's identity during the statehood debate presaged the battles that divided the state's electorate during the 1860 election, and both of those political battles caused deep concerns about the region as secession gripped the nation. Even though Oregon joined the Union as a

free state in February 1859, the proslavery element was well organized and influential. After the state constitutional convention
finished its work, it put the document before the voters. The vote
was not simply whether to approve the proposed constitution but
whether the state would allow slavery, or even free African Americans within its borders, as part of that constitution. The vote in
favor of the constitution and the prohibition of slavery won support by wide margins; however, the vote stating "No free Negro,
or Mulatto, not residing in this state at the time of the adoption of
this constitution, shall come, reside, or be within this state" won
by an eight to one margin, the widest of the three votes.[1] This was
not surprising, since the small population of whites who voted on
Oregon Territory's original Organic laws in 1843 chose to prohibit
slavery in the territory. That rule was amended the following year,
allowing slave owners up to three years to divest themselves of their
slaves. That amendment, pushed through by the head of the territorial council, former slave owner Peter Burnett, also gave freed
slaves or "any free negro or mulatto" a timeline to leave the territory (two years for men and three for women). If they refused to
leave they were to be publicly whipped until they agreed to leave.[2]
African Americans, whether free or enslaved, posed a potential
economic challenge, or so believed white Oregonians.

The Oregonian opposition to slavery and freedmen was influenced by the perception of potential economic competition and
racial bias. Joseph Lane, then Oregon's territorial delegate in the
U.S. House of Representatives, penned an editorial, calling all
who opposed the exclusion clause "negro worshipers."[3] John R.
McBride, a Missouri-born member of the constitutional convention, explained why Oregonians voted against slavery and for exclusion: "It was clear that while the new state had no relish for the
'peculiar institution' it had equally no desire to furnish a refuge
for the colored man in any condition." Furthermore, he believed
the message was that "the mingling of the races in any form in this
state was objectionable, and the vote was an emphatic expression
of public sentiment."[4]

The divisions reflected in the three votes and the subsequent
establishment of a government made up almost entirely of

Southerners continued during the 1860 election cycle. Avowed slavery supporters held all the major political posts, including Oregon's entire federal congressional delegation. Senators Joseph Lane and Delazon Smith, Representative Lansing Stout, and top state political leaders like Gov. John Whiteaker and Oregon's Speaker of the House, William G. T'Vault, were vocal supporters of slavery. Tennessee-born and -raised Judge Paine P. Prim, an original member of the state supreme court, had argued against allowing free African Americans (as well as Chinese immigrants) into the state during the constitutional convention.[5] These leaders wielded significant influence during the 1860 presidential election.

Oregon's proslavery politicians gave the Southern Democratic candidate, John C. Breckinridge, reason to be hopeful during the 1860 campaign. Having Oregon senator Joseph Lane on the ticked bolstered his chances of taking one of the two far western states. However, Abraham Lincoln had prominent supporters in the state as well. A number of influential Lincoln friends from Illinois—including Dr. Anson Henry, David Logan, Edward Baker, and the Francis brothers (Simeon and Allen)—had moved to Oregon in the 1850s. Henry and Logan engaged in local-level politics, while Baker was eventually appointed one of Oregon's U.S. senators. All three used their positions to actively promote Lincoln's candidacy. Simeon Francis, a newspaper editor in Illinois before he relocated to Oregon in 1859, provided an important voice for Lincoln when he became the first editor of Portland's *Morning Oregonian* newspaper.[6] T. J. Dryer, the editor of the *Weekly Oregonian*, also supported Lincoln's candidacy through his editorial comments.[7] While Oregon was the only state in the Pacific Northwest and therefore controlled the only electoral votes in the region, people in Washington Territory were just as passionate about the election.

North in Washington Territory, slavery had been prohibited, but unlike in Oregon, free African Americans could live there, though few did—just thirty according to the 1860 census.[8] Given the small number of African Americans in the territory, Washingtonians may have feared racial mingling less than Oregonians. The 1857 Dred Scott decision permitted the expansion of slavery into the territories, yet there is only one documented case of a slave living in Washington Territory in 1860.[9] Despite the absence of slavery in Washington Territory, there was considerable support for the South's right to own slaves, especially among the 12 percent of the population who were born in slave states. Washingtonians, however, did not want to compete with slave labor.[10] Like in Oregon, key politicians in Washington were proslavery. Washington Territory congressional delegate Isaac Stevens served as treasurer of the Breckinridge campaign. William Winlock Miller, a friend of Stevens serving in the territorial legislature, also supported Breckinridge.[11] Even as the sectional controversy caused rifts among the small farm population and the more transient miners, without any presidential electors at stake, the tension in Washington Territory did not garner anywhere near the same level of attention as it did in Oregon.

"We have," declared the article, "held our paper back for the stage from the South. It arrived an hour ago, with returns from Jackson and Douglas [counties], which we give below. Lincoln has undoubtedly carried the state by [a] 250 [vote] majority!" The news left the *Oregon Argus* staff unable to collect themselves: "Our feelings will not permit us to write with composure." Indeed, the article headline expressed their excitement: "Hooraw! Oregon for Lincoln!!"[12] Lincoln had actually carried the state by a 270-vote plurality over proslavery candidate John C. Breckinridge; he earned 1,214 more votes than popular sovereignty candidate Senator Stephen A. Douglas. Constitutional Union candidate John Bell received just over 200 votes. There was also a sense of relief in the *Argus* article; Lincoln won Oregon by a much closer margin than his national victory (Lincoln defeated his closest national opponent, Douglas, by ten percentage points; in Oregon, the margin over Breckinridge was only 1.8 percent). Lincoln's slim victory suggested that antebellum Oregon was contested ground.

As the only state in the region, events in Oregon were a bellwether for the entire Pacific Northwest. Although Lincoln only won 36 percent of the vote to Breckinridge's 34 percent, the state overwhelmingly refuted the proslavery platform. Combined, Lincoln and third-place finisher Douglas received 64 percent of the presidential vote. Lincoln may not have been especially popular in the Pacific Northwest, but support for a proslavery president was even less so.

A shift in Oregon's congressional delegation in 1860 indicated that the proslavery faction was not as strong as Breckinridge's showing against Lincoln suggested. Southern sympathizing Democratic senator Delazon Smith was replaced by Republican Edward Baker, a friend of the president-elect. The other senator, Joseph Lane, remained, but after his failed run as the proslavery vice presidential candidate on the Breckinridge ticket and the subsequent press attacks, his time in office soon ended. Lane was replaced in March 1861 by James Nesmith, a Union-supporting Democrat. Oregon's lone congressman, Lansing Stout, who had already cut his ties with Senator Lane's proslavery Democrats, also left office in March 1861. John Whiteaker, the outspoken Southern-sympathizing governor, remained and would play a key role in the creation of the First Oregon Volunteer Cavalry Regiment, albeit not in the way he anticipated. The political divisions in Oregon were not as strong as they appeared during the statehood struggle or the 1860 election. Still, the federal government could not afford to take anything for granted as the growing secession crisis engulfed the nation.

The political landscape looked similar in Washington Territory following the election. Isaac Stevens made the wrong political bet when he supported Breckinridge's proslavery candidacy. Though he eventually joined and died for the Union cause, Stevens's support for Breckinridge ruined his political career in the territory. In the wake of the election, the editorial writer at Olympia's *Washington Standard* condemned Stevens (and Oregon's Joe Lane) for engaging "in movements sustaining slavery propagandism, at the hazard of our national Union."[13] Facing considerable opposition and amid growing concern over Southern secession, Stevens, Washington Territory's first governor, withdrew his candidacy to be renominated as a delegate to Congress, ending his term in March 1861.[14]

P1. Gov. John Whiteaker. "John Whiteaker," Wikimedia Commons,
last modified August 4, 2022, http://www.waymarking.com/waymarks/
WMNBBX_FIRST_Governor_of_Oregon_John_W_Whiteaker.

Support for the Union grew throughout the region's small population in reaction to rising secession rhetoric and eventual secession. The secession of seven Southern states between late December 1860 and February 1, 1861, combined with the replacement of Southern-leaning federal office holders with Union men, dramatically changed the political climate in the Pacific Northwest. Many felt as Oregon pioneer and former state legislator Joel Palmer did, calling supporters of secession "southern fanatics."[15] Such sentiment did not alleviate fears about the vocal Southern-supporting minority, which fell off when the news of the firing on Fort Sumter reached the Pacific Northwest.

On April 30, word reached the Oregon state capital in Salem that South Carolina forces, functioning as de facto forces of the newly formed Confederacy, had attacked Fort Sumter, the federal post in Charleston Harbor.[16] After being battered for two days, the fort surrendered on April 13. While newspapers throughout the state ran extra or special editions as the news spread, initial details were scanty. The impact was clear. "HOSTILITIES COMMENCED!" screamed the front-page headline in Salem's *Oregon Statesman* on May 6. The pro-Union papers in the state—including the *Statesman*, Oregon City *Argus*, and the various editions of Portland's *Oregonian*—reported that "indignation not despondency seems to be the feeling evoked." The impact of the news, as one editor reported, "has created much feeling against secession."[17] The Southern-sympathizing Albany *Oregon Democrat* presented the news differently, declaring the South Carolina forces had been "provoked" by President Lincoln's "corrosive polic[ies]." It cautiously warned readers, "We hope the troubles which are rending communities in the Atlantic States, may not be transferred to the Pacific coast." Attempting to disguise editor Pat Malone's avowed Southern sympathies as concern for the Pacific Northwestern populace, the paper advised its readers, "It would be the greatest folly for us to be arraying ourselves in a hostile attitude to the North or South, and thereby plunge our State into a quarrel not legitimately ours."[18]

Shockwaves also reverberated from Washington territorial newspapers as reports arrived. The editor of Olympia's *Washington Standard* newspaper declared, "The traitors have taken the initiatory inaugurating civil war and the dreadful consequences attendant upon such a policy."[19] The Southern-leaning *Puget Sound Standard* and the *Pioneer and Democrat*, published in Port Angeles, said very little beyond stating the attack and surrender meant that war had commenced. Neither made any editorial comments over the coming weeks, although the *Pioneer and Democrat* eventually ran a lengthy pro-Southern account originally published in a Charleston, South Carolina, newspaper.[20]

While a few regional newspapers expressed Southern support, Union sentiment rose precipitously in the Pacific Northwest (and the entire Far West) after the attack. Most of those who had expressed their disapproval of the use of federal military power to force the seceded states back into the national union became Union men. Patriotic meetings were organized throughout the Pacific Northwest towns in the weeks after the attack on Fort Sumter.[21] One such gathering occurred in Portland, where "a large number of our patriotic citizens assembled at the theatre to manifest their adherence to the Union and the Government, and their determination to defend them to the death."[22] As many newspapers vociferously condemned the attack and predicted doom for the nascent Confederacy, more and more of the populace demonstrated their support for the Union. Soon only the most ardent Southern sympathizers publicly endorsed the Confederate cause. Circumstances changed when news of Confederate victories at Manassas, Virginia, and Wilson's Creek, Missouri, arrived in July and August. The pair of early Confederate military successes amplified concerns about potential challenges to federal control of the Pacific Northwest throughout the remainder of the year.

The most common concern was not about the region joining the Confederacy, which seemed unlikely, but about the establishment of an independent republic on the Pacific Slope. The idea of a Pacific Republic was not new, but the secession of eleven Southern states revived it. When California congressman John Burch raised the idea in the House of Representatives, it made news on both coasts.[23] Although media coverage faded rather quickly, fears of a second secession of states on the opposite side of the continent worried military leaders so much that they expressed their concerns to the new administration.[24]

When a Pacific Republic was originally discussed in 1859, it was not motivated by sectional strife. With more than 2,500 miles separating federal policy makers from the Pacific states, there was some argument for establishing an independent nation on the West Coast. This was especially true prior to the completion of the first transcontinental telegraph line in October 1861. Before that, it took weeks, sometimes longer, for communications to traverse the continent. The lack of institutions needed to sustain a nation, chiefly a protective military, kept the idea from gaining much traction until it was revived after the South left the Union.

In January 1860, outgoing California governor John Weller suggested to the state legislature that if a civil war broke out after the coming election, California should "not go with the South or the North, but here upon the shores of the Pacific found a mighty republic which in the end may prove the mightiest of all."[25] Five months later California's two U.S. senators, William Gwin and Milton Latham (Oregon senator Joseph Lane was purported to agree with his colleagues) postulated that the Pacific states and territories would form their own republic if the nation split over the election results.[26] A Puget Sound pioneer recalled that there were like-minded civilians in Washington Territory: "There was in serious contemplation [the] establishment of an American republic on this coast independent of the United States."[27] Establishing their own nation on the Pacific Coast would allow the population to avoid having to choose sides between the North and the South once war broke out.

Those arguments had been hypothetical until the Union broke apart. In late April 1861, Department of the Pacific commander Gen. Edwin Sumner observed there was "no doubt but there is some deep scheming to draw California into the secession movement;

in the first place as the 'Republic of the Pacific,' expecting afterward to induce her to join the Southern Confederacy."[28] He recognized the threat expatriated Southerners might represent. The
situation was the same in the Pacific Northwest. In Puget Sound,
Washington Territory, Port Angeles newspaper editor Charles
Prosch knew about the machinations to form a Pacific Republic
"being one of the schemes contemplated by the disloyal northern
men."[29] In early 1861 the *Washington Standard* reported a resolution
in the territorial legislature that charged its disgraced congressional delegate, Isaac Stevens, with trying "to promote disunion and a
Pacific Republic" and misrepresenting "the citizens of Washington
Territory" on the floor of the House.[30] Stevens's comments echoed
those made in the Senate chamber by California's Latham and Gwin
and Oregon's Lane. All called for a Pacific Republic on the West
Coast, a position widely criticized in the Union-supporting press.[31]

The Breckinridge supporters in the Pacific Northwest were too far
from the theaters of war to assist the Confederate armies directly,
but there were rumors they might open another front by carrying
out guerilla attacks throughout the region. Those concerns focused
on one specific group, the shadowy Knights of the Golden Circle
(KGC). An April 1861 article published in the *Weekly Oregonian*
typified the public speculation about the number of KGC members in the Far West. The author posited that there were four hundred members in Portland alone, who were "a portion of a similar
fraternity in the Southern States."[32]

The KGC was founded in 1854 by George Bickley, a Virginia-
born doctor who lived in Ohio before relocating to the South,
finally establishing himself in Texas. A prolific writer, he had a
fascination for secret societies. In the late 1850s, the KGC merged
with another secret organization known as the Order of the Lone
Star.[33] The objective of this paramilitary group was to extend the
Southern slavocracy to the Caribbean, Mexico, and possibly Central America. By the time of the 1860 election, it was believed to
have a number of "castles" (chapters) beyond the South, including in border states and the Far West. Castles were rumored to

exist in The Dalles, Albany, and Corvallis, Oregon.[34] The Southern expatriates living throughout the Far West made both regional and federal officials uneasy about a ready pool for recruitment into the group. Union supporters suspected anyone who had openly expressed support for slavery, John C. Breckinridge (rumored to be a KGC member), or the right to secede.

Early in 1861 rumors spread that the KGC was recruiting members in the Far West. In September Salem's *Oregon Statesman* reprinted an exposé (no originating source given) that explained the levels of KGC membership, listed its objectives, and described the roles leading members played in the organization—only Bickley was specifically named. While it did not tie the KGC to Oregon or the Pacific Northwest, the large front-page story makes plain the level of public fascination with the organization's presence and rumored plans in the Pacific Northwest.[35] Concerns about the KGC fueled apprehensions about a Pacific Republic.

Although Southern California and southern Oregon were seen as potential hotbeds of proslavery support, the prevailing belief was that the entire state of California was the state in greater danger from proslavery paramilitary groups. Fortunately for wartime military leaders, the army had streamlined the command structure in the Far West in late 1860, thereby enhancing the army's ability to expediently respond to any crises. Those changes followed the death of Department of California commander Brig. Gen. Newman S. Clarke on October 17, 1860. The army returned the Departments of California and Oregon to a single administrative command, the Department of the Pacific. The former Department of Oregon became the District of Oregon, a major subcommand in the Department of the Pacific that remained in place until the spring of 1865, led initially by Col. George Wright.

Though Brevet Brig. Gen. Albert Sidney Johnston had been appointed commander of the reconfigured Department of the Pacific just days before the presidential election, he did not reach his new post until January 15, 1861.[36] By then four states had seceded from the union, dramatically changing both his responsibilities and his orders. Given the fears about secession sympathizers in

California and the importance of San Francisco as the primary trading center, Johnston spent his brief tenure in command shifting troops from areas deemed less endangered or of less importance to those more endangered or more significant. Brig. Gen. Edwin Sumner replaced Johnston on April 24 and continued that policy with greater fervency. By the time news of the firing on and capture of Fort Sumter reached the Pacific Northwest in late April and early May, six companies total had already been pulled from the District of Oregon and sent south to San Francisco.[37] More than half of the military force would be transferred from the District of Oregon by the end of the next month, an area that included the modern states of Washington and Oregon along with part of Idaho.

The steady reduction in Wright's force made it difficult for him to carry out his responsibilities. After spending the previous ten years in the Pacific Northwest, he understood that his primary task remained ensuring federal control of the region against new threats as well as old ones. Relations between whites and the Indian people living in the Pacific Northwest had been uneasy for a long time, punctuated by numerous violent conflicts between 1848 and 1858. What whites called the Indian Wars began in Oregon Territory in 1848 after the murder of the Whitman missionaries by Cayuse Indians in what has since been known as the Whitman massacre. That sparked a bloody series of reprisals that flared up at various places until 1855. There were several other such "wars" in both Oregon and Washington Territories before their destructive conclusion in 1858. The defeat of a military expedition commanded by Lt. Col. Edward Steptoe, sent from Fort Walla Walla north toward Fort Colville, resulted in a one-sided destructive campaign of revenge led by Col. George Wright. After Wright ordered the killing of nearly twenty Indians, including some important leaders (some were summarily hanged and others were shot as they tried to escape); the slaughter of roughly eight hundred Indian horses near what is today Spokane, Washington; and the destruction of food supplies, the Indian Wars in that region ended until the outbreak of the Nez Perce War in 1877.[38] The decade of warfare and bloody reprisals left indelible impressions on both peoples, which influenced the relations and interactions between the Oregon Cavalry and the Indian people they encountered from 1862 to 1866.

As an active participant, Wright was well aware of the region's violent history, and he understood the three years of relative calm that followed the last "war" were misleading. Tensions rose again between whites and the regional Indian tribes, particularly in Oregon east of the Cascade Range, as more and more whites invaded Indians' traditional homelands. For the local white population, concerns about Confederate sympathizers scheming to launch guerilla attacks against federal authorities, or about others who might attempt to establish an independent republic, were secondary. Whites living in the region were far more concerned about regional Indian tribes attacking farmers, miners, and emigrants in their effort to hold on to their ancestral lands than they were about Confederate partisans.

Oregonians had historically confined themselves mostly to the western slope of the Cascade Range, particularly in the Willamette valley, just north of the California border, and along the Columbia River between Portland and The Dalles. By 1861, however, a few small towns had popped up east of the Cascades. Lightly populated and isolated, places like Canyon City in central Oregon were vulnerable to being cut off by Indians defending their lands and way of life against the newest phase of white migration. As more whites ventured into the unexplored eastern and southeastern parts of the state and farther east to the Boise area, confrontations increased, inevitably leading civilians to demand military intervention for conflicts they usually started. As the Civil War expanded in the East, the bands of mostly Northern Paiute Indians soon worried locals more than the possibility of Southern-supporting guerillas.

Despite the region's sociopolitical turn toward support for the Union, political positions espoused by prominent Oregon politicians from the early territorial days through the 1860 election left federal officials anxious. Civilians worried more about attacks by various Indian tribes east of the Cascades. Both concerns grew as the military transferred most of the U.S. Army forces out of the

P2. Brig. Gen. George Wright. U.S. Army Heritage and Education Center, Carlisle PA, Civil War Photograph Collection (CWP), RG 98, box 17, folio 109.

District of Oregon in 1861. Though skipped during the initial calls for volunteer troops, by late summer, with pressure mounting from both the local military and politicians, something had to be done to protect what appeared to be an increasingly vulnerable Pacific Northwest from external and internal threats.

TWO

Recruiting

In June 1861, after fifteen of the twenty-eight companies under his command had been transferred out of the District of Oregon, Colonel Wright warned his superior, "All that we can do is to afford general protection to the frontier settlements."[1] The situation in the District of Oregon deteriorated right at the peak of the emigration season. With just over five hundred men distributed throughout the District of Oregon, Wright could launch only a few understrength patrols along the emigrant routes coming into and through the Pacific Northwest.[2] On September 1, facing mounting political pressure caused by public fears about the safety of the eastern two-thirds of the state, Oregon governor Whiteaker asked district commander Wright "whether the forces under your command are sufficient to force these Indians to keep the peace, and if the country may rely upon [his] action for protection."[3] The answer was an unequivocal no. Wright had run out of ways to maneuver his limited (and decreasing) force from one hot spot to another. He simply did not have enough troops to mollify growing civilian fears about the dangers arising in the Pacific Northwest. His manpower situation had reached a critical moment, and there was no relief from the Department of the Pacific, which had been ordered to send most of its regular army units to the East. "The threatening attitude of the Indian tribes in the country east of the Cascade Mountains having produced much alarm amongst the settlers" forced Wright to take desperate action. As he informed Department of the Pacific headquarters on September 12, he had "to call

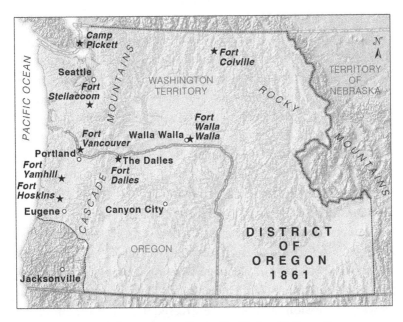

Camp
★ Pickett

★ Fort
Colville

WASHINGTON
TERRITORY

Seattle
○
Fort
Stellacoom
★

Fort
Walla
Fort   Walla Walla ★ Walla
Vancouver

Portland ○
Fort
Yamhill ★   ★ The Dalles
Fort   Fort
Hoskins ★   Dalles

Eugene ○

Canyon City ○

OREGON

Jacksonville ○

TERRITORY
OF
NEBRASKA

ROCKY

MOUNTAINS

CASCADE   MOUNTAINS

PACIFIC OCEAN

DISTRICT
OF
OREGON
1861

M1. District of Oregon, 1861. Created by Chelsea McRaven Feeney.

on the Governor of Oregon for a company for service north of the Columbia River."[4] Pacific Northwesterners were finally going to join the Union cause, albeit in a markedly different way than their Union cousins in the East. Maybe.

When Congress authorized the raising of troops for the Union war effort (seventy-five thousand in April, then an additional five-hundred-thousand-man force in July), responsibility for conducting such a massive recruiting effort fell to the states, each of which was assigned a target number of regiments to enlist. Under such circumstances, governors played crucial roles in the formation of their state's regiments. Governors in turn delegated the responsibility for recruiting and organizing regiments to selected individuals. Many of those men sought commissions in the regiments they helped raise. This gave governors incredible influence over not only the raising of regiments but the nature of the men who led those regiments as well. In Oregon that man was Gov. John Whiteaker, which proved problematic.

Whiteaker and his family left southern Indiana and arrived in 1852 in southwestern Oregon, where he established a farm. Once there he quickly became involved in local politics. He joined the Democratic Party, which supported prohibiting African American migration into the territory. This played well among a regional electorate that voted in favor of just such a law in 1858. In June 1858 he ran for and won the Oregon governorship by 1,138 votes even before statehood was official. He finally took office in 1859, after Oregon had been admitted as a state. This meant he governed over the sparkling new state during the highly contested 1860 presidential election. During the campaign he put his political influence behind the proslavery, Southern Democratic ticket of John C. Breckinridge and Oregon's own Senator Joseph Lane.[5] In the wake of Lincoln's electoral win and the subsequent secession crisis, Governor Whiteaker wasted little time expressing his views on secession. Although he stressed his commitment to the Union, he made an increasing number of Southern-sympathizing comments during the spring of 1861. Those comments culminated with a set of lengthy remarks that were widely circulated in the Oregon newspapers in June. Not only did the South have the right to secede, but according to the governor, the Confederates had the right, "if need be, to use every just means within their power to defend themselves, their property and institutions, against the unjust encroachments of the North."[6] In fact, the only question seemed to be whether the governor was a true secessionist or just an Oregon Copperhead (Southern-supporting Democrat). In either case, he seemed certain to undermine or refuse Wright's request for a company of Oregon volunteers.

Four days after Wright's request, Governor Whiteaker authorized A. P. Dennison to organize an eighty-eight-man company. What followed was a comical example of governmental graft. A proclamation announcing the calling for that company was published in the state's newspapers in late September.[7] Whiteaker chose Dennison because they shared the same Southern-sympathizing and anti-Lincoln views. Dennison, who arrived in Oregon in the early

1850s from Maine, via California, previously served as an Indian agent in Oregon. He was one of the state's two delegates to the 1860 Southern Democratic convention in Charleston, South Carolina, who nominated Breckinridge. Dennison accepted the appointment to make some money while doing almost nothing. He established his recruiting center in The Dalles and appointed four subordinates to find volunteers in the Willamette valley. The press made it clear that the governor and his operative could not be trusted, declaring, "Whiteaker, Dennison, and most of his subordinates are secessionists" and predicting that "the appointment of Dennison may prove unfortunate to the State treasury."[8] The prediction proved uncanny when Dennison and his recruiters managed to enlist just twelve men before Wright put a stop to the charade in November. Dennison racked up nearly $2,000 in expenses "for the one month he has done nothing," observed Salem's *Weekly Oregon Statesman*.[9] In the end, Dennison proved to be more of a confidence man than a military recruiter.

From the start of the sectional crisis, federal officials had concerns about the loyalty of not just John Whiteaker in Oregon but also John G. Downey in California. Both had supported the Breckinridge presidential candidacy. However, Downey, despite his previous proslavery stance, proclaimed his loyalty to the Union cause once the war started.[10] No longer worried about his loyalty, twice over the course of the summer the War Department instructed Downey to raise a total of five regiments of infantry and one of cavalry for the cause.[11] The situation was different with Governor Whiteaker. As the Dennison recruiting charade confirmed, officials in Washington DC knew they could not work through him, so they maneuvered around him. Doing so was not an easy matter, even after his popular support eroded considerably throughout the summer. It was a question of how to do it, not if they should, which was clear. The political and military leaders in Washington DC had not circumvented a governor before, so they did not have a clear alternative in place. They knew they needed to ensure that any Oregon volunteers were led by men loyal to the Union cause, but they were not sure how to go about it. Prior to the end of the congressional session in August, the War Department, almost certainly in consultation with the president (though no records survive), came up with an imaginative solution for the first step toward raising a loyal regiment of volunteers in the District of Oregon. Recruiting what became the First Oregon Volunteer Cavalry Regiment proved challenging from the start, and it remained so throughout the effort. Despite the challenges, the state formed an understrength regiment by March 1862.

On August 1, in the midst of a heated debate on the Senate floor about suppressing the rebellion, a fifty-year-old man with a partially bald head, fringed with white hair, made a dramatic entrance into the chamber. Wearing a dark-blue Union officer's coat, Oregon senator Edward Baker took his seat. As he sat, he placed his sword on top of his desk, further reminding his colleagues that whatever he said that day, he, unlike any of them so far, would take the field to put his words into action. At first he sat and listened to Kentucky senator John C. Breckinridge. The former vice president urged the Union to end the conflict, less than two weeks after the disastrous First Battle of Bull Run, and let the Confederacy form its own nation. When Breckinridge finished, Baker "sprang to the floor" and rebuffed the idea.[12] As he spoke he made his own commitment to the Union military effort clear: "We propose to subjugate rebellion into loyalty; we propose to subjugate insurrection into peace; we propose to subjugate Confederate anarchy into constitutional Union liberty."[13] One of his fellow senators remembered Baker's "striking appearance . . . in the uniform of a soldier [and] his superb voice."[14] The image of the only member of the Senate in uniform unequivocally stating his commitment to military subjugation of the Confederacy left an impression on many people that day. That militant (and military) loyalty from one of Oregon's senators provided a possible solution, awkward as it would be, to raising a loyal regiment of Oregon volunteers for the Union. Baker's remarks convinced military leaders that they had an opportunity for the federal government to sidestep Governor Whiteaker's obstructionism.

Sometime after the end of the congressional session, military officials approached Baker, who no longer split his time between the Senate and his regiment, and asked if he would oversee the organizing of a regiment of volunteers in Oregon. Given the more than two-thousand-mile distance from Oregon and his responsibilities as colonel of the Seventy-First Pennsylvania Infantry Regiment, Baker recommended three citizens to head the recruiting effort. That was something Governor Whiteaker would have been tasked with were it not for his Southern sympathies. So on September 24, the adjutant general of the Union armies informed Thomas Cornelius, Reuben Maury, and Benjamin F. Harding that they had been selected "upon the strong recommendation of" Senator Baker, who "relie[d] confidently upon the prudence, patriotism, and economy with which [they would] execute" the raising "for the service of the United States one regiment of mounted troops." The three men were informed that they would "be governed by any directions sent to [them] by Col. E.D. Baker" and would "under all circumstances report [their] conduct to the premises of the War Department."[15] With that message, the War Department removed Governor Whiteaker from having any role in forming the regiment.

Asking Baker to take on a role that was almost exclusively reserved for state governors was, by itself, a bit surprising, since he had only come to Oregon in 1859. While the senator had not been in the state he represented for very long, Abraham Lincoln's other transplanted Illinois friends had been living there since the mid-1840s. Baker knew many of them; some played a role in his appointment to the U.S. Senate by the state legislature. As a senator, he held a more prominent political position than the rest of the president's Illinois operatives in Oregon; thus, his influential position mattered more than his brief acquaintance with the people of Oregon. Of course, his most important qualification for overseeing the recruiting process that first summer of the war was his unquestioned loyalty to the Union cause and to his friend, the president of the United States.

The decision to raise a regiment of cavalry instead of the much cheaper infantry had been the logical one. While regional politicians

P3. Col. Reuben Maury. Oregon Historical Society,
OrgLot1414_0237S003_01.

and the military worried about Confederate sympathizers, civilians' concerns focused on Indian raids on whites east of the Cascade Range. It would have been impossible to protect emigrants along the various migrant trails as well as the widely dispersed mining camps in the vast territory with infantry alone. The plodding infantry, while well suited for garrisoning strategically placed forts and camps, simply could not carry out successful pursuits of mounted Indians, presumed by most whites to be Paiutes.[16] The War Department demonstrated its belief that there was a role for infantry as well. Three weeks after authorizing a regiment of Oregon cavalry, it issued orders to raise the First Washington Territory Infantry Regiment.[17] As the two regiments' service records would show, the cavalry was the key.

Just as the logic behind circumventing Governor Whiteaker had been obvious, so too were Senator Baker's reasons for recommending Cornelius, Harding, and Maury to form and then lead the cavalry regiment. Each brought different desired strengths to the endeavor that would result in creating a loyal and effective regiment to replace the departed Army Regulars. For all of the attacks on politicians' character and thirst for power throughout history, they had a valuable skill set that governors across the country recognized and used when called upon to recruit almost six hundred thousand volunteers by the end of summer. Recruiting meant persuading civilians to volunteer for military service, and persuasion was the politicians' stock and trade. Baker's politically active friends in Oregon were certainly aware of Thomas Cornelius and Benjamin F. Harding, both of whom had well-established records of political activity before Oregon was a state. Maury brought very different strengths to his new job.

A fellow political operative and judge caught up in the prewar partisan storms described Benjamin F. Harding as being "devoid of all ostentation or special accomplishment, but [he] has a big head, full of hard common sense, and much of the rare gift of keeping cool and holding his tongue."[18] Born in eastern Pennsylvania in 1832, he followed the gold rush rumors to California in 1849 but left the next year for Oregon. He ended up in Marion County, where he eventually became a lawyer and active in the territory's political world. In the years before the outbreak of the Civil War, he served three terms in the territorial legislature and as secretary of the territory from 1855 to 1859. He supported Stephen Douglas's Democratic candidacy during the presidential campaign.[19] The inclusion of Harding among the men responsible for recruiting the new regiment was wise, given the large numbers of Douglas Democrats in the state. Officially, the politically savvy Harding was appointed regimental quartermaster, a challenging task for anyone when creating a regiment from scratch, particularly one of cavalry, which required a great deal of additional equipment that infantry commands did not as well as equipment and feed for the horses.

Reuben Maury had little in common with Benjamin F. Harding beyond deciding to migrate to Oregon Territory. Born in 1821 in Kentucky, Maury was appointed from that state to the U.S. Military Academy in 1837, but there is no record that he actually attended.[20] He worked as a postal clerk in Louisville prior to serving as a lieutenant in the First Kentucky Infantry Regiment during the Mexican–American War.[21] After the war ended, he followed rumors of quick riches in the California gold fields, reaching the Sacramento Valley in the fall of 1849. Prospecting gave way to more stable work freighting between southern Oregon and Crescent City, California. He moved to Oregon in 1854, when he and a partner established a successful general mercantile business in Jacksonville. Unlike the other two, Maury had not held any political offices and, like a good businessman, seems to have been publicly nonpartisan. While he did not have the larger name recognition of Cornelius and Harding, he had strong community connections in Jacksonville, which was destined to become a key recruiting center. Combined with his military experience in the Mexican–American War, recommending Maury proved to be an excellent decision.[22]

Thomas Cornelius was seventeen when his family left Missouri and traveled to Oregon Territory in 1845. They established a homestead roughly twenty miles west of Portland. Participation in two regional Indian wars elevated his standing among the pioneer Oregonians. He served as a volunteer in both the 1848 Cayuse War and during the early part of the Yakima War, from 1855 to 1856. During the latter conflict, the twenty-eight-year-old was elected colonel of the Oregon militia, denoting the growth in his public stature since his arrival eleven years earlier. Benefiting from the reputation he gained during the Yakima War, Oregonians elected him to three consecutive one-year terms in the council, the Oregon Territorial Legislature's upper chamber, first as a Whig and then as a Republican. He maintained a seat in the new state legislature up until his appointment as colonel of the First Oregon Volunteer Cavalry Regiment.[23] Although he was five years older than Harding and had been in Oregon several years longer than either Harding or Maury, the main reason Cornelius received command of the regiment over either of them is that he combined both their strengths: political standing and military experience. Politically, as a Republican, Cornelius would appeal to the plurality that had voted for Lincoln just as Harding would to his fellow Douglas Democrats. For all three, their selection to bring the First Oregon Volunteer Cavalry Regiment to life was an honor, a great responsibility, and a daunting challenge, but one that could pay political dividends in the future.

It was a month before they received the news of their appointments: Cornelius as a colonel and commanding officer, a lieutenant colonelcy for Maury and second-in-command, with Harding accepting the regimental quartermaster's position, albeit on a temporary basis. When the order became public in late October, it effectively made the Whiteaker–Dennison farce superfluous.[24] George Wright, by then in charge of all federal forces between British North America and Mexico, west of the Rockies, got the satisfaction of asking the governor to "suspend the enrollment of the cavalry company at Fort Dalles."[25] Mindful of the need to maintain working relationships with the politicians within the Department of the Pacific, Wright's tone was more restrained than his replacement in the District of Oregon, Lt. Col. Albemarle Cady, who, nine days later, told the governor, "The raising of the company of volunteer cavalry heretofore called for has been suspended, and the men, if any, already enrolled are to be disbanded."[26] The abject failure of that effort, and the resulting dismissal of the dozen men who had signed up, eliminated any possibility of competing recruiting efforts.

Before men to replace the Regulars withdrawn from the District of Oregon in the previous seven months could be enlisted, obstacles needed to be overcome. Fortunately, by the fall the political climate had shifted even more dramatically to supporting the Union. Still, natural challenges persisted. Following Wright's promotion to department commander and Edward Baker's death at the October Battle of Ball's Bluff, Virginia, it fell to Lieutenant Colonel Cady to work with and advise the trio as they addressed the arduous challenge of recruiting in Oregon. The population was limited, and while mainly concentrated west of the Cascade Range, they were spread out from the Columbia River south to the California border. They were undertaking their job at the worst time of year, the cold late fall and winter months, which inhibited travel. "Any failure in raising this force," Cady told Wright, "may be ascribed to causes familiar to the commander of the department."[27] There was one possible benefit: recruiters could at least offer a place to live with meals and a steady (if small) income during the slowest economic months faced by miners and farmers.

The 1860 census found the population totaled just over fifty thousand people, barely meeting the threshold for statehood. Trying to fill ten companies of cavalrymen, totaling almost one thousand men, in a region without a direct physical connection to the seat of war seemed unlikely from the start. In a state with a small population and few urban centers, recruiters for each company had to spread themselves out and seek volunteers at widely separated locations instead of setting up an office in a large population center such as San Francisco. Communication between the dispersed recruiting centers proved difficult due to winter weather. Difficulty in coordination inhibited any effort at cohesion, which proved to be problematic when trying to house and feed volunteers. Once recruiters began to fill their quotas, being widely dispersed presented another problem: Where to establish training camps? The situation could have been worse; at least most of the recruiting centers had been established in the western third of the state. Unfortunately, that still meant traversing a corridor that ran roughly four hundred miles north to south, with the Cascade Range on the eastern shoulder.

Since it was November before the recruiting got underway, the weather presented a number of immediate challenges, but neither the regional civilians nor the military could wait until the spring for the regiment's ranks to be filled. Travel during the late fall and winter months would have been difficult any year, but the winter of 1861–62 hit western Oregon with generational levels of rain in the lower elevations and heavy snowfall in the mountains. North–south travel became nearly impossible due to widespread flooding, and crossing the Cascades was out of the question due to snow accumulations in the mountains. As a result, housing, feeding, and especially equipping the volunteers became almost impossible because the scattered groups could not be concentrated. Local accommodations were often haphazard; as the recruits organized in the southern part of the state marched toward the Columbia River, they rested for several days in livestock shelters at the state fairgrounds.[28] The few available uniforms and equipment were at Fort Vancouver, the site of the District of Oregon headquarters. There was no way to get any of the supplies to the volunteers encamped near Jacksonville at the southern end of the state.

The officers understood that civilian and military eagerness for troops to replace the district's depleted ranks would turn to frustration if the regiment could not take the field in the spring. Taking advantage of their local name recognition, each oversaw recruiting efforts in their home areas beginning in November. Cornelius began his effort in and about Portland, Harding a bit farther south in Salem, and Maury near the California border in Jacksonville, where his mercantile store was located. Each of the three worked with newly appointed junior officers who canvased those regions to raise troops, mostly through announcements in the local newspapers and posters. Other recruiting centers would need to be established as soon as possible to tap into other (smaller) population centers.

The public announcement that a cavalry regiment was being formed led to a frenzy of individuals seeking provisional officer's commissions. While Cornelius had been given the authority to appoint junior officers, those commissions were contingent on having enough troopers to justify all the captains and lieutenants. Approving applications was not the free-for-all that some seeking commissions hoped. Colonel Cady had advised Cornelius "to look about and select such careful, faithful, and energetic officers as might be suitable for the companies."[29] He also made every effort to select only those loyal to the Union—the War Department required each man to swear an oath of allegiance when mustered into service.[30]

Captains' and lieutenants' commissions were quickly handed out and the officers sent out to raise companies for the regiment. Most of the men commissioned in November and December proved to be at least competent during their service, and some became particularly efficient officers. Richard S. Caldwell, William Kelly, David P. Thompson, and Jacob S. Rinearson reported to Colonel Cornelius at district headquarters at Fort Vancouver. They divided up the greater Portland area, which also included Oregon City. Seth Hammer and Elijah Harding, the quartermaster's younger brother, worked the Salem area under the guidance of Benjamin F. Harding until he submitted his resignation early the next year. Initially, Lieutenant Colonel Maury worked alongside R. A. Cowles recruiting in the southern part of the state. However, early the next year Sewell Truax and William J. Matthews took over most of the work in that region.[31]

Like the other junior officers, Currey understood he would have to recruit enough men to retain his commission. While the others attempted to recruit their companies on the western slope of the Cascade Range, Currey opted to try something different. Since he lived in The Dalles at the time, he set up his office in that town, hoping to recruit his company from the eastern two-thirds of the state. There were only two minor population centers east of the mountains, where small communities had coalesced around military forts: The Dalles (Fort Dalles) and Walla Walla (Fort Walla Walla), in Washington Territory.[32] Neither town exceeded nine hundred people, which was not uncommon in Civil War–era Oregon.

Only Portland and Eugene City topped one thousand residents; however, there were numerous other towns along the western slope of the Cascades with populations between four hundred and nine hundred people where the other recruiters focused their efforts. Currey gambled that by not having to compete with any other recruiters, he could find at least seventy men willing to serve in the Oregon Cavalry. Unfortunately, "the early commencement, protracted and rigorous winter of 1861–62" forced him to confine his efforts to just The Dalles for the next several months.[33]

Regardless of where the recruiters set up their efforts, raising the First Oregon Volunteer Cavalry Regiment proved even more difficult than anticipated. Cornelius, Maury, and Harding had been instructed to fill ten companies in accordance with the general rules governing the makeup of all cavalry regiments. The May 4, 1861, general orders specified that each company should include no less than seventy-nine and no more than ninety-five men. Thus, when including such ancillary men as regimental musicians and buglers, they needed to find at least 993 recruits and junior officers (plus the four regimental officers).[34] Finding a thousand men willing to serve in a remote corner of the Union war effort in a state that had just over twenty-seven thousand males of all ages in 1860 was optimistic at best.[35] Their first step was to place "advertisements in all the State papers, and bills stuck on every public house, and in every town in the State, calling for volunteers to enlist in the service of the United States."[36]

Being the last state called upon to contribute its manpower to the Union cause did help the Oregon recruiters in one way. After almost eight months of raising volunteer commands across the country, something of a playbook had been developed. Recruiters promoted the chance to punish the Confederates for breaking up the Union and then starting the shooting at Fort Sumter. They also tapped into an individual's sense of patriotism in their efforts to induce civilians to volunteer. If all else failed, recruiters had access to monetary inducements to incentivize volunteering. Cornelius and the others saw no reason to deviate significantly from what had worked elsewhere.

P 4. Capt. (at later rank of Col.) George B. Currey.
Oregon Historical Society, 020568.

As recruiters for both the Oregon Cavalry and Washington Infantry quickly found out in the last weeks of 1861, the playbook did
not apply particularly well in the remoteness of the Pacific Northwest. When the first California troops enlisted, many anticipated
they would be called eastward to fight the Confederates. One California cavalryman recalled "how bitterly disappointed the great

majority of the boys were when this order [to proceed to Nevada Territory] came, as we fully expected to go to Washington City, and from there to the front."[37] "There was some disappointment," remembered another California volunteer, because "our expectations were that we would be called East."[38] Although not serving in the main theater of the war, some Californians did help repel the Confederate invasion of New Mexico Territory in 1862.[39] Yet five months later, they remained distributed throughout the Far West. Despite such evidence to the contrary, many volunteers and even some recruiters in Oregon also believed they would eventually be sent east to fight the Confederate armies. Such views undoubtedly encouraged some to volunteer, particularly as many of their former neighbors were already serving the Union cause.

Despite plenty of signs that the Oregon Cavalry would remain in the Pacific Northwest, some desperate recruiters certainly lured in volunteers by dangling the specter of eventual service in the East. William Colvig, a seventeen-year-old originally from Missouri, charitably speculated, "Probably the recruiting officers acted in good faith, in promising us we would soon be in active service [in the East] and on the firing line." The naive youth was certainly giving the recruiters more credit than they deserved; Company C, which he joined in 1863, had been serving in the southern part of Oregon for two years by then, which remained its home base for the entirety of its existence. Looking back on being duped in his youth, Colvig shrugged it off, remembering with some amusement that "we never got any nearer Gettysburg and Cold Harbor than the Cascade Mountains or Crater Lake."[40] Sgt. Joseph D. Myers, an immigrant from Switzerland, believed economics kept the regiment on the West Coast. He recalled late in life, "We who had enlisted could never get east because no one could get a bill through congress to pay our way to get there. It cost too much."[41] Regardless of the reason, Lt. James Waymire, who started out as a private in late 1861, remembered that the men in the ranks "hoped should the war prove a long one, and should there be no serious difficulty here they would, after becoming drilled and disciplined, be ordered East to engage in active service there."[42] Recruiters, who knew this to be unlikely, chose not to disabuse the volunteers of their wishful thinking.

Of course, the Oregon cavalrymen were not the only western volunteers to fall for the false hope of being sent east to fight Confederates. In late 1864 an Oregon infantryman's experience made it clear the misleading practice was still in use: James Shelley described how excited he was "to have the opportunity to go East and participate in the *real* struggle, though the Recruiting officer, doubtless knew we would be kept on the [Pacific] Coast."[43] Shelley spent part of his service clerking at District of Oregon headquarters and never left the district's boundaries during his enlistment.[44]

Even without promising the opportunity to fight against the Confederate forces, volunteers in the Far West were reminded that their service was a good way to prove their patriotism. However, patriotism was complex in the most distant parts of the country, particularly for the region's population of expatriated Southerners. For some, the distance had a dampening effect on their sense of connection to the rest of the country. Others felt that the war gave the Pacific Northwest the chance to prove the men there were as patriotic as anyone else in the country. As one trooper explained, the Oregon volunteers wanted the chance "to show to the world, by acts rather than by words, [their] love and veneration for this blessed heritage bequeathed us by [their] [fore]fathers."[45] When recruiting lagged behind expectations, another early volunteer chided some of his fellow Oregonians for their feigned patriotism. He reminded them how, in the early days of the war, they "arose, young and old, *en masse*, as it were to assert their love [of] the Constitution and the bright, glorious flag and our country," and yet a little over two months later, there were "only about 400, or at most, 500 of our 'patriotic citizens' who have mustered courage enough, or patriotism enough to volunteer their services."[46] Yet patriotism, even if serving in the most distant theater, did motivate some, as a member of Company D described his own decision: when "en route for the new gold fields of Oregon and Washington Territory [from California], via Jacksonville," he "found that Uncle Sam was calling upon his boys to rally and defend him against the demon of secession," so he "joined Squadron [Company] D."[47]

Captain Currey was another of those who had been moved by his "unwavering devotion for the county our forefathers gave as our heritage" to join the Oregon Cavalry.[48] Currey was born on April 4, 1833, in Crawfordsville, Indiana, where he matriculated through the school system, eventually studying law at Wabash College. His family left Indiana for Oregon in 1853. Not long after the family settled near Eugene, Currey was admitted to the Oregon bar. He got his first taste of military experience in 1856, when he participated in the Rogue River Wars. Once his volunteer service ended, he moved to The Dalles, where he was living when the Civil War erupted.[49] Despite the difficulties encountered while trying to recruit a company, Currey became the first Oregon Cavalry officer to lead troops into the field. He quickly became the most trusted company officer in the regiment.

The absence of opportunities to prove their patriotism by fighting Confederates decidedly hurt recruitment efforts, but most took it in stride. There was another common means to tempt civilians to join the Union war effort: enlistment bounties. Monetary incentives were not as important in the East until later in the war, when appalling casualty lists diminished the civilian population's martial fervor.[50] In the Pacific Northwest, however, they became a staple of the recruiters' tools. This was particularly so after the initial enthusiasm quickly passed. Pay for all Union cavalrymen was better than what the infantry received, but it was still low. Mounted troops in the West had an additional source of income, as cavalrymen were reimbursed for the horses they provided. Unlike their infantry cousins, who received just $13 (officials later increased it to $16 late in the war) per month, a private in the cavalry received more than double that, $31 per month (a significant increase over the prewar pay scale), plus seventy-five cents per day for the use of his horse.[51] Though better than the prewar rate, those sums were often not enough to induce men—primarily farmers, miners, or even laborers—to accept the government's offer. Union soldiers everywhere were paid in the much-despised greenbacks (paper currency), which merchants only accepted at discounted rates, sometimes near 50 percent of face value, if at all. This further hindered recruiting efforts in places far removed from the fighting.[52]

Generally, the white population in Oregon had left wherever they were from for better lives, and for many of them, that meant being masters of their own fate. For the average soldier, the army offered the antitheses of that at a pay rate that was insufficient to convince many to join the new regiment. The case was different for those seeking officers' commissions; social and especially political status might be enhanced by serving during the national crisis. Of course, finding men wanting to become officers was not the problem.

To make volunteering more appealing, recruiters in the northern states, including Oregon, resorted to bonus money, known as bounties, for volunteering. The important role played by the enlistment bounty system dispels some of the romantic notions that patriotic ardor was the sole reason men joined the Union cause. The state of Oregon promised to pay anyone who joined the First Oregon Volunteer Cavalry Regiment $100 (that was increased to $150 in December 1864, during the recruitment of the Oregon infantry).[53] As recruiting efforts faltered, some local communities stepped in and offered additional bounties to help entice new recruits to join. By late 1864 local communities offered as much as $50 beyond the state bounties.[54]

With bounties coming from multiple sources, some men who had no desire to serve attempted to job the system. Such "volunteers," referred to as "bounty jumpers," joined to get the bounty and then deserted as soon as possible, often to try the same thing again elsewhere. This was not only criminal; it was risky. The military, which had a host of creative methods of punishment, quickly tired of such men. As is typical where cheating the system is possible, those in control of the bounties eventually altered the way men were paid. Instead of getting all the state money up front, the bounties were distributed either in three equal installments that coincided with the anniversary payday of their original enlistment or in a lump sum upon the completion of their term of service.[55]

The state government, in addition to monetary bounties, also created a different type of bounty specifically targeting would-be farmers. Like the $150 bounties, land claims were offered for the completion of a full three years of service (or the duration of the war).[56] That bounty consisted of the promise of 160 acres of farmable land, the location of which was never very clear at the time of enlistment. Given that the vast majority of open land was in the eastern two-thirds of the state, the precise region where the cavalrymen spent much of their service, an Oregon trooper would have a much better assessment of the land he was given than a civilian buying it sight unseen. The promise of land and cash bounties worked, just not at the level politicians and the recruiters hoped. Not surprisingly, nineteenth-century historian Francis Fuller Victor's highly romanticized sketch of the Oregon Cavalry quickly breezed past how influential monetary inducements were in motivating men from "the best homes of the state" to join the cavalry.[57] As slowly as recruiting efforts went, there is no doubt that money and land bounties played an important role in motivating civilians to join the Oregon Cavalry, as they had elsewhere.

All inducements combined meant that after three years of often grueling service in the field, woven around the tedium of winter months cooped up in a fort, an Oregon trooper might walk away from his service with more than $150, plus the rights to 160 acres of land. It is difficult to assess which recruiting strategies worked best, but as the war stretched on and it was obvious there would be no chance to serve in the East, and with regional Confederate sympathizers going mostly underground, monetary reward was the one constant tool in the recruiter's repertoire.

By February 1862 it was undeniable that appeals to patriotism, hints about eventually serving in the East against Confederates, and even monetary and land enticements had all failed to fill the ten companies ordered by the War Department. Colonel Cornelius reluctantly reported the lack of progress to army headquarters in Washington DC on February 20. His report had been delayed, he told the adjutant general, because of the flooding and heavier than usual snow during a particularly severe winter. Despite his best efforts to portray things in a positive light, his recounting of recruiting efforts hinted that they had not been as successful as anticipated. Two companies had been raised by

Lieutenant Colonel Maury in the southern part of the state, Quartermaster Benjamin F. Harding had recruited just one company in the middle section of the state before resigning, supposedly due to ill health, and Cornelius himself had overseen the recruitment of three companies in the northern part of the state.[58] Colonel Cornelius's report hinted that some of the six companies had only been partially filled. In light of the disappointing news, the War Department gave Gen. George Wright, Department of the Pacific commander, the authority to form the regiment with just six full companies with the hope that the remaining four companies could be recruited later.[59]

To meet the required number of men to reach the minimum of seventy-nine troopers, some of the recruiting efforts were consolidated. Future captain William Matthews "felt some anxiety for the future" about becoming an officer "when the news came that we were likely to be discharged" for failing to raise a full company. He survived consolidation and eventually became the commander of Company F.[60] Like Matthews, Captain Currey almost ended up a victim of insufficient numbers. His gamble that he could raise a company in northwestern Oregon and southeastern Washington Territory came up short; he had recruited only forty volunteers. Fortunately for Currey, other partially completed groups of volunteers were combined under his command, and he retained his captain's commission. Others were not so fortunate. Lt. David P. Thompson also failed to recruit a full company by March, and when the men he had enlisted were merged with other incomplete companies, he was left supernumerary. Without men for him to command, he resigned.[61] Capt. Remick A. Cowles and Lt. Samuel Parsons suffered similar fates. Parsons was never officially mustered into the service, and Cowles was dropped after he failed to recruit enough men to justify his rank.[62]

Despite the desperate need for men to fill even the regiment's reduced number of companies, the recruits still had to meet the minimum physical and mental qualifications. Military doctors, if available, or civilian doctors contracted by the recruiters were to "examine him [recruit] stripped; to see that he has free use of all his limbs; his chest is ample; that his hearing, vision, and speech are perfect; that he has no tumors, or ulcerated or extensively cicatrized legs; no rupture or chronic cutaneous affection; that he has not received any contusion, or wound of the head, that may impair his faculties; that he is not a drunkard; is not subject to convulsions; and has no infectious disorder, nor any that may unfit him for military service."[63]

The prewar army also required volunteers to be at least five feet, five inches tall.[64] Designed to make certain volunteers could endure the rigors of service, physical requirements added another obstacle when struggling with the problem of too few recruits. During the war the need for men in the ranks was deemed more important, and the rules were loosely enforced as a result.[65] Few were turned away, and by the end of spring, Colonel Cornelius had six companies of volunteers.

Raising the First Oregon Volunteer Cavalry Regiment proved more difficult and less successful than the War Department had anticipated. Impeded by a small regional population that was thousands of miles from the heart of the ongoing war, recruiters had difficulty getting enough men to rally to the first Union command in the Pacific Northwest. As if the circumstances were not bad enough obstacles, when one of the worst winters in memory engulfed Oregon, it almost appeared nature was against the effort. By March, spring thaws signaled that the eastern two-thirds of the state would soon see miners and emigrant trains traversing Paiute and other Native American homelands. Another season of violence lay ahead. Desperate for a military force to join the few California companies sent to replace the departed Regulars, the War Department had little choice but to consolidate the regiment and order it into the field. It was not an auspicious start, but the five hundred–plus men who had enlisted by then had already overcome the obstructionism of a Copperhead governor (whose term had expired) and all the organizational difficulties exacerbated by the weather. Lacking uniforms and incompletely armed, they did not look like much yet, but by March 1862, the First Oregon Volunteer Cavalry Regiment was no longer just a paper command.

THREE

Transitions

When Oregon became the thirty-third state in February 1859, very few of its citizens were born in the state.[1] While the Oregon country had been part of the United States since the 1803 Louisiana Purchase, few citizens journeyed there after Lewis and Clark laid physical claim to it in 1805. It was not until after the gold rush brought hundreds of thousands to California that migration to Oregon truly picked up. Since most of the U.S. citizens had not arrived until the late 1840s, few of the roughly fifty-five thousand people living there at the time of statehood were Oregon-born. Oregon was a state of outsiders, and when, two years after statehood, the Union government finally called on it to raise a volunteer regiment of cavalry from its midst, that regiment was filled by outsiders, including a steamboat captain named John Apperson.

John Apperson, an outsider born in Kentucky who came to Oregon from Missouri, remembered the day Edward Baker, on his way to Washington DC, boarded his steamboat, the *Rival*. The senator and his family boarded in Oregon City for the journey down the Willamette River out to where it joined the Columbia and the beginning of the long trip to his senate seat in the capital.[2] As he left the *Rival*, Senator Baker thanked Apperson and told him, "Remember captain, whatever I can do for you just let me know." Although he had met most of Oregon's early statehood leading figures, Baker made a lasting impression on Apperson he never forgot: "He was a polished, courteous, knightly man and was true as tempered steel."[3] Apperson, who came to Oregon in 1847 with his widowed mother, had only been a steamboat captain for two years when the memorable encounter occurred.[4] Within a year he traded navigating the Willamette River on his steamboat for roaming the eastern two-thirds of the state on a horse. While their jobs varied, the dramatic shift was similar for most of the men who joined the First Oregon Volunteer Cavalry Regiment. The officers spent several months transforming the raw recruits into an effective mounted force. Following examinations to ensure recruits met the minimum physical standards and were loyal to the Union, the volunteers slowly transformed into troopers.

Ever since the regiment's inception, the military made efforts to prevent Southern sympathizers from infiltrating the Oregon Cavalry. First, the government sidestepped Governor Whiteaker. Then once the selection of recruiting officers began, those who raised enough recruits to keep their commissions went before an examination board. The boards were set up to weed out incompetent officers and ensure their loyalty. The most worrisome danger was that pro-Confederate officers would hobble the military effort to protect the Pacific Northwest against clandestine groups such as the Knights of the Golden Circle (KGC), or maybe even join them. Poor leadership, whether intentional or not, could easily destroy the esprit de corps and effectiveness of a command, which might also lead to high dissertation rates.

Less than a month before the War Department authorized raising the Oregon Cavalry, citizens in Eugene expressed deep concerns about secessionists infiltrating any volunteer force that might be recruited in Oregon. In response to their concerns, the Department of the Pacific commander assured them that Col. B. L. Beall, who had replaced Wright as the District of Oregon commander, had been instructed to "exercise great caution in the examination of the persons selected as officers" for any volunteer command, "and under no circumstances" was he "to accept the services of anyone 'about whose loyalty to the National Government there is the shadow of a doubt.' This, the general thinks, will frustrate any plans on the part of the secessionists to place their friends in positions dangerous to the State."[5] In August 1861, the latest department commander, General Sumner, revealed that he harbored his own concerns, informing Beall he had "reason to fear that in the event of volunteers being called for from the State of Oregon . . . [they] may not possess that character of loyalty to the General Government essentially necessary in those occupying so important a position." He made it clear to Beall that he was "particularly desirous that no one should be mustered into service" if there was any doubt about their loyalty.[6] Those hoping to earn a permanent commission in the regiment went before a review board, which assessed the applicants' loyalty. Both officers and men also had to take an oath of allegiance to the Union as part of the enlistment process.

Initially, the officers' loyalty mattered most to the military high command, but for the soldiers, it was the officers' fitness for command they cared about. In the field, even in the far-off Pacific Northwest, their lives literally depended on the officers' leadership abilities. Since only one of those seeking an original regimental commission had served in the prewar army, the trick for the examining boards was not to conflate inexperience with a lack of ability. A number of the officers admitted a lack of military knowledge, yet through hard work and humility about their need to learn, most did become at least sufficient, and some even exceptional, military leaders.[7]

John Miller Drake had no military experience when he joined the embryonic Oregon Cavalry on November 29, 1861. Born in Stroudsburg, Pennsylvania, on December 31, 1830, Drake was the oldest of ten (two of whom were born after he left home). While in Pennsylvania, he matriculated through Stroudsburg Pennsylvania Academy before he joined the migration to the California gold fields in 1849, a few months before he turned nineteen. Sometime between 1852 and 1860, he moved to Oregon, settling in Clackamas County. When he enlisted in the First Oregon Volunteer Cavalry Regiment he was living in southwestern Oregon. Drake entered the service as a first lieutenant in Company D, which was commanded by Capt. Sewell Truax at the time. Through his writings about his service, Drake demonstrates an observant mind and sharp wit, along with the capacity for biting critiques of his fellow officers and superiors. He was just as quick to appreciate their good qualities as criticize what he saw as their failings. Before he resigned his commission in the cavalry (to be appointed lieutenant colonel in the First Oregon Infantry Regiment), he was one of the most trusted company commanders, second only to Captain Currey.[8] It was an impressive achievement considering his initial lack of military experience.

In 1861, Drake was living in Jacksonville, where Reuben Maury ran a mercantile store for almost a decade before his own appointment. It seems possible that Lieutenant Colonel Maury, responsible for recruiting in the southern part of the state, knew Drake before he received a commission in the regiment. Whether the two shared stories about their time in the gold fields or did not know each other, Maury saw something in the dark-haired Drake. Although Maury had given him a lieutenant's commission, Drake remembered how all the officers eventually "went before a board of examiners at Fort Vancouver and were examined [by Regular Army officers] as to their fitness for the military service."[9] A finding of disloyalty or overt unfitness for command would have meant the end of his military service. The examination board passed Drake, allowing him to keep his commission and remain in the regiment.

While the examination process did not find any Confederate sympathizers, a few men passed by the boards later proved unfit for command. Even District of Oregon commander Col. B. L. Beall, a man in his early sixties when he assumed command in early fall 1861, sat for an examination by the board. The War Department seemed particularly concerned about Beall's abilities. A civilian employed at Fort Vancouver remembered, "Col. B. L. Beall in command of this District has been ordered to appear before a Board of Army officers for examination . . . for the purpose of retiring such officers as are incompetent to perform Military duties."[10] The War Department seemed to agree; Beall retired a few months later. It was not solely because of his age—his predecessor General Wright

P5. Capt. (at later rank of Lt. Col.) John M. Drake. Oregon
Historical Society, Org. Lot 1414, box 235, 0235S009.

was only two years younger—but because he no longer possessed
the acuity to perform the almost entirely administrative duties of
a district commander.

Given that there were more junior officers, it is not surprising
that a few captains and lieutenants managed to hide their unfitness

for command from the examining boards. Original Company A commander Thomas "Smiley" Harris resigned in 1863 rather than be forced out of the regiment because he was "an injury to the service." Specifically, his alcoholism had demoralized his company so much that it had the highest desertion rate in the regiment at that time.[11] Alcohol abuse also played a role in the dismissal of one of the regimental doctors, Dr. C. C. Dumreicher. Specifically, he was discharged for insubordination while under the influence. Astonishingly, he was allowed back into the service after the war, only to be court-martialed again in 1868 after he "was so drunk . . . as to be unable to properly perform his duty," which resulted in the death of an officer under his care.[12] The army forced a third officer, 2nd Lt. William Capps, to tender his resignation when his actions demonstrated "enough disrespect to the Country, officers of this post [Fort Walla Walla], and of insubordination in its tone to compel his commission to be vacated."[13] Those three were outliers, and most officers passed by the examining boards served faithfully and competently.

Reflecting the diversity of the birthplaces of Oregon's population, the cavalrymen hailed from a wide assortment of locations across the United States, Canada, and nations throughout Europe. There were, however, obvious trends. Most of the troopers and eleven of the officers were born in the Old Northwest—Michigan, Wisconsin, and some from Indiana, but the largest number were from Ohio and Illinois. Future Company C trooper Thomas T. Prather and provisional officer David P. Thompson were among those Ohioans who served in the regiment. Thompson had learned both blacksmithing and surveying before he drove a herd of sheep from Ohio to Oregon in 1853, six years ahead of orphaned Prather, who made the journey when he was sixteen.[14] Significant numbers of recruits hailed from the broadly defined Midwest. Cpl. David Kenworthy, born in Monroe County, Iowa, in 1838, who split his maturing years between there and Montgomery County, Indiana, typified those volunteers. Like many young men in that era, he left for opportunity and adventure in the Far West, arriving in Oregon on the eve of the Civil War. Possibly influenced by the impending long winter and uncertain earning prospects, he enlisted in Company D in December 1861.[15]

Substantial numbers of the volunteers also came from northeastern states, especially Pennsylvania and New York, Riley Barnes among them. The native New Yorker moved in stages across the country after his 1829 birth. First, when he was eight, his family moved to Indiana, then he and a brother moved to Iowa in 1855. Three years later he continued on to Oregon, where he was living when the war started. He volunteered in November 1861 and served his three-year term in Company A.[16] Significant numbers hailed from the border state of Missouri as well. In fact, native sons of every free or border state, except Minnesota and Kansas (which entered the Union in January 1861), rode in the First Oregon Volunteer Cavalry Regiment during its nearly five-year existence. Being so far from the actual fighting, it is not entirely surprising that men from every Confederate state except Arkansas, Florida, and South Carolina also served in the First Oregon Volunteer Cavalry Regiment. The largest number of the regiment's southern troopers came from Virginia and Tennessee, with a handful from Alabama. There were more Virginia-born troopers than native Oregonians in the First Volunteer Oregon Cavalry Regiment.[17]

The native-born (the government meant "whites only") Oregon population was extremely small at the start of the war for the simple reason that migration to the Pacific Northwest did not begin until the mid-1830s. Therefore, most Oregon-born white males were too young for military service during the Civil War. However, a small number of native-born Oregon men, including at least one minor, did serve in the Oregon cavalry. William Lewis, James Langlois, and Samuel Nelson Hauxhurst were among the seven native Oregonians to ride in the regiment. Lewis, who was born in Oregon before it was even a territory, joined Company G in 1863, when he was eighteen years old.[18] Langlois, the son of an English sailor, lied about his age when he joined the Oregon Cavalry, telling the recruiters he was twenty when his actual age was fifteen. Being six feet tall made it easier for him to pass as a twenty-year-old.[19]

No Oregon trooper had stronger ties to the state than Hauxhurst, who was born in 1839 to pioneer Webley John Hauxhurst and his wife, Wattiet Mary, the daughter of a Northern Kalapuyan chief.[20]

Like the antebellum U.S. Army, the Oregon Cavalry included a large minority of foreign-born volunteers, an even larger percentage than was present among the state's population. Roughly 30 percent of the Oregon cavalrymen, including five officers, were foreign-born. They came from Canada and sixteen different countries and principalities throughout Europe. Given the political upheaval that wracked the European continent at midcentury, this is not surprising. There were one or two from places ranging from Bavaria to Russia, Poland, Norway, and Saxony. Larger numbers came from Prussia, France, Sweden, and Switzerland, including Frenchman Michael Damphoffer and his son, also named Michael, both of whom served in Company C.[21] Eleven troopers hailed from Scotland, including James Harkinson, who lost his life in the service of his adopted country.[22] Eleven Englishmen also served in the regiment, along with another nine from British North America (Canada), including three officers, Charles Drew, Sewell Truax, and John W. Hopkins.[23]

Most foreign-born recruits came from Germany and, especially, Ireland, each of which went through social unrest in the mid to late 1840s. The potato famine in Ireland and revolution in Germany led to heavy migration from both places to the United States. Once here, those immigrants faced economic challenges. Germanic immigrants dealt with language barriers, while the Irish endured cultural prejudice. For both groups, the steady income of military service was often the best available economic option. Enlistment was also a good way for recently arrived immigrants to integrate into U.S. culture, William Kelly among them. Born in Ireland, Kelly arrived in the United States in the 1840s and quickly joined the army. He came to Fort Vancouver in 1849 with the Fourth Infantry Regiment, serving as a first sergeant and steward in the hospital. He remained there after his enlistment expired, working first as the postmaster at the fort and then serving as a clerk and treasurer for the U.S. district court.[24] While the antebellum army preferred its own citizens, it needed immigrants to fill the ranks. Immigrants as a whole, led by the Germans and Irish, outnumbered the native-born citizens in the prewar army.[25]

On June 9, 1863, Pvt. William Johnson was discharged by order of the Fort Walla Walla post surgeon; he was sixty-one or sixty-two years old at the time. By that time, he had shared a soldier's life with men as much as forty-two years his junior. Somewhat surprisingly, he was discharged not due to age-related infirmity but after the loss of the use of his left hand following the amputation of his thumb on that side.[26] Johnson was the oldest man to join the Oregon Cavalry, but not by much; Pvt. Patrick Kelly was just four years younger. The two were among the thirty-nine men who were forty years old or older when they served in the regiment. At the other end of the spectrum were the more than ninety teenagers who rode in the regiment's seven companies. Most of them were eighteen or nineteen, but there were several that were fifteen or sixteen years old, including all five feet, two-and-three-eighths inches of Company B's Douglas Parker.[27] Companies C and E had the broadest range of ages, forty-two years, mostly because they included the two oldest men; Companies A and B had the most teenagers in their ranks; and Companies A and C had the most men forty and older.[28]

The officers, on average, were slightly older than the troopers, with a narrower range in their ages, as would be expected, since there were substantially fewer of them. Capt. William C. Kelly was the oldest at forty-three, and James Waymire was the youngest at nineteen in 1861.[29] As a group, the median age of the Oregon Cavalry's officer corps was just over thirty years old when the regiment was formed in late 1861.[30] On average, the cavalrymen and officers were in their late twenties. That was roughly two years older than the average age of the Union military as a whole, which was just under twenty-six.[31] The reason the Oregon cavalrymen were slightly older than their counterparts in the East was the newness of the state, with an adult population overwhelmingly from someplace else. Whether they arrived as children or by themselves on the eve of war, much of the adult population left other lives behind in the hope of finding a better one in Oregon, whether as farmers, shopkeepers, or those the government sent—soldiers who chose to stay after their enlistments ended.

Recruiters in Oregon or anywhere else prized volunteers with military experience. Not only did such men know what to expect; their previous experiences, as one officer admitted, could help new recruits—and new officers in some cases—learn the art of soldiering quicker.[32] Roughly 5 percent of the troopers had served in a regular army command before, though not always in the U.S. Army. Perhaps it is not surprising, given the relatively small military presence in the Pacific Northwest during the preceding twenty years, that there was only one army veteran among the officers: Captain Kelly spent ten years in the army, eventually attaining the rank of sergeant prior to joining the Oregon Cavalry. When the call went out for volunteers to fill Oregon's first regiment, it was a perfect opportunity for both the new regiment, which benefited from his experience, and the ex-soldier, who was given an officer's commission. He led Company C in southwestern Oregon beyond the war years.[33] Company E, which was partially recruited in the vicinity of Fort Walla Walla, included over twenty former soldiers, many of them Irish.[34] No doubt the substantial bounties and promise of land grants were more appealing to some recently discharged soldiers than uncertain civilian employment or returning to the less financially rewarding and more disciplined Regular Army.

It is doubtful that any of the former soldiers had lived as adventurous a life as red-haired Charles Bruce Montague. Born in Argyll, Scotland, in 1830, Montague first came to the United States with his family in 1847. He headed to California after news of the gold discoveries spread throughout the country. Failing to strike it rich, he decided to return to Scotland in the mid-1850s. While there he volunteered for the Royal Scots Greys, a cavalry command already famous for capturing a French imperial eagle standard at the Battle of Waterloo.[35] During his time in that regiment, it served on the Crimean Peninsula, where it confronted the Russian cavalry at the 1854 Battle of Balaklava. Montague and the Greys successfully

saved the British supply wagons and then witnessed the disastrous "Charge of the Light Brigade," immortalized in Tennyson's
poem. After the expiration of his service with the Scots Greys,
he returned to the United States and then to California before
moving to Oregon in 1858. He was teaching when he enlisted in
Salem in November 1861. It is not difficult to imagine Montague
regaling his Oregon comrades, in a thick Scottish accent, with stories about his time in one of the British Army's most famous cavalry commands.[36]

Soldiering was just one of a multitude of previous occupations
claimed by the Oregon volunteers. The overwhelming majority of
them were working as farmers or miners when they enlisted. Since
obtaining the funds to purchase good farmable land could be challenging and mining rarely worked out for the actual miners, the
residents of the new state learned to be economically flexible and
opportunistic. As a result, the diversity in the volunteer's preenlist-
ment occupations was considerable. Besides farming and mining,
there were a large number of general laborers on the regimental
roster. Beyond soldiers, miners, farmers, and laborers, the regiment also included carpenters, blacksmiths, tailors, and numerous
saddlers; a banker, barber, accountant, druggist, fireman, silver-
smith, and gardener; and both teachers and students.[37]

The inability to overcome the challenges of trying to earn a collegiate education played a role in J. Henry Brown's, Benton Killin's,
and John Buel Dimick's decisions to join the Oregon Cavalry in
1861 and 1862. All three had been students at Willamette University
in Salem, Oregon; however, for different reasons none completed
his education, eventually deciding to join the cavalry regiment.[38]
For Brown, the challenge was purely financial.

Joseph Henry Brown, as he was known, was born on August 4,
1838, in Wilmington, Illinois. His parents, as he remembered,
believed they could "better their condition" in that "mysterious
country—Oregon." So after two years of planning, they crossed
the plains in 1847. He lived on the family farm for ten years before
making his way to California. Deciding there was no future for him
there, he returned to Salem. In an effort to expand his economic

opportunities and enhance his knowledge, he decided to attend Willamette University, located there. Unfortunately, he did not have any money. Undeterred, he later detailed "waiting on the tables in a hotel for [his] board, and saw[ing] wood, nights, morning[s] and Saturday for [his] clothing and tuition." All the time spent working to cover expenses took a toll, and after six months "it became evident that the toil was too much and [he] was compelled to discontinue [attending]." After a brief time working as a painter, he enlisted in the First Oregon Volunteer Cavalry Regiment on December 9, 1861.[39]

It is possible that Brown knew two future troopers during his time at Willamette University, Killin and Dimick. The Iowa-born Killin came to Oregon with his parents and siblings (including his brother Thomas, who also served in the regiment) in 1845. In 1858 at the age of sixteen, he left the family farm in southern Clackamas County to chart his own course. He worked each summer to save up enough money to attend Willamette University when the school year started in the fall. Unable to earn enough money during the summer of 1861 to enroll at Willamette, he tried his luck in the gold fields of what is now Idaho but did not remain there long. In January 1862 Killin enlisted in the Oregon Cavalry. His brother joined the regiment the next year.[40]

John B. Dimick, another Willamette University student who joined the regiment, left the university early, though not due to a lack of funds like Brown or Killin but because of an inability to focus on his courses after a great loss. Dimick, a native of Illinois, came to Oregon in 1848 with his parents and five older siblings; a younger one was born during the trek to Oregon. The family settled on a large farm in the Willamette valley. He left the family farm and started at the university in 1858 but "was called home to the bedside of [his] invalid mother," who died that September. After "her sufferings were over and her pain-racked body laid to rest," he explained later, "I returned to resume my studies. But all seemed changed. Apply myself as I would, I could make but little headway in my school work." With rumblings of war rising, he related, "My student days were numbered."[41] He enlisted in Company B on January 12, 1862. J.B., as he was called, proved to be an excellent soldier, rising to sergeant in the cavalry before being promoted to lieutenant and transferred to the First Oregon Infantry Regiment in 1865. The university's loss certainly proved to be the military's gain.[42]

Not every cavalryman demonstrated the same ability and steadfastness in the field as John Dimick, but most of the recruits proved competent and up to the tasks ahead of them. However, there were a discernable few who were ill-suited for service in the Oregon Cavalry due to either character flaws or not being able to endure the discipline and hardships that were cornerstones of service on the frontier. Training could, and mostly did, help recruits overcome inexperience and a lack of physical unpreparedness. Personal demons such as alcoholism or intentional moral failings were much more difficult to overcome, if it could be done at all.

Both Captains Currey and Drake acknowledged their own lack of experience when they first received their commissions in the cavalry. During an introspective letter to Oregon's second wartime governor, Addison C. Gibbs, Currey admitted, "I did not enter the service under the pretense that I knew all or any thing about military affairs."[43] Drake too understood that there was a general lack of experience among the new regiment's officer corps. Outside of Captain Kelly, who recruited far to the north, Drake said, "The rest of us officers knew absolutely nothing about military matters." Discussing their want of military knowledge, Drake and some of the other recently appointed officers wondered "how [they] were to obtain the necessary instruction to enable [them] to perform the duties of officers and train those raw recruits, [it] was a problem that worried [them] not a little." Though embarrassing, once the officers at Camp Baker learned there was a former U.S. Army veteran among their men, the officers swallowed their pride and asked him to train them in the manual of arms. "There was also another man," Drake later admitted, "who had been in the cavalry service in British India. He taught us the sabre exercise."[44] The officers practiced all winter long, to be ready to instruct their men when the weather broke. They needed every additional day that prolonged winter provided. New recruit David Hobart Taylor observed on the first day of drilling, "We made an awkward appearance, at first could not tell right from left." Two days later his continued struggles frustrated him: "Took one lesson in drilling was very awkward cant tell how to go through the manoever, yet but hope to become expert before long in the use of the firearms."[45]

Not all company officers went to the lengths that Drake did, but most did work to prepare themselves to turn the raw recruits into competent soldiers. Their work largely paid off. Reflecting on the Oregon cavalrymen he led for three years, Drake said, "Notwithstanding the difficulties under which we labored, the time came when we understood our business and our duties as well as any officers or troops that we came in contact with, and a great deal better than many of them."[46] In a testament to the effectiveness of their training regimen, of the seven men eventually promoted from the ranks, only one proved unfit for command. The rest served as competent officers. Two, Stephen Watson and James Waymire, developed into exceptional leaders, although neither stayed with the regiment long enough to rise further. Capt. John M. McCall described Lieutenant Watson as "a brave and gallant officer" whose comrades knew him to be "a warm and kind-hearted friend."[47] The often critical Drake remarked, "Lt Waymire is an efficient officer and the best scout with the [1864] expedition."[48] Both might have risen further, but Waymire was plucked from the cavalry to serve under Governor Gibbs and Watson was killed in action during Drake's 1864 expedition. Even the "very awkward" David Taylor became a competent soldier and was promoted to sergeant before his enlistment ended.[49]

While most members of the Oregon Cavalry steadily became proficient as cavalrymen, some were simply not suited for military service. The regiment suffered from the dual scourges of desertion and binge drinking and alcoholism. The Oregon Cavalry was not alone in dealing with those problems. The antebellum army on the frontier had been beset by both problems, undermining its effectiveness. Each challenge existed not just before the war but during as well as long after.

Isolation, routine, and boredom were the chief culprits in leading a soldier into the depths of alcoholism, either the binge drinking or daily type, or exacerbating an already existing problem.
Even though military doctors were charged with detecting problems like apparent alcoholism, which would prohibit recruits from
being able to perform a soldier's basic duties, they took a pragmatic approach. As one antebellum volunteer observed, so long as
a recruit was "sober at the time of presenting himself," he usually
passed, unless he showed signs of withdrawal.[50] The military's need
for soldiers meant doctors passed some alcoholics through. The
combination of some men who were already alcohol-dependent
with the routine, isolated service on the frontier wearing down
the resistance of others created significant problems for frontier
forces, including the Oregon Cavalry.

Oregon cavalrymen serving during the Civil War were not as
far from their homes as most soldiers in the antebellum army.
During the first spring, many recruits were encamped so close to
home that they could, as Sergeant Taylor did, visit their family and
friends. Given the prevalence of numerous references to drinking in the surviving accounts written by the Oregon troopers, it
seems that being closer to home, at the least, made it easier for
some to abuse alcohol.

One trooper believed the monthslong expeditions decreased
the propensity of his fellow cavalrymen to binge drink.[51] Unfortunately, surviving evidence does not support that conclusion.
Constant activity and the general distance from any town or other
source of available alcohol did make alcohol less accessible, but
not impossible to get. Officers could obtain alcohol more easily
than the average trooper. As an officer stationed at the Warm
Springs Reservation demonstrated, it was as easy as requesting a
favor from a friend at the supply base, in this case Fort Vancouver.
One of the officers overseeing a supply depot in eastern Oregon
asked Lt. John Apperson, on temporary staff duty at Fort Vancouver, to "please send me two (2) blankets; 3 gallons of whisky
(Com.) and 10 lbs. of crushed sugar."[52] Even if Apperson did not
fulfill the request, others certainly made sure large quantities of

alcohol made it to the supply depots in the field—and from there to the officers involved in expeditions. One trooper riding with Captain Currey's command in eastern Oregon in 1864 noted, "Lts. Currey [the captain's brother] and Hobart were almost as full of liquor as could be."[53] Captain Drake had his hands full with intoxicated officers during the other 1864 expedition into eastern Oregon. Besides the regularly drunk Dr. C. C. Dumreicher, he found "[Lieutenant] Noble and [Captain] Small [along with Captain Porter] were all more or less drunk, and were making considerable noise at a very late hour" several months into their campaign.[54] Clearly, serving on the frontier did not eliminate the officers' ability to acquire whiskey.

Problems with alcohol abuse in the field paled in comparison to what happened during prolonged periods at the forts and camps. Months of confinement at those installations and repetition led to boredom during the winter, when the weather prohibited most patrolling and too often limited even mundane camp activities. Captain Currey believed boredom and what men did to alleviate it degraded their quality as soldiers and weakened the relationship between the troopers and their officers. He felt prolonged garrisoning "destroy[ed] the efficiency of the army by leaving them exposed to the temptation to vices, and the endeavoring influences of aimless formality and self-abnegation."[55] This was not unique to those serving in the Pacific Northwest, nor new. A dragoon serving in New Mexico Territory in 1854 observed what happened all too often on payday (which was supposed to be every two months but rarely happened that frequently at isolated garrisons): by nightfall "about 80 drunken men are staggering about the [fort] grounds."[56]

While camps were generally situated at strategic locations on the frontier, the more permanent forts were built near towns or themselves became the nucleus that communities formed around. Most Oregon commands sat out the late fall through early spring months at Fort Vancouver (Portland was across the river), Fort Dalles (The Dalles), and Fort Walla Walla (Walla Walla). All three towns had their share of saloons. Those establishments benefited economically from the soldiers' thirst for "tarantula juice," a term used for the low-quality alcohol sold in the less savory establishments that tended to cater to soldiers. The rest of the businesses and the citizens had less use for drinking soldiers, who could become rowdy or even belligerent. Fortunately, drunken encounters usually involved small groups or individual soldiers, but at least one erupted into a larger fracas that turned deadly. An example of the former occurred in Portland, where "about 3 o'clock on Sunday afternoon, a soldier was seen in an alley way . . . very drunk, and almost naked." The only real damage done was likely to the soldier, whose lack of clothing made the cold December air a potential health hazard.[57]

A far more serious alcohol-fueled incident involving soldiers occurred at a theater in Walla Walla in 1862. According to an account in the newspaper, "a soldier who had been drinking too freely" interrupted the performance "by [his] boisterous conduct." An attempt to remove the drunken soldier erupted into a violent brawl. "A general fight ensued between civil officers and citizens and soldiers," during which "pistols were drawn and fired indiscriminately." One of the soldiers was killed on the spot, one mortally wounded, and several slightly so. A deputy sheriff, shot in the hip, was one of two citizens wounded in the fray; others were slightly injured in the scramble to get out of the theater once the shooting started.[58]

Regular access to alcohol in the towns adjacent to and built around the forts exacerbated the historic problem of soldiers' binge drinking. The Oregon Cavalry also had to deal with the other chronic problem facing the U.S. frontier military: desertion. Of the roughly 900 men who enlisted in the First Oregon Volunteer Cavalry Regiment, at least 125 deserted, several of them multiple times, or approximately 13 out of every 100.[59] That was noticeably higher than the Union armies as a whole, which had a desertion rate slightly under 10 percent.[60] In one strange twist, the Oregon regiment gained an experienced soldier who had deserted from another mounted regiment. Almarin Nottingham, who enlisted in Company E in October 1862, turned himself in to Major Rinearson

P6. Group of Oregon Cavalry officers, including Col. Reuben Maury and
Lt. D. C. Underwood, standing. Oregon Historical Society, OrHi 21090.

at Fort Lapwai as a deserter from the Tenth Illinois Cavalry Regiment the previous spring. Under President Lincoln's deserter
amnesty offer, Nottingham remained in the Oregon Cavalry but
was reassigned to Company B, and there he served out the entirety
of his enlistment without a problem.[61]

Nottingham was lucky; desertion was a capital offense, although
the U.S. Army infrequently executed deserters. Most often they
were imprisoned and then dishonorably discharged. The Department of the Pacific, the final military authority in the Far West,
followed the same policy. Records indicate that two cavalrymen
(Charles Garland and Francis Ely) were sentenced to death after
being court-martialed and found guilty of desertion. Despite Colonel Maury's request for clemency for Ely, who was convicted
first, from department commander Gen. George Wright, a firing
squad carried out the sentence on March 11, 1864.[62] Colonel Maury

had noted that "after almost two years service as an exemplary soldier this was his first" offense, but Wright decided the Oregon Cavalry's high desertion rate warranted an example to hopefully deter others—it had no appreciable impact.[63] Garland, who was eighteen when he enlisted, deserted from his guard post, a particularly egregious offense, two months after the army executed Ely. His sentence was "mitigated to discharge from the U.S. Service with forfeiture of all pay + allowances due + imprisonment during the war to work in chain gang on Alcatraz Island."[64] Other deserters received sentences of hard labor, with ball and chain, and were branded on the hip with the letter *D* before being drummed out of the service.[65] Some, however, were reinstated and completed their full terms as members of the First Oregon Volunteer Cavalry Regiment. Leaders in the District of Oregon did not follow a uniform policy on which soldiers were dishonorably discharged and which were given a chance to return to the ranks and serve out their enlistment.

Recruiting the Pacific Northwest's first contribution to the Union cause had not been easy and had never been as successful as anticipated. Using old strategies enhanced with regionally specific inducements, recruiters did their best to overcome a limited population that felt distanced from the actual conflict. In the end, roughly nine hundred men volunteered for Oregon's cavalry regiment. Within the limits of a racially segregated military, the First Oregon Volunteer Cavalry Regiment was quite diverse. Raised in a state of outsiders, the troopers came from a broad swath of states and countries to a degree similar to the California regiments (which also included Californios and free African Americans—the latter allowed in support roles only), but greater than many older states, where volunteers were more likely born near where they enlisted. Like the other Union states, farmers accounted for a large percentage of the recruits, but so did miners. The troopers' less common preservice occupations varied greatly, as did their ages, though most were not much older than the average Union soldier elsewhere. Despite their separation from the rest of the Union forces and the different nature of their service, their leaders did deal with the same scourges that undermined soldiers everywhere. Even though the regiment suffered higher losses due to desertion, those who remained became effective, sometimes superior soldiers who contributed to the Union cause and the exploration and opening of the frontier regions of the Pacific Northwest during their service, which began in full in 1862.

FOUR

Learning on the Job

"Perched up on the upper bunk to keep out of the way," David Hobart Taylor pulled out his diary and began to record his third day as a member of the First Oregon Volunteer Cavalry Regiment. It was January 3, 1862. Taylor, the son of Rev. Stephen Phelps Taylor, came to Oregon from Ohio with his family in 1853, settling in the southwestern part of the state, not far from Jacksonville. He enlisted in Company A in November 1861, when he was twenty-eight, and officially began his military service on January 1, when he arrived at Camp Baker "in good trim."[1] The camp, still being completed as new recruits arrived, was located about a half mile west of Phoenix.[2] The tall, dark-complexioned Taylor was stationed so close to his home that he was able to leave camp and attend his father's Sunday services and dine with friends.

Camp Baker remained the concentration point and planned training center for the three companies recruited in the southwestern part of the state. Those companies, including Taylor's Company A, remained there until May, longer than anticipated. An uncommonly cold and wet winter was the primary cause of the prolonged stay at the camp. As John Drake, a lieutenant then serving as Lieutenant Colonel Maury's adjutant, explained, it was "the hardest winter that Oregon has ever known since its settlement by white people."[3] As Taylor learned, weather played a key role in what the Oregon Cavalry did and when it did it during the regiment's nearly five-year existence.[4]

After joining the other recruits, Taylor recorded that he "slept some and froze the balance of the [first] night."[5] The next day he and his bunkmates improved their cabin, which was "made of rough logs, chinked and daubed with mud, with a rough board floor and shake roofs," until they "got it quite comfortable."[6] By the third day, he was already seeing a bland pattern in the soldier's diet. Flashing his good-natured humor, he described how "supper in great varieties was served, first bread and meat & water spoiled by adding some coffee to it. Second, meat, coffee & bread, third, coffee bread & meat." By the end of the first month, virtually no drilling had taken place; the men were restless and bored, spending too much time in their sixteen-by-eighteen-foot cabins with a confining fourteen-by-sixteen-foot interior—for sixteen men.[7] The sun came out infrequently until spring arrived, and it rained or snowed in heavy volumes. Lieutenant Drake was frustrated that "anything like drill for the soldiers was out of the question."[8] Even if the weather had cooperated, the two completed companies (A and D) lacked enough arms and equipment with which to drill.[9] The shortage was so bad that "when the sentries were relieved those on beat transferred their arms to the relief." Uniforms would not be issued for months. David Hobart Taylor, John Drake, and all six companies of Oregon cavalry got off to a rough start during those winter months in 1862.

Any hopes, misguided as they were, that the Oregon cavalrymen would be sent east to face Confederates slowly faded during the long, soggy months that followed. By the time the weather abated enough in late spring 1862 for the companies at Camp Baker, termed the Southern Battalion, to drill, it was clear that the regiment would not leave the Pacific Northwest. There would be no grand cavalry charges, virtually no practical use for their swords, no raiding deep behind Confederate lines, and no screening the movements of massive Union armies. A different experience awaited them, one that included patrolling emigrant trails and gold rush areas to protect whites from Indians trying to stop the invasion onto their ancestral lands. Despite the initial lack of equipment and training, there would be a great deal of exploration

of uncharted regions and fort building during their first campaigning season. Early on, their presence also deterred any plots to aid
the Confederacy formulated by Southern sympathizers.

Circumstances had been similar at all the concentration sites; bad
weather delayed the arrival of uniforms, weapons, and other military supplies, frustrating any ideas about getting the raw recruits
ready for service in the field just months ahead. Company B's
Pvt. James Waymire, encamped north of his comrades, near Salem,
noted, "Without arms, clothing, or equipage of any kind, rotten
pork and wormy bread for our scanty rations . . . you can imagine the condition of Company B during that long hard winter."[10]
Born on December 9, 1842, in Missouri, he crossed the plains to
Oregon with his widowed mother and grandfather in 1850. They
established a farm near Roseburg, where he lived before taking a
teaching position on the eve of the Civil War. The teenaged, blond-
haired, blue-eyed Waymire enlisted as a private in the Oregon Cavalry in December 1861.[11] On April 23, 1862, he was promoted from
the ranks after showing obvious skill and leadership potential.

In late March Captain Currey arrived at Camp Barlow, a temporary post ten miles southwest of Oregon City, with the men he
had recruited east of the Cascades at Fort Dalles. There he merged
two contingents of recruits together to form Company E. What
he found at Camp Barlow appalled him: the other recruits were
"almost destitute of everything necessary for the personal comfort of the men, and as a natural consequence the men [were] very
much dissatisfied."[12] Waymire and Company B arrived at Camp
Barlow just ahead of Currey and his men. While the conditions
were bad, the two companies at least had contact with District of
Oregon headquarters, where Company C had been organized.
Regimental commander Colonel Cornelius still had not received
any information from the southern part of the state about Maury's
success or failure due to "high water and the continued severity of
the winter, which have prevented communication with the different parts of the state for the past two months."[13]

Finally, in late February Colonel Cornelius received word from
his second-in-command. Lieutenant Colonel Maury informed him

he had two companies at Camp Baker, near Jacksonville, with hopes of being able to fill two more.[14] Cornelius passed on that overly optimistic information to the U.S. Army adjutant general. Rumors made their way to Maury and civilians in southern Oregon that the two (eventually three) companies with him would soon be ordered north. After months of almost complete inactivity, it appeared Maury's companies were destined to get out of the muddy grounds of Camp Baker. By then, Joseph Pepoon, another member of Company A, was as tired as David Hobart Taylor of the tedium: "Hadn't much of anything to do. We trained some, went through the manual of arms, sabre practice, etc."[15]

How any of the troops were able to drill or train in any way with only a few weapons, limited equipment, and without uniforms—let alone take on the appearance of soldiers—is unclear. Fully aware of the desperate shortages almost all his companies faced, Colonel Cornelius ordered Maj. Charles Drew to San Francisco "with requisitions upon the commander of the Department of the Pacific for clothing, arms, and garrison equipage for the regiment."[16] Only Company C, encamped near Fort Vancouver, and Captain Currey's portion of Company E, having been organized near Fort Dalles, received any equipment before midspring. Even though they had most of their equipment, Currey's men went without uniforms for several additional months.

While Companies C and E continued to go without uniforms, four months after joining the regiment, they were better equipped than those companies still in southern Oregon at Camp Baker. By late March, plans were finally put in motion for the Southern Battalion to join the commands in the north.[17] Maury's force now included the understrength Company F, which Private Taylor described as "a rough Set of men judging from external appearances."[18] Once there, it was hoped they would receive their weapons, equipment, and uniforms. The rumor that they would soon ride north to Camp Barlow and join with other companies and then from there continue to the fields of eastern Oregon was certainly good news for the restless recruits.

Local leaders in southwestern Oregon were not as excited about the departure of the cavalrymen. They expressed concerns about their safety to Lieutenant Colonel Maury, should all the companies leave the region. This led Maury to lobby his superiors for authority to leave a portion of his command behind. He appealed based on two of the Oregon Cavalry's responsibilities, protecting the people from attacks by Indians and helping open up new lands for whites. Maury told the Department of the Pacific commander, "The eastern frontier of Southern Oregon . . . contains large valleys susceptible of cultivations as well as extensive range for stock." He dismissed the Indian tribes living there and their claims to their ancestral lands, very little of which contained farmable land. Removing the troops, Maury warned, "will leave Jackson County especially exposed, and offer inducements to make equal cause with the Indians of the north," who both Maury and Wright presumed would begin attacking settlers and emigrants once the weather improved.[19] Maury seemed to ignore the reality that leaving a company of men without equipment, arms, or uniforms would do little to protect the citizens in southern Oregon.

White community leaders were not the only ones worried by the planned departure of the three companies of Oregon cavalrymen. The superintendent of Indian Affairs for Oregon, William Rector, wrote directly to the department commander, General Wright, to express his anxieties about Indian unrest in the region if some troops were not left in southern Oregon. Rector told Wright the local tribes—Klamaths and Modocs—become bolder and their "impudence increases as the population becomes weaker by the enlistment and withdrawal of the troops of Lieutenant-Colonel Maury's command."[20] Wright felt Rector had overdramatized the situation. Despite proclaiming he did "not believe there is any real danger from Indians at Jacksonville," General Wright decided it would be politically wise to return a company to Camp Baker. Having previously dismissed appeals for the stationing of part of the Oregon Cavalry in the region, he explained he changed his mind "to give a feeling of security to the women and children."[21] After his change of heart, he ordered that one company be left at Camp Baker. To further calm the people in the region, Wright made it clear that one of the regimental officers, Maj. Jacob S.

Rinearson, would join the cavalry company in the area. A major had more status than a company commander, so it was hoped that sending Major Rinearson to oversee a company of Oregon cavalrymen would demonstrate Wright's commitment to protecting southern Oregon. On May 12, he instructed Colonel Steinberger to order Maury to leave Company A, D, or F in southern Oregon. Unfortunately, that was a week after Maury's command began its march north.[22] It took nine more days before the orders arrived in Portland. By the time they reached Maury many days later, he "was so far on his way north as to make it impracticable to send the company back."[23]

With communications from department headquarters taking so long to reach the commands in the field, Wright decided to let Colonel Steinberger oversee the disposition of the forces in his district. Steinberger faced a dilemma: either he could order one of Maury's recently arrived companies back to the southwestern corner of the state or he could send his only available company—Company C, commanded by Capt. William Kelly. Sending one of the Southern Battalion companies back to Camp Baker would be welcomed by the local populace, as they knew those men, but this option presented an important challenge.

When Maury's men encamped near Oregon City, they were without equipment or proper arms and still wore their by now ragged civilian clothes. After so many months with only a handful of arms and no equipment, Colonel Steinberger found that even though the Southern Battalion had "been six months in service they are sadly deficient in drill and discipline." He informed department headquarters it would take time to repair "this defect, incident to embarrassments in organization of the regiment and other causes."[24] Therefore, he decided to send Captain Kelly's Company C from Fort Vancouver to Camp Baker. On June 30 Colonel Steinberger communicated this decision to Indian Agent Rector.[25] That was almost two months after Rector's plea for the stationing of a military force in the area; it took another month before Company C began the march to southern Oregon. In another change from the original idea, Maj. Charles Drew, not Major Rinearson, assumed administrative command.[26] Company C spent the rest of the war operating in the southern portion of the state, where it eventually built a fort.

On May 5 David Hobart Taylor put his foot in a stirrup, grabbed the pommel of his saddle, and pulled himself onto his horse to start the ride north.[27] Finally, after five months, he, Lieutenant Drake, and their comrades in Company A; Companies D and the incomplete F; and some unattached men set out to rendezvous with the rest of the regiment, where they would get their equipment and uniforms. As they rode away from the still muddy Camp Baker grounds, one of the cavalrymen marveled at the image they presented, in "the rags and tatters that graced many of us."[28] During the two-week trip north, their lack of uniforms and equipment confused the civilians they encountered. Some people thought they were miners, others horse traders, which hurt their pride. One of the motley-looking troopers admitted, "We thought our *soldierly* bearing should have taught them better."[29] Others believed they were California volunteers coming to Oregon to replace the departed Regulars. Only a few seemed to know their actual identity. One family that did recognize the column as Oregon's contribution to the Union cause put out a U.S. flag, prompting the men to give "them three rousing cheers and the Old Lady Said that the cheering was worth fifty dollars." Riding through an area Private Taylor described as otherwise "all Secesh, no Sense to any of them" served as a reminder that Confederate sympathizers lived throughout the state.[30]

The 250-plus-mile journey came to a temporary end for the Southern Battalion—a designation that really did not apply any longer—when it reached Camp Clackamas, near Oregon City, on May 22. After the long trek "through rain and snow and mud," during which they "went to bed cold and wet, and sometimes hungry," one of Maury's men was happy to reach the new camp. It "is very pleasantly located," he noted, "on the north side of the Clackamas river, at the grounds occupied by the State Fair last fall."[31] Private Taylor took a more jaundiced view of the camp, which lacked good grass for the horses, and the town, which he described as "not much of a place, looks like the last rose of Departed beauty."[32] His disdain for the town's aesthetics was partially offset by the fact that he had family living in Oregon City, who he visited on occasion.

The campsite was a short distance inland from where the steamers unloaded passengers and supplies. This proved convenient when some of the cavalry's equipment arrived a few days later. The things the cavalrymen needed arrived in fits and starts, which tempered some of the excitement. Notwithstanding his negative reaction to Oregon City, David Hobart Taylor's good humor had survived the long months of drilling without equipment and the cold, wet, and muddy ride from Camp Baker to Camp Clackamas. When "large quantities of Boxes, containing clothing" were dropped fifty yards from his tent, he made light of the fact that there were no pants in the crates: "Guess we will wear our high water jackets, paint our legs Sky Blue."[33] Maury's three companies were the last to receive all their equipment, clothing, and weapons—in June. They traded ragged hats for forage caps, wore light-blue woolen pants and dark-blue woolen jackets, and were issued short-barreled muzzle-loading muskets.[34] Revolvers and swords were also issued at that time.[35] At least they were armed and finally looked like soldiers; no longer would they be mistaken for miners.

The men Maury led from the southern part of the state were thrilled to finally be uniformed and armed, to finally feel like federal soldiers. Colonel Cornelius wanted to remain in camp until his command was unified before leading it into the field. District of Oregon commander Col. Justus Steinberger disagreed. He was impatient to use this new force to fill the still gaping void left by the recall of the Regulars almost a year earlier. Therefore, he ordered Cornelius to lead two of the three companies (B and E) that had already been fully equipped (Company C was the other one) to Fort Walla Walla. He directed Cornelius to establish regimental headquarters there and await the arrival of the remaining companies in preparation for service on the frontier.[36] Steinberger explained his decision to his superior, stating, "I cannot wait for Colonel Cornelius to put his whole command into position at one

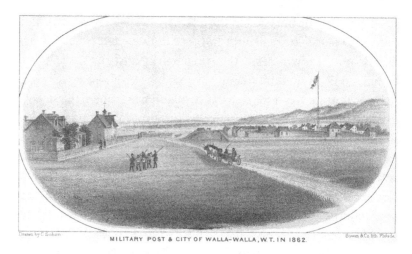

MILITARY POST & CITY OF WALLA-WALLA, W.T. IN 1862.

F1. Fort Walla Walla. Fort Walla Walla Museum, Walla Walla WA.

camp near Oregon City." Delaying "would prevent their becoming available at the moment when they will be most needed," during the emigration period from midspring to midfall.[37] Maury's companies reached their designated encampment, Camp Clackamas, the day after Cornelius started Companies B and E on their trek to Fort Walla Walla.

Colonel Steinberger clearly laid out the challenges and responsibilities facing the Oregon Cavalry in his orders sending Colonel Cornelius and Companies B and E to Fort Walla Walla. Those orders guided much of what the Oregon Cavalry did for the entirety of its service. He warned that "in the prevailing excitement about the gold mines and the large emigration to Indian country contiguous to your headquarters, there is reasonable prospect of dissatisfaction among the tribes upon whose grounds the discoveries are made, and in some instances the probability of conflict." While he did not specify, it is clear Steinberger was particularly concerned about the powerful Nez Perce tribe, on whose lands gold had been discovered. He impressed upon Cornelius the importance of preventing rather than prosecuting open conflict with any of the Indian tribes: "To prevent the outbreak of hostilities, protect settlers, and

secure justice on either side, for the preservation of amicable relations, it is expected that the force under your command is mainly
to be employed." Steinberger reiterated that "to prevent rather than
combat hostilities with the Indian tribes on our frontiers should be
the policy pursued." Steinberger emphasized to Cornelius that "in
assuming the important and responsible command of Fort Walla
Walla a high and delicate trust devolves upon you." Perhaps realizing the pressure he had put on his subordinate, he assured him,
"Much confidence is felt in the officers and troops of your command for the proper discharge of their duties."[38]

While Maury oversaw the arming, equipping, and contin-
ued training of his three companies after their arrival at Camp
Clackamas, Colonel Cornelius headed east for Fort Walla Walla.
Once Cornelius reached the fort, he assumed command of the
entire garrison, which included his own Companies B and E,
Oregon Cavalry, as well as Companies A and C of the Fourth
California Infantry Regiment.[39] It had taken his men two weeks
to get there from Fort Vancouver. Altogether they had covered
320 miles from their original encampment, according to Captain
Currey.[40] After reaching the Columbia River, the two companies
proceeded by steamship, which took them to The Dalles, where
they disembarked and took up the rest of the trip on horseback.
It was possible to take another ship that would have gotten them
close to Fort Walla Walla, but that would have cost the army
more money, something the district commander tried to limit.[41]
So the two companies got their first taste of prolonged riding as
a command, during which time trooper J. Henry Brown remembered they endured several storms. The only incident that dis-
turbed the procession occurred on May 29, when a drunken
Company E farrier named James Robinson shot Sgt. William A.
Clark, also from Company E, in the shoulder. Robinson was
in turn shot twice while trying to escape. Both men survived,
but neither served out their terms in the regiment—Clark was
eventually discharged for disability and Robinson deserted from
the Fort Walla Walla hospital.[42] By the time the two companies
reached Fort Walla Walla on June 4, they had ridden a total of

179 miles since disembarking at The Dalles, a fractional distance compared to what lay ahead of them.[43]

After five additional weeks of structured training, on June 23 Steinberger finally ordered Maury to take Companies A, D, and F and join him at Fort Walla Walla. Steinberger directed him to start one company on June 24, followed by the next company two days later, and the last one on June 27.[44] The three companies followed the same route, and in the same way, as Companies B and E had, first by steamship to The Dalles, then on their horses to Fort Walla Walla. All three companies reached Fort Walla Walla by mid-July. This was well into the most active military season in the Far West, which occurred mainly from early May to late October, when emigrant trains navigated through and miners swarmed over frontier lands. Inclement weather put a temporary halt to long-distance travel during the winter months.

Two important changes in the military command structure of the District of Oregon occurred between Lieutenant Colonel Maury's departure for Fort Walla Walla and the Oregon Cavalry's first major expedition. On June 23 Department of the Pacific headquarters in San Francisco issued orders appointing Brig. Gen. Benjamin Alvord the new commander of the District of Oregon; he took formal command upon his arrival at Fort Vancouver on July 7.[45] Four days later the department accepted Colonel Cornelius's resignation. Due to the loss (in a fire during transit) of his letter of resignation, the Department of the Pacific did not receive orders to formally appoint anyone to take over command of the regiment until 1863.[46]

Steinberger had always been an odd choice to lead a military district, so his replacement by Alvord, a Regular Army officer, was not surprising. The Pennsylvania-born Justus Steinberger had no military experience prior to being appointed an assistant adjutant general in October 1861. He promptly resigned from that post on the grounds of supposed physical disability due to abscesses that would not heal.[47] Yet somehow the pain did not prohibit him from accepting command of the newly created First Washington

Territory Infantry Regiment the next day.[48] Command of the District of Oregon devolved on him seven months later.[49] He was the fourth district commander in eight months and the only nonprofessional soldier. There is no reason provided in the official correspondence or his personnel file for his demotion back to command of the Washington Infantry, but given a professional soldier replaced him, it is likely the military's preference for Regular Army officers leading military districts cost him the command.

Thomas Cornelius's resignation generated its share of speculation—among contemporaries then and historians later. The editor at the *Weekly Oregonian* (Portland) postulated that having overseen the raising of the regiment and with it about to conduct its first field operations, Cornelius felt his job had been accomplished.[50] William V. Rinehart, who eventually rose to captain in the Oregon Cavalry, believed that "on account of [his] failure to raise a full Regiment, he resigned."[51] Historian G. Thomas Edwards speculated that he resigned due to acrimonious relations with his superior, Colonel Steinberger.[52] If that were the case, then Cornelius must have regretted resigning when he found out Steinberger had been demoted. In August 1862 Cornelius told Lt. John T. Apperson the reason he resigned was because he had failed to fill ten full companies, confirming Rinehart's view. By then he was on leave and back at his home, hoping the military would "order [him] to fill up the Redgament [*sic*] as this war appears to be farther from a close than was thought."[53] The order never came; the military moved on from Cornelius quickly, leaving Lieutenant Colonel Maury the de facto commander of the regiment and the only one of the three original officers still in uniform.

The leadership changes certainly improved the effectiveness of the troopers in the long run, but those changes came at an inconvenient time. General Alvord brought much-needed stability to the District of Oregon, which became more apparent the next year when he implemented his own plans for the campaigning season. However, he did not have time to create new strategies for the current operations, so he continued what Colonel Steinberger had set in motion. To Lt. John Drake, who had been with

Maury since the previous fall, the implications of bringing five of the six companies together were clear: "The arrival of the Oregon Cavalry at Fort Walla Walla in the summer of 1862 marked the beginning of its real military career." For Maury that meant immediately leading the largest concentration of Oregon cavalrymen yet assembled into eastern Oregon and what was then southeastern Washington Territory. Drake remembered, "On arriving at Fort Walla Walla we learned that preparations were under way for a cavalry expedition on the emigrant road on Snake River, and we began to prepare for it at once."[54]

Getting such a late start for an expedition meant Lieutenant Colonel Maury's newly arrived companies had little time to rest before setting out. Just five days after assuming command of the District of Oregon, General Alvord outlined for Maury the plans for the remainder of the summer and most of the fall. He made it clear that the Oregon Cavalry's "principal object is the protection of all travelers, and especially of the expected emigration," and that Maury was also to prevent "the introduction and sale of intoxicating liquors among the Indian tribes." Like many Regular Army soldiers who served on the frontier, Alvord was well aware that whites were usually the instigators of conflicts with Indian people, therefore he added some explicit orders regarding interaction with those he termed "peaceable" Indians. The Oregon Cavalry was not "to interfere with their fishing or other peaceful avocations" but were to ensure "the preservation of order, and especially that whenever [Maury's] command comes in contact with camps of peaceable Indians, the Indians should be vigilantly protected from injury and violence from whites, whether soldiers or citizens." To achieve his responsibilities, Maury was ordered to take three companies and "proceed as far as Salmon Falls, on Snake River, and not to return to Fort Walla Walla before the 1st of November."[55]

The prolonged stay in the field would ensure protection for the emigrant stragglers who started their journey late in the season. It would also alleviate some of the housing and feeding pressure at Fort Walla Walla. Maury chose two of the three companies he

EXPLANATION OF 1862 CAMPAIGN
—·⋗··- *Maury expedition July 28 to October 28*

N
A   0   25   50 miles

M2. Explanation of the 1862 campaign. Created by Chelsea McRaven Feeney.

had known the longest, A and D. Company F was designated for other duty, and its place in the expeditionary force was taken by Company B, commanded by Capt. Elisha Harding, former regimental quartermaster Benjamin F. Harding's younger brother.

After gathering all the needed supplies and uniforming the remaining troops, the 243-man column headed southeastward from Fort Walla Walla on July 28.[56] It was roughly 350 miles to Salmon Falls, which was approximately two-thirds of the way between Fort Walla Walla and Fort Hall, in southeastern Idaho today. It was also an area that military officials deemed particularly dangerous for emigrants because Shoshones gathered in the region to stock up on fish during the summer. After reaching Salmon Falls, Maury would be positioned to provide protection for the more vulnerable emigrant trains before they began the last leg of the journey to Fort Walla Walla. Most regional leaders believed the rest of the trip to western Oregon was less dangerous at that time and therefore did not require either military protection or an escort. Salmon Falls was also the place where he had been ordered to meet Capt. Medorem Crawford. Crawford had been hired by the War Department to organize a company of fifty armed men to lead and provide protection for emigrant trains between Omaha, Nebraska, and Fort Walla Walla, an almost 1,500-mile route through mostly open frontier.[57] The larger force of Oregon cavalrymen was additional deterrence to prevent violent interaction between the Indians and the white emigrants.

After almost two weeks of riding through the heat and dust kicked up by over four hundred horses and mules, the Oregon troopers encountered their first emigrant train of twenty wagons on August 9, on the Burnt River (south of Baker City, Oregon). They were mostly from Illinois, Indiana, and Iowa. The encounter made one of Maury's troopers reflective about his own experiences and those of most Oregonians, who should have "some recollection of this dreary, barren region, as it has not been very long since they plodded their way through." The emigrants were headed for the Willamette valley, hoping to set up farms. They told Maury that they "had no difficulty with the Indians" during their travels.[58]

The command continued heading southeastward, to the Bruneau River, where it encountered "great numbers of emigrants, in trains large and small. . . . Some of them were pretty well prepared for the journey, while others were already in need of assistance." They reached the river on August 20, where they spent ten days resting both the animals and the men. Maury left Capt. Thomas S. "Smiley" Harris and Company A on the Bruneau in a "beautiful little valley [that] affords a vast quantity of grass," perfect for the cavalry's horses or potentially for grazing herd animals in the future.[59] The rest of the command continued on toward Salmon Falls, which it reached on September 4, before setting up a camp five miles above the falls the next day.[60] Three days later, advanced elements of

Maury's command met Crawford and his men escorting a large emigrant train. The two groups mingled for parts of two days before the emigrants continued on the trail, eventually reaching Captain Harris's encampment on the Bruneau River.[61] Meeting Crawford's escort, which brought up the rear of the season's emigrant trains, marked the halfway point of the Oregon Cavalry's 1862 service. Maury and the main detachment remained above the falls until September 15 before heading back to unite with the troops on the Bruneau River. Once there, he sent out a number of small patrols to collect straggling wagon trains for the next ten days. "It was fortunate for them," wrote one of the troopers, "that we have been laying by, so much—otherwise, they would have suffered greatly."[62] Finally, in late September the Oregon troopers began to slowly retrace their original route back to Fort Walla Walla.

As they rode through the Malheur River watershed, one of the troopers made it clear to newspaper readers in the Salem area that the Malheur was unfit for man or beast: "Imagine a vast wilderness of sand and alkali hills, covered with sage brush, cactus and grease wood, and inhabited by Indians, hares, horned toads, [and] lizards."[63] For the most part, troopers commented far less on the suitability of the lands they traversed for farming, grazing, or its mineral potential during the 1862 expedition than they did in subsequent years. This was, in part, due to their chaotic adjustment and late start getting into the field and because the focus had been on providing broadly defined assistance for the emigrant trains, though the fate of an 1860 emigrant train had also drawn Lieutenant Colonel Maury's attention.

In May 1860 a wagon train made up mostly of the Van Ornum family left Wisconsin, headed for Oregon's Willamette valley. It was joined in Nebraska by the Utter family. The combined group numbered just under fifty at that point, most of whom were children. In August they reached the Fort Hall area of what is now eastern Idaho, where they were joined by six former soldiers. In early September, near Castle Creek, in southwestern Idaho, the wagon train was attacked by a large group of Indians, suspected to

be Shoshones and possibly Bannocks. The white emigrants eventually abandoned most of their wagons and animals and tried to
make their escape after a number of men were killed in a second
attack. The survivors fled at night along the Owyhee River until
they were too weak to continue. A separate Shoshone band found
this camp and traded salmon for nearly all the survivors' clothes,
some trinkets, and their last weapons. With nothing else to trade
and unarmed, the Van Ornum survivors and a couple of others
tried to escape, while others, mostly from a family named Myers,
remained at the river, hoping to be rescued. By the time troops
from Fort Dalles, via Fort Walla Walla, Washington Territory,
found the survivors' camp on the Owyhee River in late October,
there were only twelve still alive (three others had fled early on
and survived).[64] To prevent dying from starvation, the survivors
had eaten the corpses of three of the four children who succumbed
to the lack of food and the elements. The Shoshones caught up to
those who fled and killed seven members of the group and took
four Van Ornum children captive, three girls and a little boy.[65]
Zacheus Van Ornum, the captured children's uncle, spent the next
two years trying to recover his nieces and nephew.[66] The military,
in part due to Zacheus's prodding, committed to helping him, as
much as possible, to find the boy, Reuben Van Ornum; his three
sisters had not survived their captivity.[67]

    While Maury's primary objective was to prevent bloodshed
along the emigrant trails, he had also been charged with serving
as a posse comitatus and ordered "to arrest and punish murderers and other law breakers," as Pvt. James Waymire put it. Although
unsaid, this only applied to Indians and not whites, something
every trooper understood. So in mid-August Maury received
orders from Colonel Steinberger, approved retroactively by General Alvord, to assist Zacheus Van Ornum.[68] Maury told Alvord in
September, "Nothing definite has been heard of the Van Orman
[Van Ornum] children." At that time, the uncle went to Salt Lake
to pursue rumors about a surviving child.[69]

    The three companies resumed their march back toward Fort
Walla Walla without arresting anyone for breaking the law—which
meant any Indians—or helping recover the Van Ornum boy. Those

two ancillary objectives cannot be used to judge the outcome of the Oregon Cavalry's first year of service. A truer measure waited until the units were in their winter quarters and the men and horses recovered from a somewhat abbreviated yet taxing campaign season. As the other three Oregon Cavalry companies could correctly assert, they had not been idle while Companies A, B, and D provided protection along the emigrant trail.

Potential Northern Shoshone or Bannock attacks on emigrant trains were not the only tribes that concerned military and civilian leaders in the Pacific Northwest in 1862. The commitment of Maury's large expedition to protecting the emigrants from the tribal groups called Snakes was significant. However, far more worrisome to federal politicians and the military were the powerful Nez Perce tribal bands (Nimiipuu, meaning "the people" in the Nez Perce language).

The Nez Perce had maintained friendly relations with whites for more than fifty years, since their contact with Lewis and Clark in 1805. However, increasing numbers of whites coming into their ancestral lands worried military officials, who anticipated that Nez Perce tolerance for such transgressions had a limit.[70] In an effort to avoid a conflict between the growing white population and the Nimiipuu people as well as the Cayuse, Umatilla, Yakima, and Palouse tribes, Washington Territorial governor Isaac Stephens negotiated a treaty with these tribes in 1855. The treaty resulted in a much greater impact on the Yakima, whose bands were forced into a tribal confederation, than it did on the Nez Perce. Still, the Nez Perce gave up a large amount of their peripheral lands while maintaining the ancestral core, which stretched across northeastern Oregon, southeastern Washington Territory, and western Idaho (part of Washington Territory at the time). In exchange for the ceding of those lands, the government made considerable promises, almost none of which were kept—namely, to keep whites out of Indian lands until the treaty was ratified.[71]

Congress finally ratified the treaty in 1859, by which time large numbers of whites had long since moved into Nez Perce territory. The likelihood of violence escalated the next year, when gold was discovered on their lands. Not only had whites flooded in, roaming along the Clearwater River and its drainage; the government had failed to meet any of its other obligations laid out in the treaty agreement. The military leadership was sympathetic to the Nez Perce's situation. When the government sought a new treaty, General Alvord explained the prevailing military view: "Those Indians are of superior character; have always been warmly our friends, but they are now rudely dispossessed of their lands on the reservation secured to them by a sacred treaty; their women treated with outrage by the miners; liquor is sold to them by lawless whites, and great danger apprehended of collision."[72]

Gold discoveries early in 1861 led to a rush of whites onto Nez Perce land that became a tidal wave in 1862, when an estimated ten thousand to fifteen thousand brazenly ignored Nez Perce land titles.[73] That spring, Oregon's superintendent for Indian affairs, Edward Geary, wrote then colonel George Wright that "hundreds of white men are already in their [Nez Perce] country, and daily accessions will soon swell the number to thousands." Therefore, Geary recommended "the importance of having a proper military force placed so as to protect the whole reservation from the intrusion of whiskey" and unlawful interaction with the tribe. To meet the challenge of overseeing a large reservation, he suggested Wright commit a cavalry unit to such a task.[74]

Unfortunately for the Nez Perce, no action was taken until the middle of the summer due to the revolving door at the District of Oregon headquarters. Once General Alvord assumed district command in July, he took immediate (though inadequate) steps to protect the Nez Perce and prevent bloodshed. His orders sending a company to the Nez Perce Reservation followed a discussion he had with Wright in San Francisco in June.[75] Largely adopting Superintendent Geary's suggestions to Wright, Alvord ordered Maj. Jacob S. Rinearson to lead a company to the Nez Perce Reservation, where "every effort should be made vigilantly to protect all peaceable Indians from injury and violence from the whites, whether soldiers or citizens." Alvord also stressed to Rinearson that "the preservation of order and discipline among

[his] own men will be very important." Once the order reached Fort Walla Walla, Rinearson prepared Capt. William Matthews's Company F for an August 2 departure for the Lapwai Valley. Four days later the company established Camp Lapwai on the Nez Perce Reservation.[76]

Company F stayed on the Nez Perce Reservation until November 1, trying to keep whites from igniting a war with a tribe General Wright described as "large and powerful" who "have always been our friends."[77] Even after some tribal leaders granted whites the right to pursue gold and establish towns in certain parts of the reservation, the miners continued to abuse their access, spilling over into other parts of the reservation and selling liquor to members of the tribe. Rinearson was authorized to run off any "ardent spirits" peddlers, destroy "any liquor found," and tear down any buildings constructed in restricted areas, which was still most of the reservation.[78] It was an impossible task for less than one hundred men; units from the First Washington Territory Infantry Regiment joined Rinearson before the end of the year.

Fears grew so intense that General Alvord personally met with Nez Perce leaders in October to assuage their growing impatience with the military's inability to stop the white invasion.[79] During his trip to Camp Lapwai, he had a "grand council" with all the principal leaders, including Lawyer (Hal-hal-tlos-tsot), Old Joseph, and Big Thunder, except "Eagle of [From] the Light [Tipyahlanah Kaupu], who has never participated in any of the treaties." Alvord's official version of the proceedings painted a more positive picture than he shared privately. He informed General Wright's headquarters that he "dwelt upon their past fidelity [to the United States], and promised them protection to the extent of our ability, stating that the military whom [he] should leave in their country would protect them so far as possible under the old treaty."[80] Despite Alvord's assurances, the Oregon cavalrymen and Washington infantrymen could not stave off the flood of whites or prevent them from abusing the Nez Perce people. In a letter to Oregon senator James Nesmith, he lamented, "It is melancholy to see so little care taken to carry out treaty stipulations, and that with a

tribe who have adhered to us through thick and thin. It is a mira-
cle considering the mass of people upon that reservation the last
year or two, that last month the first alleged murders by Indians
occurred."[81] Alvord did not mention the number of Nez Perce who
had been murdered by whites during that time.

A member of Washington Territory's Surveyor General's Office
estimated there were almost nineteen thousand whites living on
the Nez Perce Reservation illegally in 1862.[82] Under such dire circumstances, Alvord changed the original plans that called for Company F to return to Fort Walla Walla for the winter. Instead, he
decided that both the cavalrymen and Company E, First Washington Infantry, should remain at Camp Lapwai throughout the winter, which was twelve miles from the growing town of Lewiston.
He hoped the show of protecting the Nez Perces' old treaty rights
would convince them "to form a new treaty, surrendering their
gold mines to the whites," by the following spring.[83] The military's
admittedly limited assistance would, again, come at a price: the
surrender of more native lands. Although Major Rinearson eventually served elsewhere, Captain Matthews and the men of Company F (and the Washington infantrymen) spent the entirety of
their service stationed on the Nez Perce Reservation, attempting
to prevent an outbreak of violence. That difficult task got worse
over time as the white population going through and settling on
the fringes of Nez Perce lands grew.[84]

If anyone could sympathize with Rinearson and the men
of Company F, it was Maj. Charles Drew, Capt. William Kelly,
and Company C. Like their comrades stationed on the Nez Perce
Reservation, Kelly's men were sent to ensure calm in southwestern
Oregon, to placate white fears about regional safety, and eventually to determine the suitability of the unsettled regions for development as either farming or grazing lands. Company C did less
to protect Indian rights in southwestern Oregon than Rinearson's
command at Camp Lapwai.

After a month of trying to come to a decision about the best
use of Company C, Colonel Steinberger finally ordered it to Camp
Baker at the end of June. Captain Kelly and his men began the

roughly 275-mile trek on July 2.[85] When the column reached Camp
Baker on July 28, the local newspaper hailed Kelly's men as "the
first installment of justice to Southern Oregon" and proclaimed
that "under their protecting patriotism, the broad and fertile acres
of the Klamath Lake Valley may be opened up for settlement and
civilization." His command, the paper effused, was "a fine, orderly
company of men, well mounted," which the writer predicted "will
be effective in any service that the Government they love may
require of them."[86] Despite what the newspaper reported, Company C did little during the rest of the summer beyond making
Camp Baker suitable as a winter encampment. Southwestern Oregon remained Company C's base of operations for the balance of
their service. There they provided security for whites spreading
farther into the unsettled lands that one trooper later described
as "one of the finest grass countries," with "light and dry soil" better suited for grazing than farming.[87]

With the other five companies parceled out to various encampments or in the field, Captain Currey's Company E was the only
available cavalry to watch over miners and emigrants along the
northern part of the emigrant trail. Before being tied to Fort Walla
Walla during the summer and early fall, the aggressive Currey was
the first Oregon Cavalry officer sent into the field. On March 8,
1862, he led twelve men—"that being all the recruits mustered,"
he explained—out of Fort Dalles and across the Columbia River
into Washington Territory to investigate accusations that some
unidentified Yakima Indians had murdered a group of whites
on the John Day River in Oregon. At first, they traveled through
"snow, ranging from one to two feet deep," before a "south wind
sprung up, which melted" it. The patrol soon came upon several
Indian encampments. Currey ordered the leaders held hostage
while some of the men searched the camps, where "nothing was
found among the various camps and traveling property that warranted the rumors."[88] Currey quickly realized that whites were the
root cause of most of the violent interactions with Indians and a
source of misinformation. Two months later, Colonel Steinberg

ordered Currey's Company E and Capt. Elisha Harding's Company B to Fort Walla Walla, ahead of Lieutenant Colonel Maury and his three companies.[89]

Over the course of the summer and fall, detachments from Company E were sent in every direction to respond to calls for help, leaving Currey's force stretched terribly thin throughout the 1862 operations. While Maury's three companies stayed out on the frontier for several consecutive months, Currey's men were constantly on the move on short scouts and patrols, mainly in small detachments. For Company E, "the summer of 1862 was consumed in doing garrison duty and patrolling the region about Fort Walla Walla, arresting refractory Indians and doing escort duty."[90]

In mid-August twenty-three citizens petitioned Steinberger for at least a full company to be stationed in northeastern Oregon's Grande Ronde valley to protect local white farmers. The petitioners stated a group of Cayuses who, upset by encroaching whites, were "tearing down houses and driving the settlers away from their claims, with the threat, coupled with the ability [to] enforce it, that if they returned their lives should pay the forfeit of their presumptions."[91] According to their petition, the civilians did not have the numbers to prevent the "depredations [that] have been committed here by the Indians."[92] William H. Barnhart, the Indian agent on the Umatilla Reservation, confirmed the danger.[93] In response, Colonel Steinberger ordered Captain Currey and a twenty-man contingent of men from Company E into the field on a typical assignment to "arrest and bring back to Fort Walla Walla three certain Indian chiefs who were disturbing the settlers in that valley."[94]

After a day and a half of riding, Currey reached a copse of trees within a few hundred yards of the Cayuse encampment where he believed he would find the Cayuse leaders he had been sent to arrest. In the predawn hours of August 14, he divided his force to surround a large lodge and waited for the sun to rise. At daybreak, Currey confronted two of the men he was sent to arrest and told them they must come with him back to Fort Walla Walla. They refused. After giving them until 8:00 a.m. to reconsider, Currey went inside the lodge with them to debate the matter. According to Currey, "As I entered the lodge, in advance of the men, the oldest and largest of the two drew his revolver, the younger one at the same time snatched up a rifle."[95] Currey fired first, which slightly wounded one attacker. The shot "unsettled their nerves so that their aim was too high." Currey's next shots killed both men, whom he called the Dreamer and Wainicut-hi-bi.[96] Outside the lodge the gunshots sparked a chaotic scene. Some Cayuses fired on the soldiers, who returned fire, wounding one and killing two others, scattering all but one of the rest. Currey reported that he tried to explain to the survivors that he did not intend to kill anyone and that he only came to take the leaders to Fort Walla Walla to discuss reports of their aggression toward whites. His force remained in the valley for a few additional days to ensure no further violence occurred before returning to the fort.[97]

Currey's superiors commended him for the patrol's effect. District commander General Alvord said, "The expedition was entirely successful," noting that killing the Dreamer eliminated "a baneful influence over the small party who followed his fortunes."[98] Colonel Steinberger felt the killings would "produce a salutary effect for their [Cayuse tribal members, both on and off the Umatilla Reservation] future good conduct. It convinces them of the determination and ability of the Government to protect its citizens from outrage and enforce inviolate our stipulated relations."[99] This reaction reflected the common civilian view (and Steinberger was a civilian volunteer) that killing Indian leaders who dared to challenge white claims to Native lands was the best means to force the survivors into submission.

A few days after Currey's force set out, Lt. John Apperson led twenty men to the Umatilla Reservation to suppress a separate matter of unrest. That problem was started by Agent Barnhart after he murdered one of the reservation residents during an argument, causing widespread anger among the Indians, particularly a group that refused to remain within the reservation borders.[100] He lied about the facts when he requested Colonel Steinberger send twenty-five or thirty cavalrymen to "arrest certain refractory Indians [that] are creating a serious disturbance among the settlers in that

[Grand Ronde] valley." He warned Steinberger that if nothing was done, "difficulties of a certain character must occur between them and the white settlers."[101] The deception fell apart when Apperson met with a number of the tribal leaders. He promised to investigate their charges and make certain justice was done, assuring them "if the Agent had done wrong he would be dealt with by the proper authorities." It was a promise he must have known he could not keep—punishing a white man for a crime against an Indian person was extremely rare. Amiable relations existed between the small contingent of soldiers left on the reservation during the fall and the people who lived there. Though Apperson claimed late in life that "Barnhart never returned to the Agency as agent," he was wrong.[102] Although called to Washington DC to explain "certain official transactions connected with this Agency," including "very serious charges against [his] integrity" corruption, not the murder of a young Cayuse man, concerned his bosses in Washington DC.[103] After deflecting the charges against him, W. H. Barnhart returned to the Umatilla Reservation, where he remained until he quit in 1869.[104]

Detachments dispersed widely during the summer and fall months. One went as far north as Fort Colville, Washington Territory, near the border with Canada, while another rode to the Coeur d'Alene Mission, where Jesuits ministered to and tried to convert the Coeur d'Alene people in what is now North Idaho. A detachment of five men spent the summer and fall guarding a government supply depot at the mouth of the Palouse River. As Captain Currey put it, Company E was "kept employed on various scouts and escorts that, out of eighty men then doing duty with the Company, it often happened that not a dozen was [sic] left at the fort, and sometimes not that number."[105] By November, the conclusion of most active field service, Company E had covered more miles than Maury's main force. Captain Currey estimated that his men, collectively, had ridden "something over three thousand miles."[106]

Pursuant to his original orders, Lieutenant Colonel Maury marched back to Fort Walla Walla, where his men reunited with Company E in early November. Before settling into their winter quarters, Company A was transferred to Fort Dalles in early December. There was not enough feed to sustain four companies of cavalry horses throughout the winter at Fort Walla Walla.[107] In what was perhaps an appropriate conclusion to the Oregon Cavalry's first year of service, Sgt. Joseph Pepoon wrote his sister that "the weather was very cold, about four inches of snow on the ground." He continued, "It was an exceedingly tedious trip" so that "when we got to Ft. Dalles we were a most used-up set of men."[108] With Company A's arrival at Fort Dalles, all six companies settled in for the long tedious winter of garrison duty. Captain Currey viewed that "this, of all duty the volunteer soldiers are called upon to perform, is the most harassing, tedious and abominable."[109]

Much had been learned and much had changed in the Oregon Cavalry's first year. Two of the three men responsible for forming the regiment had resigned, and four officers cycled through the command of the District of Oregon. As of December 31, 1862, the regiment lacked an official commanding officer, although Lieutenant Colonel Maury acted in that role as the highest-ranking remaining field officer. After six months as District of Oregon commander, Brigadier General Alvord's leadership brought much-needed stability to the district. The original plan for forming the regiment—with ten companies—as a unified command had been scrapped in favor of parceling out the six companies to various places of concern within the district. Another important change was the election of Addison C. Gibbs, who took office as the governor of Oregon at the end of September. Gibbs took a much more active interest in the Oregon Cavalry than had Governor Whiteaker, who refused to even acknowledge the regiment's existence.

In its first year of service, the Oregon Cavalry interacted with a number of the region's Indian tribes. Sometimes those encounters were peaceful, sometimes violent. Attitudes about and actions toward the tribes varied and were generally formed based on how compliant, in the military's view, each tribe was in submitting to military authority on behalf of white politicians and civilians. Many (perhaps most) troopers at the time already held opinions about the tribes they encountered, based largely on salacious stories and racial stereotypes. The Nez Perce were seen as powerful but friendly; the Cayuse had been dangerous but were mostly broken by defeat in the 1840s and 1850s and enduring a miserable existence on a reservation. Whites often saw the tribes on the Warm Springs Reservation, Teninos and Wascos, as potential allies, and then there were the dangerous, violent Snakes—the Northern Shoshone, Bannock, and Northern Paiute people. There were numerous other tribes in the region, but after one season in the field, the others were mentioned far less in the Oregon troopers' writings.

While things had not gone as planned, Captain Currey reported, "By our labors an Indian war which one year ago was thought very probable has been averted."[110] Generals Alvord and Wright agreed; both commended the work the regiment did during its first year. The Department of the Pacific commander singled out Captain Currey and Company E, "express[ing] his satisfaction at and approval of the handsome manner in which the duties assigned [to them] were executed."[111] General Alvord lauded Lieutenant Colonel Maury's men for how they, "in conjunction with Captain Crawford's emigrant escort party from Omaha, Neb., afforded effectual protection to the emigration, which amounted to 2,000 wagons, or about 10,000 souls."[112] He singled out Major Rinearson for performing his "duty with fidelity and discretion, and obtain[ing] the good will of the [Nez Perce] Indians" and praised Company F, which he said was "composed of excellent material, who have behaved well and have not been ruined by the temptations of a mining town."[113] Alvord even issued a circular throughout his district laying praise on all his men for their "patient endurance, the solder-like fortitude, and perseverance they have exhibited in the performance of such patriotic services." He told them he understood their frustrations about not being sent to the seat of war, which he shared: "It is but just to remember also that the troops are deprived of the stimulus which sustains our brave comrades at the East, who are engaged in a life-and-death struggle for the preservation of the Government and our national rights and liberties."[114] No actual

P7. Gov. Addison C. Gibbs. Oregon Historical Society,
Cartes-de-visite Collection; Org. Lot 500; b3.f437-2; OrHi 3467.

effort to undermine federal control of the region arose, with only a few incidents of public displays of support for the Confederacy occurring during the year. The men may have been disappointed at not being sent east to fight Confederates, but they had done what the military authorities had asked of them.

FIVE

Fully Under Alvord's Control

By the time Benjamin Alvord assumed command of the District of Oregon on July 7, 1862, the various elements of the First Oregon Volunteer Cavalry Regiment had already been given their operational instructions for the year's campaign. With five of the six companies already at their bases of operations, making major changes at that point would have only complicated the tasks before them. Therefore, whether he followed General Wright's suggestion or made the decision on his own, Alvord opted to carry out his predecessor's plans. That decision meant General Alvord managed the strategic use of the Oregon Cavalry but had nothing to do with the creation of the operational goals. Things were different in 1863. The long 1862–63 winter months doing garrison duty were something of a boon for Benjamin Alvord. He used his time during those less active months to formulate his own strategic plans for the coming campaigning season.

Experiences gained by the Oregon Cavalry during 1862 influenced the strategies Generals Alvord and Wright made for 1863. They began discussing much more complex plans for the District of Oregon, and especially the First Oregon Volunteer Cavalry Regiment, as early as October 1862. New ore strikes had drawn miners to the eastern part of the district, and the steady flow of emigrants was certain to continue in 1863. Ominous rumblings also continued to circulate about the Nez Perce reaching the limits of tolerance of white transgressions. Therefore, the two generals knew they could not tie Alvord's most mobile force down to static operations along a segment of the incoming trails. They also understood more needed to be done to simultaneously establish permanent fortifications at strategic points. Although the two generals held similar views for the coming year, implementing what they decided fell entirely on Benjamin Alvord.

Benjamin Alvord, like George Wright, was born in Vermont, in Rutland, on August 19, 1813. Like his commander, who was ten years older, he graduated from West Point (class of 1833) and already had a long military career when the Civil War started. He served during the second Seminole Indian conflict and later in the Mexican–American War, where he saw considerable battlefield service. In between he taught mathematics at West Point from 1837 to 1839. In 1854 he accepted a position as chief paymaster for the Department (later District) of Oregon, stationed at Fort Vancouver. By the time of his appointment as District of Oregon commander in July 1862, he had served in the U.S. Army for twenty-nine years, the last eight in the Pacific Northwest. Not only did Alvord bring extensive field and administrative experience to the post; he was known for being a cerebral thinker. During the course of his service, he wrote a number of articles, mostly on scientific and mathematical subjects, and in 1874 became a founding member of the Literary Society in Washington DC.[1] As a Regular Army officer who had served in the Pacific Northwest almost as long as Wright, Alvord was a natural replacement for Colonel Steinberger. Though Alvord had managed someone else's strategies in 1862, things were different in 1863; he oversaw the execution of plans he helped create.

As the foul weather began to settle over the District of Oregon in October 1862, Alvord made his first proposal for the coming year. He unequivocally stated, "I am satisfied that a post ought to be established at or in the vicinity of [Old] Fort Boise next summer." Just in case General Wright questioned the wisdom of such a move, now that he had the entire Far West to worry about, Alvord reminded the general that he had himself, "two years ago, when in command of the Department of Oregon, made a report in favor of the same step."[2] In a confident tone that bordered on hubris, he

p8. Brig. Gen. Benjamin Alvord. U.S. Army Heritage and
Education Center, Carlisle PA, CWP, RG 98, box 206, folio 1.

later added, "Everything I predicted as to the rush of miners to the
gold fields in that quarter has been more than fulfilled."[3] Alvord
did not need to worry; Wright had not changed his mind since his
recommendation two years earlier. In January 1863 he authorized
Alvord "to make the necessary arrangements for that purpose."[4]
Before the onset of the next winter season, troops would man the
new Fort Boise, though not yet any part of the Oregon Cavalry.

Fort Boise was not the only installation constructed in the District of Oregon in 1863. Generals Alvord and Wright agreed that Camp Baker in southwestern Oregon did not meet the military's needs. Therefore, during the early winter, Alvord reached out to "intelligent gentlemen of Southern Oregon" about whether or not they felt a fort necessary. Not surprisingly, they affirmed the need for a fort "to protect the emigrant road and frontier settlements."[5] Alvord recommended that Maj. Charles Drew abandon Camp Baker and have Captain Kelly's men build a new fort. The original advice was to build the fort on the western side of the Klamath River, near Lower Klamath Lake.[6] Despite good access to water, grass, and wood, the military chose a location eight miles north of Upper Klamath Lake, which also had access to all those requirements. Both forts, once built, could not only provide housing for troops permanently stationed along emigrant routes but also serve as bases of operations. Fort Boise also provided a temporary safe haven for emigrants traveling on the main trails into Oregon or skirting south to California. The new forts also extended the reach of military units, especially mounted commands like the Oregon Cavalry. Construction on both installations had to wait until after the weather improved and snow depths fell.

Static posts alone could not provide sufficient protection for the growing white population in southern and eastern Oregon and especially western Idaho, which achieved territorial status in 1863. Therefore, Alvord stressed the need to unleash offensive operations, with a substantial force, against the Northern Shoshones and Bannocks in western Idaho and Northern Paiutes in eastern Oregon. "I deem it," he explained, "important that an expedition against the Snake Indians shall be made to strike them in their haunts 120 miles east of Fort Boise, near the Camas Prairie, north of Salmon Falls." Alvord, sounding like many of the Oregon cavalrymen, hoped his men "might fight and give some opportunity to inflict a severe chastisement" upon the Indians.[7] Those offensive operations also had to wait, though not solely because of snow or high-water levels. In early summer most of the Oregon Cavalry companies were sent to support treaty negotiations with the Nez Perce in Idaho Territory.

*   *   *

The flood of whites onto lands granted to the Nez Perce by the 1855 treaty they signed with Washington Territorial governor Isaac Stevens had reached a critical point. White miners had established a number of towns on Nez Perce lands, including the bustling community of Lewiston, where the Clearwater River merges into the Snake River. Ore strikes near Boise and in Montana Territory also meant that new roads to transport trade goods to those places were inevitable. Unchecked white expansion adversely affected individual tribe members, who were sold liquor illegally and then robbed while drunk. Miners murdered Nez Perce people while crimes committed by whites were blamed on the Nez Perce, both individually and in sweeping anonymous accusations. Requests to the reservation agent for help did little good; there was not much he could do, even if so inclined.[8] The troops at Fort Lapwai did their best, but the tide of whites overwhelmed them. The government's answer was a new treaty, which the retiring superintendent of Indian affairs for Oregon, William H. Rector, felt should be negotiated immediately, in the fall of 1862. Others disagreed, and it was delayed until the next spring.

The military decided that a show of force might be useful should the nontreaty Nez Perce bands disrupt the negotiations, during which there would be considerable discussion but few concessions by the government representatives. General Alvord had left the Oregon Cavalry's Company F and Company E, Washington Infantry, at the newly built Fort Lapwai during the winter of 1862–63. Anticipating the possibility that as many as two thousand Nez Perce might show up and encamp around the meeting site, Alvord planned to send a large force to augment those stationed at the fort. Lieutenant Colonel Maury would lead Companies A, D, and E to the meeting site in the spring. They would be joined by two additional companies of infantry led by Colonel Steinberger.[9] The reason their "four Cavalry and two Infantry Companies were very actively drilling—ostensibly for the approaching campaign against the Snakes," wrote Lieutenant Rinehart, was "really for the effect it would have upon the Nez Perces."[10] As the senior officer, Colonel Steinberger commanded the combined force. He planned to establish his headquarters at Fort Lapwai, thus superseding both Maury and the fort's commander, Major Rinearson.

Pursuant to those plans, Colonel Steinberger headed to Fort Lapwai in late April.[11] On May 4 Maury, promoted to colonel that same month, followed with the three companies of Oregon cavalrymen from Fort Walla Walla.[12] One of the troopers was impressed by what he saw when the cavalry reached the negotiating site. Laid out between the agency headquarters and Fort Lapwai, "the spot selected for the grand council grounds is a beautiful little savanna, lying in a peaceful curve of the Lapwai [Creek], where the banks are dotted with a fine growth of shrubs. . . . The hills around are just wild enough in their appearance to present a picturesque surrounding to the scene. The lodges are arranged in regular order, making the encampment present the appearance of a village. Just inside of the encampment is a large, open structure, covered with sawed lumber—a kind of pavilion—where the council meets."[13] Captain Currey made a more practical observation, telling Governor Gibbs, "This is very good grazing country with limited tracks susceptible of plant cultivation."[14]

The actual discussions were delayed until May 25 by an influenza outbreak that struck the Nez Perce. As they waited, there was quite a bit of leisure time for the soldiers, some of whom, remembered Sgt. John Dimick, spent it fishing in the Clearwater River.[15] During the gathering, two incidents unnerved the negotiators enough that they called on the military to intervene to prevent a violent confrontation. Lieutenant Rinehart, recently appointed regimental adjutant general, remembered, "Just before the parley began it was discovered that a large band of renegade Indians from the north, Coeur de Alenes [sic], Okanogans, Palouses," was "mingling freely" with the Nez Perce. This made the commissioners nervous, so Companies D and E forced the group away from the treaty grounds "in a way that made the Indians know they were unwelcome visitors."[16] Captain Currey instructed Captain Drake and his contingent of Company D men to escort the unwanted Indians away from the treaty grounds while he led Company E down the Clearwater River. After twelve miles they came upon two white men who had built a house along the river, with plans to establish a claim on Nez Perce land. According to Currey, the two threatened his men if they attempted to remove them, but their courage evaporated when Currey and six men "demolished their house, threw the material in the river and returned [to the opposite side]" as the men "disappeared behind a sand hill several hundred yards in the distance."[17]

Days later, after the treaty talks were underway, remarks by some nontreaty Nez Perce leaders—the most prominent of which were Eagle from the Light, (Old) Joseph, and White Bird—convinced the superintendent of Indian affairs in Washington and Idaho Territories, Calvin Hale, that they would try to create unrest among the negotiating bands. To determine just how successful those efforts might be, Captain Currey was sent out late at night to investigate. He reached the main encampment and entered the only lodge from which light was showing. Inside he "found fifty-three chiefs and sub chiefs deliberating on the propositions for treaty." The discussion went back and forth between the nontreaty leaders and those who favored it. Currey, who held complex views about Indian people, wrote admiringly about how "the debate ran with dignified firmness and warmth until near morning," when the nontreaty leaders announced they would not participate any further in the one-sided negotiations with the white commissioners. Thunder Strikes, an important nontreaty leader whose name whites incorrectly translated as "Big Thunder," "with a warm, and in an emotional manner, declared the Nes Perce [sic] Nation dissolved." It was clear to Currey that none of the leaders intended to start a conflict. Therefore, his contingent of cavalrymen left the encampment, "having accomplished nothing but that of witnessing the extinguishment of the last Council fires of the most powerful Indian Nation on the sun-set side of the Rocky mountains."[18] Currey had not exaggerated; those who signed the treaty, led by Chief Lawyer (Hal-hal-tlos-tsot), were accepted by officials as representatives of all the Nez Perce bands, while whites viewed the nontreaty tribes as threats. The divisions, expanded by whites, weakened the strength of the Nez Perce people, and through a

P9. Chief Lawyer (Hal-hal-tlos-tsot) Nez Perce.
Wikimedia Commons, last modified September 28, 2022,
https://en.wikipedia.org/wiki/Hallalhotsoot#/media/File:Chief.Lawyer.1861.jpg.

treaty forced upon them, they ceded 90 percent of the lands they
had been allotted in 1855.[19]

Once the treaty discussions ended and the Nez Perces left, Maury
prepared to undertake his primary task for the next four months.
"The Snake Indians," Alvord told Maury, "deserve a severe casti-
gation at our hands, and so far as your time, means, and opportunity extend, I desire you to administer to them such punishment."
He hoped the Oregon cavalrymen would give them "a whipping
in battle" that would "be one of the severest lessons which can be
given them." If any Indians accused by whites were determined
to be "guilty of murdering the whites," Alvord informed Maury,
"You are hereby authorized to have them tried by military commission, and also to have them summarily punished," by which
he meant executed.[20] While the sentiment was not new, making it
an explicit part of their orders for the remainder of the campaigning season was different than the more defensive role the cavalry
played the previous year.

To achieve that objective, Alvord ordered Maury to lead Companies A, D, and E to the site of the planned new Fort Boise, where
the expedition would be joined by Companies H and I, Washington Infantry. From there the five companies would continue on to
Fort Hall, north of the present city of Pocatello, Idaho. Along the
way Alvord wanted the expedition "to clear the road of all Snake
Indians."[21] After reaching the fort it would retrace its path back to
the site of the new Fort Boise by October 1, where Maury would
leave Company I of the infantry before leading the Oregon Cavalry
and Company H of the Washington Infantry back to Fort Walla
Walla by October 26. During his return he was advised to send
small patrols out from the main force, looking for both emigrant
trains and Indians. The orders reflect Alvord's view of keeping
the mounted force in the field for as long as the weather allowed,
which not only helped emigrants still traveling late in the season
but also reduced the stress on the supplies at Fort Walla Walla.

There had been, or soon would be, some changes among the
company commanders from the previous year. Capt. Thomas S.

Harris led Company A at the start of the campaign but would not
return with it. Capt. John Drake replaced Capt. Sewell Truax at
the head of Company D after Truax's promotion to major. Only
Company E had its original commander at the end of the campaigning season, Captain Currey. Currey, the most experienced of
all the company commanders, had led more independent operations than any of the others and had the most interaction with the
various Indian tribes, yet the less experienced Truax received
the promotion.

Maury led his command out of Camp Lapwai on June 15, heading out along Lapwai Creek. Maintaining a decent pace proved
difficult. While the 175 mounted men and officers could move rapidly, such columns were also composed of a quartermaster's unit,
including civilian employees, and cattle, which were slaughtered
along the way for food. According to Lieutenant Apperson's cal-
culations, besides the 175 cavalrymen, twenty-two mounted civilians, and five Nez Perce scouts, there were 152 mules and fifteen
head of cattle. The sizeable column covered just six miles the first
day, a pace that dramatically increased in the future, even with the
slower-moving animals.[22] The average pace for a full day's march
ranged between eighteen and twenty miles, but smaller contingents, not encumbered with quartermaster's employees and cattle, might cover more than thirty miles in a day.

The command rose before dawn and mounted by 5:00 a.m.,
which became the norm for the remainder of the campaign. As
the column moved south it gained elevation, riding along the western edges of the Clearwater and Salmon River Mountains before
heading down toward the Salmon River. The trail was nerve-
wracking in places. While nothing happened to any of the men, two
pack mules lost their footing and tumbled down a two-hundred-
foot embankment; one was dead before it reached the canyon
floor, while "the other got up, walked a few minutes, and fell over
dead."[23] The constant ascending and descending "reminded" one
of the troopers of "Bonaparte crossing the Alps."[24]

After two weeks the command reached lands frequented by the
Northern Shoshones. From this point on, they paid extra attention

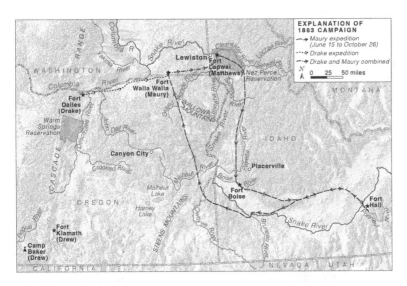

M3. Explanation of the 1863 campaign. Created by Chelsea McRaven Feeney.

to any indication that the Indians had recently been in the area. The determination to find any Indians clouded their judgment on at least one occasion. In late June Lieutenant Apperson led a small patrol to confront two riders seen on the column's flank, presuming they were Indians watching them. His patrol caught up to the men, who were not Indians but white packers loaded down with supplies. The two packers were headed toward the upstart gold towns. As the patrol neared the gold country two men deserted; ore strikes had long been a threat to military cohesion in the West because of the lure of better pay in the gold fields. At least nine others followed during the next three months.[25]

Getting lost among the constantly churning mass of humanity during the mining rushes gave some deserters hope they would get away. On June 28 Maury ordered Lieutenant Apperson to take five men to Placerville, looking for deserters. Apperson came across a chaotic scene when he rode into the town, a rather typical upstart gold rush district. He reported, "For some miles before reaching this place we found the hills and ravines full of miners. Placerville is such a town (if I may be allowed to call it a town) as one might suppose would be built up in a few months, and is filled up with the roughs of this coast. There seem to be a great many men here. Dramshops and gambling houses are all the go." He shared the common Oregon troopers' belief about such places, noting, "The impression seems to be that two thirds of the men of these towns are rebel sympathizers and [I] learn that it is no unusual occurrence for them to meet and have a 'big drink' drinking success to the Southern rebels." The truth was that so long as Southern sympathizers did nothing more than toast the Confederate cause, they were not breaking any laws. Besides, leading just five men, and with the main column many miles away heading to Fort Boise, there was little Apperson could do.[26]

On the Fourth of July Maury and the main force set up camp in the Payette valley, which he estimated was twenty-five miles northwest of Placerville. This was not his original intended course, but operations in the Far West were often altered by both the weather, as had been the case in 1862, and the terrain. As Maury explained, he slightly altered his line of march because conditions were "very bad" for the animals, with "grass and water very scarce." As the column snaked through the challenging country, he reported that after twenty days they had "as yet met with no Indians, nor any evidence of their proximity." They had not met any emigrant trains either.[27] Three weeks into a long campaigning season and the only thing to show for their efforts were their reports describing the ruggedly beautiful land that was ill-suited for anything but the mining already engulfing the region.

Four days later the column reached the Boise River and followed it toward Boise. The march slowed considerably when Maury's command finally met up with Companies H and I, First Washington Territory Infantry. The inability of supplies to keep up with troopers forced Maury to establish a camp on July 13 and wait. A few wagons of emigrants came upon the cavalrymen while they were still encamped. Those emigrants told them they had seen, but not had any interaction with, some unidentified Indians on Camas Prairie. With no signs of trouble, the emigrants pressed onward while Maury waited. Frustrated by the delays, he worried about the negative impact "the consequences of much delay in camp, both upon its health and morale," had on his command. Prolonging his stay was detrimental to the animals as well; "alkali in considerable quantities exists in this vicinity, which with the scarcity of good grass has affected [their] animals unfavorably."[28]

Once supplies reached the temporary camp, Maury immediately continued the march toward the fort and town of Boise, which one of the troopers called "the juvenile city."[29] The town was indeed in its earliest stage. One trooper colorfully described its rudimentary state, writing, "As of yet, it is only a city in name. The forests that are to enter into its construction, and the mortar which is to cement its fair proportions, together with the population that is to inhabit it, all are in the prospective, in the dim distance; the stately trees move as before, the soil that is to form the gigantic adobes for its foundation still bristle with wild rye and sage."[30] Just prior to Maury's arrival, Maj. Pickney Lugenbeel, Ninth U.S. Infantry Regiment, reached the site of the proposed fort with three companies of Washington Infantry and took charge of constructing the fort.[31] The Oregon troopers played no part, at this point, in the building of the fort but instead, after a few days, pressed on toward Fort Hall, more than two hundred miles to the east.[32]

Before leaving Boise there was a change in command of Company A. Captain Harris's alcoholism had become so debilitating that he was forced to resign once the column reached the Fort Boise site. Replacing a company commander in the middle of a planned four-month operation gives a strong idea of just how bad things had become.[33] Lieutenant Apperson, who had proven himself a reliable officer since mustering in the previous April, assumed temporary command of the company as the combined force moved eastward, where Indians had been more frequently sighted.[34]

John T. Apperson's 1847 migration from Missouri to Oregon was not only arduous; it was marked by tragedy. During the course of the long trek across the arid and rugged lands, his father died in what is today Wyoming, leaving his mother with nine children, one of which was a baby. Apperson was only thirteen at the time of his father's death, an event that impacted him for the rest of his life, since it forced him to give up any further education. The family settled in Oregon City, where his mother remarried two years later. Perhaps spurred partially by his mother's marriage, he left for California during the first wave of the gold rush, when he was only fifteen. He returned to Oregon in 1859 and bought a steamboat, which he operated on the Willamette River for parts of three years. Then in 1862 he accepted a second lieutenancy and commission to recruit a company for the First Oregon Volunteer Cavalry Regiment. When he failed to raise a full company, his recruits were merged with the men from other incomplete recruiting efforts, creating Company F. He was quickly promoted to first lieutenant on April 2, 1862, and transferred to Company E. Despite a successful turn as acting commander of Company A, he was sent into his home region on recruiting duties in November 1863.[35]

The Oregon troopers' long trek south from Fort Lapwai had taken them through Nez Perce lands, then into Bannock, and finally into Northern Shoshone territory. Those troopers hoped they would finally "have an opportunity for being of some service in chastising the murderers of so many emigrants to Oregon."[36] From the white perspective, all murders on the frontier were, of course, perpetrated by Snakes, who must be punished. The Oregon troopers, despite no reports of Indian attacks on emigrant trains, hoped the time had finally arrived.

Captain Currey remembered, "The pleasant news came that we would take up the line of march" for Fort Hall.[37] In early August the advance to Fort Hall came to a temporary halt when Colonel Maury received reports that "a considerable band of hostile Snake Indians were encamped" fifty miles from his location, along the Malad River. In response, he sent several detachments on short patrols fanning out from his encampment, hoping to increase the chance of making contact with this band of Indians. Maj. Jacob S. Rinearson, Lieutenant Apperson, and Captain Currey led the shorter patrols. Rinearson, who had joined Maury's expedition with the two companies of Washington Infantry, did not find any of the so-called Snakes. Apperson's twelve-man detachment did not fare any better. Only Currey's column made contact with any Indians.

Maury ordered Currey to lead a twenty-man detachment from Company E to investigate along the Malad River.[38] Even though Currey had a reputation for "always [being] on hand when there is any Indian fighting to be done," he admitted his men were "all glad to leave the dull, dusty road"; they were looking for a change of scenery as much as they were eager to confront the Shoshones.[39] For three days Currey's column followed the "industrious little stream," the Malad River, which "literally morticed its way through a lava bed." On the fourth day, "amid several thousand acres of fertile soil," they found "an abandoned camp and fishery, with fires still burning."[40] They headed downriver, riding along the banks above the Malad. Currey's force crested a bluff above the river in the early afternoon and noticed "almost beneath [their] feet" a camp of eleven brush huts. Currey ordered his men to the river to surround the encampment, planning to summarily kill all the adult males, likely Shoshones. When the "Chief of the band came out to treat, and to make his desire for peace more emphatic, [he directed] all his men to stand in a conspicuous place and show [the Oregon troopers] that they were unarmed and did desire peace, by holding up their hands." By doing so, he changed Currey's mind. Currey reported, "Although we had then trailed the party for four days, one day without rations, I could not consent to fire upon an unarmed and supplicating foe," though he did so in the future. That "foe," who he dismissed with common prejudice as "decidedly the lowest specimen of humanity [he had] seen," was destitute and fishing for their sustenance.[41] Despite the fact that they were unarmed and did not pose any threat, Currey imprisoned two influential men and impounded some of their desperately needed salmon for his own men before returning to the main force. He reached Maury's camp after "five day's hard traveling through mountains and over lava and sage brush plains." Once there, the two men were interrogated as to the whereabouts of other, less cooperative bands. After the interrogation Maury released them, now far from their encampment.[42]

Although, once again, only Currey's detachment encountered any Indians, the Oregon cavalrymen believed, as one of them put it, their efforts would "at least keep the Indians beat back into the mountains and allow the emigration to pass through the country safe and secure."[43] General Alvord had made it clear that he wanted Maury to engage and chastise—the convenient white phrasing for "kill"—any Indians found raiding the emigrants. However, making the emigrant routes safe for whites did not require confrontations. In that sense, they were achieving the government's desired outcome by their presence and the threat of military action they posed.

Mindful of another important objective, recording the suitability of the lands they rode over for white development, Maury and a number of his troopers wrote in detail about what they saw in that part of Idaho Territory. The colonel reported from his Camas Prairie campsite about the "extensive and fertile valley" that was "thirty miles in length and from six to eight miles in width, and is watered by many fine streams that take their rise in the mountain range dividing the waters of Salmon and Boise Rivers from those of Malade [sic] River, and crossing the valley at intervals of from two to four miles." He pointed out that the "growth of grass throughout the entire valley is luxuriant, and the mountains on either side afford pine timber in large tracts on spots, not more than five miles distant from the margin of the valley."[44] One of the troopers concurred, telling newspaper readers there was "plenty of water and an abundance of grass" in the area. "In fact," he continued, "the whole distance from here to Boise river is a vast meadow."[45] The rich soil particularly impressed another member of the expedition.[46] The area was so perfect for grazing and possibly farming that one cavalryman postulated, "Had a Fort been built here I will venture to assert, and I believe every intelligent person in this command will bear me out in it, that within the next twelve months there would be at least five hundred permanent settlers in this valley."[47] As the column kept moving eastward into a less hospitable landscape, one trooper described "the haze that hung over that somber region [that] seemed to come up from the smouldering hell beneath. The heat shimmered upward as from a furnace."[48]

Captain Currey explained best how the Oregon Cavalry's monthslong expeditions were as much exploratory as offensive operations: "Going and coming enabled me to see the larger portion of the Cammas [*sic*] Prairie country, which in time is destined to become one of the most important agricultural districts in Idaho Territory." He too noted it had "good soil for grass, and in many places [is] exceedingly fertile."[49] By the time the regiment disbanded, five-plus years of mounted expeditions placed hundreds of Oregon volunteers, many of them farmers, in a position to assess for themselves the potential for developing those frontier lands. Some of their views were shared publicly in the press and some officially in reports. The frequency with which local newspapers printed their descriptions makes it clear that civilians in Oregon as well as parts of Washington and Idaho Territories were eager for the information.

Camas Prairie's potential as farming and grazing land held future consequences. However, at the time it was more important that it was a good site for establishing a temporary depot. Fortunately for Maury, such a depot would require protection, which justified leaving the two companies of Washington Infantry to guard it. That, in turn, freed the mounted forces up to move faster, which he needed to do after hearing the latest rumors of large Indian encampments ahead.[50] He also left a small contingent of the cavalry at the depot to perform localized protective patrols for the emigrants as they came over the western end of Camas Prairie.

After disentangling his remaining mounted troops from the slow-moving infantry, Maury resumed the march toward Fort Hall. Although able to move faster, it took Maury's reduced command thirteen days to reach the Fort Hall area, 170 miles from his supply depot on Camas Prairie. A meeting with Capt. Medorem Crawford, who was again providing protection for trains on the emigrant trails, had caused the delay. The Oregon troopers met Crawford's escort and eighty emigrant wagons at a ferry crossing on the Snake River, some twenty miles from Fort Hall on August 17. Crawford said there had "been no difficulty or trouble of any nature with the emigration this season up to this point [the crossing of the Snake River]."[51] He also informed Maury that he believed he was leading the last trains of the season.

The presence of Crawford's emigrant train presented the soldiers with a greatly appreciated distraction from their long rides. In particular, they enjoyed the chance to get "up a fine dance with the prettiest kind of emigrant girls," where "bon-fires and torch-lights set the camp aglow." Lieutenant Rinehart remembered that Captain Currey's younger brother Lt. James L. Currey, met his future wife at the dance.[52] After a few days, Crawford restarted the trains toward Fort Boise, leaving a number of "forlorn bachelors" among the Oregon troopers. The cavalry remained at their camp a few additional days before setting out for Fort Hall.[53]

In something of an ironic twist, Maury's command finally had frequent contact with Indians while encamped at Fort Hall, though not in an anticipated way or, frankly, a desired one. Rather than hostile encounters, Maury reported, "A good many of the leading men of the tribes treated with, now living farther east, have visited my camp, generally having letters of recommendation from [Utah] Governor Doty." There were two reasons for the unanticipated nature of the interaction with the Shoshone people. First, in January, District of Utah commander Col. Patrick Connor and a combined force of California infantry and cavalry almost wiped out a large band of Shoshones led by Wirasuap (Bear Hunter) along the Bear River, just over the Utah Territory border in southeastern Idaho Territory. That encounter, known today as the Bear River Massacre, resulted in the deaths of roughly 250 men, women, and children.[54] The level of human destruction, combined with the execution of dozens of Indians from a number of tribes by other California commands, caused tremendous fallout. It convinced a large number of Indian leaders to negotiate treaties with Connor and Utah governor Doty. As more and more treaties were signed over the course of the summer (and into the fall), the tribes tried to limit contact with whites. Second, as Maury himself noted, the growing white migration into these lands had a destructive impact on all the Indian people in the region.[55] The regional tribes, to use a term whites then employed, were no longer deemed "hostile."

Maury's stay at his camp on the Portneuf River, near Fort Hall, only lasted a few days. While there some of his men found the body of a murdered Indian, which rightly worried Maury. He warned that "such acts will certainly lead to retaliation, and most likely unsuspecting parties [will] be the sufferers."[56] Since his command had less than seven weeks to make it back to Fort Walla Walla, he could not wait to see if a threat developed. Running out of time, on August 27 the advanced contingent of Oregon cavalrymen began their return to Camas Prairie, where they met up with the rest of the cavalry and the infantrymen they had left at the temporary camp. While the operational season was winding down, Maury still hoped to "satisfy the desire of [his] command and the ends of justice by inflicting punishment upon such Indians as have not been braced in the treaties made by General Connor and Governor Doty."[57] The effect of Connor's treaty negotiations frustrated one trooper, whose nom de plume was the rather unimaginative "Snake Hunter." He did "not understand how Gen. Connor is to effect a treaty with this portion of the Snake tribe [in Idaho Territory], especially as they come within the jurisdiction of a different Department."[58] The Oregon troopers—at least Companies A, D, and E—were desperate for a fight, but so far only Captain Currey had much luck finding any Indians to engage, and little action came from those encounters.

Maury's advanced contingent met up with Major Rinearson and the rest of the Oregon Cavalry and the two Washington Infantry companies at the supply depot on Camas Prairie on September 5. From there the cavalry took up the march for Fort Walla Walla on September 11. First, Maury planned to take a detour to Salmon Falls Creek, where he hoped they would find more aggressive Snake Indians than those encountered previously. Rinearson and the infantry continued on to Fort Boise, where they would go into winter quarters.

After a six-day respite, all three mounted companies began the march toward Salmon Falls amid rumors that "hostile" Indians were in the area. One of the men in the column admitted, "Our trip, so far as regards chastising the Snakes, has been fruitless."

"The great difficulty," he explained, "is to find the Indians. Such a force as ours, with the necessary transportation, make[s] so much 'sign,' that the Indians can always discover us in time to depart" before the Oregon cavalrymen made contact.[59] Thus far, neither the band Currey found fishing nor those at Fort Hall presented any threat to whites. Up to then, the Oregon Cavalry had not found an "enemy" to fight. Since, as some of them noted when they volunteered, fighting Indians along the emigrant trails was their only real chance to prove their patriotism, their sense of frustration comes through clearly.

Maury's command did not find any Indian bands that fit his definition of *threatening* when it reached the Salmon Falls Creek region on September 15. As he reported to General Alvord, "The few Indians we find are miserably poor and almost destitute [and] represent themselves as very friendly and ask permission to live undisturbed in the vicinity." What he told the leader of one small band (which he estimated numbered between thirty and forty people in the camp) reflects both one of the Oregon Cavalry's main objectives—maintaining peace on the frontier—and the general attitudes of most white westerners at the time. "I have represented to them," he informed Alvord, "that as long as they remained here without molesting in any manner our people who may travel through the country they might expect to live in peace," but if they did not, "they could expect nothing but extermination." Maury admitted, "Neither during the last nor this season have I heard of any complaints against them." However, he held the general view: "They are of course like all Indians, and have probably been guilty of acts of violence and robbery."[60] The Regular Army, more so than most volunteers, preferred to avoid conflicts with Indian tribes. Besides being dangerous, most Regular Army officers, and probably many soldiers as well, quickly realized that white civilians caused the majority of problems, then turned to the military to save them from suffering the consequences their actions initiated. While Regular Army soldiers often pointed to white transgression against various Indian tribes as the root cause of unrest in the West, volunteers more often reflected the attitudes of the communities from which they came and blamed the Indians.

The command remained at that camp, which Maury recorded as Camp 56, for ten days, during which time he sent out a number of scouting parties that traveled varying distances. Neither Captain Drake and Company D nor Lieutenant Apperson and Company A reported any "signs of Indians made this season." Even Captain Currey had little success, only encountering a Shoshone family consisting of an adult male, his two wives, and their seven children during his two-hundred-mile circuit. Currey admitted he would have murdered the man except he did not want to leave the women and children to fend for themselves "in that far off and inhospitable region."[61] His men did get a break from the heat afflicting their comrades when they took a route high enough into the mountains that it snowed several inches during his ride, causing a reverse problem for Currey's force.[62]

Unlike the others, Lt. James Waymire's scouting party did engage a group of Shoshones. In late September Waymire was ordered "to march with twenty men of Co. 'D,' two Nez Perce scouts, and supplies for three days up the valley of the [Bruneau] river, and to inflict summary punishment upon any Indian that might be found in the region of the country," apparently regardless of any news of attacks on whites. On the afternoon of the second day, Waymire wrote that the Nez Perce scouts reported "a large body of the enemy encamped in the river cañon about a mile ahead. Fearing that the Snakes would get information" about their approach and flee, he took eleven of his men and rushed to the reported campsite, which was at the bottom of the narrow canyon he estimated was two hundred yards wide. Waymire's approach was detected before he could find a way down. The Shoshones rightly judged that the cavalrymen planned to attack, so they fled across the river, taking up concealed positions on the other side of the Bruneau. At that point, Waymire left his horses with four men and led the other seven scurrying down the canyon walls. As his men moved down their side, the Shoshones opened an erratic fire. The Oregon troopers halted and took position on the rocky slope to return fire. According to Waymire, "A few volleys from our men demoralized them, and drove them from their concealment." As they fled out of the canyon, "they were greatly exposed to our fire."

Despite the considerable distance, Waymire's men killed four Shoshones. After a few volleys, "the men clambered down the precipice,
waded the river, and followed in hot pursuit, but they (the Indians)
were soon out of reach." When they returned to the campsite they
found "a large quantity of ammunition, also an extensive supply of
provisions," which his men destroyed. Before leaving they discovered a woman and two children hiding in the brush, who "were left
undisturbed" but without shelter or food.[63] After destroying the
campsite, Waymire's patrol rejoined the main command. Maury
continued southwestward toward the Owyhee River, with Currey joining the main force after concluding his extended scout.[64]

The column moved at a steady pace but made a number of stops
of several days' duration. Those stops helped preserve the worn-
down animals (so long as there was ample water and grass in the
area) while also enabling Maury to send out scouting patrols "to
collect in all the Indians on either side of the [Bruneau] river or
to attack in the case of finding any considerable force of them."
A patrol led by Lieutenant Waymire came upon a group of thirty
Indians about twenty miles north of Maury's camp and attacked
without provocation, killing four, wounding an uncertain number
of others, and forcing the survivors to abandon their campsite and
flee for their lives.[65] No evidence was reported tying this group of
Shoshones to any attacks on whites. They were victims of the volunteers' frustration at not having had the chance to "chastise" the
so-called Snakes during the summer and fall. Other bands were
more fortunate. The remaining scouting parties gathered between
eighty and one hundred Shoshones and determined that "they
expressed great desire for peace and a willingness to do anything
or go anywhere they might be directed." Having "no evidence of
guilt or of complaints" against them, Waymire impressed upon
them the consequences they would suffer if the band attacked
any whites on the emigrant trail and then let them go. Probably
unaware of the irony, Maury reported that one of his patrols found
the remains of seven Indians killed by miners, yet he expounded
on how the Indians in the region "never fail to kill and steal whenever opportunity offers."[66]

With the campaigning season nearing the end, Maury accelerated the pace of the return march. The column made only one additional layover when it reached the Owyhee River on October 10. Following a couple of days' respite, Maury's command began the northward ride out of that desolate region toward Fort Walla Walla. Despite the lack of good grass and water, which weakened their mounts and pack animals further, Maury pressed onward at a quick clip. Companies A, D, and E reached Fort Walla Walla on October 26. Maury reported that his command was in "good health and fair condition." After riding through everything from snowstorms to choking dust and wilting heat for four months, it was time for two companies to settle into their calm, if monotonous, winter quarters. Company D was not so fortunate; it had one more ride to make before its 1863 operations were concluded. After three short days of rest, Maury ordered Captain Drake to lead his company to Fort Dalles, where it could finally rest for the winter.

Although Maury's command received nearly all the newspaper coverage about the Oregon Cavalry, the other three companies had not been idle. Each in their own way performed important duty in 1863. Following the negotiations with the Nez Perce, Company F spent the rest of the summer and fall trying, with only limited success, to keep whites off the Nez Perce lands. Administration of that responsibility changed just prior to the treaty negotiations when Maj. Sewell Truax replaced Major Rinearson as commander of Fort Lapwai in April 1863.[67] Even before the treaty was ratified by Congress, the news spread that the reservation borders would be dramatically reduced. Consequently, whites began to spill into the Nez Perce Reservation before the bands moved out of their old lands and legal sales of it occurred. General Alvord rightly saw this as a danger that could threaten the fragile treaty should violence break out between the white interlopers and the Nez Perce. Therefore, he informed Major Truax, "You will aid in every way in the protection of the Nez Perces, and in securing to them their rights under the treaty of the 9th of June, 1863." Truax was also to ensure that whites did not violate the Indian Intercourse Act,

which prohibited the sale of alcohol to Indians. This meant sending Company F (and Company E, Washington Infantry) out to
remove encroaching whites and, if necessary, to destroy liquor
inventories, as they had done in 1862.[68]

Rather than wait for Congress to open up the Nez Perce lands,
some whites tried to force the military off the reservation by burning between twenty-five and thirty tons of needed hay in the fields
around the fort. Although whites blamed it on the Nez Perce, Truax
had proof those accusations were fabricated, explaining to General Alvord that "one white man was seen by two sergeants of this
command on horseback, and was seen to dismount several times
and set fire to the prairie."[69] Without further guidance from the
federal government (the treaty was not ratified until 1867),
Truax's command faced a hopeless situation that kept them occupied throughout 1863 and beyond.

Company B had also been present at the treaty negotiations,
along with Companies A, D, E, and F. At the conclusion of the
treaty, Capt. Richard S. Caldwell received orders to lead it to Fort
Dalles—about twenty miles from the John Day River, in north-
central Oregon—after the deaths of three miners, reportedly killed
by Indians.[70] Once there, Company B used the fort as its base of
operations for the next two months. During that time, the company functioned as something akin to the department's reserve
force, ready to be used wherever needed. Hearing the usual rumors
(often true) about raids by Snake Indians, Northern Paiutes in this
case, along Canyon City Road, General Alvord ordered Captain
Caldwell "to move first with your command beyond the outer-
most mining camps near Canyon City, giving pursuit to any hostile Indians who may show themselves," and then to proceed "about
forty miles this side [west] of Canyon City, and there select a suitable site for a permanent camp and depot, from which during the
season scouts should be made for the protection of the whites."
Alvord emphasized the need for "the most energetic steps [to be]
taken for the pursuit and chastisement of hostile Indians."[71]

General Alvord eventually countermanded his very specific
original orders. He explained to General Wright that there were
multiple reasons for the decision to keep Company B encamped

six miles from Fort Dalles. Militarily he pointed out that "incursions of the Snake Indians have not been very hostile of late," and the ubiquitous "rumors reach[ing] this office that there was great danger that the Nez Perce Indians would become troublesome in consequence of misinterpretation of the late treaty, the whites claiming that they were entitled to settle up the boundary of the new reservation before the ratification of the treaty." These were legitimate reasons not to commit Company B to patrolling the Canyon City Road area, particularly since it "was the only disposable company"; therefore, he "deemed it prudent to hold it in reserve." Money, however, may have been the ultimate factor in not sending Caldwell's command nearly two hundred miles southeast. The firm that had a monopoly over supply packing in The Dalles increased their rates for government goods by over 100 percent. Therefore, Alvord could not justify the expense of moving all the supplies Caldwell would need away from Fort Dalles at that exorbitant rate.[72] As a result of all three factors, Company B spent the rest of July through the end of September frittering away their time just outside The Dalles before it was ordered to "proceed by water from Fort Dalles to Fort Vancouver." Company B was the least effectively employed Oregon Cavalry command in 1863.

Captain Kelly's Company C was the only Oregon Cavalry company absent from the Nez Perce treaty negotiations. Stationed at Camp Baker, near Jacksonville, since the previous summer, it did not participate in a long-range expedition until 1864. In many ways it was an orphan company. Captain Kelly led the company, but Maj. Charles S. Drew was the military authority in the region, and he reported not to the District of Oregon, nor to regimental commander Colonel Maury, but directly to Department of the Pacific headquarters in San Francisco. Although the command served in Oregon, it was stationed almost equidistant between San Francisco and Fort Vancouver. The administrative boundaries were a relic of the prewar military borders in the Far West.

Even though General Alvord had no direct authority over the Oregon cavalrymen at Camp Baker, General Wright sought Alvord's views on the military situation in southwestern Oregon. This was largely because there was a good chance Company C would be called east of its base to protect emigrants and miners traveling through the southern part of the District of Oregon. It was an awkward arrangement that frustrated Alvord, especially during the coming year, and left Drew uncertain about to whom he reported.

Civilian pleas for one of the Oregon Cavalry companies to be permanently stationed in southern Oregon led to Captain Kelly's Company C being sent to Camp Baker the previous summer. Camp Baker, however, was not fit to serve as a permanent base. Well aware of the camp's shortcomings, General Alvord reached out to Department of the Pacific headquarters to make a case for building a fort elsewhere in southwestern Oregon. He reminded General Wright, who had spent so long serving in the Pacific Northwest, that "many emigrants have at different dates been murdered upon that road [from South Pass, in southern Oregon], and it is proper that protection should be given to the route and to settlements near the lakes [Klamath and the adjoining lakes]." The site recommended to Alvord by Oregon pioneer Jesse Applegate was seventy miles southeast of Jacksonville, on the western banks of the Klamath River. Applegate felt the site provided maximum protection for emigrants and local communities, presumably from the Klamath and Modoc tribes.[73] Since he had no authority over the forces in southwestern Oregon, Alvord passed the recommendation on to General Wright. Alvord had known Wright for nearly ten years, and they seemed to value each other's views; therefore, Wright trusted his assessment of the need. Despite Alvord's lack of jurisdiction, Wright supported the call for constructing a permanent fort somewhere in the region and sent his recommendation to the War Department.

Agreeing to build the fort and actually building it were not the same thing. Although Wright had quickly approved Alvord's call for building a fort in southwestern Oregon, final approval rested with the War Department. Hoping to avoid delays, he did not wait for the torturously slow communication process to confirm his decision; in mid-March General Wright gave Charles Drew, recently promoted to lieutenant colonel, the task of selecting the best site.[74] By April 20 Wright was under the impression that Drew was "making preparation to move from his camp, near Jacksonville, east to the neighborhood of the Klamath Lakes, to establish a post in that vicinity for the protection of the emigrant route." Unfortunately, Wright was overly optimistic; Drew continued to do virtually nothing for the next two months. Snow levels certainly impeded travel for part of that time; however, weather conditions alone did not seem to explain Drew's lethargy. General Wright, still occupied with the fallout from an attempt by Confederate sympathizers to steal a ship in San Francisco Bay in mid-March, did not press Drew on his tardiness. Some local citizens were not as tolerant. Lieutenant Colonel Drew's casual regard for finding a site for the new fort fueled growing criticism.

Complaints against Lieutenant Colonel Drew came from two sources: the local Indian subagent and those who wanted to be paid to supply the garrison. The former stemmed from Agent Amos E. Rogers's accusation that Drew did not provide him assistance when asked. That charge was summarily dismissed later in the year when an investigating officer did not find any reason to censure "Colonel Drew's conduct," nor did he "reflect indiscretion upon his judgement." The other charge was potentially more troubling because it suggested a Confederate sympathizer had infiltrated the Oregon Cavalry's officer corps. During the investigation, "respectable citizens of Jacksonville" implied that Drew was a Copperhead because he had given army contracts to a suspected Confederate sympathizer. The investigating officer determined those accusations did not have "the slightest foundation in reason or fact" and were probably leveled because those making the charges did not receive government contracts. The military, rather than being suspicious of Drew, felt he acted wisely, since the supplier in question, a Mr. Glenn, charged the lowest prices.[75] Whether these charges, which were discussed publicly from Jacksonville to Governor Gibbs's office, contributed to Drew's delayed action is unclear. After Drew sent a six-page letter to the Department of Pacific headquarters defending himself, it does suggest they did distract him.[76]

Finally, more than three months after receiving the task to establish a new fort, Drew set out to find a good site. The party included Lts. Frank White and David Collins (D. C.) Underwood and thirty men from Company C as well as a number of civilians; it left Camp Baker on June 22. The scouting party headed northeastward toward Upper Klamath Lake. The citizens reported they went along "for the purpose of visiting the Klamath Lake country" to determine its agricultural potential. Their presence had an adverse effect on Drew, who seemed to let their interests override the military purpose of the scout. The civilians were disappointed once it was determined the lower end of Upper Klamath Lake was "surrounded almost entirely by [a] tulle marsh, with little or no tillable land on the lower side." They had been "led to suppose that [they] should find a rich valley, with good water and timber" at that location. Encumbered with the frustrated civilians, "the Colonel decided [on] leaving the examination of this portion of the country for another trip."[77] The party returned to Camp Baker on July 1.

The nine-day scout had largely been a waste of time and, based on how one of the civilians described it, nothing more than a campout. Drew laid over an extra day during the return so the civilians could enjoy the refreshing waters of an unnamed lake. It seems he paid less attention to trying to find a site for a fort than focusing on "the numerous little accidents and funny circumstances of frequent occurrence, the recital of pioneer experience and wonderful stories, only to be appreciated around a camp-fire," which along with the "novelty of mountain life, made [the civilians'] trip a pleasant one."[78] That pleasant trip was also antithetical to the military objective.

Having failed to find a suitable location for the fort, Drew set out again six days later, planning to explore beyond the farthest point of his first scout, heading east and north of Mount McLoughlin. He was accompanied by Lieutenant White, thirty-three men from Company C, and another group of civilians. This scout proved more successful both in military terms and for what the civilians hoped to find—land with agricultural potential. During the return trip, the group came across Klamath Chief La Lake's encampment, a band that did not alarm the whites. After questioning those in the camp, Drew's party continued their return ride toward Camp Baker. The civilians, unaccustomed to so many long days in the saddle, left Drew's troopers and opted to try a shortcut, which ended up being worse than the route taken by the cavalrymen. The contingent from Company C reached the camp almost two weeks after they started.[79]

This trip, unlike the first one, had been a success; Drew found the location for the fort. The two scouts, however, had been poorly conducted. This was the only time that influential local civilians, not working for the military, accompanied a contingent of the Oregon Cavalry during its military operations. Recording their assessment of the land's potential for development was a key part of the Oregon Cavalry's service. However, bringing along unprepared civilians to do the actual assessing was a mistake. In both instances the civilians had shown they could not endure the challenges of being in the field for even two weeks. While the civilian account of the first scout almost sounds like they were out on a lark, Drew certainly cut the ride short to accommodate them. Had he not been burdened with civilians, he almost certainly would have found the location for the fort during the first scout. Instead, their presence added an additional two weeks before he eventually started the construction of the fort.

Once official approval for the significant monetary and military commitment finally came through, Alvord's role in the Fort Klamath project ended.[80] From then on, Wright dealt directly with the military authority in the region, the slow-moving Lieutenant Colonel Drew. It fell to Captain Kelly's Company C men to do much of the construction of the fort. Having the enlisted men work as common laborers to keep construction costs low was not uncommon. Still, the Oregon Cavalry's adjutant, Lt. William V. Rinehart, bristled at the use of soldiers for such work. He understood the need for troopers to do manual work in the field, where there were no other options, but "in garrison [officers] should not require such work from soldiers." Emphatically he argued, "I have no doubt but that the practice of compelling soldiers to do such work is highly detrimental to the service."[81] Unfortunately for the men in Company C, his complaints came from afar, since he served on Colonel Maury's staff and not in southwestern Oregon. The Company C men would provide the main source of labor when it came time to build the fort.

Finally, three months after Wright had informed the army's adjutant general that construction was just around the corner, Drew showed an urgency that had been absent previously. To get material and supplies to the fort grounds, a portion of Captain Kelly's men hacked out an eighty-five-mile-long road between Jacksonville and the fort. Capt. James Van Voast, who General Wright sent to southern Oregon on an inspection tour, was impressed by how quickly the road was carved out of the wilderness: "The work expended upon it shows that the men must have labored with more than ordinary industry to have finished it in so short a time"—about one month.[82] The only way Drew could devote his men so thoroughly to building the fort was if the region was protected from Indian raids. General Wright assured Drew that other forces would "be so dispersed as to give the necessary protection without having to call upon any part of [Drew's] force to quell disturbances that may spring up." Thus, most of Drew's men could focus their "whole energies to the erection of the post, using as many of the enlisted men of [Drew's] command as can be made useful and spared from other duties."[83]

Captain Van Voast described the location of the fort in greater detail, noting that it

> is situated eight miles north of the waters of the Upper Klamath Lake. It is about eighty-six miles from Jacksonville by the new wagon road leading to it, about twenty miles south of the Rogue River and John Day turnpike, which runs from Jacksonville to the Boise mines, and about fifty miles north of the present southern emigrant road leading into Oregon. The fort is placed in the most beautiful and pleasant part of the valley. It

has southern exposure, and is surrounded by wood and water in greatest abundance. The soil appears of a peculiar nature, but the luxuriance of the grass would seem to indicate that it was capable of producing grain and many of the vegetables [needed to feed the soldiers] in great profusion.[84]

Numerous civilians complained about the fort's location, mainly because it was too far from Jacksonville, but Captain Von Voast was satisfied: "There can be no question as to the fitness of the place selected for this new fort" for both "the health of the troops and the economy in their support." As a "strategic position, taken for the purpose of holding in subjection Indians that are considered hostile, it offers very many advantages."[85]

The fort buildings were rather rudimentary that first winter due to the need to complete them before the cold descended over the region, but enough of it was finished that Company C passed through the coming winter relatively comfortably. Since the plan was to house two companies at the fort, it had plenty of space—a second company did not arrive until the spring of 1865. According to Oregon infantryman Sgt. Orson A. Sterns, a soldier assigned to Fort Klamath in 1865, "The post consisted of some five one-story frame buildings on the east side of a square, with the company quarter[s] on the south side, consisting of a rough lumber one-story box building set up on wooden posts about two and one-half feet from the ground, and with a division across the centre of its length to accommodate two companies. The entire structure was 120 feet long by 24 feet in width. It was unceiled and unlined, but had battens over the cracks between the siding boards. There was a large double fire place in the centre." It included a "mess house and kitchen building about 30 feet wide by 80 feet long, which was built at right angles to the company quarters, forming a T." All buildings were made of "cheap box lumber construction, and elevated from the ground." The officers' quarters were at a right angle to the company quarters. There was a guardhouse, and an "adjutant's office was at the southeast angel of the square, on a line with both the officers' quarters and the company quarters."

The post hospital was "at the northeast corner of the square," with the quartermaster's and storehouse in the middle. By 1865 a few houses had been constructed for soldiers' families as well. Stables, large enough to hold the horses of two companies if need be, were located "about 300 feet south of the officers' quarters."[86]

The work had undoubtedly been taxing and somewhat rushed, since the cold fall winds and snow were not far off—the altitude of the fort site was over 4,100 feet. However, Sgt. William Colvig had fond memories of the fort. During the off days, Colvig remembered, "We spent our time, off duty, riding over the sagebrush plains, hunting the game, which was plentiful, fishing in the lake or river and playing cards in camp." Once the site had been chosen, the military ordered Chief La Lake's band to relocate near the fort, which led to rather routine interaction between the soldiers and the Indians. Sergeant Colvig described seeing "the old [Klamath] 'piece chief' Lalek [La Lake], who indeed seemed most friendly" to the soldiers. He continued, "His tall figure, unbowed by age, was often seen among our tents, and all the soldiers held somewhat the same reverence for him that his own tribe did." Despite having a degree of respect for the chief and at least a tolerance for that band of Indians, Colvig still harbored the attitudes common among whites at the time. Years later, and removed from his actual interaction with the Klamath chief, he reflected, "We did not know the Indian character well enough to understand that the passive attitude they assumed was but a sign of the smoldering treachery in their hearts." In a more contemplative moment, Colvig touched on the true state of white–Indian relations in parts of the District of Oregon, not just in 1863 but over the course of many years: "Of course we were foolish to think that these people were going to give up their land and the freedom they loved so well and be led to the reservation without a murmur of protest in a struggle for their rights."[87] The struggle, over the land and for freedom, intensified the next year.

The change in Oregon governors after the June 1862 election of Addison C. Gibbs influenced the First Oregon Volunteer Cavalry

Regiment in a very direct way. Unlike Copperhead John White-aker, Gibbs maintained direct and regular communication with a number of the regiment's officers and even a few of the troopers. The new governor got along well with many of the Oregon cavalrymen, probably because they had many things in common. Although he was slightly older than "his" cavalrymen, and from New York instead of the Midwest, as were so many, Gibbs, like the men in the regiment, had come to the West in search of gold. Like many of them, once he concluded he would not get rich in California, he headed north to chart a different course in Oregon Territory in 1850. He was a ten-year veteran of Oregon's political battles when he was elected governor in 1862 as a Republican. Like many Oregonians, he had not been a staunch Lincoln man until secession and subsequent events pushed him into that position. By 1863 he was as eager as the volunteers to do his part for the Union cause and to enhance awareness of the region's frontier expanses.[88]

On January 6, 1863, Governor Gibbs did something his predecessor had not: he issued a proclamation calling for recruits to serve in the U.S. Army to fill the First Oregon Volunteer Cavalry Regiment to full strength. His proclamation stated the new companies "will be needed the coming Spring on the frontiers in this State and Washington Territory," which referred to that portion that shortly became Idaho Territory, "for an expedition against the Snake Indians." Being optimistic, he did not "doubt that the citizens of Oregon, who have always promptly responded to any demand for their military services . . . [will] respond to this call." Governor Gibbs emphasized the opportunity for individuals to perform patriotic duty by volunteering, echoing strategies used during the initial recruiting in 1861. He declared that by volunteering they would have the chance to demonstrate "their loyalty to the Government, and aiding in chastising marauding bands of Indians which infest our frontiers." While the governor did not mention pay or additional funding, there were two differences from the original recruiting efforts. First, volunteers were not required to provide their own horses, but if they did, they would be paid at a higher daily rate—forty cents instead of thirty. Second, in a nod to the depleted ranks of the original six companies, the new companies were to have one hundred enlisted men, not seventy-nine, making it easier to parcel them out in the field as needed.[89]

Already being four companies short of full strength, every desertion had an amplified effect on the Oregon Cavalry's strength. Reports about desertions in 1863 were troubling. Lieutenant Rinehart stated that twenty-two men deserted from Company A before Maury's command reached the site where Fort Boise was being constructed.[90] An August 19 article in the Jacksonville *Oregon Sentinel* noted that just four or five men had deserted from Captain Kelly's Company C. Given that they were being employed to build Fort Klamath, and not in a way any recruit could have anticipated, that number is surprisingly low. Kelly and the other officers, the newspaper reported, were not bothered by the few desertions because "they were such worthless characters that the company is profitably rid of them."[91] One of the troopers with Maury agreed, believing, "Uncle Sam does well to get rid of all such profligate characters. These deserters in nine cases out of ten rid our Regiment . . . of the trash."[92] Company B had the lowest number of desertions in 1863 (and over the course of its enlistment); just three men deserted from the company as it lolled away the summer and early fall months around The Dalles.[93]

With Governor Gibbs's support, recruiters once again tried to drum up enthusiasm for service in the state's only Union regiment.[94] Initially, recruiting offices were set up in Portland and The Dalles. Efforts were later expanded to Salem and Eugene, and eventually southern Oregon, by the end of the year. In light of how difficult recruiting had been when the national enthusiasm for serving in the Union forces was high, trying to find four hundred men to fill four companies in Oregon was ambitious in 1863. Henry C. Small and John F. Noble got to work quickly, though the military relieved Noble from his recruiting duty in November while he awaited the outcome of a court-martial.[95] Others involved in the effort included William Hand, Patrick McGuire, and Looney C. Bond, all of whom hoped to form their own companies.[96]

Some papers took delight in the early struggles, when there were more officers than recruits. The Walla Walla *Washington States-man* managed to mock both Governor Gibbs and the limited success of the recruiting effort: "His Corpulency, Governor Gibbs, is very much bored by applications for commissions."[97]

Rather than enlist the four companies of one hundred men each, recruiting, once again, proved a challenge. In addition to the recruiters, many newspapers also leaned into the effort. One Eugene newspaper referred to "trains being stopped and robbed by" Indians, "and there is every reason to apprehend that they will add murder to their other crimes." This, the newspaper stated, "is a conclusive argument in favor of the immediate filling up of the Oregon Cavalry Regiment. The troopers are needed, and if Oregon fails to furnish them her interests will suffer." Stressing the populaces' responsibility, the newspaper reminded its readers, "They who will not help themselves are unworthy of assistance."[98] With most efforts faltering, it looked like the exonerated John F. Noble would have the most recruits and thus be given the captain's commission, with Small appointed first lieutenant. However, when the first (and only) company reached the required number of men and was mustered into service in August 1863, Noble and Small flipped ranks. Henry C. Small was appointed captain, while John F. Noble was appointed the first lieutenant. William Hand, the second lieutenant, filled out the officer corps of the newly created Company G. Both McGuire and Bond's efforts failed, and neither was formally mustered into the service.[99]

Despite the poor results, efforts were renewed at the end of the year when Lt. John Apperson was transferred from temporary command of Company A and put in charge of the latest recruiting effort. The move partially explains why the popular Apperson was not promoted to captain and given permanent command of the company. There was reason to believe that if anyone might be able to convince men to volunteer, he was the one.[100] Unfortunately for Apperson, he failed miserably and was transferred to a staff position. By that time, command of Company A had been given to William V. Rinehart, most recently the regimental adjutant.[101]

With the conclusion of the failed effort to recruit a new company, 1863 came to a close for the First Oregon Volunteer Cavalry Regiment, though not for Lieutenant Apperson.

While the cavalry companies settled into the various forts for the winter, Apperson had two more tasks to perform. Despite failing to recruit another cavalry company, Apperson did succeed in a different type of recruiting effort during the winter of 1863–64. Writing to Apperson in November from Fort Dalles, the man who soon took command of Company A, Lt. William V. Rinehart, besieged his friend: "If *recruiting* fails us this time, then indeed is our (my) condition hopeless. The honor of the Regiment, my own happiness, indeed everything sacred and dear should serve to promote energetic and decided action." Rinehart implored Apperson not on behalf of the regiment; he wanted Apperson to be his proxy in his pursuit of Amanda Gaines. Rinehart, realizing Mrs. Apperson might not appreciate her husband spending time with Ms. Gaines, enjoined Apperson to remind his wife "*she* [once] had a laudable sympathy for *you* in your soldier bachelorhood, so you have a kindred sympathy for me . . . poor devil . . . in my long, long struggle on the road to bliss." How much influence Apperson had on keeping the flames of the Rinehart–Gaines romance alight is unclear, but Rinehart and Amanda married a year later.[102]

Like Rinehart, Captain Currey had a Gaines sister on his mind throughout the winter at his encampment at Fort Walla Walla. Though not as desperate as Rinehart, he too sought Apperson's help with his romantic interests. As he planned for the spring 1864 campaign, he asked Apperson if he and his wife could let Jennie stay with them during his six-month campaign. Currey informed his friend, "Though you may not know it yet I write you the fact in a very quiet manner that I intend to make her legally my own upon my return." He wished the Appersons to "accommodate her or add to her happiness," which would "greatly oblige [him]."[103] Whether or not the Appersons reminded Jennie of Currey's commitment to her during the long months he spent on the Oregon and Idaho frontier, the two married at the end of the year. Lt. John T. Apperson may have failed at recruiting a new company for the regiment, but he apparently helped his friends "recruit" their wives.

Just as many Oregon cavalrymen had been disappointed they were not sent east to face Confederates in 1862, troopers were disappointed the next year, when only a few of them engaged the so-called Snakes. Frustrated as they may have been, General Alvord's strategy for 1863 had been mostly successful from both the military and civilian standpoints. It was true that the Oregon Cavalry had failed "to inflict a severe chastisement" upon the Northern Shoshones, Bannocks, or Northern Paiutes. However, they had achieved most of everything else that Alvord had originally wished, as well as what he later added, for them to do during the campaigning season. He praised the five companies of Oregon Cavalry (and the two of Washington Infantry) for helping maintain calm during the Nez Perce negotiations, saying, "This assemblage of troops at Lapwai had thus a most salutary effecting, evincing that the power of the Government was not gone, as rebel sympathizers had endeavored to instill" in the Indians.[104]

Two troopers who spent the summer and part of the fall riding from Fort Lapwai to Fort Hall before turning back for Fort Walla Walla realized that failure to engage the Indians was not really a failure. One reflected that "the expedition will be attended with a great many good results, while it will at least keep the Indians beat back into the mountains and allow the emigration to pass through the country safe and secure in both person and property."[105] Echoing those sentiments, another cavalryman from the expedition added, "One fact, however, speaks well, and shows that our presence had some" good results, since "not a single depredation has been committed to the present season anywhere from Burnt river to Fort Hall."[106]

Not all contributions occurred in the field that year; two forts were built at strategic locations. While the construction of Fort Boise was completed under the guidance of the Ninth U.S. Infantry's Maj. Pinkney Lugenbeel and the labor provided partially by Washington infantrymen, the presence of the Oregon Cavalry had made work on the fort possible. Had Maury's expedition spent less time between Fort Boise and Fort Hall, the infantry units would have had to patrol the region. Once enough of the structures were completed to house a permanent force, an Oregon Cavalry officer (Major Rinearson) was put in charge.

Unlike the lesser connection to the establishment of Fort Boise, Company C was directly involved in the creation of Fort Klamath.[107] From choosing the site, to building the road to it, and finally, to providing the muscle to construct the fort itself, Company C made the fort a reality. Like Fort Boise, establishing Fort Klamath in a key location on the emigrant trail was a long-term achievement. The search for a site, as badly handled as that had been from a military efficiency standpoint, did contribute to one of the cavalry's secondary but important goals, frontier exploration. Even though there had been significant criticism of Lieutenant Colonel Drew by a number of civilians, the local newspaper understood how important his exploration had been. In September the editor wrote, "Klamath Lake Valley, proper, had been almost entirely unexplored until up to the time that Col. Drew and his command went there, and all information in regard to its extent, the character of its soil, its climate, etc., cannot fail to be of interest to the people of Oregon."[108]

In truth, whether it was making the emigrant trails safe for whites, providing a visual show of federal strength during the Nez Perce negotiations, or building and manning strategically located forts, the First Oregon Volunteer Cavalry Regiment had done almost all that the district commander had asked, and the people could hope for, in 1863. Alvord admitted to Oregon governor Gibbs, "The gallant spirit of the First Oregon Cavalry, who have borne like good soldiers the hardships of the campaigns, are entitled to my thanks for the efficient and cheerful manner in which they have discharged the duty, although they had not the good fortune to meet an enemy."[109] Though satisfied with the results of his first full year in charge of the district, Alvord had bolder plans for 1864; he was determined to make sure the Oregon Cavalry got a chance to meet an enemy.

SIX

Bold Plans

As Benjamin Alvord contemplated the operational season that had just concluded from Fort Vancouver, he had every reason to feel satisfied with his first full year as District of Oregon commander. Almost everything he had asked of his forces, especially the First Oregon Volunteer Cavalry Regiment, had been achieved. The only thing his mounted command had not done was largely out of their control—namely, "chastise" the Snake Indians. To do that, as Colonel Maury could point out after two years, one needed to find them first. During the winter of 1863–64, General Alvord mulled over how to make certain the Oregon Cavalry found the Snakes. On February 10, 1864, he mapped out his plans for the coming campaign in a letter to Oregon governor Addison Gibbs. Alvord told the governor, "I shall recommend to the general commanding the department that troops [most of the Oregon Cavalry and some Washington Infantry] be sent to traverse thoroughly the whole region" from Canyon City to the California border and as far east as Fort Boise. While the Oregon Cavalry had spent the past two summers and falls in the field, Alvord planned to deploy them differently in 1864. As Alvord detailed, "I hope to put two expeditions in the field the whole season for that purpose against the Snake Indians—one from Fort Dalles southeasterly and one from Fort Boise westerly and southwesterly. I shall also recommend a movement from Fort Klamath easterly; but as that post is not in my district I cannot speak so definitely in reference to it."[1]

The plan was textbook military strategy: Alvord's idea was to constrict the open spaces as the various Oregon Cavalry companies moved toward one another (somewhat similar to the Union's Anaconda Plan used against the Confederacy). If all worked well, one or more of the cavalry contingents would finally have the clash they sought with the Indians. This differed in two ways from what the Oregon Cavalry had done the previous two years. First, the operations area would be shifted; instead of spending most of their time from Fort Boise eastward, along the emigrant trails, they would operate in eastern Oregon and western Idaho Territory, south of Canyonville, Oregon. Next, this would entail multiple expeditions taking place at the same time. Alvord "requested the authority" to put the "troops in the field as follows: From Fort Boise west and westerly, two companies of Oregon cavalry (A and E), under command of Capt. George B. Currey. From Fort Dalles, southeasterly, two companies of the same regiment (D and G), under the command of Capt. J.M. Drake."[2] Coordinating with the third pincer of Alvord's strategy was the most complicated, since Fort Klamath was outside his jurisdiction. A month after explaining how he would move his own forces around, he recommended to his superior "that two-thirds of the company at Fort Klamath be sent in the direction of Goose Lake [eastward, just above the California border], to remain out all summer."[3]

Alvord understood this was likely the last opportunity the Oregon Cavalry would get to use its weight of arms against Indian raiders; most enlistments expired in less than a year. He empathized with the Oregon cavalrymen, knowing that the "ardent desire of many of them would be to join in the war in the East."[4] Since that had never been possible, a well-coordinated military campaign to stamp out any Indian resistance along the emigrant trails was their only chance to prove their patriotism and support for the larger Union cause. It was also likely the last opportunity to have so many mounted troops focused on such a singular objective. Coordinating three operations, separated by hundreds of miles, under two military jurisdictions was an ambitious plan. It also gave off an air of desperation.

The emigrant trains were not Alvord's only concern. Sending multiple columns out specifically looking to engage Indian raiders would also protect the growing influx of miners. Alvord believed miners would rush to "that portion of Oregon east of the Cascade Mountains, which is now a center of great attraction" because "it contains no doubt immensely valuable mineral deposits." Alvord declared, "It is my earnest wish to give them all the assistance and protection in my power." Perhaps exceeding his authority, he emphasized to Governor Gibbs that "to aid in such an interesting development should be the aim and policy of the Government." If the Oregon Cavalry succeeded, as Alvord envisioned, both emigrants and miners would reap the benefits.[5]

Even before an Oregon trooper mounted his horse to set out on General Alvord's large-scale expeditions, changes had to be made. Alvord's original plan called for Captain Currey to lead two companies westward from Fort Boise. Unfortunately, those companies had wintered at Fort Walla Walla, 250 miles to the northwest. Two companies of Washington Infantry were the only troops stationed at Fort Boise during the winter of 1863–64. There was a practical reason why the cavalry had not diverted to Fort Boise instead of continuing on to Fort Walla Walla at the end of the 1863 campaigning season: the still unfinished Fort Boise could not accommodate two companies of cavalry and their horses.[6] If there was to be an eastern pincer in Alvord's planned campaign, Captain Currey would have to lead his two companies on a roughly two-week trek just to get into position before they could turn west and move in coordination with the other two columns. Wisely, it was decided the additional fatigue on the horses would be too detrimental just to get them in place at Fort Boise. Also, waiting for them to get into position there might force Alvord to delay the other two columns. For these reasons, Captain Currey's two companies would start their campaign from Fort Walla Walla instead of Fort Boise.

The 1864 campaign started earlier than anticipated when events in the late winter forced General Alvord to send patrols out from

both Forts Dalles and Walla Walla. The first detachment of the
Oregon Cavalry activated in 1864 left Fort Walla Walla on February 16 under the command of the always-ready Captain Currey. Currey led fifty-nine men, pulled from Companies A and E,
and three civilians, whose property had been stolen, northward.
They investigated reports of armed Indians harassing miners above
where the Palouse River joins the Snake River. Three days later the
patrol finally crossed over to the north side of the Snake River and
encountered some Palouse Indians. Believing they would betray
his presence and intention to "the band [he] was in quest of," Currey reported, "I gave out that I was en route to [Fort] Colville,"
near the Canadian border, "and as soon as it was fairly dark and
all the Indians had left camp I took up the march and moved on
for five hours without halting." Foul weather hindered his progress the rest of the fourth day, but his command finally found the
people he was looking for on the fifth day, about eighty miles north
of Fort Walla Walla.[7]

Doing what he had in previous situations, at about 8:00 a.m.
Currey ordered his men to surround the seven dwellings they
found. That no one came out seems to have perplexed Currey.
Unsure of what to do, he ordered two platoons to fire three volleys into the camp, but apparently not into the dwellings, to avoid
hitting anyone. Unfortunately, at least one of the shots went into a
lodge and "wounded one Indian in the neck, probably mortally,"
Currey reported. The terrified Indians, who Currey believed were
"renegades from neighboring tribes," came out to avoid being
slaughtered in their own abodes. After lining up the men and
letting the civilians inspect them to identify the perpetrators of
the theft of some of their goods, Currey bound three of them and
took them back to Fort Walla Walla, where they would be tried
and almost certainly found guilty, then punished.[8]

The entire expedition lasted just seven days, but Currey's superiors felt his actions, once again, would have a salutary effect.
Lt. Col. Thomas English, of the First Washington Infantry and
commander of Fort Walla Walla, felt "the expedition prov[ed] a complete success."[9] General Alvord was even more impressed, stating

Currey's actions "will have a very good effect on those Indians. They will be apt to hereafter to let the miners alone."[10] The irony is that the Indians, most likely Palouses, were already trying to avoid the miners, who were encroaching further into their lands.[11] As Captain Currey observed, the band had "selected their present location because of its seclusion from and difficult approach by the whites."[12]

Currey's patrol was not the only Oregon Cavalry operation during the late winter. Like Captain Currey, Lt. James Waymire and a twenty-five-man contingent of Company D cavalrymen moved into the field earlier than planned. The origins of Waymire's late winter–early spring operation began in January in response to reports Colonel Maury received about Indian thefts of livestock and attacks on white settlers along the Canyon City Road, an important trade route in north-central Oregon. On February 20 Maury first suggested to General Alvord "that twenty-five or thirty men be sent as soon as they can be started to camp in that vicinity."[13] The impatient colonel followed that up two days later with another letter, declaring, "Considerations of my letter of the 20th instant are increased in importance." The thieving had gotten worse, but he admitted that "many robberies are, however, committed by white men." Regardless of who the perpetrators were, the presence of some cavalry would "repress or detect the operations of whites and Indians."[14] General Alvord agreed and sent Waymire an order to move as soon as he could for "the South Fork John Day's River and encamp at some point best calculated to protect the whites against the incursions of the Indians." Alvord reminded the young lieutenant that "the friendly Indians from the Warm Springs Reservation should be treated with kindness."[15] The reservation, which had been established after the 1855 Stevens Treaty near Walla Walla, was home to Wasco and Tenino people, who the whites most often lumped together and called Warm Springs Indians.[16]

By 1864 Lieutenant Waymire had become one of the regiment's more trusted junior officers. A year after his promotion he was about to embark on his first independent expedition, providing protection for the few whites trying to scratch out an existence along the Canyon City Road. Though this was the twenty-year-old's first independent command, he had earned the respect of Captain Drake over the course of the previous two years, a considerable achievement. Drake felt Waymire was one of the very few officers who he could trust to conduct independent scouts.[17]

On March 1 Waymire and his twenty-five men from Company D left the relative comfort of Fort Dalles and headed out into the cold air of the arid high plains on the way to find a position on the South Fork John Day River.[18] Waymire's force took seventy-five days of rations in anticipation of it being out until it could join other units as they headed into the field for the major 1864 operations.[19] Alvord wanted Waymire to investigate the allegations to see if the reservation's Indians were truly to blame for the attacks and thefts or if it was whites. There is no hint that Alvord wanted Waymire and his men to mount a major offensive operation like those planned for the coming season. However, Waymire shared Captain Currey's opportunistic, aggressive tendencies and ended up exceeding the intent of Alvord's orders. His men paid a price for his brashness.

The command rode southeast for two weeks before coming to a spot along the South Fork John Day River where Waymire established a supply depot, which he named Camp Lincoln. According to a civilian riding with the column, the location was nearer the "centre of the Indian depredations than any other feasible point, and is well situated as to wood, water and grass."[20] This became his base of operations, requiring him to leave men behind when he went on scouts looking for the livestock thieves. The locals believed the culprits were Paiutes, but Waymire doubted they were working alone, telling Colonel Maury, "White men are probably at the head of the band of Indians who are committing the depredations."[21] The early season of the operations had been hard on his mounts due to the "scarcity of grass and the severity of the weather."[22] Not long after choosing the depot site, information reached the young lieutenant that one hundred head of livestock had been stolen near Canyon City, and whites presumed the theft

P10. Lt. James Waymire. Oregon Historical Society, 020574.

had been done by Indians.[23] Leaving ten men behind to complete the depot, Waymire and the other fifteen headed to Canyon City, east of Camp Lincoln, the next day. They reached it on March 19.[24]

Upon reaching Canyon City, Waymire learned that about forty mules and horses had been stolen from a rancher named Davis. His ranch was located two miles below the town. The ranch owner and approximately thirty locals had already left in pursuit of the

animals and the thieves, heading southeastward. Without sufficient supplies and unsure of how long the civilian pursuit would
last, Waymire returned to his depot rather than follow their trail.
Before departing he left word in town to be contacted once something definitive was heard from the civilian pursuers. A messenger reached Camp Lincoln three days later, informing Waymire
that rancher Davis had returned to Canyon City to gather supplies
and reinforcements. He let Waymire know they had found the raiders' trail near Harney Lake and that he planned to return there soon.

Lieutenant Waymire gathered eighteen men and headed south
and slightly east on March 24, toward Harney Valley. The troopers found the trail "very rough and [going] over the mountains
almost impassable on account of the snow and ice." Three days later
a severe snowstorm brought the march to a halt for a day. Finally,
on March 30 Waymire found the civilians, now totaling fifty-four,
in Harney Valley. Cincinnatus Miller, who became famous under
the pen name Joaquin Miller in the 1870s, led the group. After discussing what to do next, it was decided that Miller's civilians would
march "toward the upper portion of the valley," hoping to find a
place to cross Silvies River to look for signs of recent Indian presence. At the same time, Waymire and the Oregon troopers followed
the trail left by the stolen animals, which led to the southeastern
end of the valley. Another snowstorm made the river unfordable,
so Miller's civilians turned back and caught up to Waymire on
April 1 as he and his men waited out another storm. The chase,
which was interrupted by yet another snowstorm, continued for
six more days, during which they came across the site of a weeks-
old Paiute encampment about twenty miles beyond Harney Lake.[25]

Finally, after two weeks on the trail, traveling across rugged terrain and over mountains in excess of five thousand feet through
frequent snowstorms, Waymire's scouts reported seeing numerous fires in an adjacent valley. With the cavalry in the lead, the
cavalcade remounted their worn horses and headed farther south.
They found "an Indian village, lately built of sagebrush, willows,
and grass, having contained probably 100 souls [that] had just
been deserted. Baskets, ropes, furs, half-cooked meat (horse flesh)"

scattered throughout the camps, along with "fires still burning," gave clear evidence the Paiutes "had been forced to leave hastily," likely after having seen Waymire's scouts.[26]

Eager to catch the fleeing group, Waymire picked fifteen of his men while Miller selected thirty of his, and they started after them at 3:00 a.m. on March 7.[27] Just after sunrise Waymire noticed smoke rising in the early morning sky three miles from the trail. He sent Sgt. Robert Casteel with four men (three troopers and a civilian) to investigate while the rest of the force continued. Not long after Sergeant Casteel departed, some civilians riding in advance of the main body spotted what they thought was a herd of horses in a valley two miles below the patrol. Without any reconnaissance they charged for the herd, riding at full speed for such a distance it "rendered their animals almost ineffective for the rest of the day." Their exuberance was misguided; rather than capture a herd of stolen or Paiute horses, all the civilians managed to do was surprise a large flock of geese and scatter themselves in small groups of tired riders and blown horses across the valley.[28]

The civilians' lapse in judgment proved costly for Waymire and Miller, who had a much smaller force at hand when they saw a lone Paiute at a distance of approximately two miles. Miller and five men set off in pursuit, leaving Waymire and his shrinking force in an area cut by numerous sage-covered ridges and dry creek beds. The landscape provided perfect concealment for a much larger gathering of Paiutes than Waymire and Miller had anticipated during their monthlong pursuit. At 10:00 a.m. the Oregon troopers heard a shot from Miller's direction. Waymire changed course to head toward the sound of the shot and soon saw large numbers of mounted Paiutes "file down out of a cañon and take position on a prominent sage ridge" about four hundred yards in front of him.[29] The pursuers quickly found themselves in a dangerous position.

With some of his men and some of the civilians miles back at the temporary depot watching their supplies, Waymire had less than a dozen troopers with him. Miller's civilians, most of whom had proven unreliable, were not within supporting distance. He dismounted his men, sending two-thirds of them forward (the others held their horses). According to Waymire and a civilian employee who had accompanied him, the Paiute numbers had increased to maybe two hundred since he heard the first shot.[30] The two sides exchanged ineffective fire, with those Paiutes on foot keeping up the firefight while a mounted force tried to move behind Waymire's dismounted men and get to their horses, thereby cutting them off. As the situation became critical, Waymire dispatched a messenger to the goose-chasing civilian group, whose horses were still partially blown, telling them to come up on his left flank. Their leaders had difficulty in getting the civilians to move to Waymire's aid. While the civilians inexplicably demurred from a fight they had so boldly sought, Waymire decided to fall back to the horse holders. Eventually, Cincinnatus Miller reorganized most of the civilians and rejoined the now remounted Oregon cavalrymen. One of Miller's men had been slightly wounded in the initial moments of the firefight, but no one else was hit.[31]

Dramatically outnumbered and in danger of being surrounded, Waymire ordered his men to draw their sabers, something that was uncommon even in the main theaters of the war. They charged toward the Paiutes at their front. Mounted Indians peeled off on both sides of the advancing Oregon troopers, firing their revolvers at Waymire's men. The departure of the mounted men revealed an organized body of Paiutes on foot "who greeted us with a heavy fire," Waymire reported. The bold gamble had not intimidated the Indians but instead had made his own situation worse. Still, Waymire wanted to mount another charge with Miller's group riding in his wake, firing their revolvers, but Miller refused, telling Waymire that "this was not his way of fighting Indians." The second charge was abandoned, and the group fell back toward a hill, with six troopers making "a brisk race over the sage plain and up the rocky hillside" to secure the position before the Paiutes closed the escape path. At 2:00 p.m., the lieutenant, "seeing that the enemy's horses were fresh and ours already nearly worn out, very greatly outnumbering us as they were and as well armed [we were], a retreat to camp was resolved upon."[32]

Waymire continued the retreat for over twenty miles, all the way back to the temporary depot, where he had left several of his own men and over twenty of the civilians. Not certain if the Paiutes had gotten between him and the campsite, he led a force of skirmishers "at the gallop" to "the plain twelve miles in advance, in line of skirmishers," where they "scoured the brush and grass to camp." This movement put Waymire well in advance of the main body as it fell back. While the Paiutes followed him, they did not ride ahead and cut off his retreat. Once at the campsite, he waited for the rear elements to come in, which did not happen until late at night. The Paiutes did not pursue all the way to the temporary depot, thus ending a long day that included a four-hour firefight followed by a long retreating skirmish. Waymire believed that five Paiutes had been hit, but since they held the ground, "it is impossible to ascertain their loss," he reported. Besides the slightly wounded civilian, a number of their horses had to be abandoned, and his own mounts were badly jaded after the twelve-mile gallop to end an exhausting day.[33]

Given the condition of the horses and lack of sufficient supplies, Waymire almost certainly would have started back to Canyon City the next morning, but he had not heard anything from Sergeant Casteel and his men. Eventually one of the troopers made his way back to the campsite. He told Waymire that the onset of the measles had left him too sick to continue, so Casteel sent him back to camp while the sergeant and the three others continued on. Worried the small group had not come in during the night, Waymire led fourteen men to find them. That they went on foot is a clear indication that their mounts were badly worn down.[34] They were able to follow Casteel's track to a hot spring, which Waymire had mistaken for campfires. From there Waymire followed Casteel's trail to a site that showed evidence of a fight, after which "all sign of them was lost."[35] The onset of darkness forced the patrol to give up and return to its campsite, which they reached "after 2 o'clock in the morning of the 9th and waited until night for them." Afterward, they "began the homeward march, being now on half rations."[36] Waymire's command was left "with the conviction that the worst fears of their fate were correct."[37] Two years later, an unsubstantiated report indicated that unidentified Indians attacked Casteel's patrol, killing troopers Ingraham and Himbert and the civilian in the initial melee. Casteel escaped, leading the Indians on a four-day pursuit before they caught up to and killed him.[38]

The exhausted group reached Canyon City on April 13, at which time the civilians returned to their homes. One of Waymire's men noted, "[We] had been out 24 days—a portion of the time on short rations, over a desolate country in snow and rain, mud and mountains. It stormed on us 14 days out of the 24, and snowed with the exception of two or three days, more like mid-winter than the middle of Spring."[39] The Oregon cavalrymen left the next day for Camp Lincoln, reaching it that day, where they learned Indian raiders had run off all the depot's stock. Also, while a large group of local civilians and the contingent of cavalrymen were far to the south, a band of Paiutes raided a number of the farms, stealing livestock and killing two white men. Waymire had not protected the locals around Canyonville, had lost some of his own stock, had been drawn more than a hundred miles from the site of his depot, and had engaged in a firefight and was forced to make a quick (albeit organized) retreat. His misjudgment of the hot springs steam for smoke had cost the lives of three cavalrymen and a civilian, who were "undoubtedly surprised, separated, and killed." Sgt. Robert Casteel and Pvts. Cyrus R. Ingraham and John Himbert were the first Oregon troopers to lose their lives in combat.[40]

Waymire's expedition was an undeniable failure and an ominous beginning to General Alvord's plans for the 1864 campaign, something Alvord did not take lightly. In his view, Waymire had shown "cool and gallant [conduct] in the fight," but Alvord continued, "He ha[d] converted his humble task into a regular campaign into the Indian country," which "far exceeded the programme intended for him" when detached on a reconnaissance.[41] Colonel Maury felt similarly, telling Captain Drake, "Waymire had made a mistake and had pursued the Indians too far."[42] Waymire was undeniably guilty of exceeding the intent of his orders, but the defeat on April 7 might have been avoided if the civilians had maintained their cohesion at the start and held their ground later in the day.

Realizing "the hard service performed by Lieutenant Waymire's men in the early spring, and the jaded condition of his cavalry horses," Captain Drake ordered Waymire's contingent to replace Lt. Stephen Watson's force at the Warm Springs Reservation.[43] A reliable force was required to watch over the reservation to keep the Indians from leaving it and whites out. There was also a supply depot that needed to be guarded. It was hoped that such easy duty would give Waymire's men the chance to recover. The switch freed up Lieutenant Watson to join Drake's prong of Alvord's plan, which was already underway.

By 1864 Capt. George B. Currey was well established as the most experienced company commander in the Oregon Cavalry; he was also the second most senior of those still in service. Only Capt. William J. Matthews, at Fort Lapwai, had been appointed before him. Capt. William Kelly's commission was dated a day after Currey's, giving the latter seniority over him by one day. The rest of the original company commanders were gone, Elisha Harding had resigned, Thomas S. Harris was forced out, and Sewell Truax had been promoted. When crafting his plans for the 1864 campaign, General Alvord wanted Currey to lead one of his expeditions due to both his seniority and his experience. Alvord chose Capt. John Drake to lead the central expedition. Drake, the most senior of the second generation of company commanders and generally the most trusted, had replaced Truax as commander of Company D. He left from Fort Dalles. Captain Kelly would lead the southern expedition from Fort Klamath, taking his orders directly from Department of the Pacific headquarters. While his comrades spent the spring through early fall on the frontier in the boldest campaign of the Oregon Cavalry's existence, William Matthews continued his difficult task of trying to keep the peace on the Nez Perce Reservation by keeping whites off Nez Perce lands.

General Alvord's original orders to Captain Drake, issued on March 19, directed Drake to lead his own Company D and the recently organized Company G "into the Indian country" on April 5, or as soon thereafter as possible.[44] The idea of Drake being ready to start his expedition in less than a month was overly optimistic.

Company G, commanded by Capt. Henry C. Small, had not yet reached Fort Dalles from Fort Vancouver when Alvord suggested the start date. Fortunately, most of the trip between the two forts was by boat; therefore, the horses would not be heavily fatigued by the movement. Still, both men and mounts would need some time to be fully rested. Waiting on Company G, however, was not the main cause of delay for Drake.

All of the 1864 expeditions required a tremendous amount of time not just to get the men and their own horses ready but to gather vast quantities of supplies and the pack animals and wagons to carry those supplies. Although supply depots would be established in the field, which Forts Dalles and Walla Walla would resupply, the initial outlay of everything from food for men and horses to medical supplies and military equipment was substantial. Gathering everything was time consuming, in part because it was difficult to assemble all that was needed. Drake started with "eight wagons and six mules each for the same, and 132 pack and riding mules, or 180 mules each"—all of which were handled by civilian employees of the Quartermaster Department under Capt. David W. Porter. This was in addition to the two companies of cavalry. Finally, Drake's column was accompanied by roughly twenty Wasco Indian scouts, something Captain Currey had repeatedly and vociferously advocated.[45] The Indian scouts would join Drake's column when it passed by the Warm Springs Reservation. When Drake finally led his column out of Fort Dalles on April 20, just five days later than Alvord had desired, it consisted of eight wagons; thirty-nine civilian employees; 120 Oregon troopers on their mounts, meaning there were at least three hundred horses and mules; and a number of heads of beef, all of which required substantial food.[46] The food for the men was also supplemented, whenever possible, by hunting. Some food for the animals was also packed, but mainly the plan was for them to subsist on grass along the way. Each column was a considerable logistical operation; later on when Lieutenant Colonel Drew led Company C toward Fort Boise, he faced the same issues on a fractional scale, since his force was much smaller.

Drake was confident about his own company, which "had made two Indian campaigns before this one," but "Company G was a

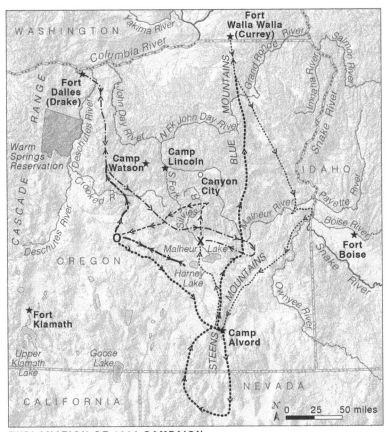

EXPLANATION OF 1864 CAMPAIGN

—·➤·— Drake expedition before joint operation (April 20 to June 30)

····➤···· Currey expedition before joint operation (April 28 to June 30)

--➤-- joint operations (July 1 to August 2)   **X** contact   **O** separation

—➤- Drake expedition after joint operation (August 3 to October 26)

···➤·· Currey expedition after joint operation (August 3 to October 11)

M4. Explanation of Currey's and Drake's 1864 campaigns.
Created by Chelsea McRaven Feeney.

raw company, without any experience in campaign life."[47] He was
equally troubled by Company G's officers, Captain Small and
Lts. William Hand and John F. Noble, who he felt needed "a good
deal of instruction for campaign life." Drake was especially critical of Hand and Noble, who "know nothing at all about their
duties." He continued, "Hand I don't think wants to learn anything. Noble is willing enough, but is too flighty entirely to rely

upon in any contingency."[48] While Drake came to appreciate how Noble's "good humor is inexhaustible; always lively, always jolly," his disgust with Hand only worsened over the many months of the campaign.[49] An exasperated Drake felt Hand "never will make an officer; it is not in him," which created a problem while they were in the field. Drake knew he "did not dare entrust him with anything," saying, "He is so utterly worthless that I could not put the lives of men under his care."[50] While extreme in tone, even for Drake, if he felt he could not rely on Hand, it could pose a genuine problem during the next six months.

As much as Lieutenant Hand's failings posed potential danger during the campaign, Drake could do his best to mitigate the risk by never allowing him to lead an independent scout. Unfortunately, there was no way around the negative impact caused by the expedition's medical officer, Dr. C. C. Dumreicher. The German-born doctor held the rank of major, which he felt gave him the authority to countermand or ignore Captain Drake's orders during the expedition. That view eventually led to him being court-martialed for disobedience of orders and insubordination, although he was found not guilty by a court led by an army surgeon.[51] Drake's biggest problem with Dr. Dumreicher was that he was a full-blown alcoholic with access to plenty of liquor. That problem first manifested itself on the second day out from Fort Dalles, when Dumreicher arrived late for his rendezvous time with the column, and drunk.[52] Two days later he somehow lost the trail, possibly while again drunk. While Drake, who was not much of a drinker, disliked the doctor personally, he worried more about his role as a medical officer with the command. He stated that Dumreicher "cannot take care of himself much less take care of others."[53]

Not surprisingly, Drake had more confidence in the officers in his own company, Lts. John M. McCall and James Waymire (who did not rejoin the command for some time after his defeat weeks earlier). Unlike most officers, McCall did not generate any of Drake's censure; in fact, when his actions under fire were criticized, Drake deflected the accusations, saying McCall had used "wise precaution."[54] Lieutenant McCall was deemed competent

enough that he was eventually promoted to captain in 1865. Waymire, in Drake's view, was the only officer, besides McCall, he
trusted on an independent scout, even after Waymire's failure
in the early spring.[55] Two other officers impressed Drake: the assistant quartermaster, Captain Porter, and Lt. Stephen Watson, who
eventually joined the column with his twenty-five-man contingent
of Company B men from his camp on the Warm Springs Reservation. Drake felt Captain Porter was "active and diligent, a live officer."[56] Lieutenant Watson was a brave and "active, efficient officer."[57]

Drake did not get far the first day, going into camp at 11:30 a.m.,
just five miles from Fort Dalles. The quick halt allowed the pack
mules and wagon teams to disentangle themselves from the crowd
of well-wishers in The Dalles. The easy pace continued the next day
as well, when the column headed out at 6:00 a.m. but only rode
ten miles before going into camp on the east side of the Deschutes
River, just four hours later. These short rides allowed Drake to ease
the inexperienced Company G troopers into the routine that would
dictate their lives from then until October. Though veterans, after
six months in winter quarters, the Company D men also needed
to ease back into campaigning condition. Regimental commander
Colonel Maury took advantage of the column's nearness and rode
out on the second day to confer with Drake. Undoubtedly they
discussed the news about Waymire's defeat, which had reached
Fort Dalles the day before. The next day regimental supply officer Lt. Jesse Robinson led a herd of beef cattle for the expedition
to Drake's camp. The pace picked up on April 23, when the column covered seventeen miles before going into camp. From this
point on, things settled into a routine for the third summer: start
by no later than 6:00 a.m. and ride somewhere between a dozen
and twenty miles.[58]

For the next five days, the column headed in a generally southern direction before Captain Drake ordered a halt on April 28
on Trout Creek, a little more than ten miles east of the Warm
Springs Reservation. Thus far Drake's only problem was that supply
officer Robinson had unloaded "the weakest and poorest" mules
pulling wagons "that were hurriedly fitted up expressly for this

expedition; they are utterly unfit for the severe service expected of them."[59] The halt allowed Drake to confer with Lieutenant Watson, who rode over from his camp on the reservation. He informed Drake he would return in three days with his entire contingent of Company B men. Drake also learned that Stock Whitley and a group of Warm Springs scouts were on their way. The Wascos' and Teninos' history of conflict with the Northern Paiutes partially motivated the men from the reservation to serve as scouts.[60] The layover dragged on until May 4, days longer than planned. Drake was waiting not just for Watson and his men but also to meet with Lieutenant Waymire on his way to the Warm Springs Reservation.

Unable to wait any longer, Drake finally resumed the march the next morning, with Watson's force added to his command. Increasingly worried about Waymire, the column only made it four miles before Drake halted again. Knowing his hundreds of horses and mules were leaving ample tracks to follow, his concern reached a critical point when Waymire had still not appeared. Drake commented that he felt "worried about Waymire" but also impatient, since "the expedition is being delayed on [Waymire's] account."[61] Frustrated with the delays, the command put in a more normal ride the next day, covering fourteen miles before going into camp a few miles outside the southeastern corner of the reservation, not far from the modern town of Madras. Despite the delays, Drake laid over for another day, hoping to see Waymire, who finally arrived in the camp at 3:00 p.m. the next day, May 7. Drake observed, "His horses and men are a good deal jaded, and look very rough" after their prolonged stay in the field.[62] Yet another day was lost when Drake remained encamped, conferring with Waymire, who was deeply disappointed that he was being sent to patrol the reservation instead of joining Drake. With the disposition of Waymire's command completed, Drake was elated "that the expedition will get off entirely without further let or hindrance, all impediments to its onward course being removed." He expressed, "We hope tomorrow to cut loose from civilization entirely."[63]

While the command only covered ten miles the next day, partially due to the steepness of its path, the troopers were "in high

glee and good humor" to be fully back on the expedition.⁶⁴ Drake
was impressed by the western vistas, which included Mount Jefferson and the Three Sisters of the Cascade Range, writing, "The
view of these peaks from camp is a magnificent one." The captain
shared his men's good mood, in part because of the antics of Lieutenant Noble. Drake admitted, "Buffoon though he is, our time
would frequently hang heavy but for his rollicking fun. I think
better of him, the more I see of him."⁶⁵

Unfortunately for Drake, his good mood was dashed the next
day, when new orders from General Alvord arrived. Drake was
instructed to "proceed to the northeastern end of Harney Lake
and effect a junction with the force of Captain Currey, First Oregon Cavalry, who will command the whole force. Captain Currey
will decide when the two commands will again separate."⁶⁶ These
changes were directly opposite of the original orders, and Drake
felt they "will destroy the effective strength of both" his and Captain Currey's expeditions. Drake wondered, "Why could the Gen.
not have left each free to govern himself?"⁶⁷ Things worsened over
the next few days. First, Dr. Dumreicher got into an argument with
Captain Porter at the beginning of the next day's march, leading
an exasperated Drake to complain that the doctor "wants half the
command to wait on him and is not worth a curse for a trip of
this kind; can't help himself at all."⁶⁸ Then on the night of May 13,
fifty horses broke free and ran up into the mountains, including
Drake's own mount. Two days were lost retrieving the animals.

Four weeks into his campaign and Drake had nothing to show
for his efforts except growing frustration over the numerous delays.
As a result of those delays, the column was only roughly 125 miles
southeast of Fort Dalles. While he and some of his men took note
of the vegetation and nature of the terrain they had ridden over,
most of that land had been explored before. The fact that his column had ridden on existing, though rough, roads most of the way
made it clear they had yet to explore any truly frontier regions.
Worse, given General Alvord's objectives, the only Indians Drake's
command encountered so far during the campaign were their
Warm Springs scouts. Time was running out for Drake, who was

angling farther southeastward toward the forced junction with
Currey's command near Harney Lake. He sent small patrols of
cavalry and some of his Indian allies fanning out on his forward
flanks, trying to find Paiute encampments or at least some indication they had recently been in the area.

Finally, on May 17 patrols reported back to the main body that
they had found evidence that a Paiute band was in the area. The
discovery occurred two miles below Drake's camp, which was at
the junction of the North Fork Crooked River and the main river
channel. He immediately sent patrols out to find their current
campsite. One of the Warm Springs scouting parties discovered
a Paiute "camp about 12 or 15 miles [northeast] distant, numbering 9 lodges, and a large band of horses, 100 or more." Eager to
engage the Paiutes, whether in a confrontation of arms or to warn
them against attacking whites, Drake moved quickly. He ordered
Lt. John M. McCall to make a night march to the site of the Paiute camp with a force including twenty-six of his own men from
Company D, Lieutenant Watson and ten men from Company B,
and twenty-one Warm Springs scouts led by Stock Whitley. The
plan was for McCall to surprise the camp in the predawn hours,
despite having no evidence they had done any raiding. Drake would
follow with the rest of his force in the early morning.[69]

At 9:30 p.m. McCall left Drake's camp on the Crooked River and
headed in a northeasterly "direction over an extremely rockey [sic]
country for some 12 miles" before coming into "the vicinity of the
camp, where [they] found [their Warm Springs] scouts."[70] Traveling in the dark and trying not to give away his approach, McCall's
force did not reach his scouts' location until about 2:00 a.m. He
sent four of the Warm Springs scouts ahead of his main body to
find the best way to close the mile gap between his men and the
Paiute camp. The scouts reported they could safely move within
five hundred or six hundred yards without being discovered.
McCall quietly moved his force as close as possible. Finally seeing the campsite for himself, he noted it was on a flat, under some
juniper trees and opposite a gradual rise. The Paiute horses were
herded together in two groups above and below the camp. As it

neared 3:00 a.m., McCall developed his attack plan. On the advice
of his scouts, he approached the camp from the west. He divided
his force into three groups, with Stock Whitley and his twenty-
one Warm Springs scouts moving to the left, or south, while Lieutenant Watson took up a position in the center, and McCall led
his Company D men to Watson's right, or north.

The crucial coordination between the three columns, made
more challenging in the dark, quickly unraveled after the advance
started at roughly 4:00 a.m. Watson, whose eagerness combined
with having the easiest path, quickly outpaced the other two wings.
McCall's men were literally bogged down when they advanced "over
an extremely rockey [*sic*] and rough country" before reaching "a
quagmire, and with difficulty got across." By this point the Paiutes
had discovered they were being attacked by an unknown force of
undetermined size, so they sent a man out to gather their horses.
McCall's men drove the man off and "immediately secured these
[horses], and put them in charge of a corporal and two men."[71] The
struggle through the quagmire and disorganization caused by capturing the horses left McCall well behind Watson's center group.
The Warm Springs scouts made steady progress on the far left.

After detailing the three men to take charge of the horse herd,
McCall moved the rest toward the Paiute encampment. McCall
reported, "[We] heard firing to our left, and turned in that direction, but found we were going directly under the fire of Lt. Watson's
men." Shifting to the right as they moved forward to avoid friendly
fire, McCall's men "found Lt. Watson's party all cut to pieces."[72] As
Watson's men emerged into the open, the Paiutes had fallen back
to a defensible position among some rocks on the hill, where they
fired both guns and bows. One of his men stated, "Lieutenant Watson was the first to arrive in front of the Indians, and on the first
fire fell mortally wounded from his horse—two of his men were
killed at the same time."[73] Others were hit during the ensuing firefight, including five additional troopers. A civilian named Richard Barker was shot in the thigh, breaking the bone, and one of
the Warm Springs scouts was also hit. The scouts' leader, Stock
Whitley, was struck at least four times. One of the bullets "entered

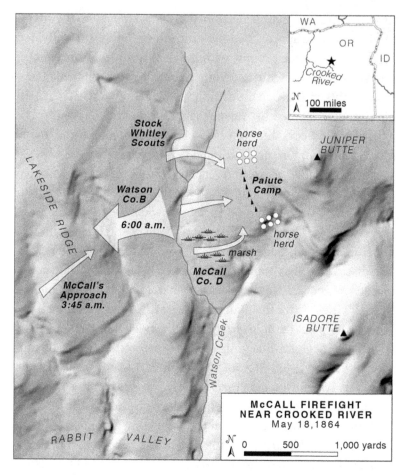

M5. The 1864 McCall firefight. Created by Chelsea McRaven Feeney.

just under his ear and came out of his mouth carrying away two teeth, another fracturing his collar bone."[74]

After emerging on the right, McCall "found on examination that the Indians were completely fortified in a cliff of rocks." With both Watson's troopers and the Warm Springs Indians receiving heavy fire and his own group of troopers starting to come under fire, McCall decided that if he was going "to save [his] wounded men and the horses, [his] only recourse was to retire to a safe place, and send for reinforcements." At 6:00 a.m. McCall's situation was precarious; he believed reinforcements were almost thirty

round-trip miles away. A worried McCall "reached what [he] considered a safe place" near a spring at about 8:00.[75]

Fortunately for McCall's force, Drake had led a patrol out of
camp at the usual time, heading generally in McCall's direction.
Thus Drake was already an hour out of his camp when he saw two
riders "approaching at full speed." Learning from the messengers,
a trooper and one of the Warm Springs Indians, that Watson had
been killed and McCall was in danger, Drake "and a detachment
of 40 men" from Captain Small's Company G "proceeded with all
possible speed to the scene of the conflict."[76] Riding "at a plung-
ing trot," Drake arrived at McCall's defensive position three long
hours after McCall had sent for reinforcements. While his surgeon attended to the wounded, Drake rode the extra mile to the
scene of the firefight.[77] As near as Drake could tell, the Paiutes had
left in considerable haste about an hour earlier, leaving a large
quantity of provisions and some equipment. They fled on foot
because the Warms Springs scouts managed to capture the horse
herd after the three cavalrymen fell back with the rest of McCall's
command, abandoning their prizes. Drake's men also recovered
the bodies of their dead comrades, who had been stripped and mutilated. A Warm Springs scout had been disemboweled and scalped.[78]
After burning the Paiute encampment, with "an immense amount
of provisions, robes, saddles and plunder," Drake's men gathered
the remains of their dead comrades and headed back to McCall's
position.[79] From there, the wounded able to ride mounted their
horses, while the two most severely wounded were carried on
impromptu stretchers. They returned to the campsite selected by
Lieutenant Hand slowly, finally reaching it at 11:00 that night—
"weary, tired and gloomy," in Drake's words.[80]

May 19 "was consumed in the necessary preparations for the
burial of our fallen comrades," Drake recorded in his journal.
"Their graves were dug side by side on a small knoll south of camp
in the edge of the timber and the three bodies were buried with
appropriate [military] honors." The surviving Warm Springs scouts
gathered the bodies of their dead and returned to the reservation.
Drake acknowledged that "a sad feeling pervades the command

on account of Watson," who one of his men said "was about the most popular officer in the regiment."[81]

Once their dead comrades were buried and the initial shock wore off, the camp was rife with talk about Lieutenant McCall's conduct during the firefight. Most blamed him for the disaster. John Drake, however, did not. While he repeatedly criticized his fellow officers when he felt they did not perform their duty effectively, he was pragmatic and restrained in his assessment of McCall's actions. Drake told Lt. John Apperson, "I am not disposed to censure McCall in this matter at all. He obeyed his orders. I did not send him out there to get a lot of men butchered for the mere glory of the thing." Drake dismissed camp talk that McCall had not moved fast enough to relieve Watson's force, noting the Paiute's position was strong and they had already shown their ability to crush a frontal attack. Even the criticism that McCall could have used his remaining force to pin the Paiutes in their position did not impress Drake, who noted McCall had no way of knowing how long it would take before help arrived. In the meantime, "the wounded were groaning and writhing in their agony, and a man whose heart is not very hard, could not be blamed much for trying to alleviate their sufferings as much as possible."[82]

Needing to improve the site to serve as a supply depot and having to catch up on paperwork, Drake's expedition remained in the camp, which he named Camp Maury, for the next seventeen days. One of the civilians with Drake described the camp being "up a little canyon, at the head of which there is a heavy forest of pine, and numerous clear, cold mountain springs."[83] Drake tried to keep the men busy by regularly sending them out in groups of twenty-five on three-day patrols or having them construct a rudimentary warehouse for the supplies and a large corral for the horses. Captain Small and Lieutenants McCall and Noble each led patrols, but none found any Paiutes, despite (unsuccessful) nightly raids on the corral. Shots were fired several times in the dark when nervous sentries saw, or thought they saw, Indians attempting to steal horses or mules.[84]

During the recovery time at Camp Maury, Drake ordered Lieutenant Waymire to leave his encampment on the Warm Springs

Reservation and join the expedition with his men, which he did on May 29. This brought the overall strength of the command to 160 cavalrymen. He sent for Waymire not to enlarge his command so much as to help offset the impact of having to leave a strong force to guard Camp Maury when he finally resumed his march to meet up with Captain Currey's expedition.

Another force that could have augmented Drake's strength considerably came into camp two days later. On May 31 sixty-six Warm Springs Indians reached Drake's encampment. Eager for revenge for what happened to their friends, including Stock Whitley, whose condition had not improved, they were "pretty well mounted" and said they were "well armed." Drake had a very different attitude than George B. Currey about the martial bene-fits of employing Indian allies. Unlike Captain Currey, Drake felt they would "wilt like a leaf and stampede for the Warm Springs like a herd of deer" if they were in a serious firefight. He contin-ued, "As scouts they might make themselves very useful if they can muster energy enough to get themselves actively at work." While he hoped they would be useful, he doubted it, believing, "They are going to give us some trouble in some way."[85] Some of Drake's pessimism was likely based on his impression of the origi-nal group of Warm Springs men, who returned to the reservation not long after the firefight. He misunderstood their motive. They left to return their wounded and dead friends, not because of an unwillingness to pursue the Paiute band.

In early June Drake finally resumed the move toward Harney Lake and a meeting with Currey. The depression caused by the defeat near the Crooked River on May 17, his strong opposition to tying the two expeditions together, and the resulting loss of his autonomy were all factors in the incredibly long delay at Camp Maury.[86] The night before Drake resumed the march, Stock Whit-ley died from his many wounds. The death of the Warm Springs leader affected Drake, who felt he "was the noblest Indian [he] ever knew."[87] One of the survivors from McCall's disastrous expedition described how Stock Whitley had "showed himself a brave man on the battle-ground, and, though almost shot to pieces, walked off to where he could receive assistance."[88]

The next morning Drake started southward again, finally moving toward Harney Lake. Due to various delays, some unavoidable and some of his own choosing, he was almost a month behind General Alvord's modified timeline. He left Captain Small with fifty-eight men to guard the supply depot, leaving just over one hundred troopers and some civilians with the Quartermaster Department in his column. Drake was certain Currey would "beat [him] to Harney lake [by] ten days" and "wonder where in the devil I am at."[89] Being so far behind schedule, Drake worried Currey might have moved on after not finding or hearing from him and tiring of waiting. Really, the only way Currey might still be anywhere near the rendezvous region is if he too had encountered delays in executing his prong of Alvord's strategy.

Just ten days after Captain Currey returned to Fort Walla Walla following his short February patrol, the base commander, Lt. Col. Thomas English, suggested that General Alvord adjust his original plan for the coming campaign. English, who also led the First Washington Territory Infantry Regiment, told the general, "It does not seem to me necessary that Captain Currey should be required to go all the way to Fort Boise prefatory to making a start." English felt it was better for Currey to begin the campaign from Fort Walla Walla and to establish a supply depot along his route to be used during the coming months. English argued the time spent in building the depot somewhere near the mouth of the Owyhee River "would have a good opportunity to improve [the horses] during the interval." The colonel also lobbied for a detachment of Washington infantrymen to be sent there to guard it because Currey's command could not spare the manpower to garrison the depot.[90] General Alvord heeded both suggestions, which changed the course Currey traveled but did not significantly alter the region where he spent the 1864 campaigning season.

Lieutenant Colonel English was not the only one concerned about the strength of Currey's force. Currey argued that he be allowed to augment his force with as many as one hundred Cayuse Indians serving as an irregular force assigned to his command.

Currey, the Oregon Cavalry's most aggressive officer and the one responsible for the killing of more Indians than any other company commander, was also the strongest advocate for utilizing men from allied tribes in the fight against the Northern Paiutes, Bannocks, and Shoshones. Currey believed, "For ten dollars per month, a few clothes and rations, the use of arms and ammunition, one hundred bold riders, fine marksmen, and trusty warriors, can be procured from among these Indians at any time."[91] He felt such an alliance would cultivate "in the Indians a stronger feeling of friendships towards the whites." Furthermore, employing them as allies would ensure "that their unruly young men will not, while chaffing through the monotonous days on a reservation, plot war against us."[92] Despite demonstrating a more prescient awareness of the fate of many Indians forced onto reservations, Currey's arguments mostly fell flat with his regimental commander, Colonel Maury. General Alvord was more pragmatic; he authorized Currey to recruit twenty Cayuses as unpaid scouts.[93]

While the order sending Currey out on his long campaign was issued on March 31, he did not receive General Alvord's detailed instructions for more than ten days. In those orders Alvord reminded Currey, "You will consider the object of your expedition is to protect the whites in mining, in the exploration and occupation of the country not included in the Indian reservations." Alvord expressed his view that Currey's command should make "two circuits of nearly sixty days each," the first of which should head in a more southwesterly direction; the second should "extend east of the Oregon line, and possibly protect any emigrants coming in over the more southerly road south of Snake River." Alvord also expected Currey to protect the mining operations along the Owyhee River as well as emigrants traveling west and southwest of Old Fort Boise. The general also informed him it was possible he would order his and Drake's columns to unite at some point during the summer. If that happened, Currey was to command the joint operations. It was a lot to ask of Currey, who clearly did not have as much freedom as Alvord stated when he told him the course he took was "left entirely to [himself]."[94]

One of the men in Currey's column, speaking for many, observed, "Now, in the closing months of our service, we are sent to do that which would have been done months and even years ago, i.e.—to chastise those marauding and predatory bands that have so often proven a source of trouble to the emigration, as well as the frontier counties of Oregon."[95]

Currey had already started preparing for the campaign when Alvord's more explicit orders reached him. He gathered 104 pack mules as well as eight 6-mule wagon teams to carry supplies, including rations for his men for ninety days. His force of ninety-one troopers was "in good condition and fine spirits." They were drawn from Company A, commanded by Capt. William V. Rinehart; his own Company E, under his brother Lt. James Currey; and a contingent from Company F, led by Lt. John Bowen.[96] Captain Currey and his men finally left Fort Walla Walla on April 28, eight days after Captain Drake had started his portion of the 1864 campaign from Fort Dalles. On the third day out, Currey's command was joined by ten Cayuse Indians and their war chief, whose name, Umhowlish, Currey spelled a variety of ways, never correctly.[97] "The Indians," Currey pointed out, "undertook a campaign. . . . without pay, they furnished their own horses (two apiece) and left their homes to fight the white man's battles."[98] After crossing the Blue Mountains, he went into camp on the Grande Ronde River, near the eastern base of those mountains, where he rested his animals for a day after the climb over the mountains.

The day layover allowed Currey to ponder the dramatic changes that occurred in the two years since he first rode into the Grande Valley. "When I visited this valley in August 1862," he reflected, "what is now a thriving little village of over a hundred houses, consisted of a single house without any roof on, and another up to the top of the valley. Now the whole valley is dotted with farm houses."[99] Clearly what Currey saw as he began his third year of a monthslong expedition assured him how important it had been for the Oregon Cavalry to serve in the Pacific Northwest.

Currey resumed his march at 6:00 a.m. the next morning—"my usual hour for commencing the day's march," he noted.[100]

Nine uneventful days later, the column reached the Malheur River. He sent Captain Rinehart up the river to find a trail for the next day's movement while the rest of the command went into camp. Before Rinehart returned, a messenger from Fort Boise found Currey's camp and reported that "a considerable band of Snake Indians were encamped on the Owyhee river some distance from its mouth." The news excited Currey; the "Snake Indians being [his] objective point," he ordered his column to retrace its path on the Malheur the next day and push on for the mouth of the Owyhee River, in heavy rain. There they were joined by Capt. Edward Barry and a portion of Company G, First Washington Territory Infantry Regiment. This brought the strength of Currey's force to 133 soldiers and nearly two dozen civilian employees in the Quartermaster Department.[101]

The presence of the infantry allowed Currey to take his entire mounted force on an excursion on May 18 to both look for a suitable site for a long-term supply depot and search for the reported Paiutes. The second day's course ascended far above the river and onto an arid region, forcing both men and animals to go without water. Currey reported, "We toiled on from ground swell to ground swell until late in the afternoon when both animals and men began to show evidence of considerable suffering from thirst." The situation deteriorated as the exhausted and thirsty column began a descent into a valley, where the temperature was much hotter. "On, on the little column dragged its heated, thirsty length," recalled Currey. Finally, with daylight fading, Currey himself found an abundant source of water, though down a steep canyon. The phrase "in the nick of time," comes to mind: "Although the packers declared often during the afternoon that the mules would all give out, but [only] one failed to reach camp."[102] Currey's experience on May 21 was a reminder of one of the natural dangers facing the military as it ventured into Northern Paiute lands (as well as when it was trying to find Shoshone bands to the east): the scarcity of water could cost lives.

After such a grueling experience, Currey allowed most of his command to rest the next day, although that was more for the animals than the men. He did send out some scouting parties, apparently on foot, to investigate their surroundings and to try to find the Owyhee River. Fortunately for his column, the river was found only a few miles from where they were recuperating. He resumed the march the next day, May 22, still in search of a practical site for his supply depot and any recent sign of Paiutes. Four days later Currey finally found a good spot for his supply depot, where water was accessible and good grass plentiful. He established Camp Henderson, named after Oregon's congressman-elect James H. D. Henderson, 330 miles south of Fort Walla Walla and on Gibbs Creek, about 8 miles from its junction with Jordan Creek.[103]

In an effort to keep transportation loads lighter, Currey had previously left all the tents with Captain Barry's Washington Infantry and the supply wagons and pack mules. After establishing Camp Henderson, he ordered the wagons at the supply base to continue on to Fort Boise while he directed all supplies that could be carried on pack mules brought to Camp Henderson. The lack of tents forced his men to become "very expert in constructing 'wickiups' [sic] or huts made out of such material as happened to be found in the vicinity of camp; sometimes willows were weaved into very picturesque conical huts," and if nothing else was available, the troopers piled sagebrush "to afford a shade, better than in the sun without any effort to mollify it."[104]

While he waited for the supplies to reach Camp Henderson, Currey dispatched patrols on short scouts to find any signs that Paiutes had been in the region. Despite the camp's good location for grass and water, Currey was disappointed to learn "that the present camp was not within reach of any place very often frequented by the Snakes." Therefore, he set out with a detachment of men from Companies A and E on May 28 in a southerly direction, hoping to make contact with any Paiute bands possibly in the area. The first day out, the Oregon troopers found enough evidence that Paiutes had been in the area that Currey believed it was the site of a regular summer encampment. Eager to make contact with this band, they rode well past nightfall the third day, crossing "over ridges, down slopes, with the clamp, clink, clug of the horses' feet against the loose rocks."[105] After not finding further evidence that Paiutes were still in the region, Currey's men returned to Camp Henderson on May 31.

Thus far Currey had not found any Paiutes; however, he did finally come across lands that had potential for future white development. Northeast of Camp Henderson, he reported, "there is [a] considerable quantity of very good looking soil along the alluvials of Jordan Creek, which if the country ever becomes safe enough for farmers to live in, will become [a] thrifty neighborhood."[106] Despite the importance of exploration, Currey took limited solace in successfully performing that aspect of his mission.

Currey's scouts finally brought him the news he had been waiting for: they reported finding a small Indian camp to the north, on Jordan Creek. Not wasting any time, he gathered thirty troopers and led them northeastward late on the evening of June 2. The next day the patrol came across four (or five; Currey gave conflicting numbers) men fishing, who wisely attempted to flee at the sight of the cavalry. They had no chance; the troopers ran them down and, as Currey reported, "killed them and moved up the creek in search for more, but only found one—killed him and then returned to Camp Henderson" on June 5.[107] This was a typical encounter between whites, particularly a volunteer or militia command, and any band of Indians. Their mere presence in the region was a presumption of guilt for often unspecified "crimes," as was too often the white attitude toward most Indian people. Since Currey had not heard of any recent attacks on whites, summarily killing the five men was not justified, even by their standards.

Currey's command remained at Camp Henderson for the next ten days, during which only one incident of note occurred: "On the 8th of June a settler came galloping into the camp and reported a large number of Indians on Jordan Creek." The civilian estimated the group numbered eighty or more. "By sundown," Currey explained, "I started with the Cavalry again, for Jordan Creek; but on arriving there satisfied myself that it was my own Indian scouts who had accompanied me on the previous scout up the creek." Bemused, he admitted, "In fact, my night ride was a forced march in pursuit of myself!"[108] After eight more days at the camp, the command resumed its march westward for the Alvord Valley, the day after the supplies arrived, only to halt again for two days to let one of his recently arrived patrols recuperate. He also established another temporary supply depot at the base of Steens Mountain.[109] This was the same location where Lieutenant Waymire had established a rudimentary camp during his disastrous winter patrol. Concerned about a possible attack on the supply base once he led the cavalry in search of Captain Drake, Currey had his men build rudimentary earthworks in a star fort formation to make the camp "as easily defensible as possible."[110] He named the impromptu fort Camp Alvord. It was located three hundred miles south-southeast of The Dalles, in what Currey described as "the finest grass valley" he had seen since he "left the broad prairies of the Mis[s]o[uri] Valley."[111]

For three weeks after leaving the supply deport, Drake's column headed in a generally south-southwesterly direction, constantly hoping to come across any sign of Currey's column.[112] They rode through "dry sage plain, loose sand, which with a high wind on our backs was sent flying over the command, making it very disagreeable." In a letter sent to a newspaper in Boise, one of Drake's troopers informed the readers, "The country is a burnt district," with "no quartz or other gold or silver bearing rock."[113] Still hoping to encounter Paiutes as he moved toward Currey, Drake sent the few remaining Indian scouts fanning out in front and to both sides of his march. On June 9 the scouts found a solitary Indian camp, which Drake surrounded with men from Company D. The scouts captured the only people there, a woman and her child, along with three horses. They also found a large quantity of foodstuffs and a cavalryman's top shirt, indicating she was present at or in contact with the men who participated in the firefight with Lieutenant Watson.[114] Drake interrogated the woman but learned nothing from her.[115]

During the remainder of Drake's ride to Harney Lake, his force experienced a full range of weather. First, a heavy snowstorm caused them to halt and wait it out for a day. Four days later as they continued southward, the temperature reached the lower seventies before falling again and then rising considerably. They found a substantial valley at the head of a site he called Big Meadows that was a "good grass country but of too high an altitude for agricultural purposes." Closing in on the designated meeting area, Drake called it "the most dangerous part of the Indian Country." Pressing on at an average of twelve miles per day, they reached the south fork of the Malheur River before having to retrace their steps for eight miles. Drake's march was delayed again for four days while he waited for the express, which might include changes to his orders. While there, Lieutenant Noble's "unremitting gas" made the layover bearable. Drake said, "He always has something fresh and original—true, it is not of the most chaste and refined quality, but better than none, a good deal."[116] Receiving nothing official with the mail, Drake continued southward, finding one of Currey's abandoned camps. That energized Drake, who scouted ahead of his command to be certain that Currey's column was moving toward the eastern side of Harney Lake. Since his command was south of the lake by this time, he turned his men north toward Harney Valley on June 29 while simultaneously sending scouts ahead to find Currey. They went into camp on a summit above the valley, which gave Drake a tremendous view. Seeing the lake, he judged he was roughly forty miles from it. His force descended into Alvord Valley and continued on toward the lake, hoping to hear that his scouts had made contact.

Believing Drake must be approaching the designated meeting area near Harney Lake already, Currey left the infantry and those cavalrymen whose horses were too fatigued to continue and started for the lake on June 22. Two days later they reached the southeast corner of Malheur Lake, which did not relieve their thirst because the shallow alkali lake was "brackish and filled with the excrement of wild geese and other water fowls."[117] Continuing westward below Malheur Lake, Currey reached the eastern side of Harney Lake on June 27. That left the column diagonally opposite of where they were supposed to find Drake. By this time a sense of urgency to reach the rendezvous point seems to have limited Currey's search for Paiutes beyond what was directly in front of his path. Unable to ford the narrow water connection between the two lakes because of deep quicksand at the bottom of the channel, Currey's men ended up riding a west then north circuit around the lake. Not finding Drake or any sign he had been in the area, Currey shifted his focus back to looking for Paiutes and led his command toward Silvies River. Finally, at midnight on June 30, one of the men Drake sent on Currey's trail, Cayuse George, rode into his camp.[118] Three months into the 1864 campaign, the commands finally connected on July 1 on Rattlesnake Creek.[119]

SEVEN

Missed Opportunities

Alvord's decision to unite the commands forced both Captains Currey and Drake to give up their own efforts and move away from their original patrolling regions. Drake railed against the diminished effectiveness of bringing the two forces together into one large column, writing, "Binding the command[s] down in orders to a course of action that will prove futile to accomplish anything whatever."[1] Though his predictions proved prophetic, both cavalrymen and officers were happy to see their fellow Oregon troopers. Even Drake admitted, "The meeting of the two commands was rather a joyful one. Everybody was glad to see everybody."[2] One of Currey's troopers simply called it "a jolly time."[3] Being from the newest company in the regiment, it is not surprising that Lt. John F. Noble talked to Currey's men about their officers. His assessment was that "Capt. Currey [is] much like[d] by his comd. Treating men very kindly & friendly—so also all the Lieuts. of his Comd."[4] This was the largest concentration of the First Oregon Volunteer Cavalry Regiment in the field since the summer of 1862. It consisted of parts of Companies A, B, D, E, F, and G.

Drake was both happy to see his comrades-in-arms and relieved that the search was over. He had wondered "what Currey will propose or rather what he intends to do when he gets the two commands together."[5] The combined force rested for two days, during which Currey explained his plan to keep the whole force "continually on the move, through the brakes and along the creeks of the Blue Mountains, clearing the Cañon [Canyon] City [Road area]

of Indians." Part of that work included "marching through, scouting and hunting the haunts along the South side of the" Canyon
City Road for the duration of their thirty-day joint operations.[6]
Drake shared his colleague's goals but felt that Currey's methods
were impractical. "I fear," Drake wrote, "that Currey's project will
be impracticable, unless well managed. Currey is such a regular
storm that I fear he'll break down our trains by his infernal rapid
marches." Additionally, Drake was convinced that a large command
could not find the Paiutes: "I do not think the Snake Indians in
these mountains can be hunted down in that way. They will have
to be spied out and surprised, suddenly attacked wherever they
make a stopping place for a few days."[7] Time would prove the cor-
rectness of Drake's rather chilling description of "hunting down"
any Paiutes the cavalry could find. For the immediate future, the
campaign resembled what the Oregon Cavalry had done the previous two years.

Drake's tactical reservations were somewhat mollified when
he considered Currey's plan from a slightly different perspective.
Drake, just as much as Currey and the men they led, wanted the
chance for a great encounter with the only enemy they would
face during their service. Since forcing all Indians away from the
emigrant and trade routes was the real objective, how the Oregon
Cavalry achieved that was less important. A large body of cavalry
roving through regions where emigrants, farmers, and commercial
packers had been attacked might be sufficient to force the raiders
to leave the area. "Something in that line," Drake admitted, "may
be accomplished." Still, he hoped Currey would only keep the two
commands together for no more than two weeks.[8]

The joint operations began on July 3, heading northward in the
general direction of the upper Silvies River. The next day, gaining
elevation as they went, Company A's Sgt. Joseph Pepoon spoke for
many when he observed Independence Day: "One more Fourth in
the wilderness. The last, I hope."[9] Midway through the last summer of enlistments, Pepoon was not the only one feeling service
fatigue. Just days later Drake recorded hearing among his men
"a remark indicating disgust at the kind of service the [Oregon]

Cavalry are engaged in." Thus far, counting all the side patrols that spun off from the main expedition, the troops had ridden over five hundred miles, failing to force the Paiutes into a large-scale engagement (which was antithetical to their way of fighting). Traveling mostly through inhospitable desert lands that were not fit for future cultivation during the past two months, the Oregon troopers' esprit de corps was undeniably faltering. A change of scenery, at least, was at hand as the column reached a wooded region, leaving the sagebrush-covered deserts behind. Drake noticed the shift, thankful for "the change afforded by these timbered mountains [which] is decidedly refreshing in comparison with the sage desert of Harney Valley."[10] Captain Currey agreed, noting, "Although mountainous, this was a most delightful region to travel through."[11]

The march continued in a jagged pattern, mostly westward by north at first but turning southwestward until going into bivouac on a tributary of the Crooked River on July 11. While encamped there, some of the Indian scouts returned and reported finding a Paiute campsite ten to fifteen miles to the northeast. They returned to the site that night, where another group had remained watching the encampment, presumed to be Chief Paulina's band. They were discovered and attacked the next day; the scouts reported they killed one of the Paiutes and dismounted another. Currey immediately organized a pursuit with fifty of his men along with Drake and thirty of his troopers. Sergeant Pepoon found himself in the midst of "a great hubbub in camp, the men getting their arms on and falling into line, and the horses sent for."[12] When they reached the site of the encampment, it was predictably deserted.[13] They picked up the trail the next day and found themselves under attack while in a vulnerable position at the bottom of a canyon. Captain Currey described what happened: "While following the trail across the South Fork of John Day's River, the Indians fired upon us from the overhanging rocks." Captain Drake, leading his column, "noticed some few of the men getting a little shaky, and even indisposed to fall in at all, others manifested evident signs of being scared."[14] It was reported that Chief Paulina walked to the edge of the lip of the canyon and taunted the cavalry about its inability to catch him.[15] Fortunately for the Oregon troopers, the distance was considerable, and being on the rim above, the Paiutes overshot, which Currey observed "is usually the case in firing down steep hill sides, and owing to this fact none of the men were hurt, and only one horse slightly wounded." The Oregon troopers shooting uphill at long range were just as ineffective, leading Currey to honestly admit, "I am satisfied our lead was equally harmless."[16]

Unable to defend themselves properly from the bottom of the canyon, Currey ordered Captain Drake to dismount his men and scramble up the slope and attack the Indians. As the Company D men "moved slowly up the mountain," they "succeeded in getting an advantageous position and opened fire at once." Once they fired a volley from a level field, the Paiutes quickly fled. Drake dismissed a report that one of the Paiutes was wounded, noting it "was a wonder considering the distance, 1,000 yards at least."[17] Drake fell back while Currey took over the pursuit, to no avail. Captain Currey ended his chase once he was "satisfied that [the Paiutes] had abandoned the region, and would not stop until they got beneath the cooling shadows of Stein's [Steens] mountain." One of the troopers was less convinced: "Most of the men are indignant because he did not follow them further."[18]

Currey's enthusiasm for continuing the joint operations seems to have steadily fallen off as the combined force moved closer to Captain Drake's supply depot at Camp Maury, which they reached on July 18. As far as Drake was concerned, Alvord's orders had ruined "a period of time that should have been devoted to active operations against the Indians"; instead, they spent it "marching up the hill and then marching down again."[19] Once the two commands reached Camp Maury, Drake and Company D relieved Captain Small's Company G. Drake's men recuperated while Small's command, "glad enough to get out once after having been confined to this camp for upward of 40 days," were finally sent out on an independent scout.[20]

Having reached Camp Maury, Currey explained, "[With] no further evidence of Indians in that country being ascertained, I resolved to separate the command, leaving Capt. Drake to his original programme."[21] Currey sent Drake on one final scout before the two commands separated. It proved to be the longest one undertaken since uniting the two forces. While Drake was unclear where the "rather mystical locality" of Sheep Rock was located, he admitted, "I do not care much on this point; neither does Currey," just so long as Currey could "report that he had sent a scout to Sheep Rock." Mindful that exploration was a goal for each campaign season, Drake admitted he did "not regret the trip" over the region between the Crooked and Deschutes Rivers: "I succeeded in gaining a knowledge of the country that I could not have acquired by any other means. As for the country I have no desire to visit it, or any portion of it again. It is a desert to all intents and purpose, utterly worthless, sandy, rough and rugged."[22] Following Drake's return, Currey ended the joint operations and headed southeast toward his own supply depot at Camp Alvord.

As inhospitable as so much of eastern Oregon had proven to be, some of the troopers found it rewarding for a different type of exploration. Captain Drake, Company A's Sgts. David Hobart Taylor and Joseph Pepoon, and other unidentified soldiers were keenly interested in the geological aspects of the region. Drake wrote on July 16 that some soldiers at Camp Maury had "discovered some very fine geological specimens on the crest of a low ridge," which "consisted of fossil shells imbedded in a hard sand stone. In most cases, the imprint of the shell only is left in the rock." The next day "some very fine specimens of petrified wood were found," and "a large number of them were gathered by the soldiers and others."[23]

Sergeants Pepoon and Taylor, serving with Currey, bought a two-volume geology book the previous winter and spent "a great deal of time that winter roaming around over that country hunting up geological specimens." During the march to meet up with Drake's command, Pepoon "gathered a large number of curious stones." Weeks later he was one of the men who found the fossils that impressed Drake, ultimately lamenting they were "all too large to carry away."[24] Unlike the noncommissioned officers, Drake had better access to a means of transporting specimens, which he sent to Thomas Condon, a geologist who discovered the John Day Fossil Beds.[25] In late July Drake sent Condon a number of samples his men had found, including some fossils, explaining, "I had begun to despair of finding anything of considerable interest in that line," but while "in pursuit of a party of Snake Indians, some soldiers made a discovery that I take to be of interest geologically." At one point, "our entire camp," Drake told Condon, "[was] converted into a vast geological cabinet."[26] Such news, along with a supply wagon full of specimens, must have thrilled the geologist.

Despite Drake, Taylor, and Pepoon's enthusiasm, the public (outside of Thomas Condon) cared very little, if at all, about finding and collecting geological specimens unless they contained ore. Both Captains Currey and Drake came under scathing attacks by newspaper editors for the perceived failure of their campaigns so far. This was particularly true after Indian raids occurred in other parts of eastern Oregon while the cavalry was in the southeastern section of the state. It is clear that the criticisms were having a negative impact on both captains. A Salem newspaper swiped at the joint command, saying, "Capts. Currey and Drake seem entirely inadequate to keep them [the Paiutes] in subjection."[27] Currey responded to the mounting criticisms from those sitting safely behind their desks by pointing out the obvious: "While we were thus taxing the energies of man and beast, we were accused both by the press of California and Oregon of being tardy." The "unjust criticism that we received from the Oregon press," he reported, "did more to make my command lag than a thousand miles of hard marching over the most inhospitable desert."[28]

Captain Drake was himself critical of Currey's handling of the joint operations but explained his critique from a military perspective. Drake did not "like Capt. Currey's way of pursuing Indians, he moves to[o] slowly. Yet with 120 men, the size of his command, and a train of 60 pack animals it is impossible to move fast enough to accomplish anything." Though Drake's disapproval held validity, it was opposite of previous complaints about Currey's movements, when Drake called Currey "a perfect storm."[29] However, the unified force's pace was almost the same as Drake's when operating independently.[30] Despite his criticism of how Currey conducted the joint operations, Drake also endured considerable criticism by *The Dalles Mountaineer*, a paper that did not support the Lincoln administration, Gov. Addison C. Gibbs, or the Oregon Cavalry. Drake raged over the characterization of his part of the campaign being called "Drake's fishing party" and complained about being "defamed beyond measure."[31] One of the critical articles had been penned by a member of Company G.[32] The paper had another ally in General Alvord, who publicly criticized the Oregon Cavalry's failure to stop raids. Since the two captains were following Alvord's orders, his criticism was both disingenuous and hypocritical. Frustration over a third summer and fall in the mostly arid lands of eastern Oregon and southwestern Idaho Territory was beginning to undermine the effectiveness of the various parts of the First Oregon Volunteer Cavalry Regiment.

As things deteriorated and men started thinking about the end of their service, the two commands finally separated on August 2. By that time unrest was compounding in Drake's command. Somewhat surprisingly, his problems did not start from his own Company D or the detachment from Company B, both of which were in the last months of their three-year enlistments. Instead, the disruptions came from the officers of the more recently formed Company G and, of course, Dr. Dumreicher. Drake noted that Captain "Small and [Lieutenant] Noble quarrel, Noble and [Lieutenant] Hand quarrel, and the Doctor quarrels with them all. They are a troublesome crew."[33] Perhaps the return to independent operations would prove more effective militarily and lead to more cordial relations among the officers.

Captains Currey and Drake were not the only ones criticized for their 1864 operations. Lt. Col. Charles Drew also came under heavy criticism for his role in Alvord's coordinated three-pronged campaign. Salem's *Weekly Oregon Statesman* explained, "We think Col. Drew more to be censured [than Currey or Drake] because he did not move the troops two months sooner to operate against the Indians."[34] This was a dramatic turn from the compliments he received just a year earlier, when the Jacksonville newspaper praised Drew and Capt. William Kelly "for the untiring energy displayed by them in building the road to Klamath Valley."[35] Building roads in 1863 proved vastly different than trying to confront Paiutes in 1864, particularly Chief Paulina. As Captains Currey and Drake found out, achieving success as the public defined it during the 1864 campaign was difficult.

While Lieutenant Colonel Drew, Captain Kelly, and most of Company C were key elements in General Alvord's 1864 plan, he had limited interaction with them. Since Fort Klamath was located outside the District of Oregon through prewar boundary making, Drew took his orders directly from Department of the Pacific commander Brig. Gen. George Wright. Technically, Fort Klamath was within the District of California boundaries, which, in another administrative quirk, Wright commanded as well. This truncated situation made coordinating Drew's actions with those of Captains Currey and Drake, to the northeast, difficult. Given this awkward arrangement, it was General Wright who instructed Drew on March 18 to "go with a detachment across the country to the Owyhee." Wright added, "After the completion of the reconnaissance you will return to Fort Klamath."[36] Not specifying a start date or at least giving a range of dates proved to be a mistake in the coming months.

Three months after receiving his initial orders, Lieutenant Colonel Drew still had not started his reconnaissance. At first traveling conditions prevented Drew from starting; the higher elevations were still covered in snow. He reported, "The greatest difficulty under which I labored before starting out was in obtaining the requisite means of transportation."[37] While Jacksonville, the nearest town, was on the trail into California, the whole region was fairly isolated; therefore, it is not surprising that there were insufficient mules available to pack Drew's equipment. Acquiring those mules, mostly in California, consumed more time. Just when he was finally ready to get started in late June, Drew reported he could not leave Fort Klamath just yet. "An effort is being made by Ou-a-luck, a considerable chief of the Snake Indians," Drew informed General

P11. Lt. Col. Charles Drew. U.S. Army Heritage and Education
Center, Carlisle PA, CWP, RG 98, box 82, folio 54.

Wright, "to induce the Klamath Lake, Modoc, Goose Lake, and other bands of Indians to join him in warfare upon citizens." He warned that while the target area of Indian raids would be more than two hundred miles northeast, near Canyon City, "he [Ou-a-luck] would doubtless extend his operation toward this post and elsewhere."[38] Therefore, Drew delayed his departure for a few more days to investigate how the local tribes were responding to the inducement to attack whites. This latest delay further damaged the already embattled Drew's standing among the local civilians.

While local feelings toward the Canadian-born Drew had been positive in 1863, by the spring of 1864, everything had changed. His numerous delays led to questions about his willingness to take the field at all. The Jacksonville newspaper made the biting observation, "If Col. Drew has ever before tried to get leave from his superior to take an expedition into the unexplored country east of us, we have never heard of it; and we presume he never has."[39] Far worse, however, were the increasing accusations that Drew was a Copperhead. The basis for those charges ranged from where he established Fort Klamath—giving lucrative government contracts to Copperhead businessmen, with whom he associated too freely, some said—to the charge that he tried to influence the 1864 election by keeping the soldiers from voting.[40] Criticisms grew louder the longer Drew delayed his participation in the 1864 campaign. Almost two months after Captains Currey and Drake started their prongs of Alvord's plan and ten days before finally leaving Fort Klamath, the newspaper declared, "Drew has long been scattering, cropping out" his "copperhead leaven."[41]

The complaints about Drew's distribution of government contracts reached Department of the Pacific headquarters the previous year, leading General Wright to initiate an investigation. When Wright sent his most trusted investigative officer, Capt. James Van Voast, north to Jacksonville in late October 1863 to inspect Fort Klamath, he entrusted him with another mission: investigating the charges against Lieutenant Colonel Drew. Captain Van Voast determined there was no substance to any of the charges against Drew. After completing his investigation, he reported back to department headquarters "that petty jealousies, personal interests, and party prejudice have more or less to do with its formation it would be folly for anyone to deny."[42]

The truth about Drew's actions was far from incriminating. Both the location of the fort and decisions about who he purchased supplies from were driven either partially (the former) or entirely (the latter) by concerns about costs. Drew had been instructed to run his operations as inexpensively as possible. Those lobbing charges against him were upset he did not purchase their more expensive goods for his command. As Captain Van Voast had correctly deduced, Lieutenant Colonel Drew had done nothing wrong. The sudden evaporation of attacks against Drew once he led his men into the field underscores the manufactured nature of most of the charges. That Drew was friends with individuals who showed Southern sympathies was known before his appointment in 1861. Concerns about his failure to get Company C into the field before the end of June were warranted. Yet his sloth-like activity was entirely consistent with his conduct during the two previous years and should have surprised no one.[43]

Finally, after three and a half months, Lt. Col. Charles Drew prepared to lead most of Company C into the field and join the majority of the other Oregon Cavalry companies as they participated in the 1864 campaign. He designated Lt. D. C. Underwood to remain at Fort Klamath with a small portion of the company to protect the post while the rest of the cavalrymen headed across the southern expanse of Oregon.[44] On June 28 Captain Kelly led forty-seven troopers, along with Dr. G. W. Greer, assistant surgeon, and twenty-seven civilians, most employed to wrangle the supply animals, eastward from the fort. The civilians included twelve packers, eight quartermaster's employees, a teamster, a blacksmith, a guide, and two unidentified Indian scouts.[45] There was one person among the civilians who stood out, William M. Gabb, a member of the California Geological Society. Gabb hoped to do some surveying while protected by the cavalry column.[46] Given that this expedition was much smaller than those led by Currey and Drake, Drew needed fewer supplies. Even so, the accompanying supply

P12. Lt. D. C. Underwood. Oregon Historical Society, OrHi 3471.

train of eighty-six pack mules and one six-mule and one four-mule team made the entire column a substantial undertaking.[47]

The methodical (some said overly cautious) Drew followed two days later. Though much later than had been anticipated, all three prongs of General Alvord's grand plan were finally in the field. The first two hoped to deliver a crushing blow to the Snakes, while Drew's expedition seemed different from the start. As much as his focus on the minutia and penchant for record keeping over action was frustrating from a military perspective, those were skills that served him well as an explorer. Drew kept excellent records of the geography and landscape during his delayed expedition. He, like Captains Currey and Drake, would pass through under-explored parts of southern Oregon and southwestern Idaho Territory. However, unlike the two company commanders, Drew did not show a great interest in pursuing any purported Indian raiders, despite harboring even more dehumanizing attitudes about Indians than either Currey or Drake.

From Fort Klamath Captain Kelly led the entire procession east, by a slight angle southward, to the Williamson River. After Lieutenant Colonel Drew joined them on July 1, they continued slightly east then southeastward to Sprague Valley. Drew reported the valley was skirted with pine trees and "abundantly watered by rivers." Most importantly, it possessed "all the natural requisites for a good stock range."[48] A shift in command occurred on July 5, when Drew ordered Captain Kelly to return to Fort Klamath, pending reassignment for recruiting duty in Portland.[49] It appears personal animosity led Drew to take that highly unusual action with a campaign underway. Various newspapers speculated that the two held differing views about how to conduct the reconnaissance. If this was the case, it is not surprising the volunteer lieutenant colonel did not want to debate Captain Kelly, an experienced former Regular Army sergeant.[50] Transferring Kelly fueled new criticism of Lieutenant Colonel Drew, leading one paper to write, "It seems incredible that Col. Drew would assign so valuable and efficient an officer as Capt. Kelly to recruiting services when his services in the field are so urgently needed."[51] Whatever happened from then on, Drew bore the sole responsibility.

While in the Sprague Valley, Drew's force came upon a small group of white packers who had been attacked by an unidentified group of Indians. The packers decided to remain with the Oregon cavalrymen for a bit, taking advantage of the security they provided. During this time the Oregon troopers came in contact with a small band of Klamath Indians. They informed Drew that Paiute Chief Paulina "tried to induce them, with [all] the

EXPLANATION OF 1864 CAMPAIGN
—➤— *Drew expedition (June 28 to October 18)*

N 0   25   50 miles

M6. Explanation of Drew's 1864 campaign. Created by Chelsea McRaven Feeney.

Klamath's [*sic*] generally to join in the murderous operations he was then conducting." Fortunately for any civilians traveling through the region, "the chief remained steadfast for peace." Despite the assurance of peaceful relations, Drew and several civilians, including one from a party of whites attacked in late June, made an unannounced visit to their camp. The objective was to see if this band of Klamaths had been involved in the recent attack. Finding no evidence, and after the witness declared they were not the ones who attacked his group, Drew and the survivor determined that "these Indians would not be in any way held accountable for what transpired."[52]

The next day the column continued southeasterly to the northeastern end of Goose Lake. As they moved to the eastern shore of the lake, Drew's Indian scouts came down from the surrounding mountains with three Snake leaders to meet with the colonel. On the way back to the cavalry encampment, they came across twenty white miners who accompanied the scouts to the encampment. The Indian leaders came in on foot and unarmed, leaving both their horses and weapons with an undisclosed number of friends. Conversations with Drew were amicable, and he did not believe the Snake leaders, probably Paiute, presented any threat. Both the miners and the three Indians remained near the cavalry camp overnight before leaving at separate times in the morning. The miners left first, planning to ambush the three Indians. Drew described what happened as "one of those incidents, that are unfortunately too common on [the] frontier." The whites had seen the Indians' horses the previous day and "seemed to have made up their minds that an Indian has no rights that a white man is bound to respect." Four of the miners set out to ambush the Indians, planning to kill them and steal their horses. After firing on the three and taking two of their horses, the Indians, who had reached their friends and were now armed and reinforced, returned fire. One of the whites named "Burton was shot with a rifle, directly through the head." Drew related that the Indians' defense led to "the dispersion of [Burton's] three comrades in as many directions."[53]

Drew had sensed what the white men were up to, so he "ordered a detachment in pursuit, to prevent any outrage upon the Indians." His men reached the ambush site after the melee was over and all parties had fled. Over the next two days, cavalry patrols brought in the three surviving Indians. Drew was reassured that "the Indians seemed to have comprehended, however, that the troops were in no way responsible for the outrage."[54] The incident was a reminder that unprovoked white attacks on Native people often caused Indians to retaliate violently toward whites. As Drew knew, those whites who attacked, murdered, or otherwise abused Indian people rarely suffered the consequences themselves; instead, other whites suffered retaliation.

As Drew's column left their camp on the northeast side of Goose Lake on July 20, several packers and emigrant trains from California joined them. The military provided substantially more security than the insufficiently armed civilians could provide themselves. They were headed for Boise, a possible turnaround point for Drew's reconnaissance. The presence of these groups quickly turned Drew's expedition from part exploratory and partly offensive operations against the Paiutes into an escort mission. Now encumbered with more than one thousand additional grazing and pack animals, Drew's procession moved very slowly through Surprise Valley. The valley impressed Drew with its abundant timber and grass, patches of excellent tillage, and "game of all kinds." He had concerns about the forty or so residents living there: "All the population of this valley is in dangerous proximity to the ever hostile Indians."[55]

The escort plodded along northeastward until reaching the southwestern base of Warner Mountain (known as Hart Mountain today).[56] Despite not encountering any "hostile" Paiutes thus far, Drew believed he had found one of their base camps. He stated, "In military point of view, this mountain is the Sebastopol of the Snake Indians; producing subsistence and forage within, its walls impregnable, and to high too [sic] render artillery effective from their base, offering but few approaches to its summit, and these capable of an easy defense from the numerous impregnable bastions and watch towers that guard their entrance on either side."[57] He determined that it was not a permanent camp and turned southward toward Guano Lake. What he did not know then, but learned later on, is that Chief Paulina and his band were watching the Oregon Cavalry and their new charges the entire time as they approached the lake.[58]

While Drew did not know his movements were being watched (Chief Paulina later described the nightly procedure of assembling the mountain howitzer and placing it in the middle of the camp), his scouts had apparently let him know the Paiutes were above the valley.[59] Had either Captains Currey or Drake been informed a group of Snakes were within riding distance, both would have immediately gone in pursuit. Drew, however, explained, "Having a force of only thirty-nine enlisted men, and several families under our charge, and property to the value of perhaps one hundred and forty thousand dollars to guard, not including our own supplies in the estimate, I deemed 'discretion the better part of valor' and avoided acting upon the offensive, though always choosing ground for the alternative should it be forced upon us."[60]

Beginning in mid-August Drew led his force and the cavalcade they were protecting around the southern end of Pueblo Mountain. This course took the column across the Nevada border before turning northward toward Currey's Camp Alvord. The early part of the route had been brutal, with "hardly a spot of grass that was in any way beneficial for [their] animals to eat" and with so little drinkable water that they had to dig "holes along its [Guano Lake's] banks." According to Drew, by doing so, "[they] obtained water that was barely endurable for cooking purposes, but not at all palatable to drink."[61] During the latter part of this leg of the journey, they encountered some Indians who appeared friendly, but Drew did not trust them. That was probably derived from his negative views about all the regional Indians: "Among nearly all the Indian tribes of Oregon and northern California, murder, rapine, robbery and theft, are virtues of their highest order."[62] Thus far Drew had written with more conviction about his views than he had achieved through his (in)action. He had failed, through a lack of effort, to find any of the bands of Paiute raiders while taking on the role of military escort for civilian pack and emigrant trains and their massive herds of animals, which effectively ended any offensive patrolling. While he kept good records of the suitability of his course of travel for white development, once he reached Camp Alvord, his colleagues had already done that.

Just a few days before reaching Camp Alvord, on August 26, the troopers came across "some of the bones of the feet and hands" and partial remnants of a soldier's clothing. Drew believed they were the remains of Sergeant Casteel or one of the other men who disappeared from Lieutenant Waymire's expedition in April. Whether he shared that information with Currey when he arrived is unclear, but it did not make it into any of Drew's official reports or communications.[63] By then orders had been sent from District of California headquarters directing him to return to Fort Klamath immediately. His circumstances prohibited him from obeying those orders.[64] He explained, "[Our] supplies, too, [had] become too short for our return trip, in consequence of the escort duty we had performed and not anticipated before leaving Fort Klamath, and it was necessary to replenish them either from Camp Alvord or Fort Boise."[65] He also felt obligated to protect his train of civilians all the way to Fort Boise: "Rumors of Indian difficulties ahead, too, rendered it apparently unsafe for the trains we had brought in safely in this point to continue their journey unguarded." Therefore, after five days he left half his men at Camp Alvord and moved on with the rest of them and the civilians northeastward to Fort Boise. Reducing his force was an interesting decision, considering his stated fears about the safety of the civilian train and with illness rampant among the men at Camp Alvord.[66]

Now aware that he was expected back at Fort Klamath, Lieutenant Colonel Drew picked up the pace. Moving northeasterly up Jordan Creek in the direction of Boise, his men encountered the same problems that Currey's men had dealt with earlier in the summer: there were stretches with limited grass, wood, and most importantly, water. On September 9, ten days after leaving Camp Alvord, Drew's caravan reached Boise, which one of his men described as "a thriving place, but like a great many towns that have sprung up almost by magic, is outgrowing its breeches." Drew pressed farther northeastward for one more day, reaching the Idaho City mining district before leaving his charges and returning for supplies at Fort Boise.[67]

Drew's outward reconnaissance had taken two and a half months. After five days of rest and resupplying at Fort Boise, his men began the return, retracing their "steps, making the same stopping places and camps as [their] outward trip." Drew stopped at Camp Alvord to collect the other half of his men and then set out immediately for Fort Klamath. Unencumbered by the civilian pack and supply trains and feeling the pressure to adhere to the orders recalling him, Drew's column covered the same ground in half the time, reaching Fort Klamath on October 18. During his sprint back, Drew's men did far less exploring, in part because they had covered most of the route on the way out. Not surprisingly, they also failed to come into contact with Chief Paulina's Paiute band or any other bands described as hostile Snakes. Ironically, even though he started so late, his rapid pace after leaving Fort Boise enabled Drew to return to his base of operations at generally the same time as the other two prongs of Alvord's 1864 movement. He reached Fort Klamath on October 18.[68]

* * *

When Currey and Drake's joint operations ended on August 2, Captain Drake did not mince words about his relief that he was once again on his own, stating, "I am glad he [Currey] is gone." Drake "did not object to serving under him at all," but he disliked being "placed in such an anomalous position of having command of an expedition yet having no control over it." He was now free to conduct his operations as he saw fit for the remaining two months of the 1864 campaign season. He wasted little time, sending Captain Small and thirty-two men out on a fifteen-day scout north along the Canyon City Road on August 4. Drake took a forty-two-man party out the following day, patrolling southeastward to the head of the John Day River.[69]

A harbinger of what to expect for the rest of the campaign, Drake's only substantial outcome was finding a new location for his supply depot and base of operations. Moving from Camp Maury was inevitable after the available grass had been exhausted by his animals. The move was completed on August 22; the new depot was named Camp Dahlgren in honor of Union colonel Ulric Dahlgren. The colonel had been killed in March during a cavalry raid on Richmond. The naming of the camp was a reminder that even when out in the remote regions of eastern Oregon, the cavalrymen had access, albeit delayed, to the current news about the fighting in the East. Since supplies came down from Fort Dalles, the primary source of news was William H. Newell's The Dalles *Daily Mountaineer*. Though known to be unfriendly to both Governor Gibbs and the First Oregon Volunteer Cavalry Regiment, this was Drake's main news lifeline.[70]

The growing signs the service was beginning to wear down the men and especially the officers that Drake noticed earlier were worsening. It was his opinion that "all [the officers] wish to go out without exception." He admitted he agreed: "I am tired of it myself." Drake was not so much tired of military service as feeling he was not contributing to the larger Union cause.[71] With months of the campaign remaining, Drake complained that "camp duties are very few and very dry."[72] Another officer, Capt. William V.

Rinehart, suffered purely physical fatigue. He had led Company A in Currey's expedition but had been badly bruised in a fall from his horse during the long-range firefight on July 14. Since the firefight took place much closer to Drake's depot than Currey's, Rinehart was taken to Camp Maury, confined to bed, and "quite used up on arrival at camp." When Camp Maury was abandoned, the injured Rinehart endured the ride to the new campsite.[73] The prolonged stay at Camp Dahlgren was good for Rinehart but had a corrosive effect on many of the other officers. At different times during the month's stay, Drake found Captains Small and Porter, Lieutenant Noble, and of course Dr. Dumreicher drunk, although apparently not while on duty. Their drinking was undoubtedly caused by the "universal monotony of a dreary camp life."[74]

The enlisted men were likewise feeling the effects of a long campaign season, the last one for most of the men. Unruliness among the men reached a critical point when Sgt. Thomas Baker and a detachment were ordered to subdue some agitating soldiers. While the cause of the problem and the number involved are unknown, during the ensuing brawl, Baker was seriously injured.[75] Lieutenant Waymire referred to the incident as "a very unfortunate affair."[76] Discipline was unraveling with less than two months remaining before the expedition's scheduled return to Fort Dalles.

Activity was the best available means to maintain any sense of esprit de corps. Drake sent Captain Small's Company G, less physically worn down but just as in need of activity after their long service protecting the supplies, on short patrols.[77] Even Lieutenant Hand was sent on an independent scout, despite Drake's belief that he was entirely unfit for such responsibility. The only reason he did so, besides Hand's complaining, was because he did "not think there [was] any danger of [Hand] being attacked by Indians anywhere in this section now."[78] This was a vastly different attitude about finding Paiute encampments from when the expedition started out in April. Had it been five months earlier, Drake would have sent several probing expeditions in multiple directions, leading at least one himself, in an effort to make contact with the Paiutes. When Captain Small reported seeing some signs

P13. Capt. William V. Rinehart. Fort Walla Walla Museum, Walla Walla WA.

of recent Indian presence, Drake dismissed it rather than immediately sending him back out to investigate. His reluctance was at
least partially influenced by his lack of trust in Captain Small.[79]

Two things did occur to break the monotony of camp life before
Drake started back to Fort Dalles. First, he was joined temporarily

by Capt. Richard S. Caldwell and a portion of his Company B in late August. Caldwell and his men had been scouting along the Canyon City Road in response to news of Indian attacks in the area. Caldwell remained at Camp Dahlgren for two weeks.[80] Drake also ordered Captain Porter to take some of the men and build a wagon road that connected to the Canyon City Road, which he started on September 11. The only other interruption to the camp routine was the need to move most of the command again. The move was precipitated by the exhaustion of the available grass. Drake explained the reality of having mounts and pack animals living mostly off the land: "It is remarkable how quick four or five square miles of even good grazing ground fails under the hoof of three or four hundred head of stock." This had changed his plans for the final month in the field, during which he had anticipated staying at Camp Dahlgren.[81]

Prior to leaving Camp Dahlgren, an order arrived outlining plans for a winter encampment. General Alvord, probably influenced by arguments made by Captain Currey, ordered Company G to remain in the field throughout the winter at Camp Watson. The unpleasant duty, which Drake termed "a terrible punishment to Small and Hand," fell to Company G for the simple reason that the enlistments for most of the Company D men, including Drake, were set to expire before the winter ended.[82]

Before relocating the camp, Drake and his remaining men (Captain Small and Lieutenant McCall were out on short patrols of several days duration) participated in one last expedition. They left Camp Dahlgren on September 19—Drake left some of the supplies and a small guard behind. Although they headed to Little Summit Prairie the first day and then toward a way station named Mountain House, this was really the beginning of their return to Fort Dalles. The slow but steady move back toward the fort ended on October 11, when Drake's column, minus Company G, reached Fort Dalles. Drake probably spoke for many of his men when he wrote, "I am heartily sick of these campaigns in the plains. Three years in succession appropriated to that kind of service is sufficient for most anyone."[83]

*   *   *

Drake's command was not the only one to lose some of its fervor for campaigning after the joint operations ended in August. When Captain Currey's column headed eastward from Camp Maury, angling slightly south, it was different in spirit than it had been in July. Part of the challenge for Currey was to maintain discipline without enough officers. With Captain Rinehart confined to a bed at Camp Maury and Lt. John Apperson temporarily assigned to the Quartermaster Department at Fort Dalles, Orderly Sgt. W. T. Leever led Company A. Currey was replaced at the head of Company E by his brother, Lt. James L. Currey, which left the company short one officer. Lt. John Bowen led the detachment from Company F. Though tired and down a few officers, Currey still had work to do until October.

Just two days after separating from Drake's command at Camp Maury, Currey's men came across an abandoned wagon near a creek that fed into the Crooked River, with personal effects and mining equipment scattered about. They recognized the wagon as belonging to four young miners they had seen at Camp Maury. The oxen were gone, there were moccasin tracks in the dirt, and the cart had bullet holes in it. However, there were no bodies, which led the soldiers to speculate that "the men saw the Indians coming and grasped their guns and ran up into the bluffs where the Indians could not follow them with their ponies, and there made their escape." Sergeant Pepoon was convinced the men had been attacked by Chief Paulina's band, though there was no way to confirm that.[84] Leaving the debris behind, Currey's command continued its march southeasterly toward Steens Mountain and its supply deport at Camp Alvord. Much had changed about the environment since they had left the area in late June. The Silvies River had withered under the summer sun; instead of flowing water, its course was marked by a series of pools. The swampy areas at the head of the river had completely dried up. Nine days after leaving Camp Maury, Currey's command reached Camp Alvord, guarded by the men from Company G, First Washington Infantry, and the cavalrymen left behind to get their horses back to good health. One of the troopers was happy to be done "beat-ing around in those horrible sand and wild sage brush deserts, traveling some 25 to 30 miles over the rockiest, sandiest, dreari-est and most monotonous country under heaven."[85] Given such conditions it was no surprise that "the horses and mules were beginning to look thin and weary." Currey explained, "[Because] quite a number of the men were suffering from the 'bloody flux,' I was forced to give them some rest." He limited his activity to "sending a scout under Sergt. Major Gates to Jordan Creek, and to open communications with Col. Maury," who had led an expe-dition into the region after reports of Indian attacks on whites in the area.[86] The circumstances with his men were serious; between his arrival on August 12 and September 1, 106 of his men either were or had been too sick for duty. Worst of all, his medical sup-plies ran out. Some supplies were obtained when Lieutenant Col-onel Drew's escort column arrived on August 26. Drew's medical officer shared what he had, but that was quickly exhausted, leav-ing Currey to suggest a naturalist's remedy of a tea made from wild geraniums.[87] When Drew left about half of his force at Camp Alvord as he and the rest continued on for Fort Boise, it further strained the medical supplies at the camp.

Despite the devastating impact of dysentery, some of Currey's healthy men had an encounter with a band of Paiute Indians who came within sight of Camp Alvord. According to Sergeant Pepoon, the group numbered "about forty, two-thirds of whom were women and children."[88] As Currey put it, the Indians "were more surprised at finding our camp than we were in seeing them." It became clear to Currey that they were heading for the mountains across a dry lake bed south of his camp. Responding as the military typically did, he sent his available mounted men dashing at that Paiute band, which instinctively fled as fast as they could.[89] Sergeant Pepoon reported disappointedly that "the men followed them until nearly dark and fired several shots but did not succeed in killing any of them."[90] Damage had been done to the small band, however, as they lost six horses. Currey further described the results of this unprovoked attack on the band: "A considerable quantity of camp equipage and Indian commissary was strewn along the road."[91]

When Sergeant Major Gates's scouting party returned on September 1, it brought news that revived Currey. Gates informed his captain that he had not met Colonel Maury during his four-hundred-mile expedition to Jordan Creek, but it appeared Maury had forced a group of Paiutes out of the Jordan Creek area. Currey's scouts expressed the view that the Indians were headed south, into Nevada. In response to this news, he quickly assembled a pursuit force and started out the next day with thirty men from Company A and forty-six from Company E, along with twenty of the Washington infantrymen, "to follow them as far and fast as the condition of [his] command would permit."[92] The pursuit passed through a new mining district in the Pueblo Mountains, just north of the Oregon–Nevada border. After riding more than forty miles into Nevada, Currey's column caught five Indians who proclaimed their friendship toward the whites. Currey dismissed their assurances and planned to hang them on the sport—and certainly would have if the local miners had not prevailed upon him to spare the five. It was pragmatism and not necessarily any sense of humanity that led the miners to intercede on behalf of the Indians. They judged, probably correctly, that if Currey executed the five, particularly since there was no evidence they were guilty of anything, local Indians would retaliate against the miners. Currey reluctantly freed his five captives and pressed farther south for a few more days. By then it was clear his men and animals had reached their limits: "My convalescent men could not endure the fatigue, and I was reluctantly compelled to change my original plan and be satisfied with a less extensive circuit." He turned his column around on September 12 and reached Camp Alvord four days later. It was his last serious expedition of the year.[93]

Currey kept his command at Camp Alvord for two more weeks before breaking it up and heading back to Fort Walla Walla. During that time, he reflected on the Alvord Valley, noting that due to its mild climate, abundant grass, and water, "this valley has been, and will continue to be, until occupied by the whites, the grand rendezvous of the Snake Indians." He predicted the "valley will, as soon as the Indians are subdued, furnish homes to a population equal to that of Jackson County."[94] While Captain Currey reflected and prepared to break up his supply depot, Sergeant Pepoon spent much of his remaining time exploring and gathering rock samples, as he had, when possible, the entire summer, remarking, "I never before beheld such a sparkling mass. I selected a few of the most beautiful I could find."[95]

On September 26 Captain Currey's men began their march back to Fort Walla Walla. Captain Barry and his company of Washington infantrymen, along with the wagons, were sent to Fort Boise. Initially, Currey moved toward the Malheur River and followed it and other mountain streams as his cavalrymen moved northwestward. The return was tedious, according to Currey: "The men had been so constantly in the saddle during the summer that they were nearly fagged down, and the horses were 'dog poor.' The cold nights of autumn and the crisped grass upon which the animals now subsisted, aggravated their difficulties." The weary column halted on October 26 near Fort Walla Walla, where it was formally dissolved. Company A went into winter quarters there, while Lieutenant Bowen's detachment from Company F proceeded back to Fort Lapwai to winter with the rest of that company. Unfortunately for Captain Currey and the men in Company E, they were directed to make the long march to Fort Dalles and to prepare to put down a rumored uprising by Southern sympathizers on election day. Company E arrived at Fort Dalles on November 6 and was finally able to rest when nothing happened on election day.[96] The 1864 field operations had finally stumbled to a close.

As each of the three columns staggered into their winter quarters, a sense of relief pervaded their ranks. The end of this campaign season coincided with the approaching end of most Oregon troopers' enlistments. Those who volunteered in early 1862 still had a few months left, but for those who rushed to the colors in November and December 1861, it was only a few weeks until they were discharged. As Sgt. Joseph Pepoon, one of the earliest volunteers, observed, "The boys were naturally hilarious, on account of this being our last summer campaign."[97] The sense of both relief and excitement that Pepoon's friends felt was not shared by General Alvord, who was about to face a critical manpower shortage. Refilling the ranks weighed on Alvord for over a year. In July he had informed General Wright that the enlistments for 401 Oregon cavalrymen would expire between late November and the following March. He had not been involved in the initial recruiting effort but was the district commander early in 1863, during the next recruiting attempt. The memory of that disaster, when just one company had been enlisted, gave every reason to be concerned. As Alvord reminded his superior, the dismal response forced the governor to finally abandon "the undertaking, revoking the appointment of the second lieutenants and recruiting officers" responsible for recruiting the other five companies.[98] Under those distressing circumstances, recruitment became the fourth major military operation of 1864.

During the original attempt to raise the regiment, recruiters had pushed the patriotic and economic aspects of serving while letting would-be volunteers think they might be sent to the main front of the war in the East. Things had changed dramatically since then, making recruiting even harder. While it was impossible to anticipate how much longer the war would last, it was clear the Confederacy's ability to keep fighting was fading. With the war's end in sight, recruiters would not be able to use the same patriotism to entice men to join the Oregon Cavalry. Similarly, after serving for three years in the Pacific Northwest, it was not possible to suggest any units raised in the region would be sent to the seat of war. The third leg that had helped provide the precarious foundation for recruiting efforts had been monetary need. By late 1863 that was no longer as effective as it once was either, although steady pay still held some appeal over potentially higher, yet uncertain, civilian wages.[99] Unfortunately, as Lt. William Hand explained to Governor Gibbs, the army's reputation for not paying its soldiers on schedule undermined the notion that the military provided steady pay.[100] If monthly pay failed as an incentive, as previous attempts suggested it might, then General Alvord would need to try something else.

The job of raising a regiment of new recruits began a year before the veterans' enlistments expired. On November 13, 1863, Lt. John T. Apperson was relieved of temporary command of Company A and reassigned to recruiting duty. The move was not a criticism of his handling of the company during the last part of the 1863 expedition but a nod to his value as a recruiter. Even after two years of service, the former steamboat captain retained some name recognition in the Salem area, where he established a recruiting office in mid-December. For unexplained reasons, Apperson ran just two weeks of announcements in the Salem *Weekly Oregon Statesman* before abandoning the effort. Whatever the reason, he was transferred to the Quartermaster Department in early spring, meaning his recruitment work might have lasted for as little as two weeks or, at most, four months.[101]

Apperson was not the only active Oregon Cavalry officer pulled out of the field to serve as a recruiter. Captain Kelly's reassignment to recruiting duty in Vancouver initiated a convoluted journey that eventually resulted in his appointment to command Fort Klamath, twice. While reassigning Apperson made sense in several ways, including opening a path for William V. Rinehart to assume command of Company A, pulling Kelly out of the field was less logical on the surface. Kelly's time as a recruiter was brief; shortly after arriving at Fort Vancouver to start recruiting in July, he was sent back to Fort Klamath to assume command. In the span of a month, Kelly had been pulled from the field and ordered to assume command of Fort Klamath, only to be sent north to start recruiting to refill Company C before receiving renewed orders to assume command of Fort Klamath. The last orders stood, and he took charge of the fort. Kelly's experience demonstrates the administrative challenge of trying to recruit a command that served in two separate jurisdictions. The Department of the Pacific commander felt better with the Regular Army veteran in charge of the fort than the volunteer Lt. D. C. Underwood, leaving the recruiting to others.[102]

Regardless of who was put in charge of the recruiting efforts, there were two possible paths to refilling the ranks before there was a manpower shortage. Neither option had much hope of success. The first was to canvas the veterans to see how many of them would reenlist. This had a tremendous upside for the military, but convincing a veteran to sign on for three more years on the alkali plains was a hard sell to men who knew the truth about the brutal conditions of such service. Still, every veteran who reenlisted was instantly ready for the rigors of service, whereas new recruits needed a good deal of training and seasoning in the field to be as effective as the men they replaced. If there was a key to keeping men who knew exactly what to expect but whose patriotic fervor had been eroded, it was monetary appeal. Such veterans would want more than they had been paid initially. In fact, since the public had a general idea of what to expect in the Oregon Cavalry, new volunteers would also want more money than the original cadre. With soldiers' monthly pay set, General Alvord and Governor Gibbs needed to come up with a means to supplement the army's paltry wages.

Bounties had already been used, but they had been a mix of money and land grants. By fall 1864, with the disintegration of all six original companies eminent and the last recruiting effort a confused failure, both General Alvord and Governor Gibbs felt that a more expansive bounty was the last chance, short of conscription, to refill the regiment's ranks. In October, with the Oregon legislature about to recess for the year, Governor Gibbs finally presented the dire situation to the state leaders, informing them that without a bounty to motivate enlistment, Oregon would face forced conscription to refill the cavalry regiment's ranks and raise a regiment of Oregon infantry. The governor laid out the situation in terms that made it difficult for the legislature to ignore. He used self-evident rhetoric, reminding the chamber that "no well informed man can truthfully say that troops are not needed" to protect the populace and trade routes east of the Cascades. He included General Alvord's recognition that the work of the still incomplete First Oregon Volunteer Cavalry Regiment had "been of the utmost importance in protecting that region against the Snake Indians" and stressed the small force had been stretched to its limits. To emphasize how events in the lightly populated part of the state could impact them, the governor posed a hypothetical scenario: "Suppose the avenues of trade are closed up by Indian highwaymen east of the Cascade Mountains, the property holders will be the greatest loser."[103]

Looking to make opposition impossible, he added three more reasons the legislature should approve funding extensive bounties. First, he reminded the legislature that Oregon had failed to meet the original quota set by the federal government. Next, he called on the specter of pro-Confederates rising up "to bid defiance to the law and the authority of the Government" and to "light the torch of the incendiary and inaugurate civil strife." Governor Gibbs based his rhetoric in truth and not just political hyperbole, even if the war was winding down. Captain Rinehart confirmed such threats still existed when he encountered secessionists who tried "to pick a quarrel with our recruits" in the Eugene area.[104] Finally, Gibbs informed his fellow politicians that if civilians could not be incentivized to volunteer, the federal government might implement conscription, "a just and proper method to be used when enough volunteers cannot be otherwise obtained," to which "enlightened nations not unfrequently resort."[105] It is impossible to know what influence Captain Currey had on the governor's consideration of using conscription, but in April he had suggested to Governor Gibbs that the regiment "will have to be filled up during the following winter by some means more potent than has heretofore been employed."[106]

It was a tour de force call for funding bounties to help in recruitment. The governor had managed to wrap together protecting the underdeveloped part of the state, economic self-interest, patriotism, and the state retaining self-determination into his call. He even managed to turn what was a negative factor that had disappointed many early volunteers into a positive for politicians three years later. While most individual troopers (at least among those who left a record) had wanted to be sent East to fight against the Confederates, with the war winding down, such an argument did not appeal to the state's politicians. Governor Gibbs made it clear, "This call is made for our own protection. None have been heretofore required to go east of the Rocky Mountains and none will be hereafter."[107]

The combination of pleas and cajoling worked; the legislature approved paying new recruits or veterans who reenlisted each a $150 bounty beyond any federal bounties, which had increased to $300.[108] Additionally, the veteran cavalrymen were to receive $5 extra per month. The focus, however, was no longer on the cavalry but on raising the First Oregon Infantry Regiment. Still, efforts to replenish the cavalry's ranks were part of the plan. One of the most important elements of the bounties is that they would be redeemable in gold, not the detested paper currency the men received from the federal government. Lt. William Hand, during his earlier recruiting effort, summed up the impact of paying volunteers in paper currency: "This is quite a drawback to recruiting."[109] The federal government never understood (or did not care) that the exchange rate for paper currency added another challenge when recruiting volunteers. With a paper currency exchange rate of roughly 50 percent of its face value in gold coins, the promise of payment in gold coins was a more effective incentive and a more equitable treatment for the volunteers.

Armed with large bounties in gold and additional money for reenlisting veterans, the recruiting process was restarted in the fall of 1864. The governor called on local officials to get behind the effort, which they did, but almost exclusively in regard to recruiting the infantry regiment.[110] While the civilian focus was on the new infantry regiment, work to convince veteran cavalrymen to reenlist started immediately, since their terms began expiring just a few weeks after the bounty approval vote. Predictably, the effort fell flat. Only twenty-eight veterans opted to reenlist between late 1864 and early 1865, seven of those in Company D.[111] This was a bad, though predictable, omen. The effort to raise new recruits fared just as poorly. The emphasis on recruiting the infantry regiment had drained the pool of potential recruits even now that the government did not require cavalry volunteers to supply their own mounts. The dismal cavalry recruiting results were problematic for the military, which needed a highly mobile force to conduct operations the infantry simply could not do. In the end, only Company A managed to fully replenish its emptied ranks. The other original companies fared much worse, only raising a combined ninety-five replacements. By the eve of the 1865 campaign season, the new recruits, reenlisted veterans, and the smattering of men who joined one of the six original companies in late 1862 or early 1863 added up to roughly 225 troopers. When combined with the 77 men who enlisted in Company G in 1863, General Alvord had at his disposal a mounted force of just over 300 men to perform the work done the year before by roughly 525 overly taxed men. There was no way around it: the final recruiting effort had failed. What was left of the First Oregon Volunteer Cavalry Regiment would be asked to do more with considerably less for the remainder of its service.[112]

Brigadier General Alvord had set out to use the First Oregon Volunteer Cavalry Regiment's various companies for one last grand operation before the expiration of most men's enlistment. It was based on sound military logic and appealed to most of the officers tasked with carrying it out. Moving three large expeditions simultaneously toward the same general area would, it was hoped, force the various Paiute bands to either flee precipitously or be crushed in a military engagement with one or more of the cavalry forces. If the former happened, then they became a danger outside the District of Oregon, which, frankly, was someone else's problem. However, if the latter happened, which Alvord and his officers hoped would be the case, then the surviving Paiutes would have to seek a treaty, much in the way the Shoshones had signed treaties with then colonel Patrick Connor after the Bear River Massacre in 1863. The larger outcome, whether achieved by military defeat and treaties or by flight, was the same, making the area from the Cascades to Fort Boise, between the Columbia River and the California–Nevada borders, safe for whites traveling through or staying in the region.

After each of the expeditions had ended, all three of the principal commanders reflected on what they had achieved. Two of the three did not feel entirely satisfied. Captain Drake candidly admitted, "The results achieved are not all that I hoped for at the beginning."[113] Captain Currey, who had been even more excited about the 1864 campaign than Drake, lamented that his command "did no very decisive injury to the Indians." In truth, it was the Paiutes who had defeated the Oregon Cavalry, twice, during the 1864 campaigns, including at the firefight near the Crooked River, which was the bloodiest day of the war for Oregon's cavalry. However, both believed their efforts had reduced attacks on whites in the region. Currey pointed out that his campaign "explored their [Snakes'] haunts, and claims the honor of being the first command that ever traversed Southern Oregon without meeting with defeat," something Drake could not say. However, Drake felt "a good deal has been done. The hostile Indians have been driven out of the country near the Canyon City road far to the south."[114] He went on to predict, "They are not likely to disturb the settlements north of the mountain for some time to come."[115] Ironically, Lieutenant Colonel Drew was the only one entirely ebullient about what he had achieved. Drew pointed out the "discovery of many of the haunts, strongholds, and hiding places of the most dangerous portions of the Snake and Piute [sic] Indians that will be useful to the public, and beneficial to the service in future operations."[116]

Despite mixed feelings about their effectiveness at pushing the Paiutes and other tribes questionably accused of being hostile out of the region, each had done a great deal of exploration of the areas of operation. Lieutenant Colonel Drew emphasized this more than the others, but both Captains Currey and Drake had also kept detailed records of the lands they traversed from April to October.[117] Perhaps more important, since official reports were not printed until volume 50 of *The War of the Rebellion: A Compilation of Official Records of the Union and Confederate Armies* was published in 1897, were the letters written by troopers out on campaign to the various regional newspapers. In an extremely detailed report of his expedition, which was made public in early 1865, Drew summed up the work his column had done. "The exploration of country between Fort Klamath and the Owyhee region, of which comparatively nothing had been known," was a public benefit, he stressed.[118] While Drew was describing his own expedition, each had explored regions that had been at least partially, if not mostly, unknown to whites. Success in this secondary goal held long-term importance, but for the more aggressive Currey and Drake, it did not offset their inability to bring on a momentous confrontation with the Paiutes. While some were disappointed at missing their last chance, to use the common vernacular, to "chastise" the Paiutes, General Alvord's grand 1864 campaign had been mostly successful.

EIGHT

Doing More with Less

Translating the metallic clatter into words, the telegraph operator was the first to know. Once the transmission ended and he finished the transcription, he handed the communication to a messenger, who took it to Benjamin Alvord's office at Fort Vancouver. Once there it passed to one of his aides, likely either Lt. John W. Hopkins or his acting assistant adjutant general, Lt. Washington Irving Sanborn. Whether one of them read it first or handed it directly to General Alvord is impossible to know. Regardless of who brought it to the general, they would have known the gist already, if not the exact wording: "Turn over command of district to next officer in rank, and repair to Washington City [DC], and report in person to Adjutant General."[1] The original orders relieving Alvord from command of the District of Oregon were issued seventeen days earlier, on March 7, 1865, and carried from Department of the Pacific headquarters in San Francisco to Vancouver on the ss *Brother Jonathan*.[2] Although the order was for Alvord, it impacted Hopkins and Sanborn, both staff officers.

The orders were a surprise to others, including Department of the Pacific commander Maj. Gen. Irvin McDowell, who acknowledged that he "received with regret and surprise the order for General Alvord's relief from command." McDowell admitted, "How or why he was removed I am entirely ignorant." Although no one on the Pacific Coast knew the reason, Alvord's removal was instigated by Lt. Gen. Ulysses S. Grant, commander of all Union land forces. Grant, for unclear reasons, had gone out of his very busy way to fire Alvord, saying, "I know Alvord well. I do not think he is fit for the command, and he ought to be called East." Grant professed to believe Alvord was a good man but entirely unfit for any service beyond a desk or review board position.[3] It took eight months for Grant to get his way.

Relieving General Alvord from command was the latest, but not last, change in the leadership up and down the District of Oregon (more broadly) and the First Oregon Volunteer Cavalry Regiment (more specifically) since November. The resignations, transfers, and expiration of terms touched off dramatic changes in the regiment's officer corps. General Alvord's departure had an immediate impact on the regiment's command structure. Since Col. Justus Steinberger had mustered out earlier in March, it left Col. Reuben Maury as the most senior officer in the district.[4] As such, district command devolved on him. His promotion left the regiment without a commander, since all the other field-grade officers had departed. The War Department accepted the resignations of Colonel Cornelius in July 1862; Maj. Sewell Truax on October 31, 1864; and Lieutenant Colonel Drew on January 31, 1865. Maj. Jacob S. Rinearson had mustered out on November 16, 1864.[5] The truth was that by March 24, when Maury assumed command of the district, the First Oregon Volunteer Cavalry Regiment no longer existed. At least the undersized regiment no longer existed, although three nearly full companies and the fragments of the other four remained. The combined force amounted to little more than a battalion in a full-strength cavalry regiment. Had Colonel Maury not been elevated to district command, the reduced number of men in the Oregon Cavalry would have left him supernumerary.

A number of the company officers had also left the Oregon Cavalry by March 1865. Its two most experienced company commanders, Captains Currey and Drake, along with Capt. William V. Rinehart, transferred out to oversee the formation of the First Oregon Infantry Regiment. Though their resignation became official in the late spring of 1865, they had moved on months earlier. Lt. James Waymire, one of the regiment's better young officers, resigned in November 1864.[6] Capt. Richard S. Caldwell, technically the Company B commander in 1864—when not on various administrative duties as assigned by the district headquarters—tendered his resignation in March 1865.[7] The terms of service also expired for 2nd Lt. James L. Steele and surgeons William Watkins and Horace Carpenter.[8] All those departures left William Kelly the senior company commander. The harsh truth was that so many leadership vacancies impacted its effectiveness. While some of the leadership vacuum could be filled by promoting men like Lts. Frank B. White and John M. McCall to captain in 1865, none of the new officers had the command experience of those who had departed. With the departure of its senior officers and most of its companies greatly diminished, it was difficult to anticipate how effective it would be going forward.

The departures were not the only changes that impacted the remaining years of the Oregon Cavalry's existence. The cavalrymen and those from the First Washington Infantry Regiment were increasingly replaced by the First Oregon Infantry Regiment, with the trio of familiar faces in command. Having Currey, Drake, and Rinehart leading the Oregon Infantry provided some consistency when the 1865 campaign season began. Given their collective field experience as company commanders in the cavalry, they knew how to employ the remaining cavalry forces during joint operations. This proved significant as the Snake War intensified and spread in 1865. For the remaining members of the First Oregon Volunteer Cavalry Regiment, their last year and a half of service looked markedly different than what the original members experienced. The increasing violence between the military and tribes labeled Snakes necessitated distributing the greatly reduced Oregon Cavalry to more locations, in smaller bodies, to confront a worsening situation. As the violence spread and the military leaders allocated larger numbers of infantry forces to the district, the Oregon Cavalry served less independently than in previous years. From 1865 to 1866, the Oregon troopers increasingly served in conjunction with the infantry, never repeating the large, concentrated campaigns that occurred between 1862 and 1864. With the focus on stopping more frequent Paiute raids, exploration and mapping ceased. While a great deal had changed from the previous three years, the remaining Oregon cavalrymen endured two more seasons in inhospitable conditions, suffering through freezing temperatures and snow at one place and choking heat without water in another, fighting a widening conflict.

After "succeeding unexpectedly to the command of the district," Colonel Maury did his best to acquaint himself with his new responsibilities. Fortunately, General Alvord "was very kind in his efforts to impart all desired information" before he left for Washington DC. Even with Alvord's help, Maury was understandably overwhelmed. Even though the First Oregon Infantry Regiment, which numbered well over 1,200 men when it was fully recruited, was the largest unit in the district, the cavalry remained Maury's most effective force. As the regiment's former administrative commander, the colonel reported what he wished to be true and not what was happening with the efforts to fill the mounted ranks. Colonel Maury informed Maj. Gen. Irvin McDowell, who had replaced General Wright as Department of the Pacific commander on July 1, 1864, that "recruiting for the cavalry is progressing rather better in the last weeks than at first." Since it had been going so poorly for so long, even a slight improvement made little difference toward filling the planned ten companies. He also told McDowell that he already had "about 500 enlisted men in fragments" of companies. That number was incorrect. At most there were around 350 cavalrymen manning the seven existing companies.[9] As bad as it might appear, most regiments serving in the main theater of the war were similarly reduced through attrition by this point.

Maury's rosy assessment of the cavalry's strength and prospects for completing its full recruitment led the new district commander to suggest dispositions for the coming operational year that were incompatible with reality. Although he did couch his vision as dependent upon successfully filling the ranks of both Oregon regiments, Maury had already conveyed an overly optimistic tone about it coming to fruition. During the coming year, he planned to distribute one company to Fort Colville, near the

Canadian border, and leave one company each at Forts Dalles, Walla Walla, Lapwai, and Klamath. Three companies would be sent to Fort Boise, while three dismounted companies would be held at Fort Vancouver. Finally, a detachment would establish a supply depot on Jordan Creek, with the rest of that company assigned to patrol the main mail route.[10] Using the forts as bases for shorter operations was the opposite of sending the cavalry into the field on monthslong expeditions, as had been done the three previous years. Maury's plan, or rather hope, reflected his own unsuccessful experience leading two of those campaigns in 1862 and 1863. Unfortunately for Maury, the Oregon Cavalry's true strength was just over a third of a full regiment when he wrote his thoughts down on April 7, making his vision impossible.[11] Making matters worse, recruitment for the Oregon Cavalry was halted in the wake of the collapse of the Confederacy and President Lincoln's assassination.

General McDowell did not respond to Maury's wishful proposal for a month. By the time he did, he had been apprised of the true situation regarding troop strength in the District of Oregon. Fully aware that new recruits and reenlistments had not filled the empty ranks, McDowell replaced Maury's overly optimistic proposal with a modified plan for the Oregon Cavalry (and the rest of the forces in the district). Instead of manning every fort with multiple stationary commands during the coming operational season, McDowell told Colonel Maury, "The post of Forts Vancouver, Dalles, Walla Walla, and Boise will be regarded simply as depots, and ordinarily will have but a guard sufficient to protect the public property and furnish escorts, not to exceed a company at each." Recognizing the tremendous deficiency in the number of cavalry available, he added that if Maury did not have "sufficient cavalry for the escorts and for Sub-District of Boise [he] may replace the company at Lapwai [Company F] by a company of infantry." There would also be a road-building undertaking that required cavalry protection in the coming months. McDowell had not abandoned Maury's plan, just amended it to reflect the inability to replace the departed cavalrymen.[12] While the changes reflected a sense of reality about available manpower

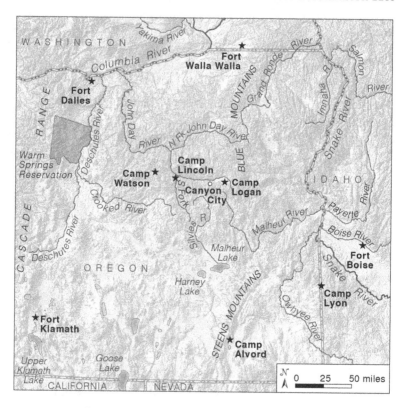

M7. Oregon, 1865–66. Created by Chelsea McRaven Feeney.

in the district, McDowell's meddling only served to undermine the new district commander's authority, who would now have to question his decisions knowing the department commander was not above countermanding his plans.[13]

Without enough cavalry, military operations in the District of Oregon in 1865 were focused on using the infantry, which was best at establishing strong points to provide centers of protection for white emigrants traveling through the district and miners working the ore strikes. Of course, the infantry lacked the ability to cover a lot of territory quickly in response to reports of attacks on whites, so they were mostly relegated to guarding the regions around their posts. To remedy this problem as best as he could, Colonel Maury ordered the various cavalry companies and fragments of companies to the temporary posts in the eastern part of the district. As a result of this change, the remaining Oregon Cavalry forces went into camps with their infantry counterparts, where the infantry did the protective guard work in the area and the cavalry chased after reports of recent Indian raids. The thinking appears to have been that this would provide whites with two types of protection. First, the infantry, which might conduct short patrols or sweeps, would establish stationary strong points. Second, small cavalry commands could conduct reconnaissance operations to search for and attack any Indians (who were arbitrarily deemed hostile) in the region. McDowell's modifications left the military operations far less aggressive than what the original Oregon troopers had known. The new approach seemed more reactive in nature.

Taking so long to develop a strategy for the operational season would have been unthinkable in the prior years, but a brief calm had settled over the District of Oregon since the peace treaties were signed the previous fall. Still, not all tribes had agreed to cease attacking the steady stream of whites coming into their homelands. Even with the temporary calm in much of the district's frontier regions, none of the leaders believed it would last. In fact, Captain Small's Company G, marooned in the snow at Camp Watson, conducted a number of small operations during the winter in response to nontreaty bands attacking whites on the Canyon City Road. According to Dr. David Walker, who was later sent to evaluate the environmental health conditions at Camp Watson, the camp was situated in an area "comprising mountainous country of every kind, interspersed with rolling table land, and occasionally prairies. Sage brush and alkali dust cover the country, while most of the streams contain more or less alkali," and "in general the nights are cold, and in summer the noontide heat is great. At all times of the year snow may fall, and thunder showers are frequent throughout the summer."[14] Unfortunately for Captain Small and his men, the camp was strategically located near the vital Canyon City Road, requiring a permanent military presence to protect travelers. Anticipating increasing attacks in the area in 1865,

F2. Camp Watson. Oregon Historical Society, Mss5279_001.

the military reinforced Camp Watson with Company H of the new First Oregon Volunteer Infantry Regiment.

Any mounted operation starting from Camp Watson had to be limited because almost all the company's horses had been taken to Fort Vancouver for the winter. While the men had been trying to improve their insufficient quarters since November, the first active patrol of the new year occurred on January 11, 1865. Responding to civilian claims that a threatening band of Indians had been seen near Cottonwood Station, east of The Dalles and north of Camp Watson, Captain Small gathered Lt. William Hand and twenty men to investigate the report. After a short three-day trip, he reported the patrol returned "without accomplishing anything."[15] The civilians had proven again to be overly edgy. Four days later, during a heavy snowstorm, Lieutenant Hand led eight men out for a patrol to the Canyon City Road. This patrol also returned without achieving anything.[16] Rather than sending out regular patrols between Camp Watson and Cottonwood Station, on March 1 Small sent Hand and a ten-man detachment to establish a temporary camp near Cottonwood House, on the stagecoach line north of Camp Watson.

Three days after sending Hand's detachment to establish a temporary presence at Cottonwood House, Small set out for Fort Vancouver because "nearly half of the company were down sick with the scurvy for want of proper food and medicines." The lack of vitamin C in the troopers' diet was a serious problem. Small had combated this as best he could by purchasing potatoes and onions from local farmers, but that supply quickly ran out. His absence meant Lieutenant Hand was in charge of both Camp Watson and the temporary encampment near Cottonwood House. Not only had Small gone looking for vegetables with which to ward off scurvy; he gathered up the company's horses and brought those back to the camp. When he returned, he learned the situation had worsened considerably during his absence.

The temporary camp near Cottonwood House had been established in response to increasing complaints from civilians about their livestock being stolen by (unidentified) Indians. Hand's small force was there to protect the settlers living at and near the station. With such a limited command, he had not been given approval to go out on any patrols, which would leave the encampment and Cottonwood House unguarded. While Hand and his men remained at their encampment, a group of locals left on March 7 to recapture the stolen animals. Five days later, according to testimony from the civilian posse, they somehow induced a band of twenty-eight Indians to come back with them to Cottonwood House, presumably to turn them over to the military. Apparently realizing they were in danger, the Indians attempted to flee from their white captors, at which point the whites immediately "commenced firing on them, killing 12 and wounding nearly all the rest." Two women were also "accidentally killed" in the chaos. Attesting to the one-sided affair, not a single member of the posse was hit. The whites captured twenty-three horses and mules but did not mention if any of those were the stolen animals, which they certainly would have if that was the case. The incident was not uncommon in eastern Oregon, but the scope of the butchery was unusual. Believing the Cottonwood House station would be a likely target for future attacks (retaliation) along the Canyon City Road, Hand suggested that "it would be well to leave this detachment here for the present."[17] Small agreed, so a detachment was kept at the camp.

Small also learned of the recent thefts of livestock and the civilians' murder of most of the small band when he returned to camp with the vegetables and horses on April 13. Concerned about the escalating raids on the settlers' animals and worried by Hand's warning, Small decided to lead a mounted patrol out to determine if any Indians were still in the area. Without taking time to rest, Small headed out the next day with twenty-one men, riding back toward Cottonwood Station along the South Fork John Day River.[18] At Cottonwood, Lieutenant Hand and his detachment joined the reconnaissance.

Unlike the first two patrols of the season, this expedition was able to use the stolen animals' tracks to make contact with the Indian raiders. After two days, 1st Sgt. George Dichtl and an eight-man contingent patrolling ahead of the rest of Small's force were fired on near the road that ran between Red Bluff, California, and Canyon City. At 5:15 p.m. on April 16, Small, with nine men and the surgeon, raced in the direction of the scouting party.[19] The trail led to the foot of a steep prominence from which the Indians had fired on Dichtl's party, wounding him (breaking his leg) and Pvt. A. Q. Church (three shots to the body).[20] Small began to lead his men up the slope for thirty feet when they received "a hailstorm of bullets," forcing his men to dismount. They slowly made their way to the top of the slope on foot, exchanging fire as they went. As they crested the rise, the Indians fled a mile to another hill, where they remained, watching the Oregon troopers. Small claimed three Indians were killed while four of the cavalrymen were wounded during the firefight. He believed the Indians numbered thirty and were in such a strong second position that it would have been fruitless, and likely costly, to try to dislodge them.[21]

After putting the wounded men on makeshift litters, they started for their camp. Small reported his "men cheerfully and willingly undergoing the arduous duty of packing three of the wounded twenty miles to Cottonwood, wading the river when necessary"—the fourth man was apparently able to ride.[22] First they came to the temporary camp near Cottonwood Station. The next day they fell back farther to the better facilities at Camp Watson. Corporal George Washington McKinny and another trooper were sent out to bring refreshments to the wounded. They "met the wagon about 4 miles from camp," where they "found the wounded getting along as well as could be expected."[23] Captain Small tried to put his best spin on what had happened, writing in his report, "I feel thankful that we succeeded in driving off the enemy with so few casualties." Small undermined his effort to whitewash what had really happened; he reported the Indians' second position was so impregnable that he did not dare attack them.[24]

The day after bringing his wounded into Camp Watson, Small and Dr. Walker tried to make a dash back to Cottonwood Station, where he had left Lieutenant Hand and his men. Soon they noticed roughly a dozen Indians just forty yards away, forcing Small and the doctor to attempt to quietly back away. It was too late; the Indians discovered them and, according to Small, "raised the war-whoop and came after [them] at full speed." He admitted, "We only escaped by being mounted upon the best horses."[25] Forced back to Camp Watson, Small, Dr. Walker, and three cavalrymen started again for Hand's camp at 1:00 a.m. When they reached the point where Small and the doctor had encountered the Indians, they "found three citizens who had been killed—two of them scalped."[26] The five men moved on quickly to Lieutenant Hand's camp, which they reached at dawn. Small immediately ordered a patrol to pick up the Indians' trail and determine which direction they had headed. At the same time, he sent a wagon team back to pick up the bodies of the three dead men, which they buried near the temporary Cottonwood camp. The patrol returned later in the day without seeing any Indians. Their report convinced Small that he had vastly underestimated the size of this group. Alarmed, he reported to district headquarters, "The force under my command will prove insufficient to afford the necessary protection to travelers and settlers." The early spring maneuvering had left both men and horses "much fatigued, having been almost constantly on the march for the past eight days and nights."[27] The new campaign year was off to a rough start for Company G.

Camp Watson remained a hive of activity well into October. While the camp was located in the high desert frontier, given its proximity to the Canyon City Road, it was regularly visited by expressmen. The mail rider brought both military communications and newspapers, which included both regional and national news. National news and orders from District of Oregon headquarters at Fort Vancouver traveled via boat to The Dalles. From there an express rider took orders as well as newspapers to Camp Watson. That somewhat circuitous route was faster than it might seem. Lieutenant Noble noted the camp received news of President Lincoln's assassination on April 21, just five days after the president died and four days after it ran in the Portland *Oregonian*.[28]

Neither the death of the president nor the earlier news that Robert E. Lee had surrendered the Confederate Army of Northern Virginia had any impact on the men at Camp Watson.[29] Given its key location, Company G (later joined by Company H of the Oregon Infantry) was guaranteed to spend the remainder of the spring through the early fall in the field, regardless of what happened in the East. The theft of livestock and killing of the three men Small found suggested the area would remain a focal point for violence. Each subsequent report of livestock being run off, an attack on whites, or even the "threatening" presence of any Indians sent the cavalrymen off on a reconnaissance. This type of activity continued throughout the rest of the season. Small reported the men of Company G remained busy on scouts throughout the early part of the summer. Acting quartermaster Lieutenant Noble recorded a number of those typical patrols and escorts in his diary.[30] Most were two-day, out-and-back escorts or rides along the stagecoach line to the station at Cottonwood House.

The arrival of Company H, First Oregon Infantry Regiment, commanded by Capt. Loren L. Williams on May 21 finally allowed Small to be more aggressive.[31] Two days after the infantry arrived, Small sent several forces on simultaneous reconnaissance. Having the larger force at his disposal and more officers (there had been just three at Camp Watson since November, Small and Lieutenants Hand and Noble) enabled Small to replicate, albeit on a small scale, the lessons he learned the previous year. The largest patrol, led by Captain Small, consisted of forty men from his own Company G and Captain Williams and forty of his newly arrived infantry. This joint force moved off southwestward toward Camp Dahlgren. At the same time, twelve cavalrymen, led by one of the sergeants, were sent back to the camp near Cottonwood House, while Lt. Jesse Applegate and ten infantrymen headed northeastward to Bridge Creek.[32]

The expeditions left behind a camp filled with sickness. According to Lieutenant Noble, most of the men remaining at Camp Watson were sick and "unfit for duty"—and getting worse. Both Noble and his wife, who had come to stay at the camp during the winter with their children, were among the sick. He had wanted his wife to leave the camp for The Dalles, but due to the severity of her illness, there were concerns she could not endure the stage ride. After recovering enough to travel, she left for The Dalles on May 26. Whether or not it was because there was no room on the stage, their children remained at Camp Watson. Within days, as the sickness spread, Noble's daughter, Ella, fell ill. Noble believed part of the reason for the widespread sickness was due to the erratic weather, which changed quickly from warm and pleasant to snowing during this time. Noble could not shake the illness, writing at one point that he had "suffered much with a cold[,] sore throat & hoarseness today." He also admitted, "I am having the shakes." While it took some time, both the lieutenant and his two-year-old daughter recovered.[33] The weather continued to swing from extremes, and then the meat rations ran out at the end of the month, which only contributed to the men's discomfort, but they also eventually improved.[34] Sickness and a poor diet were taken very seriously at the isolated camp. Earlier in March Pvt. Matthew Fitzsimmons died from scurvy due to the lack of a proper diet. Therefore, it was a relief when no one else died during this latest wave of illnesses.[35]

John F. Noble received a welcomed surprise on May 30. On that day part of Company A and the few new enlistees in Companies B, D, and E, led by Lt. Charles W. Hobart, arrived at Camp Watson. Hobart was in charge of the amalgamated force because senior Lieutenant McCall was assigned to escort duty with the bulk of Company A. The previous year the four companies would have numbered between 225 and 260 men, but Noble counted just 100 troopers as their column moved to a site just above Camp Watson. Though still under the weather and worried about his daughter, it was good to see at least a handful of familiar faces. Lts. Silas Pepoon and James L. Currey, who were with Hobart's column, had ridden in Captain Currey's expedition in 1864 but had gotten to know Hand during their joint operations. Corporal McKinny, who had not gotten sick, was equally glad to see "several of my old companions and fellow sufferers of last summer's campaign through this desert and barren country."[36] Company G had spent the entire 1864 season in Captain Drake's expedition, so McKinny knew the few remaining old hands in Company D well. The pleasantries lasted just a few days before Hobart continued on to Fort Boise.

Charles W. Hobart had spent much of his early service as a staff officer at District of Oregon headquarters before requesting field service in 1864. Then in January 1865, he was appointed commander of Company A, replacing Lt. John W. Hopkins.[37] While he had less active experience than most of the remaining veteran officers, he had seniority over almost all of them, having been appointed second lieutenant in December 1861 and assigned to duty at that grade on January 16, 1862.[38] He was appointed first lieutenant on March 30, 1863, but eventually declined the promotion because it would extend his term of service.[39] With the most experienced and senior lieutenant in the Oregon Cavalry, John M. McCall, slated to command half of Company A as it provided protection for the Central Military Road survey, command of the amalgamated force fell to Hobart. On May 12 Colonel Maury ordered Hobart to lead parts of Companies A, B, and D east. First they would go to Fort Dalles and then continue east from there, angling southward at the same time.[40] This provided John Drake, now second-in-command of the First Oregon Infantry Regiment and the commanding officer at Fort Boise, with a desperately needed mounted force. Civilians had been calling for military assistance to stop raids on their livestock between Fort Boise (in the east) and the Malheur River region (in the west). It was nearly hopeless to try to catch mounted Indians with the slow-moving infantry. The cavalry would be kept busy once they reached the fort.

After his stop at Camp Watson on May 30, Hobart continued on toward Fort Boise, which he reached in early June. Just a few days after Hobart's detachment arrived, Drake sent it out to establish a base of operations for the remainder of the campaigning season. Hobart found a site with enough wood, water, and grass on Cow Creek, which he named Camp Lyon after the Idaho territorial governor Caleb Lyon. This eventually grew into a substantial encampment before the end of operations that fall. At 11:00 a.m. on July 2, Hobart led his first patrol from the new camp. With forty-four men, he picked up the trail of stolen livestock and followed it for five days, during which time the unidentified Indians "went in a very circuitous direction and every method had been used" to make the trail difficult to follow. As Hobart's men closed in on the Indians and the stolen animals on the Malheur River, his scouts were seen by "three Indians who were gathering berries. They fled to the brush" where, despite every effort "to find them, so that they would be unable to transmit intelligence" of the cavalry's presence to the main body of Indians, they were able to evade the cavalry.[41] The next day Hobart left his pack train in camp with a guard while he followed the livestock trail at a rapid pace. They came across abandoned campsites but were unable to maintain contact with the trail when it appeared the livestock were scattered in several directions. This forced Hobart to divide his command further, sending small groups in several directions, but none came upon either the stolen animals or any of the Indians before they gave up the pursuit for the night.

They had no better luck the next day, but in the predawn darkness of July 9, the campsite guards reported Indians near camp. Hobart responded by bringing in the pack mules, calling the men to arms, and saddling their horses. He also had the mountain howitzer unpacked and set up. Those lightweight artillery pieces had long given the military a psychological as well as firepower advantage in their confrontations with Indians. The activity in the camp proved the Indians had been discovered, at which point they opened fire from all directions, according to Hobart. He ordered the howitzer to fire several times, mixing spherical shots with canister. While canister was devastating at close range against massed men, it was still effective against the more spread-out Indians due to the numerous projectiles scattering in the air and the noise. As Hobart had hoped, the howitzer fire sent the attackers fleeing out of range. The eruption of rifle fire, punctuated by the deeper boom from the howitzer, spooked ten horses and a number of mules so thoroughly that they broke free and ran from the camp. Miraculously, none were hit, and all later returned to camp.[42]

When the animals fled, Hobart ordered Sgt. Joseph Wallace and Cpl. James Walker to head them off before they fell into the Indians' hands. With the animals returning on their own, Wallace and Walker turned their attention to the Indians, who were now fleeing from the cavalry's "quick and well directed" fire. Hobart sent reinforcements with them, and the group kept up a running firefight for five or six miles before giving up the pursuit. Hobart's men captured nine horses and claimed to have killed five Indians; three he said were carried off from around the camp, while the Indians were forced to leave one body behind. A fifth Indian was killed during the pursuit. Hobart was unsure about the number wounded but did note that the captured horses were covered in blood and therefore deduced, "Quite a number of Indians must have been wounded."[43]

The Oregon Cavalry's casualties had been light; two horses and a mule were lost and two cavalrymen wounded. During the initial firefight around the campsite, Company D's Pvt. William R. Jones, fighting at the front of the camp, was shot in the arm.[44] During the pursuit, two men from Company B, Corporal Walker and Pvt. William B. Phillips, were cut off from the main body of cavalry, forcing them to rush through the Indians to get to safety.[45]

Phillips was seriously wounded and might have been unhorsed had not Walker killed one of the Indians. As some of the cavalry broke through to their comrades, the Indians fled. After an uneasy quiet settled over the campsite, the Oregon cavalrymen searched the area and found "considerable soldiers' clothing among them and [they] appear to have plenty of arms and ammunition." Less certain and more shocking, Hobart believed there were white men among the band, because "they told us in good English to 'come on, you sons of bitches, we can whip you anywhere.'" He also believed some of the Indians had been scouts, since "the gun captured is one of those that were stored in the quartermaster's storehouse at Fort Boise."[46]

After returning to Camp Lyon on July 13, Hobart reflected on the encounter, believing there were a large number of Indians in the region. This view was reinforced by continued attacks on civilians and more thefts of livestock. In response to another report of livestock thefts, this time from the Jordan Creek area, Hobart sent a detachment led by Sergeant Wallace (Hobart was the only officer) south of the camp to try to recover the animals and kill "this band of thieves." Wallace's patrol found the Indians in an eight-hundred-foot-deep Owyhee River canyon on July 17. Realizing he could not surprise the Indian encampment, Wallace left his horses above on the plain while two groups of cavalrymen scrambled down into the canyon. One group approached the camp from above and the other from below. Sergeant Wallace intended that the group led by Cpl. Charles Phillips, of Company B, would hold its fire until they heard Wallace's men firing, catching the twelve to fifteen Indian men in a cross fire. Things did not go as planned when Phillips's group was discovered as it approached, forcing them to open fire. Wallace's men picked up the pace and soon began firing from its position. Surprised by the attack, the Indians gave no resistance but tried to flee instead. Four of them were killed in their camp, while the survivors crossed the Owyhee and escaped into the forest on the other side ahead of the gunfire. Sergeant Wallace reported that most of those who escaped were wounded. The cavalrymen found "several hundred pounds of dried meat, a large amount of dried berries, trinkets, & [et]c, robes, furs, blankets and all the stuff in their camp," which they burned before returning first to Jordan Creek and then Camp Lyon on July 18. For all the devastation inflicted upon the Indians, Wallace's patrol only managed to retrieve two horses and one ox from those stolen; the rest had been killed for food.[47]

Following the departure of Lieutenants Hobart, Currey, and Pepoon and the reduced Companies A, B, and D toward Fort Boise in early June, life at Camp Watson returned to the routine of periodic patrols for both the Company G cavalrymen and the Washington infantrymen in Company H. While Captain Small did a good job of keeping his men in the field in smaller detachments, boredom quickly set in for those taking their turn staying in the camp. That the quartermaster had run out of beef on May 31 only made matters worse at Camp Watson.[48] On June 10, after a week of no patrols being mounted and a day after getting their first beef rations in ten days, some of the men broke open their stash of liquor and got drunk. Sergeant McKinny remembered "several in the guard house" and "one tied to the flag pole" as punishment for their transgression.[49] One of the men was still confined to irons two days later. The best remedy for such behavior was to get back into the field, where alcohol was harder to come by (although available for the officers, if so inclined). On June 14 Small sent out two expeditions; Lieutenant Hand led twenty-six Company G cavalrymen toward the Deschutes River on a fifteen-day scout, while Captain Williams led a group of his infantrymen to the North Fork John Day River. Two days later Small sent Sgt. John M. Reid with another nineteen Company G troopers to the South Fork John Day River on a ten-day patrol.[50]

Hand's and Williams's patrols returned to Camp Watson on June 25 and 28, respectively. Neither had encountered any Indians. Only Sergeant Reid's patrol remained in the field as long as Small had planned, not returning until July 8.[51] The lack of commitment suggests the officers were losing some of their enthusiasm for that type of work. These relatively short reconnaissance operations had become routine. They were marching into the same general areas, rarely seeing any Indians, and returning to camp having failed to achieve the one thing most of them wanted—namely, a confrontation with Indian raiders. Sergeant McKinny did record one incident that briefly disrupted the boredom: he was jarred awake by the firing of the mountain howitzer on July 4, when some of the men decided to start the celebrations with a boom of the cannon.[52] Despite enjoying a day to celebrate the nation's birth, things quickly slid back into the routine. While attacks on miners and thefts of livestock were reported, the summer months passed without the men at Camp Watson finding, let alone engaging any of the raiders.[53]

In the midst of the summer operations, some of which had devolved into repetitive activity, two administrative changes occurred that impacted the military commands serving in the Pacific Northwest. Not long after Lieutenant Hobart arrived at Fort Boise, the War Department changed the military structure in the Far West by doing away with the Department of the Pacific and replacing it with the Division of the Pacific. At the same time, the District of Oregon was replaced by the Department of the Columbia, which included Oregon and the Territories of Washington and Idaho. Maj. Gen. Henry Halleck became the new commander on the West Coast. He had proven himself far more capable as an administrator than a field commander during the recently ended war. While Halleck was new to the Far West, the military appointed Brig. Gen. George Wright, the most well-known soldier in the region, to command the Department of the Columbia. Wright had served in the Pacific Northwest for nine years before taking over the entire West Coast military operations in late 1861. His return was welcome news for many locals; just before his assignment to the new department, one Oregon newspaper declared, "We know [General Wright] to be fully alive to the interests and welfare of this frontier."[54] Unfortunately for those reassured by news of his return, the good feelings did not last long. The general, his wife, and his staff died when their ship, the ss *Brother*

Jonathan, sank off the coast of northern California on July 29.[55] As a result, Department of the Columbia command fell to its senior officer—at least temporarily—until the War Department could find a suitable replacement. Command of the new department did not fall to Colonel Maury, who had been relieved.[56] Maury's departure left George B. Currey, who had been promoted to colonel of the First Oregon Infantry Regiment in May, the senior officer in the Department of the Columbia. It was an impressive rise from captain leading Company E in the First Oregon Volunteer Cavalry Regiment in early 1862 to department commander three and a half years later.

Wright's return had been especially popular with those who came to the Oregon country before statehood, largely due to his brutal exploits against a number of Plateau tribes in the 1850s. Now guiding the changing department became Currey's responsibility. He had acquired hard-earned experience serving in the challenging conditions and terrain in the old District of Oregon, both exploring and especially trying to force the regional tribes to make way for white development. However, department commander was an administrative job, something quite different than leading a company in the field for three years. His administrative experience was extremely limited; he had only been in charge of the First Oregon Infantry Regiment for seven months (at first, before it reached regimental status, as lieutenant colonel, then in May 1865 as colonel). Even worse, he soon faced the same thing that bedeviled Colonel Maury: he did not have a great deal of control over the operations in his department. This was particularly true when it came to operations that had been planned before he assumed department command.

There was one final change that impacted the organization of the Oregon Cavalry. With all recruiting efforts canceled, it was obvious that some of the seven cavalry companies existed more on paper than in reality. Therefore, the decision was made to consolidate some of them. In July Companies D, E, and F were folded into other companies. This in turn required a shuffling of the remaining officers. Capt. William J. Matthews, the original commander of Company F at Fort Lapwai, was elevated to battalion command when his six new recruits were merged into Company B.[57] Lieutenant Bowen, leading Company F, was in the field near Auburn with a forty-five-man detachment when the consolidation order was issued. Although he would not know it until an expressman found him, he and his force were transferred to Company A.[58] Orders mustering out Company E's remaining officer, Lt. James L. Currey, were issued at the time of the consolidation. However, they were countermanded in August; Currey continued to serve until the end of the 1865 operational season.[59] With Captain Drake's transfer and promotion and Lieutenant Waymire's resignation, there were no officers left in Company D. The consolidation meant there were only four companies of Oregon Cavalry after July: Company C was headquartered at Fort Klamath, Company G at Camp Watson, and Company B along with a portion of Company A operated from Fort Boise, with the remainder of Company A about to begin escorting a survey crew. Companies A and B were the benefactors of the consolidation when the few men from D, E, and F were blended into their ranks.

These changes were certainly needed—it was ridiculous to have a company of seven men—and they correlated the paper strength more accurately to the available force. Currey oversaw these changes even though he had not been involved in the decision to consolidate. Furthermore, by August all four of the remaining companies had been assigned their duties for the 1865 operational season. The one that Currey knew the least about was Company C at Fort Klamath. While Company C, minus Captain Kelly, had participated in the coordinated campaigns in 1864, the area around Fort Klamath had been outside the old District of Oregon until early 1865. Captain Kelly and Company C were something of a mystery to Currey when he assumed command of the new Department of the Columbia in August.

The last six months may well have been the most relaxed of Capt. William Kelly's service in the Oregon Cavalry. His commanding officer and longtime nemesis Lt. Col. Charles Drew had submitted his resignation after returning from the 1864 campaign. Rather than wait out its acceptance, Drew left the post on leave, supposedly to help process the discharge of most of his men. The true reason for his quick departure may have had something to do with a report Captain Kelly sent to District of California headquarters regarding Drew's conduct during his delayed 1864 campaign. Kelly reported he learned that Drew "was going to take it slow, and wait[ed] some days on the way so as to have the men receive pay for a longer time for the use of their horse and horse equipment." According to Kelly, "The men understand his [true] motives to be for the purpose of keeping in Service a pack train of about eighty mules at three dollars per head per day." When Drew left part of his command at Camp Alvord, he did not turn around at Fort Boise but continued to Bannock City, which served no military purpose. Kelly relayed the prevalent theory that "it is supposed [he kept going] to get funds to purchase Mining Stock" in one of the upstart mining companies in the area. Perhaps most offensive in Kelly's view, a belief likely supported by General Wright, was that "Col. Drew studiously avoided all difficulties with the Indians."[60] Since Charles Drew lived in California after his service, it seems he did not invest in any mining operations near Boise; still, the new accusations certainly undermined his position in the Oregon Cavalry.

Drew's departure in mid-November left Captain Kelly not only in command of Company C but also in charge of Fort Klamath. Having served as an enlisted man in the prewar army, he had undoubtedly dealt with officers who avoided their duties before. However, it is unlikely that any of those instances had changed so much in his favor as what he experienced at Fort Klamath. The onset of winter, which made it almost impossible for the cavalrymen to conduct any patrols, also limited the communication he had with Department of the Pacific headquarters, to whom he reported. Isolated and freed from having to interact with Drew, Kelly rode out the cold months with his men in the frontier comfort of the fort, trying to fend off the boredom. While that monotony, as Captain Currey had suggested, could erode the men's effectiveness, they were not suffering during expeditions in the cold like Captain Small's force at Camp Watson.[61]

Things remained relatively calm and at the mercy of the winter snows until Captain Kelly received some shocking news. In early April 1865, a message arrived at Fort Klamath from Paiute Chief Paulina saying he wanted to negotiate a peace treaty with the white officials (the military represented by Kelly and J. W. Perit Huntington, superintendent of Indian affairs for Oregon). The most feared and despised Indian in Oregon suddenly, if not entirely unexpectedly, was prepared to submit to white rule. Chief Paulina's wife and child had been captured not long after negotiations with the Klamaths and Modocs in October 1864. Since then they had been held prisoner at Fort Klamath as leverage, which apparently worked. Achieving peace with the Paiute chief (or his death) had been on the agendas of all three of the 1864 expeditions. Finally, without conducting another campaign, Kelly and Superintendent Huntington could achieve that goal. The chief wanted to begin the negotiations "as soon as the snow is off the ground," allowing him to bring his band to the Fort Klamath area. The climate continued to dictate what could be done.[62]

The treaty negotiations were still months off and were not finalized until August 1865.[63] Even though Colonel Maury had relinquished command of the District of Oregon (in April) to Colonel Currey by then, he had laid out how the forces at Fort Klamath were deployed.[64] In many ways, Maury's plan reflected his own experiences in the field from 1862 to 1864. In his May 11 orders to Kelly, he directed Kelly "to protect the travel on the trail leading from Northern California and Southern Oregon to Canyon City, Boise, and Owyhee mines, and to chastise any hostile Indians that may be found." Maury was sending Company I, First Oregon Infantry Regiment, to Kelly to be used as a stationary defense force. Specifically, he was ordered to establish a supply depot for his summer operations "at or near Silver Lake, on the trail from Yreka and Southern Oregon to Canyon City." Kelly was to station some of the infantry at the depot to protect the supplies. Maury envisioned using Kelly's command just as the other companies had done in

previous years, to "scour the country in all directions" throughout
the summer and fall. He was to keep an eye out for other expeditions Maury hoped to put into the field for the summer, which
he believed "will be very likely to drive the Indians into the section of country to be traveled by you."[65] Kelly was to operate west
of Harney Lake and focus on protecting the road from the Willamette valley to Canyon City. It was clear from those instructions
that Maury still felt the best way to stop Indian attacks and thefts
was to continue the same types of campaigns the Oregon Cavalry
had done for three years. The orders also revealed that the district
commander did not fully grasp the limited mounted force available.

Colonel Maury had included one caveat in his orders that could
alter how and where Company C served during the coming operational season. He left open the possibility that the company might
be used to provide a military escort for the Central Military Road
survey expedition planned for the summer. This potential alter-
ation to his orders was a holdover from the previous summer,
when both Captains Currey and Drake had been ordered "to furnish them [Oregon surveyor general Byron Pengra's survey party]
with such escort of cavalry as [they] shall be able to spare."[66] In the
end, neither of them had to divert any part of their force because
Pengra's survey crew did not cross into eastern Oregon. The orders
Maury sent to Captain Kelly were far less direct: "Further instructions may be sent you in relations to the party establishing what is
known as Willamette military road."[67] Kelly's experience of being
issued contradictory orders by Lieutenant Colonel Drew and District of Oregon headquarters the previous fall was being repeated
by Maury in May 1865. In the end, serving as an escort for the road
survey was Company C's major activity in 1865.

Byron J. Pengra arrived in Oregon in 1853, when he was thirty
years old. Within five years he had become a prominent Republican, who, as a newspaperman, operated more in the political back
rooms. After the election of Abraham Lincoln and the correspond-
ing rise in stature of the state's Republicans, his political support
netted him the appointment as the surveyor general of Oregon.

In such a role, he hoped to be chosen to oversee the construction of a railroad through the state, but that job went to someone else. However, in 1864 he was put in charge of building a military road from Eugene east to the Idaho line, near the Owyhee mining district. The path would be an economic boon for both western and eastern Oregon as well as beneficial for the military as a better roadway—free of charge because of the government's involvement in the project.[68]

Pengra conducted the first phase of the survey west of the Cascade Range in 1864. As he prepared to continue to survey east of the mountains, construction crews began work on the eastern portion of the road in June 1865. Weather and snow levels delayed the start of the second phase of the surveying operation until July. Unlike the western route, surveying a path between the eastern slope of the Cascades and the Idaho border would require his crew to cross through regions where Indian attacks had occurred in the past. Treaties with the Klamaths and Modocs in late 1864 and impending ones with some of the Northern Paiute bands, including the one led by Chief Paulina, certainly lessened the chance of being attacked. However, it did not eliminate it; an already nervous Pengra had requested a military escort at the beginning of the year, before Chief Paulina and other Paiutes signed a treaty with the government's representatives.

The civilians were there to construct roads and were not properly equipped or trained to provide their own protection if they were attacked by any of the Indians whose lands they would travel through. Escort duty was a different type of work than what the Oregon Cavalry had done the previous three years. The exploration was different than what Lieutenant Colonel Drew had done in 1864, although the Pengra team planned to explore some of the same area. For the military, it was not glamorous duty, but it was important. Connecting the western and eastern parts of Oregon would expedite development and make trade between distant places easier and more profitable. Therefore, rather than place one of the former desk officers in charge of that important

duty, Colonel Maury assigned the responsibility to his most experienced available officer, Lt. John M. McCall. The critical Captain
Drake had trusted McCall enough to send him out on numerous
independent patrols in 1864, something he would have avoided if
he did not believe McCall was up to the job.

Earlier in the year, General Alvord laid out for Department of
the Pacific headquarters the vision for the cavalry's involvement
in the road surveys. Surveyor Pengra's crew would move southward from Eugene, then through the Cascades, before heading
along the state's southern line to its eastern border. McCall would
lead a patched-together cavalry escort for Pengra's wagon road
survey. Alvord, channeling three successive years of orders to the
Oregon Cavalry, suggested that "these expeditions would remain
out all the season, and could not return probably before the latter part of October," which indicates he had more in mind for the
military escorts than just protecting Pengra's crew.[69]

From the start, Alvord hoped Pengra's cavalry escort detail would
"move independently of Mr. Pengra" so it could "give protection
to the miners and travelers who may be employed and prospecting through that region."[70] This may have been the reason Colonel Maury selected the experienced Lieutenant McCall to lead the
escort. McCall had come west with Company D to Fort Vancouver
after the conclusion of the 1864 operations. With the expiration of
most of Company D men's terms of enlistment, he was assigned
to recruiting duty at the end of the year, headquartered in Salem.
He remained at that unsuccessful task until he received orders
on May 29 to dispose of public properties related to his recruiting effort in preparation for commanding a military escort for
the wagon road survey.[71] Once he closed the accounts in Salem, he
was ordered to head to Eugene to prepare a force of forty-five men
from Company A, two Oregon troopers (one each from Companies B and D), and one infantryman from Company A, First Oregon Infantry Regiment.[72] It is unclear how selective McCall was
when he chose the men who went on the escort, but at least one
of them, German-born Alexander Stauff, had been a lumberman
before the war.[73] Colonel Maury issued his final orders on June 27.

P14. Capt. John M. McCall. Oregon Historical Society,
Cartes-de-visite Collection; Org. Lot 500; b4.f690-1.

Maury reminded McCall that "the opening of the proposed road
is one of importance to Oregon, and every reasonable effort for its
successful exploration is enjoined." He further informed McCall,
"As soon as your party is supplied with the necessary outfit you
will move [out]" and "be governed in your route by the wishes
of B. J. Pengra." Maury was particularly interested "to have more
and better information of the route [they were talking] generally, and especially of the later portion," since Pengra might follow

a different course than previous efforts across the southeastern section of the state.[74]

After spending three weeks finalizing his preparation, McCall led his column southward out of Eugene on July 17. Pengra and the survey party had completed their preparations already and gone ahead; they planned to meet on the east side of the Cascades, where the potential danger began. Nineteen civilians accompanied the soldiers on this first stage of McCall's march. The column continued south, gradually angling eastward until it crossed the Cascade Range. While the first week had gone well, the ascent up the heavily forested mountains was costly. There was a rough road, but a recent storm had covered the path with fallen pine trees. Crews already working to improve the roadway found themselves having to do repair work first. "It was difficult to get past the working parties owing to the quantity of the timber that is cut down," McCall recorded. Finding it was in his best interest to assist the road crews, he "put some 15 or 20 men at work to assist" in opening a path, which they did in just under three hours. The fallen timber proved problematic, but it was not dangerous, whereas the steep climb on narrow trails was both difficult and dangerous. A number of his seventy-six mules gave out and had to be left behind. Worse, "the report came that some of the animals had fallen from the trail and [were] killed." Some fell nine hundred feet down a steep and rocky hill, taking the supplies with them, including over two hundred pounds of bacon, some flour, and syrup.[75] Some mules simply wandered off, and many of those that made it almost gave out before they finally began the descent to the eastern side on July 26, which was also treacherous, though not quite as exhausting. Quantities of supplies were also lost when packs were torn open by the timber along the trail—McCall used the word *road*, but everything he describes makes it clear it was more of a trail.

The escort duty really began on July 27, when McCall's patrol met up with Pengra's survey team, which was encamped on the Deschutes River three miles from the eastern base of the Cascade Range. On July 30 Pengra proceeded to Fort Klamath, hoping to observe the formal treaty conference with Northern Paiute Chief Paulina. The treaty was scheduled to begin on August 10, along the Sprague River, but the actual agreement did not happen for two more days. While McCall's little command did not provide the show of strength that Colonel Maury had displayed during negotiations with the Nez Perce bands in 1863, having additional troops, beyond Captain Kelly's company, nearby probably heartened the government's spokesperson, J. W. Perit Huntington, superintendent for Indian affairs for Oregon.[76]

For whites living within the boundaries of the District of Oregon and the military who served there since 1861, Chief Paulina was ubiquitous. If raids were conducted, livestock stolen, or individual miners found dead, whites blamed his band almost reflexively. While the chief aggressively challenged whites throughout much of the lower half of eastern Oregon, in some cases his band was accused of committing attacks on whites hundreds of miles apart almost simultaneously. He was the one Indian person above all others the whites in the region, civilian or soldier, despised the most. Given his prominent status, McCall was shocked when he saw the band at the negotiating site. Though infused with the standard racial tropes of the times, he seemed genuinely surprised: "They are [a] miserable lot of looking rascals. Apparently capable of committing almost any fiendish acts. There [sic] wardrobe is in a seedy condition, giving evident token that they have either been very unsuccessful in their recent plundering excursions or else they have a *cache* in the mountains somewhere."[77] McCall was one of the few Oregon Cavalry officers to actually see the Paiute chief. Therefore, it must have been a surprise after more than three years chasing the name Paulina around the south-central and southeastern part of the district to witness him agreeing to the treaty, which was finalized on August 13.

Once the treaty was signed, Pengra's crew and McCall's command started back on the survey, heading south to the north side of the main branch of the Sprague River. In an effort to find the best route for the military road, Pengra divided the survey team into two bodies. Captain Kelly and a detachment of Company C men escorted the team led by a man named O'Dell along the same path from Steens Mountain that Lieutenant Colonel Drew followed in 1864.[78] Pengra and McCall moved north toward Silver Lake, a lake without any permanent sources of incoming water called *Kalpshi* by the Klamath people. The escort and survey crew found drinkable water widely dispersed in this region and usually "standing in holes."[79]

The survey expeditions continued eastward during the rest of August. They crossed over rugged hills, descended into Warner Valley, skirted some small shallow lakes, and pressed on toward Steens Mountain. Having assessed the southern trail, Captain Kelly's men and Mr. O'Dell's survey team turned north and headed toward McCall's patrol, halting at Honey Creek. McCall's column found them there on August 28. By the time Captain Kelly's force and the other half of the survey crew rejoined McCall and Pengra, McCall's column had run into two groups of Paiutes, both assuring the soldiers they were friendly—the first group was led by Chief How Luk. Had Chief Paulina not signed a treaty just weeks earlier and assured the commissioner that the other bands of Northern Paiutes wanted to do the same, it is likely McCall would have attacked How Luk's band.

Odell and Pengra discussed what each had seen and decided the route Lieutenant Colonel Drew took the previous year was the best course for extending the Central Military Road. McCall even stopped at a campsite Drew used the previous year. Having determined the best route upon which to start laying out the road, the entire body turned back on August 29. Captain Kelly left his wagons in McCall's hands and dashed back to Fort Klamath ahead of the main body. McCall and the surveyors followed slowly for the next seventeen days before Pengra separated from McCall's force on the Williamson River. Pengra's survey crew, with a few cavalrymen for protection, headed up the Deschutes River while McCall's main body rode to Fort Klamath, which they reached on September 17. With the weather getting colder and snow likely to start falling at any time, this was the end of McCall's active service.[80]

Not long after returning to Fort Klamath, McCall received an overdue promotion to captain, which he certainly deserved for his long service, including leading a company since the previous fall. Even though there were almost no Oregon cavalrymen left to lead by the time his promotion came through, McCall remained in uniform through the summer of 1866. Captain Kelly resumed command of Fort Klamath after participating in the Oregon Central Military Road survey escort. He also remained with the ever-dwindling Oregon Cavalry until July 1866.[81] By then, not only was he one of the few remaining officers; he was the most senior one in what had been, in all practical sense, a battalion for a year. As such, he was appointed to the somewhat superfluous position of battalion commander. More years of active service lay ahead of him, but not with the Oregon Cavalry. For both men, their role in escorting the road survey marked the end of the most active part of their service in the Oregon Cavalry.

While providing the military escort for the Central Military Road survey was not a glamorous end to their careers in the Oregon Cavalry, it had important results for the future, something McCall came to understand. He felt his portion of Company A, along with Captain Kelly's Company C, had traveled "over a district of country heretofore unexplored" even though "sometimes inconvenienced for want of good water or grass." In his view "the exploration and location of the Mil. Road in a military point of view is one of vast importance." He predicted, "If this road is completed it at once opens a highway or thoroughfare into the heart of their homes"—*their* referring to what he termed "bands of Indians that are or have been hostile." Such a road "where troops can be rapidly thrown into their midst, and experience of all Indian warfare goes to prove that that is the place to strike them."[82] Although McCall did not know it, his predictions about the military importance of the Central Military Road rang true over the next three years as hostilities intensified between whites and various bands of Paiutes. The work had been dangerous, but not because of confrontations with any Indians, and it had an important impact on the future, though by then, few remembered the contingent of

Oregon cavalrymen's role. It was for McCall, Kelly, and most of
their men a metaphor for their service.

Service in the District of Oregon changed a great deal between the
first expedition in 1862 and the 1865 operational season, though
some aspects remained the same. Company C and part of Company A spent their summer conducting a somewhat different type
of exploration than had been done the previous years. Companies B
and G, along with the rest of Company A, continued operating
similarly to previous years. Company G, along with Company H of
the First Oregon Infantry Regiment, continued to send out expeditions from Camp Watson, which was something like the center
of the wheel from which the spokes extended. Farther to the east,
Company B, with part of Company A—reinforced by the men
consolidated from Companies D, E, and F—provided the subdistrict of Boise with a much-needed mounted force.

Captain Small, Lieutenant Hand, and their patrol did not return
to Camp Watson until July 8, rejoining the rest of their Company G
comrades. The men missed the celebratory firing of the cannon,
and the officers missed a reunion with Hobart and Pepoon. Small
put the other Company G men back into the field just three days
later and issued orders sending part of Company H of the Oregon Infantry into the field the next day. Though there were some
deviations, this was the routine they followed for the remainder of
the summer and fall. A slight change in the routine for the shorter
patrols occurred when Lieutenant Hand was sent out to link up
with Lt. John Bowen. Hand led the few remaining members of
Company F from near the mostly abandoned mining boom town
of Auburn, Oregon, south of present-day Baker City.[83] Both forces
returned to Camp Watson on August 20.[84]

The addition of Bowen and his handful of men was not the only
change in manpower that occurred at Camp Watson in the late
summer. Company K, First Oregon Infantry Regiment, arrived
on August 11, scheduled to replace Captain Williams's Company H,
some of which had been ordered south to a camp on Willow

Creek along the Boise Road. The rest of the company remained on extended reconnaissance. Then on August 26, the acting assistant quartermaster, Lieutenant Noble, received orders transferring him to Fort Walla Walla.[85] While changes in manpower were authorized losses, more troubling was the steady drip of desertions. Most of the time a single person deserted, but occasionally a pair left their posts. Some were captured, others not, but having to pursue the deserters taxed already worn horses and tired men. The deserters came more frequently from the infantry commands and not the cavalry, which had served at Camp Watson since the end of the previous year. By summer 1865 only the committed members of Company G remained.[86]

Even as the temperatures dropped, the men at Camp Watson remained active throughout the fall. In September, during a planned joint infantry-cavalry operation, Lieutenant Bowen led a patrol to upper Silver Creek, not far from the Silvies River. His patrol came across three Indians, who fled at the sight of the cavalrymen, but Bowen's men killed two of them before they could escape and captured the third one. The captive was killed during an escape attempt.[87] The Paiutes retaliated; attacks continued and were not limited to civilians. On October 22 two privates were attacked on the Canyon City Road between Cottonwood and Camp Watson. Both were severely wounded in the melee, and two Indians were killed before the soldiers abandoned their wagon and team of mules. Such incidents kept Small's command so busy, he could not mount a reconnaissance until November 13, the last major effort of the year, because he "did not have a sufficient number of men to go in pursuit of the Indians."[88]

In mid-November Captain Small found himself in a bind. With no other officers then at Camp Watson, he could not lead a pursuit of a group of Snake raiders attempting to steal livestock from Cottonwood Station. Small's challenge turned into an opportunity for 1st Sgt. George Garber. Small ordered Garber to lead twenty-two Company G cavalrymen in pursuit of the raiders. Four days later Garber's patrol found "about twenty-five or thirty Indians camped upon the west side of the South Fork John Day's river, near the upper crossing of the road leading from Yreka, Cal. to Canyon City." The weather was in an "awful state" as Sergeant Garber took the point with eight of his men and attacked the camp. Garber was hit in the initial exchange of fire, the intensity of which drew the rest of the patrol to the scene. The sustained fire from the cavalrymen killed four or five of the Indians and wounded eight or nine others. They abandoned their camp and fled to survive. The troopers found blankets, furs, a large quantity of ammunition, and an estimated six thousand pounds of dried meat; this was clearly a winter encampment for this band. Before leaving with the wounded Garber, they burned everything.[89]

The patrol retraced its path back toward Cottonwood Station while sending an express rider to Camp Watson to inform Captain Small of what had happened. Small took eight men as well as the post doctor and immediately raced to meet up with the patrol. Contact was made beyond the stage station on November 18. There was nothing the surgeon could do for Garber, who had been shot in the bowels. He died the next day.[90] Small stated that he wanted to take up the pursuit of the Indians, but "the jaded condition of [his] animals," he explained, "and the awful state of the weather would not permit of [his] going out again."[91] For the men stationed at Camp Watson for another winter, it was a depressing end to the campaigning season.

Lieutenant Hobart's consolidated companies had been equally busy once they reached Fort Boise. The merging of Companies D, E, and F gave Hobart more than one hundred men, which was a much-needed addition to Lt. Col. John Drake's Boise subdistrict. Hobart's consolidated command reached the fort in early June, whereupon it was allowed to rest and recuperate from its 350-mile overland ride from Fort Dalles. With Idaho Territorial governor Caleb Lyon demanding action to protect miners and guard the road to Boise, Drake was eager to "hurry Lieutenant Hobart into the field with the utmost dispatch."[92] Once rested Drake sent Hobart and a portion of his force out to establish a camp southwest of the fort as a base of operations on both sides of the Oregon–Idaho Territory border. This was the post Hobart named Camp Lyon, located about sixty miles southwest of Fort Boise and less than a mile from the border with Oregon. As one of his troopers recalled, "This was our headquarters, and from there we scouted the country in every direction, and some times were near two hundred miles from our headquarters."[93]

During one of the first patrols from the new camp, Hobart led his men in pursuit of a group of Paiute raiders accused of stealing horses from whites in Silver City, Idaho Territory. Begun at the end of June, the pursuit went on for eight days of hard riding before they reached the Malheur River, near what is now the boundary between Grant and Baker Counties. With a hint of sarcasm, one trooper wrote, "Had a jolly time chasing them over rocks and sage brush," wearing down their mounts so much that Hobart ordered the command to lay over for a day to rest. That gave the Paiutes, reportedly led by Chiefs Winnemucca and Weahwewa, an opportunity to gather their numbers and surround Hobart's camp. The Paiutes fired a fusillade of shots into the camp, causing a chaotic situation as some cavalrymen loaded the mountain howitzer with deadly grapeshot and others mounted and prepared to drive off the attackers. As had been the case in 1864, the presence of the artillery piece prevented the situation from going very badly for Hobart's command. The mountain howitzer helped neutralize the Indians' larger force, which one trooper believed outnumbered Hobart's command roughly six to one. The grapeshot proved lethal whenever the Paiutes gathered together. The combination of the artillery piece and the mounted counterattack killed an estimated dozen Paiutes. A running fight ensued once the Indians gave up the attack on the camp and fled.[94]

Although they had driven off their attackers, two of the cavalrymen had been wounded, and the command was in the precarious position of being a long way from their temporary base. Worse, according to one of the troopers, Lieutenant Hobart had shown considerable incompetence and a bit of cowardice during the thirty-minute firefight. The nearly two-hundred-mile return to Camp Lyon was brutal for the two wounded men, who had been placed on impromptu litters. For nine days the wounded men suffered, to the point that one trooper remembered, "Often did [William] Phillips beg us to kill him." Once they reached Camp Lyon, Hobart sent an express rider to Fort Boise to bring the surgeon back to remove the bullet. Miraculously, the more seriously wounded Private Phillips survived the long period before Dr. Cochrane arrived and removed the bullet. Both men recovered well enough to shortly return to duty.[95]

The command rested for two weeks before setting out on a number of patrols during the month of July, one of which extended south into California. While they chased after some Indians, they never encountered any during July. Some of the troopers were also detailed to escort a load of quartz to Yuba City, Idaho Territory. Early in August a detachment of Oregon troopers found a Paiute camp on the Owyhee River. They immediately attacked, quickly killing two men and then shooting an elderly man who had tried to swim the river to escape, at which point "one of the boys went over and scalped him, as he said, 'just for fun,'" illustrating that whites were capable of the barbarity they decried about Indians. Other expeditions spun out from Camp Lyon, but there were no additional encounters with the Paiutes during the waning days of the operational season. Finally, just before abandoning their camp and returning to Fort Boise, scouts reported an encampment with roughly twenty lodges seventy-five miles south of Camp Lyon. A detachment was sent out to investigate. After a rough and cold ride through snow and over rocky terrain, the patrol came so near the site where the scouts had spotted the encampment that the Oregon troopers were not allowed to start fires. The next morning, they moved to the edge of where the camp was said to be, only to find "nothing more than twenty huge rocks lying in such a manner as to resemble a camp with lodges in rows in the Indian mode." Although Hobart's men had engaged in a number of skirmishes during his 1865 campaign, this was an appropriately symbolic conclusion to their efforts. As one of his men admitted, "It was a long time before the boys heard the last of the Owyhee sell."[96]

Lieutenant Hobart was not the only officer with the merged force of Oregon Cavalry at Fort Boise. The amalgamated command included Company E's Lt. James L. Currey and supply officer Lt. Silas Pepoon, which allowed Lieutenant Colonel Drake to send out another contingent elsewhere while Hobart worked out of Camp Lyon. Drake had sent Lieutenant Currey with a contingent of cavalry along the road to Rock Creek Station. In early August Indian raiders stole some of the beeves from Currey's herd and horses from the station. Currey pursued with twenty men, eventually overtaking the raiders, who killed two of the beeves before abandoning the rest and fleeing into the scrub brush. The lieutenant, according to some civilians who accompanied the force, refused to rush the brush, opting to attempt to surround them. The attempt failed and the Indians escaped, leaving Currey in possession of the stolen horses and the two surviving beeves. The civilians wanted to keep up the pursuit, but Currey demurred, sending a sergeant and seven men with them but keeping the rest with him. According to the civilians, after another six miles, five soldiers tired of what they felt was a pointless effort and gave up the pursuit. The civilians and the three remaining soldiers continued and did eventually catch up with the Indians. After a quick skirmish, they killed three of the raiders, while the rest got away. Again the civilians proved they were just as savage as they accused the Indians of being, scalping the three corpses. The local press mocked the soldiers for Currey's performance. It was a far cry from his good service as a subordinate officer the previous year.[97]

Increasingly, the new Oregon Infantry were taking over the responsibilities of their mounted comrades. While the infantry could not keep pace with the usually mounted Snakes—whether they were Northern Paiutes, Bannocks, or Northern Shoshones—military forces were closing in from all directions. As the Oregon Cavalry units conducted their final operations, California and Nevada volunteers pressed from the south, and Oregon infantrymen spread out throughout the eastern part of Oregon and southwestern Idaho. Finally, after the final Confederates surrendered by June, the end of the Civil War freed up forces for service in the Pacific Northwest.

The arrival of the Second Battalion of the Fourteenth Infantry Regiment at Fort Vancouver in December marked the transition away from almost exclusively volunteers who had taken over the military responsibilities in early 1862.[98]

The end of the Civil War meant it would be economically prudent to start dismissing the roughly two million volunteers who had been called up to crush the rebellion. This included the troops in the Far West. On October 9, 1865, the War Department ordered Major General Halleck to "muster out all volunteers on the Pacific coast, as many as possible, at once." Halleck let the War Department know this was not possible regarding the remaining Oregon cavalrymen, telling his superiors plainly, "This cavalry can not be mustered out until some other comes to take its place" because "the services of mounted troops are absolutely necessary."[99] Despite Halleck's urgent need for mounted troops, there was little he could do to retain a good portion of the only cavalry in the Department of the Columbia. Knowing enlistments for most of the men in Company G would expire in March and April, the majority of them were ordered to Fort Vancouver for the last months of their service. The enlistments were also up for the handful of men who had enlisted in the other companies in 1863. Further indication that the professionals were taking over occurred when half of the forty-seven men who had enlisted in mid-1865 were discharged before the start of the 1866 operational season. Only those who had volunteered during the prior enlistment push in late 1864 and early 1865 remained. Some Company A and C men remained at Fort Klamath, but most of the others wintered at Fort Boise, where one of them remembered, "We had a very pleasant time and little to do until spring."[100]

The men were not the only ones leaving the service. Colonel Currey resigned in November. Maj. William V. Rinehart, formerly a captain in the cavalry but serving in the Oregon Infantry since early 1865, would resign later in the year after being censured by the War Department for initiating a winter campaign. Currey was

a long and vocal proponent of the strategy, something Rinehart
called a "bold move," which he boasted "was in fact 'the beginning of the end' of our Indian troubles."[101] Although Currey did
not stay to see things through, there were ten camps established
in the heart of where the Paiutes wintered. With only a handful
of Oregon cavalrymen remaining, manning the camps fell to the
infantry, which was good for the cavalry, since "it was a winter of
severe cold."[102]

    As had been increasingly the case at the end of 1865, the infantry
did more of the work in 1866. Still, the few remaining cavalrymen
were active, if only briefly, once the weather permitted. Rinehart,
who closed out his military career as the commanding officer at
Fort Klamath, had the two most experienced officers at his disposal. Captain Kelly, whose career in the Oregon Cavalry was
just about over, still had over twenty-five Company C men. Captain McCall still had the men who volunteered in 1865 in his
Company A. There were also two companies of infantry at the
fort, which gave the major a potent force to work with once
the snow melted enough in the mountains to permit their use. Fortunately for the cavalrymen, the weather had only started to break
when the War Department's order dismissing most of the volunteers was actualized. The enlistments for the remaining members
of Company C expired on May 21. Captain McCall remained for
several weeks longer, but he had no force to command. Captain
Kelly accepted a captain's commission in the U.S. Cavalry and also
left by the start of summer.[103]

    The winter and spring did not pass as quietly for the remain-
ing troopers at either Camp Watson or Fort Boise. Not every man
stationed at those locations lived to be mustered out with their
comrades. The long winter and access to alcohol led to the death
of Company A's Pvt. Thomas Shea. Shea had been placed in the
guardhouse for desertion and was awaiting his trial when the prisoners somehow obtained "whiskey" and "got on a glorious drunk"
and ran off the guard on December 27, 1865. The drunk prisoners,
"some of them . . . being almost like maniacs," apparently took the
guard's weapons, barricaded themselves in the guardhouse, and

threatened to shoot anyone who tried to arrest them. The threat proved hollow when a force of thirty men broke open the door and stormed inside. In the chaos Shea was shot and killed.[104]

Shea was not the only Oregon trooper killed in the Fort Boise guardhouse. On April 9, 1866, Pvt. Perry McCord was shot and killed in a bizarre sequence of events that started days before. An accused murderer was taken to the Fort Boise guardhouse in an attempt to prevent vigilantes from hanging him. Somehow the lynch mob managed to get to the guardhouse and take the prisoner, who they lynched. The incident set the military guard on edge, so when Private McCord rushed into the guardhouse unannounced one night, the guard shot him as he came in, killing him. McCord's death was "a sad affair" in the words of one trooper stationed at Fort Boise.[105]

McCord's tragic death occurred as the remaining cavalrymen were about to begin their first field service of the year. Attacks on regional ranchers and miners in southwestern Idaho Territory and below the border in Nevada increased in the early months of the year. Numerous stage stations were attacked, livestock was stolen, and buildings and supplies were burned. In early March two miners on their way to the Owyhee mines were killed, their bodies mutilated. In response the new commander at Fort Boise, Maj. Louis Marshall, Fourteenth U.S. Infantry Regiment, led a patrol to find the perpetrators. Marshall had replaced Lieutenant Colonel Drake after the latter was promoted to Department of the Columbia commander in November 1865.[106] His column marched south toward the Bruneau River but only found a camp of unarmed and unidentified Indians.[107] As incidents continued, Marshall sent periodic patrols to the sites of the reported Indian attacks but did not encounter any raiders.

There were so few Oregon cavalrymen remaining in the Boise subdistrict that they mostly accompanied bodies of infantry as scouts. Responding to news that a group of brigands made up of both whites and Indians was attacking travelers along the Snake River, a patrol made up of men from Company D, Fourteenth U.S. Infantry, accompanied by ten Oregon cavalrymen set out to find the criminals. They were given authority to execute them on sight. Once again, they failed to find those responsible for the attacks. This was typical of the remaining Oregon troopers' last months of service.[108]

In mid-May reports came in of large groups of Chinese miners being killed by a band of Paiutes led by Chief Pony Blanket on the Owyhee River. Other Chinese miners were attacked in Battle Creek Canyon, not far from the Owyhee. They were particularly vulnerable because they had no sense of the dangers in the region and because whites were reluctant to sell them firearms.[109] The boldness of the attacks on the largely defenseless Chinese led Major Marshall to send an expedition of thirty-five men heading southwest to the Jordan Creek area. From there they continued toward the Owyhee, long considered a hot spot of Snake activity. At the same time, the veteran campaigner, Lt. Silas Pepoon, led a force of almost fifty Oregon cavalrymen from the consolidated companies out from Camp Lyon to the spot where the miners had been massacred. After seeing to it that they were buried (a task done by fellow Chinese miners), he led his men to meet up with Marshall and the infantry. On May 27 the combined infantry and cavalry force encountered a large group of Indians numbering several hundred—including women and children. The two bodies began firing at each other from opposite sides of the Owyhee River. Marshall moved his men down the river to find a place to cross and get behind the Indians. Using a rudimentary raft, half the men crossed before their mountain howitzer broke the raft apart. The howitzer sank into the river, and Marshall was left with part of his already outnumbered force on each side of the river.[110]

After building another raft on the night of May 27, he ferried the rest of his men to the east side of the river the next morning. Marshall sent two Oregon troopers to ride up out of the gorge and find a path out for the rest of the command. As the two men reached the top, a crash of gunfire erupted, bringing down both of their horses. One of the men was able to escape, but Pvt. William B. Phillips, who was one of the rare veterans who reenlisted,

"was lassoed and drawn up over the cliff in sight of the command," according to one of the mounted men at the riverside.[111]
He was never seen again, nor was his body recovered.[112] Lieutenant
Pepoon gathered ten men and prepared to try to at least retrieve
his body, but Major Marshall ordered him to stand down. Correctly believing his force was in real trouble, with the Owyhee
at their back and being fired on by a vastly larger body of Paiutes
than his own, Marshall focused on getting out of his precarious
position. The men recrossed the river on the rebuilt raft during
the night and retreated toward Camp Lyon, which they reached
on June 1. Unfortunately, four men did not make it across. By
the time Marshall became aware, he did not feel he could send
anyone back for them. It was a bitter end to what was, for most
of them, their last field service before being discharged.

The 1866 operational season was brief for the other Oregon
Cavalry company still in service. After its second winter at Camp
Watson, Company G was in no condition to mount patrols,
deferring to the infantry commands at the fort. Captain Small
reported, "Owing to the poor state in which we found our horses
and the almost daily diminution of the company from the expira-
tions of their terms of service and the severity of the weather, no
scouting was done until the month of March."[113] The few scouts
conducted by the remaining men from Company G were unre-
markable except that Pvt. John McLaughlin "drowned by falling off his horse in crossing the South Fork of John Day river,
while on a scout with Lieut Dichtl" on April 20.[114] He was one
of three Oregon troopers to drown while in service. The reduc-
tions reached an extreme point in April, "the company being
reduced to fifteen men, for duty." Captain Small told department
headquarters, "It was perfectly useless to attempt doing anything
toward hunting Indians with that number of troops." With most of
the Oregon troopers already discharged, the military concurred. The
last Company G men were ordered to Fort Vancouver on May 10
for discharge.[115]

By June there were only a few Oregon cavalrymen left in the
Boise subdistrict. They were the last members of the First Oregon

Volunteer Cavalry Regiment still active. Still, Major Marshall had declared his determination to return and hound the Indians who had defeated his force on the Owyhee (and presumably retrieve his cannon from the bottom of the river) until they gave up. The Oregon Cavalry did not, however, join any such operation. By the time he sent new patrols chasing reports of Snake attacks, the enlistment for all but a few of the Company B men had expired; the very last troopers still serving were discharged by August 11.[116] After almost six years, the First Oregon Volunteer Cavalry Regiment had finally ceased to exist.

Many things had changed for the Oregon Cavalry after the expiration of the original enlistments in late 1864 and early 1865. The regiment, which had never been filled to full strength, was reduced to slightly more than a battalion, stripped of many of its veteran officers, and increasingly serving alongside volunteer infantry and eventually U.S. Army Regulars. During its last twenty months of existence, the remaining members of the old regiment were asked to do much more militarily with considerably less manpower. They were often distributed out to smaller camps from which they carried out shorter scouts, frequently in joint operations with infantry. They were simply needed in too many places, and their numbers were so reduced that they could not engage in long campaigns like the first three years. Also, twelve troopers died during those last twenty months; some were killed in combat, some died from disease and sickness, and some through accidents. That was 40 percent of all Oregon cavalry fatalities. In that sense, the final months of its existence were especially costly. Except for Lieutenant (eventually Captain) McCall's escort of the Central Military Road survey, the Oregon Cavalry's role in exploration ended in 1864. While few of the men who mustered out in 1865 or 1866 served as long as the original enlistees, they could easily agree with Captain Drake's sentiment about his service: "Three years in succession appropriated to this kind of service is sufficient for most anyone."[117] For most men, it was more than enough, but those who wrote about their service in the Oregon Cavalry did not regret it. It was their way to serve the Union cause, if obscurely and from afar. So when the last few men mustered out of the shell of the First Oregon Volunteer Cavalry Regiment and put on civilian clothes, they undoubtedly were relieved to be out of the service, but over time they appreciated what they had done in the far corner of the Union during and beyond the Civil War.

NINE

To the End of Their Days

Whether they were one of the first to enlist in the First Oregon Volunteer Cavalry Regiment or joined in early 1865, every trooper who chose to was a civilian again by September 1, 1866. With the exception of the few who joined the Regular Army, they melted back into civilian life. By the time the last Oregon trooper, John McDonald, died in 1938, the former cavalrymen's experiences had varied as much as the men themselves. Over the course of their lives, they worked in a wide variety of fields, and while most remained in the Pacific Northwest, especially Oregon, others scattered throughout the country, thereby influencing the development of many parts of the nation. Some found incredible economic success, while others struggled on the opposite end of the spectrum, battling to live marginal lives. Numerous former troopers played important sociopolitical roles on a regional stage, with a few even achieving some national importance and influence. Most, however, became hardworking members of their local communities, even beloved by their neighbors, but anonymous in the grand historical sense. What became of most of them is unknown; they have been obscured by the passage of time. It is, nonetheless, possible to reconstruct the postwar lives of enough of them to have a sense of what happened to the rest.

After being discharged "every man went his separate way, many of them to never meet again," remembered one Company A trooper.[1] Some returned home as quickly as they could, while others, less sure about their plans, drifted about. Sgt. John Dimick, from Company B, may have had the best start to his postservice life. After taking a boat ride to Oregon City on his return trip home, he and a group of discharged veterans were met by civilians "at the dock, headed by a band of music, [which] escorted them to Washington Hall, where a sumptuous feast and hearty welcome home greeted them all."[2] J. Henry Brown, another Company B veteran, immediately headed home to Salem once discharged, where he became a clerk for the state legislature at the beginning of the next session.[3] Unlike Brown or Dimick, William Byars, another Salem-area veteran, lounged around Portland for two weeks before getting a cousin to take him home.[4]

During the seventy-six years between the resignation of Benjamin F. Harding in early 1862 and the death of trooper John McDonald in 1938, the majority of former Oregon cavalrymen remained in Oregon. Though they lived, worked, and eventually died in almost every part of the state, most ex-troopers, like the majority of the state's population, lived on the north–south line between Portland and Jacksonville, just above the California border. The possible exception was the brutal southeastern corner, which so many of them rode over—and generally disliked. John Drake was one of the many who lived out their lives in the northwestern part of the state, in the Portland area. During his lifetime he worked as a store clerk, a state labor official, and for many years, a purchasing agent for the Oregon Railroad and Navigation Company.[5] John T. Apperson, a good friend to so many of his brother officers, lived nearby in Oregon City.[6] Cpl. Enoch Churchill, a Company B trooper, was one of a number of the regiment's veterans who settled in Salem. His father, Joseph, also a Company B veteran and one of the regiment's oldest members, also lived in Salem.[7] George Riddle, a trooper in Company C, settled farther south in Riddle, a southwestern town named after one of his brothers.[8] Teenager Jasper Roberts, who enlisted in February 1865 and mustered out on July 26, 1866, lived near Canyonville during the last thirty-five years of his life.[9] Former sergeants William Colvig and W. T. Leever both established themselves in Medford, less

P15. Former Company C trooper Judge William M. Colvig.
Southern Oregon Historical Society, Medford, #1360.

than thirty miles north of the California line, after their respec-
tive discharges.[10] Morgan L. Peden, a deserter from Company E,
lived even closer to the California border, in Jacksonville, for many
years before moving into the state's Soldiers Home.[11]

Even though most of the men who remained in the Pacific
Northwest lived on the western slope of the mountains in Oregon,

others established themselves elsewhere. George B. Currey, the aggressive captain whose meteoric rise ended when he served as Department of the Columbia commander before resigning his commission in 1865, ultimately settled in La Grande, in northeast Oregon. There he worked as a lawyer and ran a newspaper. During one of the phases of his multifaceted career, former Company A trooper John L. Sperry served as a sheriff in Pendleton, about sixty miles northwest of La Grande.[12] Simon Bolivar Carthcart, who had served as a corporal alongside Sperry in Company A, lived nearly as far west as one could go and still be in Oregon. He settled in Coos Bay, a Pacific Ocean inlet a little more than halfway between the Columbia River and the California border. While living there it is possible Carthcart ran into Company D trooper Orvil Dodge or Company A man Alexander Stauff. The tall, dark-haired Stauff served in many different positions in the area after leaving the service, including as county assessor, deputy sheriff, and deputy customs collector.[13] Dodge ran a general store in Coos Bay for a number of years.[14] Some, like William V. Rinehart, relocated to Washington. Rinehart became a pioneer for a second time when he settled in Seattle before Washington achieved statehood. As the Oregon Cavalry veterans spread throughout the state and into nearby states such as Washington, Montana, and California after their enlistments ended, their contributions were felt throughout the Far West.

One of the reasons so many former Oregon cavalrymen remained in the Pacific Northwest (and more broadly the Far West) was the same as what drew them there before the war. As the region's population, economy, and even political power grew, it was clear the Pacific Northwest burgeoned with potential after the Civil War. During the next forty years, lands that had been frontier in the 1860s gave way to towns, cities, and counties, which in turn resulted in Montana (1889), Washington (1889), and Idaho (1890) becoming states. Those places needed energetic people with unbreakable wills to help them develop. Many Oregon Cavalry veterans helped fill those needs—at every level, from small towns to state legislatures, and in a wide array of occupations. It was a successful marriage of need and opportunity, which benefited both the region and many of the veterans.

Between the end of the Civil War and the turn of the century, many of Oregon's state legislators, county officials, and city and town leaders were men who had once ridden in the First Oregon Volunteer Cavalry Regiment. Initially, it was the regiment's senior leaders, men already well established, who moved (back) into politics, but steadily over the next four decades, both junior officers and troopers became political leaders as well. Although none of them ever became governor, many found their way to the Oregon state legislature at one time or another. One former trooper served as a U.S. ambassador and another spent time in the U.S. Senate. More served in civic positions in their local communities as commissioners, sheriffs, and mayors. This was not unique to the Pacific Northwest; five of the seven presidents between Grant and McKinley were Civil War combat veterans. However, given the apathy the post–Civil War generation had about the Oregon troopers' service, it is somewhat surprising. In those early days after the war, service in the Oregon regiments did not carry a great deal of sociopolitical weight by itself; however, having survived the trials and dangers of service on the frontier for three years (or more, for a few) imbued some with an unconquerable confidence in themselves and a desire to help develop their communities and states.

The first to go into politics after leaving the Oregon Cavalry were the ones who had already held political positions before the war. Recruiting volunteers in the dash to fill the Union ranks led to a marriage of necessity between local politicians and the federal government (and its military leadership). The government needed to raise troops as quickly as possible to fight the Confederacy (or in the case of the Far West, to exercise additional power after the Regulars were transferred to the war). Therefore, it asked governors to select men to recruit regiments. Speaking to crowds and stirring them into a patriotic fervor came as second nature to good politicians, so governors leaned heavily on their state political leaders, particularly the ones from their own party.

Military service, as most politicians knew, usually had tremendous political value when running for office in the future. Holding on to a military rank for the remainder of their lives was well
worth the time spent in uniform, which was short for some by
design.[15] The wave of high-ranking commissions given to political leaders, especially during the first year of the war, attests to the
mutually beneficial partnership of that relationship. Some famous,
politically motived commissions worked out well, while others were
disastrous. John Logan, a U.S. House of Representatives member
from Illinois, was among the former, while Massachusetts political opportunist and prewar governor Nathaniel Banks was one
of the many poor choices. Both became prominent politicians after
the war. The Far West was no different. When the War Department outflanked Governor Whiteaker by asking Oregon senator
Baker to oversee the recruiting, he asked fellow politicians to do
the actual work of establishing the regiment. Reuben Maury was
seen as the military man among the original three officers, but both
Thomas Cornelius and Benjamin F. Harding were well-established
politicians by the fall of 1861, and both reentered politics almost
immediately after resigning their commissions.

Thomas Cornelius had been chosen as the regiment's first commanding officer because he was a successful Oregon pioneer who
had served in both the political and military arenas long before
being appointed colonel of the regiment. During his brief tenure
in command, he served dutifully as an administrator overseeing
his dispersed companies from his headquarters at Fort Walla Walla
before resigning in July 1862. He might have remained longer had
there not been friction with his superior. In an age when militia rank was carried throughout a man's political career, Thomas
Cornelius was already addressed as "Colonel" for leading militia
forces during the 1855 fighting against the Yakima people (he held
a lesser position in the so-called Cayuse War in 1848). His time
in the Oregon Cavalry did little to enhance his already considerable political standing, nor was it an impediment. He returned
immediately to the Oregon senate after resigning his commission and served until 1876, when he moved, with his second wife

and children, to an area in Washington County known as Free Orchard, west of Portland. Although he later ran as the Republican gubernatorial candidate in 1886 and lost, he focused his energies on building up his holdings, particularly after a railroad line was constructed through the area. Before his 1899 death, he had established the town of Cornelius, where he owned a sawmill, warehouse, and a 1,500-acre farm.[16] During the thirty-seven years between his resignation and death, Thomas Cornelius helped the maturing state not only as a political leader but also as a businessman and town builder.

Benjamin F. Harding also continued a political career very quickly after his short service in the Oregon Cavalry. Unlike Colonel Cornelius and many other former troopers who served at the state level, Harding represented Oregon on the national political scene in the U.S. Senate. Benjamin F. Harding had made no secret that his involvement with the regiment was purely temporary, so when a political opportunity arose, he resigned in December 1861 (accepted in January 1862).[17] The Oregon legislature had yet to permanently fill the Senate seat vacated by Edward Baker after he was killed at the October 1861 Battle of Ball's Bluff, Virginia. After resigning from the cavalry, Harding, who had served in both the territorial and first state legislature, began maneuvering to take over from a temporary appointee and fill the remainder of Baker's seat. Lobbying as a Democrat to replace the martyred Republican senator probably made it more challenging than it should have been for Harding (some were wary about both senators being Democrats; James Nesmith was the other senator). Nonetheless, after thirty votes, the legislature selected him to replace Baker on September 12, 1862. Surprisingly, given his political scheming to get the senate seat, he left the U.S. Senate at the end of the term in March 1865 and returned to Oregon, never to hold a political office again. This effectively ended his political contribution to the developing region. He lived a quiet life on his farm near Salem before moving to Cottage Grove, south of Eugene, where he died in 1899. His transition out of the public arena was so complete that when he died, state newspapers hardly mentioned his passing.[18]

Only one other member of the Oregon Cavalry rose as far in the political arena as Harding or sustained it as long as Cornelius, David P. Thompson. Although already a successful businessman when the war started, Thompson achieved a more spectacular rise than any of his former comrades after he left the Oregon Cavalry. The nineteen-year-old had already apprenticed with a blacksmith and learned surveying in Ohio before his long walk to Oregon Territory in 1853. Both skills served him well in the future. In the eight years before the war started, he found steady work, initially as a blacksmith and then as a surveyor for the first railroad planned for Oregon. His work as a surveyor paid great dividends in the future when he became a land speculator after the war years, benefiting from what he learned while surveying to determine the best places to lay railroad tracks and assessing the suitability of the land for development.[19]

Desperate to raise the full number of companies for the regiment, the twenty-seven-year-old successful businessman made a perfect junior officer recruiter. The start of Thompson's tenure in the Oregon Cavalry is a bit difficult to determine, since records indicate he mustered in as a member of Company F on December 28, 1861, yet he does not seem to have served a day in the company. What is clear is that he was appointed as a provisional recruiting officer, with the rank of lieutenant, in February 1862. When he failed to enlist enough men, his recruits were merged with other incomplete efforts to form a full company, leaving him supernumerary. He officially left the service in 1863. His failed foray into military service was one of the very few endeavors that were not (spectacular) successes during his busy life.[20]

Despite his continued focus on economic opportunities, Thompson steadily became more involved in politics after the war. In 1866 he was elected to the state senate, a seat he held until 1872. That same year he became manager of the Oregon City Woolen Manufacturing Company. He remained concurrently busy in both arenas for the rest of his life. Eventually he served two nonconsecutive terms as mayor of Portland before being appointed governor of Idaho Territory. Later he returned to the Oregon legislature, but in the lower house in 1882 and again in 1889. In 1892 President

Benjamin Harrison appointed him minister to the Ottoman Empire. He served for a year before returning home in 1893. During this same period, he became active in railroads and transportation. He eventually became director of the Oregon Railway and Navigation Company. He also owned part of the Sterling Mine Company in southern Oregon and served on the boards of over a dozen banks before retiring in 1891. His enormous financial success enabled him to generously support charities and especially education in the state at both the primary and collegiate levels. He retired from politics after returning from his ambassador's post in 1892. In 1901 he and his wife embarked on a trip around the world, but poor health forced him to return to Portland, where he died in December of that year. Ironically, though he failed in his recruiting efforts for the Oregon Cavalry, David P. Thompson was the most successful member of the regiment in the decades after their service. His work with the railroads contributed greatly to the development of the state, just as his patronage and promotion of education helped create a new generation of leaders.[21]

Although none of his former comrades approached David P. Thompson's postwar achievements, opportunity abounded throughout the West after the war, and many ex-troopers took full advantage of it. Some eventually shared the stage with their former leaders as they guided their towns and cities into the future. Men like John Dimick, Louis T. Barin, and Peter Gates typified those whose persistence and hard work enabled them to take full advantage of the growing opportunities after the war, which in turn led them into public office. John Dimick, who inherited his father's farm, was held in such regard by his neighbors that they elected him to three terms in the Oregon legislature, first to the house as a Republican in 1886, then in 1900 and 1902 to the senate as a Democrat.[22] While in the state senate, he had a public spat with a writer at the *Oregonian* about honoring Oregon's Civil War regiments. That confrontation helped fuel the creation of the Association of the First Oregon Cavalry and First Oregon Infantry Volunteers.

Former sergeants Louis T. Barin and Peter Gates were just as involved in the state's political activities as Dimick, and at more levels. Barin, who was from Rhode Island and descended from Polish immigrants, was one of the many ex-cavalrymen who became a lawyer after the conclusion of his service. He served in the Oregon House in 1872, then as the prosecuting attorney for Oregon City in 1874 and 1875 before being elected its mayor. He was later elected to the state senate and appointed a U.S. marshal in 1890. Described as heavyset and of middling height, it was not entirely surprising when he died from a heart attack on his way back to Portland after visiting his farm on April 18, 1904.[23] Pennsylvania-born Peter Gates had a similarly varied public career before an untimely death. After circumstances prevented him from accepting a commission in the Fifth U.S. Infantry, he was elected sheriff of Yamhill County in 1868 and reelected in 1870. Sixteen years after he stepped down as sheriff, he was elected Yamhill County treasurer and then to the state senate in 1890. He did not seek reelection when his term expired. He might have returned to public service later, as others had, but he was killed when a tree fell on him in August 1894.[24]

These men and many others participated in state and local government for more than four decades after they left the Oregon Cavalry. However, the majority contributed to the development of the region in their own communities, such as the red-haired Benton Killin, who had been a corporal in Company B, and William Byars, who enlisted in 1865. After his service ended, Byars finished the college education that had been interrupted when he enlisted in the Oregon Cavalry in March 1865. After completing his degree, he had a short career in education, including serving as the superintendent for the Douglas County Schools, before transitioning to surveying. He eventually served as the state's surveyor general for a time before finally settling into the newspaper business, first running Roseburg's *Plaindealer*, then the *Oregon Statesman* in Salem. He also found time to briefly serve as commandant of Roseburg's Soldiers Home. His busy life ended on April 22, 1922.[25]

The Illinois-born Killin brothers, Benton and Thomas B., represented the locally engaged experience common among most of their former comrades after the war years. With one exception,

when President McKinley sent him to Alaska Territory to assess
the ability to grow certain crops there, Benton Killin focused his
energies in northwestern Oregon. After his enlistment expired,
he earned a law degree from Pacific University. He then served
two years as school superintendent for Clackamas County before
fully embarking on his legal career. He quickly became a busy
lawyer with a firm in Oregon City, where he specialized in real
estate law for two decades before declining health forced him to
retire in 1892. The combination of his public service and a highly
regarded legal career made him a prominent person in Oregon
City until his death in 1905.[26] Thomas Killin, who joined Company G with his younger brother, served eight years as a Clackamas County commissioner, from 1890 to 1898.[27]

"Captain" John T. Apperson also held local and state political
office during his long life. The appellation *captain* reflected his prewar occupation as a steamboat captain on the Willamette River
and not any military rank, which did not exceed first lieutenant.
After his enlistment expired in April 1865, Apperson returned,
briefly, to steam boating.[28] In addition to his career piloting a
steamboat, he retained an interest in farming held since his youth.
Later in life he found a way to support agricultural development
while working for many years as a public servant. Not long after
the end of the Civil War, he served one term each in the state house
(1870 term) and later the state senate (elected in 1878) and held
the office of sheriff in Oregon City during the years between the
two terms. A firm believer in the importance of education, Apperson served on the state board of education for ten years. He was
also a member of the Oregon Agricultural College's (now Oregon
State University) board of regents for thirty-one years, six of those
as president. Not only did he and his wife fund an educational
scholarship; after they died—he passed away in April 1917 and his
wife, Mary, died six years later—they bequeathed their estate to
the college.[29] As one writer put it while Apperson was still alive,
"His interest in the growth and development of his adopted state
is sincere." In what could have been said about many of his comrades and not just about Apperson, the writer made it clear "it is

P16. Former Company G trooper Judge Benton Killin. Oregon Historical
Society, Cartes-de-visite Collection; Org. Lot 500; b4.f610-5; OrHi 3248.

to such men that the present generation owes a debt of gratitude that will never be paid."[30]

Supporting the educational system in the states where they lived provided another avenue for Oregon's ex-cavalrymen to help the state grow and modernize. Some taught in the classroom or worked as school administrators, others served on various educational boards, and some did a combination of all three. Some former soldiers engaged at the primary school level, while others supported regional colleges. Like John Apperson, Benton Killin also served on the Oregon Agricultural College board after retiring from his law practice. As noted, John Dimick and William Byars both taught school.[31] Maj. Sewell Truax taught school in Massachusetts in the early 1850s and in Oregon Territory a few years later.[32] Company D's Francis Marion Brown also taught school for a time, although in Missouri; William Colvig taught in Illinois before his return to Oregon.[33] Eli T. Boone and his brother-in-law Joseph Pepoon taught school before migrating to Oregon on the eve of the Civil War and did so again after returning to the Midwest at the expiration of their service—in Nebraska.[34]

The regimental surgeons and assistant surgeons—Drs. Horace Carpenter, D. S. Holton, Edward Storror, and William H. Watkins (Dr. Dumreicher was a U.S. Army surgeon assigned to Captain Drake's 1864 expedition)—were all educated men before the war started. In Horace Carpenter's case, he earned his initial medical degree from the University of Iowa before gaining more training at the Long Island College Hospital and then in Michigan.[35] Three of the four enjoyed highly successful medical careers after leaving the Oregon Cavalry. While Dr. Holton did not rise to the heights of his medical peers, he lived near Grants Pass until his death in 1912 as a revered Oregon pioneer.[36]

While Holton contributed to his local community in multiple capacities, Drs. Watkins, Storror, and Carpenter demonstrated exemplary commitment to their profession. Dr. Watkins continued his practice in the Portland area after his service. In addition to being a general practitioner, Dr. Watkins offered specialty treatment for eyes and ears. He agreed to serve on the faculty of the short-lived Oregon Medical College. After its dissolution he served as a faculty member in Willamette University's Medical Department. He died suddenly from a heart attack during a church service in 1888.[37] Edward Storror quickly took his medical skills to a leper colony on Molokai, Hawaii, and from there tended to French officials in China before finally relocating to the San Francisco area before his 1910 death.[38] After the expiration of his enlistment, Horace Carpenter made an important impact in Oregon during his remaining twenty-three years. He helped found the Oregon State Medical Society and the Willamette University Medical Department. He served as a professor of civil and military surgery for nine years, then two years later he accepted the position as the university's first dean of faculty. He resigned from Willamette University in 1875 and moved to Portland, remaining active in the state's medical association, which he helped found. From 1883 to 1886, he served as the first superintendent of the Asylum of the Insane. Throughout it all, he remained an active surgeon, known for using what were then advanced surgical techniques. Through his support and work at Willamette University—which one admirer said, "Over that institution he has always watched with a parent's interest and care"—he helped provide a young generation of Oregonians with opportunities to further their medical careers, just as he had received.[39]

It is not surprising that a number of Oregon cavalry veterans like Dr. Carpenter actively supported education in light of how it opened doors for many of them. John Apperson was the outlier; though he strongly committed his later years to supporting Oregon Agricultural College, his progressive support for its importance may well have been tied to his own lack of education. Others had been well served by their college studies. John Dimick, J. Henry Brown, Benton Killin, and George Durham all attended Willamette University, though the latter two finished their academic careers at Pacific University in Forest Grove, Oregon. Other collegians included Byars, Louis Barin, William Colvig, and Reese Clark; Lts. James Waymire and Seth Hammer; and Maj. Sewell Truax, who graduated from Norwich University in Vermont. All

P17. Lt. Seth Hammer. Oregon Historical Society,
Cartes-de-visite Collection; Org. Lot 500; b3.f471-3.

of them enjoyed varying levels of socioeconomic success before
becoming public servants at one time or another, primarily in
local or state government.

Most former troopers, like Pennsylvania-born Francis Marion Brown and Indianan George Conn, lived quietly in their

communities, contributing in ways that did not receive publicity or garner a great deal of historical attention. Brown left Oregon soon after his service ended in December 1864 only to find his way back to the Far West. He might not have left at all after his enlistment expired except for a solemn duty he had to perform. After his discharge he headed east to recover the remains of his brother-in-law, who had been killed during the war, and brought them home to his sister in Pennsylvania. With that completed, he headed to Missouri, where after a short stint teaching, he married and started a hotel. Apparently he had not forgotten his time in the Pacific Northwest, and after selling his hotel, the family moved to Lewis County, Washington, north of Portland, in 1886. He remained there for the last twenty-four years of his life, a quiet member of his local community until his March 1910 death.[40]

George Conn, the oldest of three brothers that joined Company A in March 1865, during one of the last recruiting efforts, served just a year before the government disbanded the remnants of the regiment. All three were farming in the Melrose area, just a few miles west of Roseburg, when they enlisted. The brothers returned to farming after their brief sojourn in the cavalry. After seven years of farming, George received a patronage appointment—something that rarely happened for veterans of Oregon's two regiments. The second Grant administration appointed him recorder in the U.S. Land Office in Klamath Falls. He held the post under two more Republican presidents before resigning during the abbreviated Garfield administration to go into the mercantile business. Conn continued his mercantile business until he retired, sometime between 1910 and 1914. After retiring he relocated to Oakland, California, where he died in March 1916. As proprietor of a local mercantile store, he provided an important service to his small-town neighbors.[41]

Not every former Oregon cavalryman got the chance to take advantage of the opportunities an expanding Pacific Northwest offered the veterans from David Thompson to George Conn. Some found trouble after the conclusion of their service in the regiment. Others simply did not live long enough to participate in the growing region—and nation. Mental illness, the early onset of poor health, and premature death prohibited some veteran Oregon cavalrymen from the opportunities enjoyed by their former comrades over the years. At least one trooper continued his violent criminal behavior, landing in jail both during and after the expiration of his enlistment.

Nelson Hauxhurst, one of the few Oregon-born men in the regiment, had been in trouble with the law even before he volunteered. In fact, his questionable past followed him into the service. He was absent from Company B between April and December 1862 and then discharged because he had been jailed for burglary.[42] By the time the last Oregon volunteers were discharged, Nelson Hauxhurst was a prisoner in the state penitentiary system. According to later folklore, he stabbed two men to death on separate occasions. Whether he did kill a second person is speculative; however, he was definitely tried and convicted of manslaughter in 1865.[43] What became of Nelson Hauxhurst after he was released from the remainder of his ten-year sentence in 1870 is unknown, but all indications are that he left the region, with the folktales suggesting he went to South America. Whatever the case, there is no record he remained in Oregon. Speculation was that the mixed-race Hauxhurst, who one early Oregonian remembered as having superior intellect, with a quick mind that excelled at mathematics, became bitter over the racism that kept him from fulfilling a desire to become a doctor.[44]

Whatever the root of Hauxhurst's violent crimes, extant records show that he was an anomaly among the men who served in the First Oregon Volunteer Cavalry Regiment. Others suffered misfortune beyond their control in the years after their service. Pvt. Virgil Newsom, a Company B trooper, suffered from mental illness for decades before his death, at a time when the only treatment was to remove a person to an asylum, which is what happened to him.[45] Morgan Peden, one of Captain Currey's original recruits, who deserted two months into his service, committed suicide on the grounds of the Soldiers Home near Roseburg, Oregon, where he had been living for almost a year.[46] Adrian Nappy, who rode in

Captain Drake's Company D, suffered from increasingly degenerating health, leading him to spend several multiyear stays at various Soldiers Homes during the last twenty-plus years of his life. He died at the Columbia Falls, Montana, facility in 1916.[47] Unlike Nappy, whose ill health plagued him for multiple decades, fellow Company D trooper Zephaniah D. Bones died just five years after his service ended. Employed as a brickmaker when he enlisted, the twenty-seven-year-old's death deprived "the temperance cause . . . of the aid of a practical and earnest supporter."[48] While many veterans of the First Oregon Volunteer Cavalry Regiment found numerous ways to contribute to the communities where they lived, a few never overcame the challenges in their lives, including criminal behavior, ill health, and premature death, which kept them from sharing in the opportunities a growing region (nation) provided.

Steady emigration to the Pacific Northwest did not begin until the mid-1840s, and even then it was only a trickle. By 1866 the state was still inhabited by a white population of mostly outsiders. Therefore, it is not surprising that a number of the ex-troopers, who came from the eastern half of the country, left the region not long after their enlistments ended. Some continued their economically driven wandering, but most of them returned to where they had been living before emigrating to the West. Former Oregon troopers (re)settled in the Midwest, the plains states, and the Northeast, and at least one relocated to the Southeast. Like their comrades who remained in the Pacific Northwest, the former Oregon troopers who lived out their lives in those regions engaged in a wide variety of professions, with varying levels of success, over the next sixty years. In doing so, they impacted communities distant from where they served, just as their former comrades did throughout the Pacific Northwest.

Joseph Pepoon, who had only been in Oregon for a year when he enlisted with his brother Silas and future brother-in-law Eli Boone, did not really have a home in Oregon. So it was not surprising that he returned to the Midwest as soon as he could. At the expiration of his enlistment, he went to The Dalles and found a job clerking in a general merchandise store, waiting out the 1864–65 winter. He remained "until sometime in June 1865, when [he] started back to [his] old home in Warren, Ill."⁴⁹ Eli Boone went with him. Boone, who married Joseph's sister Eunice, along with Joseph and his new bride, Bessie, all moved to Pawnee County, Nebraska, in 1867. There Joseph and his wife established a school. Three years later he began a political journey that eventually saw him elected to the Nebraska state senate in 1877 to fill a seat vacated by his brother. The tenure of his last political office expired in 1886. Bessie died that same year, and he retreated to his farm, where he remained until 1900, when he sold it to one of his sons. He seems to have lived in semiretirement for the last twenty-one years of his life, eventually dying at a daughter's home in Lincoln, Nebraska, on August 25, 1921, at the advanced age of eighty-three.⁵⁰

Blue-eyed private George P. Ockington, who served in Company F, emigrated from much farther east than the Midwestern-born Pepoons and Boone. Ockington, who did not enlist until 1865, lived for thirty-five years after his enlistment expired in 1866. Following his separation from the Oregon Cavalry, he returned to his native New Hampshire, where he ran a store in the town of Stark. Like most of his former comrades, his life is mostly shrouded in mystery, only mentioned in the extent newspapers a few times, such as when his store burned down in January 1888. Two years later he filed for the invalid pension the government gave Union veterans. He was just fifty-two at the time. He appears to have taken the insurance money and gone into farming rather than rebuild the store. He died in 1901 in Stratford, New Hampshire. His wife, who was sixteen years younger, lived in New Hampshire for another forty years.⁵¹

Other former troopers, like Ockington's fellow New Hampshire native Sgt. Maj. Francis Flagg Putney, moved to states that were entirely new to them. Initially, Putney returned home at the expiration of his enlistment but remained only briefly. He soon sought better opportunities outside the Granite State. Instead of returning to the West, Putney pursued anticipated opportunities elsewhere. He had gone home to organize some of his relatives to head to the South, to set themselves up in impoverished postwar southern Georgia. Putney and his relatives, all Union veterans and Republicans, were quintessential carpetbaggers. They settled in rural Dougherty County, south of Albany, Georgia, either in 1866 or 1867, roughly eighty miles north of Tallahassee, Florida. Unlike most carpetbaggers, Putney succeeded in winning over both his white and African American neighbors, eventually becoming extremely prosperous.

Surprisingly, despite amassing large land holdings and becoming incredibly successful in the midst of a devastated white population, it seems his white neighbors held no animosity toward him. In a history of the state, the authors, one of them a former Confederate general, wrote that Putney was a "sterling and influential citizen," who "is a man who commands the respect and confidence of all who know him."[52] This is somewhat remarkable considering that he encouraged the former slaves to vote and even served one term in the state legislature before home rule resumed. Doing both was incredibly dangerous in the midst of white Southern efforts to keep power from the former slaves and outsiders. Putney learned this firsthand in 1868 during the Camilla Massacre, where at least nine freedmen trying to hold a political rally were murdered, and one of his fellow white Republicans was beaten. Somehow Putney survived; was elected to the state legislature two years later, presumably by the freedmen; and yet was highly regarded by all when he died more than forty years later.[53]

Before his death in 1928, he amassed complete or partial control over nearly thirty thousand acres of farm and timberlands where several farmsteads were established along with grist and cotton mills. Eventually a general store was erected to serve the growing population of farmers and lumbermen in the unincorporated community named Putney, which still exists today. In Putney's case, not serving directly against the South during the war probably allowed his white Southern neighbors to more readily accept him.

Few former Oregon troopers relocated as far from Oregon as Francis Putney, but Almarin Nottingham, who simply wandered for eight years after the expiration of his enlistment, traveled farther.

He migrated to foreign countries and back to the United States before settling down. Despite having deserted from an Illinois cavalry regiment in the early months of the war, he remained in good standing throughout his three years in the First Oregon Volunteer Cavalry Regiment. It is reported that after being mustered out in October 1865, he traveled around the Pacific Northwest, eventually crossing the border into Canada. From there he made his way to Panama, then at some point boarded a ship for New York, before finally returning home to Ashland, Illinois. Not surprisingly, the wanderlust struck again, and he soon headed to Texas, where he herded cattle northward to railheads in Kansas and Nebraska that linked up to the rail hub in Chicago. During his seemingly endless roaming, he met a woman in Kansas. He not only came back to her in 1873; she influenced him to remain in one place, near the infamous town of Lawrence, which had been attacked by William Quantrill's murderous band of Confederate raiders in 1863. He continued in the cattle business, operating from his farm and ranch until numerous accidents in old age left him nearly bedridden in his last months before passing away in June 1917 at seventy-seven years old.[54]

Not every trooper who took their bounty money and left the Pacific Northwest fared well after relocating. Just as had been the case for some of the ex-troopers who remained, surviving evidence shows some Oregon cavalrymen found life filled with challenges, hardship, and premature death far removed from the Pacific Northwest. Some struggled financially, while others suffered from poor health after the end of their service. Those are precisely the types of individuals who left the least historical imprint, making it difficult to determine how many died prematurely, struggled throughout their lives, or both. The fates of Capt. Richard S. Caldwell, former Sgt. Newton Fortney, Cpl. David Kenworthy, and Pvt. Riley Barnes give a sense of how difficult life was for an uncertain number of the Oregon veterans after they relocated far from where they had served the Union.

After resigning his captaincy in March 1865, Richard S. Caldwell quickly returned to his native Massachusetts. Less than four years later, he died in Providence, Rhode Island. It is unclear if he was visiting or living there at the time of his death. What is clear, however, is that at not yet forty years old, the former Company B commander did not live long enough to show what he might have done.[55] Newton Fortney, who made sketches of Shoshone Falls during his service that were donated to the Smithsonian, returned to (West) Virginia.[56] He was discharged in December 1864, too late to make the crossing back to his native state until the next spring. When the weather broke the next year, according to a newspaper account, he "returned a much richer man than he left, in exuberant health, and with an experience of wild Western life rare in one of his age." He was twenty-six. He had seen opportunity during his service in the Oregon Cavalry "and in a fortnight was off again to the far West"—specifically, chasing ore strikes in Idaho and then Montana, accompanied by a younger brother. Instead of finding success in his return to the West, death awaited Fortney the next year. While working a mine in Montana, one of the heavy ore buckets slipped from its pulley and "struck him directly on the head, crushing his skull and killing him instantly" in February 1867.[57]

While Company A's Riley Barnes lived a relatively long life, it was marred by steadily declining and debilitating health, beginning shortly after his discharge. After leaving the cavalry, he waited out the winter in Oregon and left for Indiana in early 1865. Initially, he planned to help take care of an ailing father but moved to Minnesota in the spring of 1866. There he began remodeling a farmstead he had purchased, probably using some of his service bounty money. However, he was plagued by poor health for the next sixteen years, punctuated by the steady loss of his sight. After total blindness set in, one of his brothers and his family took care of him for his remaining years. His impaired health steadily worsened, starting in 1890. By January 1892 "his sufferings were great," and he "often expressed a wish to pass away and be at rest." Those sufferings finally ended on February 1. Though he had lived into his early sixties, ill health combined with blindness left him an invalid those last nine years.[58]

Unlike Caldwell, Fortney, and Barnes, Cpl. David W. Kenworthy lived a long life surrounded by a large family. Even so, he confronted economic challenges. After three years of service in Company D, he was discharged in December 1864 but, like others, had to wait out the winter before making the trek eastward, back to Iowa in his case. Waiting to get his bounty money may have been another factor; the $180 bounty paid on February 26, 1865, provided him with a financial boost before leaving. One year later he married Elizabeth (McCreary) Wellman, a widow with a son. Over the course of his life, he seems to have struggled financially, trying farming and raising bees but mostly working as a laborer. During that time, he and Elizabeth had five children together while living in Jackson, Iowa. David W. Kenworthy represents the unknown number of former Oregon cavalrymen who lived economically challenging lives. Despite what appears to have been a financially unstable existence, he was an active member of his community, belonged to fraternal organizations, and was seen as "a true and representative citizen of the county" before his 1914 death.[59]

As their enlistments expired, most men agreed with Captain Drake that three years of service on the frontier was enough for a lifetime.[60] However, there were a few who either reenlisted in the cavalry or sought a transfer to the First Oregon Infantry Regiment. Ironically, Drake was among the latter group. When both Oregon regiments ceased to exist, some even chose to continue in the military by joining the U.S. Army. The military evaluated volunteer officers' fitness for command before they considered offering them commissions in the army, though there does not seem to have been a similar effort to assess the men. Negative evaluations for some who received commissions make it clear that the army did not rely solely on assessments. Four officers and an unknown number of cavalrymen enlisted in the army at the expiration of their service in the Oregon regiments. Those officers were Capt. William Kelly and Lts. Silas Pepoon, James Waymire, and Charles W. Hobart. The evaluator felt Captain Kelly possessed a good character and fair fitness for command but lacked the education to rise very far in the army. Charles W. Hobart had good character and a good education, but his fitness for command was "unexceptional."[61] What motivated them is uncertain, but Kelly, who had served in the army before the war, knew what to expect. The other three, however, had never served in the military prior to joining the volunteer First Oregon Volunteer Cavalry Regiment. Only one of them was still serving ten years later.

It was not surprising when the prewar veteran William Kelly sought an officer's commission in the army at the conclusion of his Oregon Cavalry service. He had been one of the few to remain with his company after his initial enlistment expired. Before he finally resigned, he was the senior officer in what was by then a battalion. After his July 1866 muster out of what was left of the Oregon Cavalry, he was appointed a captain in the newly authorized Eighth U.S. Cavalry's Troop C. He remained with his troop, operating in Oregon for the next two years. During that time, his command engaged in a firefight with an unidentified Indian band in 1868. In 1869 the entire regiment concentrated in Arizona, where Kelly's troop remained active trying to recapture stolen livestock and attacking bands of Apaches into 1870. He died from chronic dysentery while on furlough in Denver on December 28, 1871, when he was fifty-three. His remains were sent to Fort Vancouver, where he was interred in the fort cemetery.[62]

Unlike his brother and future brother-in-law, Lt. Silas Pepoon decided to remain in the army rather than head to Nebraska. Pepoon was appointed a second lieutenant in the Tenth U.S. Cavalry Regiment in 1867 (his recommendation was dated the year before). The Tenth was one of the four regiments made up of all Black soldiers, led by white officers. With the reduction in the size of the army, some officers accepted positions in the "Buffalo Soldier" regiments to avoid being without a command, despite viewing the regiments as less desirable assignments. Pepoon came from a staunchly abolitionist family, and while the lieutenant's commission was an inducement, he viewed his soldiers more positively than some of the other white officers. Pepoon and the Tenth saw considerable action, including riding to the rescue of Maj. George

Forsyth at Beecher Island, Colorado, in September 1868 and later trying to force the surrender of Cheyenne bands on the Great Plains. By October 1874 he had been stationed in Texas as well as back in the Indian Territory (present-day Oklahoma), including near Fort Sill.[63]

By then Fort Sill, where some "Buffalo Soldier" units were headquartered, including Pepoon's command, had earned a toxic reputation. Unfortunately, Pepoon, according to the Fort Sill surgeon, "had been suffering during the past summer much from malaria in conjunction with which he had exhibited great mental depression, at intervals even to temporary dementia." Given his worsening condition, the malignant atmosphere in and around Fort Sill (Pepoon's command was camped eight miles from the fort), and the approaching winter, this was the worst place for him. Things deteriorated much further after he was accused of cheating while playing poker with some of the other officers—a court-martial offense. On October 16, while waiting for the court to convene, he discharged his pistol "with the muzzle held apparently against the nasal eminence of the Frontal Bone," which was almost certainly "instantaneously fatal."[64] It was a tragic end for someone who had been popular among his fellow officers in the Oregon Cavalry. The fragility of Pepoon's mental state had been noticed in 1864, when Capt. George B. Currey observed he was "in a terrible rage" about something related to his duties with the Quartermaster Department. Currey informed John Apperson, "How long he will maintain his mentality is a serious question."[65] Pepoon's suicide was not entirely uncommon for men serving on the frontier.

Despite deciding to enlist in the army two years after his volunteer service ended, James Waymire did not remain in the army long. Waymire's decision to enlist must have surprised his former commander, Captain Drake, who observed in 1864 that Waymire was "so anxious to get out of the service."[66] Drake's assessment was correct at first, but after two years of civilian life, Waymire sought a commission in the Regular Army. Whatever his motive, he accepted a second lieutenant's commission in the First U.S. Cavalry on January 22, 1867. Unlike Kelly or Pepoon, he never left the old District of Oregon boundaries. He served at places such as Camp Lyon, Idaho Territory, and when his regiment relocated to Arizona Territory, he remained in the Northwest on detached duty at Camp Warner, Oregon.[67] His interest in the army waned after two years, and he resigned his commission on August 2, 1869—it was accepted the following month.[68]

He initially went to Salem to resume the study of the law but soon accepted an offer to serve as a legislative reporter in Sacramento, California, for the *Union*. He continued his studies while working as a reporter and eventually passed the Oregon bar in September 1870, despite living in California. From there he steadily rose through California's legal ranks. After another turn as the legislative reporter for the newspaper during the 1871–72 secession, he accepted a position as court recorder for the California Supreme Court. Following a move to San Francisco in 1875, both his legal practice and economic standing rose swiftly. For six years he expanded his law firm, which grew so successful that he was eventually able to purchase an estate in Alameda. In October 1881 California governor George C. Perkins appointed Waymire to fill an open seat on the state's superior court. Given his earlier interactions with both the state's political and legal leaders as a reporter and then as the recorder in the state supreme court, Waymire was a well-known choice. Despite his general popularity with the state's leaders, he was a Republican in what was a Democratic environment, and he lost the subsequent election eighteen months later, ending his judicial career.[69]

After leaving his brief tenure as a judge behind (but retaining the title "Judge" for the rest of his life), Waymire resumed his law practice in San Francisco. At the same time, he started a long involvement with the Union veterans' group, the Grand Army of the Republic, even presiding over the California branch for nine terms. The golden touch that had rewarded him and his family so well for two decades failed in the 1890s, when he speculated on one disastrous project after another. Despite the string of economic setbacks, he did serve two terms in the California legislature in the mid-1890s. Unfortunately, Waymire's continued financial problems led him to invest in ever riskier schemes to make back the money he had lost on previous bad investments. Finally, in 1906, unable to repay his creditors, he and his wife were evicted from their estate. It was a very public collapse from which he never recovered. James Waymire died from a heart attack four years later, on April 16, 1910. Few former Oregon troopers rose so high in another state, or fell so publicly, as James Waymire.[70]

Although William Kelly almost certainly would have retired from the army had he lived, Charles W. Hobart was the only one of the four officers to do so. Staying in the service was the best choice for the former Oregon Cavalry lieutenant. By the time he retired from the army in 1898, he had attained the rank of lieutenant colonel. Like Kelly, Hobart served in the Oregon Cavalry until it ceased to exist and then made the leap to the newly formed Eighth U.S. Cavalry. Lacking Kelly's prewar experience and never having anywhere near his command responsibilities (and being twenty-five years younger), he was offered a lieutenant's commission. During the next seven years, he was stationed throughout the Southwest with the Eighth Cavalry. Then after receiving a promotion to captain, he was transferred to the Third U.S. Infantry. After the transfer, Hobart shuffled around to installations in the Deep South, various posts in the Midwest, and then up to Montana (during the Nez Perce War) over the course of the next twenty-five years. He was promoted through the grades, gaining his lieutenant colonelcy in 1896 before retiring two years later. During his more than thirty years in uniform, he achieved a record of reliable service. He died in 1919, survived by his much younger wife, Flora, and two children. Not only was he the last former Oregon Cavalry officer in uniform when he retired; he was also the last survivor of that small group.

More soldiering did not appeal to most former troopers, but some found another way to remain connected to the Indians they had tried to remove or kill during their time in the Oregon Cavalry. At least five former Oregon cavalrymen worked on Indian reservations at the conclusion of their service as Indian agents, post traders at agency headquarters, or teachers at reservation schools.

As Capt. William V. Rinehart observed, it appeared incongruous: "As Indian Agent I fed for six years these same Indians whom I had fought for four years." It was not as odd as it might seem. With an increasing number of treaties signed starting in 1864, there was a need for low-level government officials to serve as intermediaries between the reservation population and local and federal authorities. Former cavalrymen, just finishing three or more years living in the same regions where reservations were established and now needing employment, were a ready, if unique, pool of potential agents and reservation employees. Historically, Indian agent positions were rife with graft, where limited oversight gave agents semiautocratic authority over the people they were supposed to be serving. Not all agents saw their positions as an opportunity to enrich themselves or the chance to lord their power over their charges, but many did. William V. Rinehart was among the group of agents who hoped to do both. His time as an agent was marked by growing unrest on the Malheur Reservation resulting from his mistreatment of the Northern Paiute and Bannock people living there. Despite being accused of selling food allotted for the reservation residents to whites and allowing whites to move onto reservation lands, Rinehart left voluntarily, rather than the government replacing him. He moved to the Seattle area and became a prominent pioneer in a second state.[71]

Chauncey M. Messenger, who had been a farrier first in Company G and later Company F, also served as an Indian agent. After his enlistment ended, he obtained an agent's position on the Nez Perce Reservation at Lapwai, Idaho Territory. Messenger may have been seen as better suited for such a job due to personal connections. His first wife was an Indian woman, although surviving records do not indicate from which tribe. There is no record of mistreatment of the Nez Perce or corruption during his five years as an agent at Fort Lapwai.[72] Maj. Sewell Truax and his brother, Sgt. Charles Truax, also served on the Nez Perce Reservation, although not as Indian agents but as post traders.[73] Maj. Jacob S. Rinearson found different employment on a reservation. After the expiration of his enlistment, Rinearson taught briefly at a school for Indian children on a reservation in eastern Washington Territory.[74]

None of the former Oregon troopers remained employed in the reservation system for very long. Only Rinehart worked with the Indian tribes for more than five years. Sewell Truax found surveying work and eventually ended up in Spokane, Washington, after living many years in Walla Walla. Rinearson returned to Oregon, and Messenger left for Illinois and then moved on to Kansas in 1871, remaining there for the majority of his life, outliving all three of his wives and two of his ten children. Despite his questionable tenure at the Malheur Reservation, Rinehart went on to enjoy great economic success as a land speculator in Washington. Eventually he held public office both in Seattle and at the state level before his death in 1918.[75]

Just as the experiences of the members of the First Oregon Volunteer Cavalry Regiment varied widely, so too did the way they saw their service in the regiment and their contribution to both the region and the nation. Their experience in the Pacific Northwest's first Civil War military unit was complex. That was in large part because of how much the region changed and how their service was judged against that of others. The pulsing excitement to expand and develop the West partially explains why the veteran troopers went silent about their service for several decades. Generally lauded for the protections they provided during their years of service, things changed quickly after the regiment was disbanded.[76] Migration into the region grew, eventually leading to the creation of the states of Washington, Montana, and Idaho. Many of those moving to the Pacific Northwest from east of the Rocky Mountains were Civil War veterans. The presence of so many veterans of battles whose names resonated in the public obscured what the Oregon troopers did. Those Oregon cavalrymen who moved to the Midwest or East after the war found themselves surrounded by veterans from famous fields. For the former Oregon cavalrymen, there was no Gettysburg, no capturing of a major Southern city, no service under a famed leader like Grant or Sherman to talk about. The former Oregon troopers (as well as their brethren in the Oregon and Washington Infantry regiments) could not compete with these outside veterans when the conversation turned to what they did during the war. Even their service against the various Indian tribes, in particular the Snakes, did not measure up to the far more famous regional "Indian wars" against the Nez Perce or even the Modocs, both of which took place more than ten years after the Civil War, following the substantial migration into the Pacific Northwest. Still, as time passed, the Oregon Cavalry veterans began to take pride in their service, including it in town and county histories, political biographies, and their obituaries. They accepted that they fought a different war, that their service was not like the cavalry fighting in the East. At the same time, they stressed the dangers of so many little combats against a foe whose numbers they amplified and whose brutality they embellished beyond an already gruesome belief. Some also emphasized their role in opening more of the Pacific Northwest to white expansion and development. By then, however, the next generation, many of whom still came from elsewhere, were ambivalent about a military unit most knew nothing about.

In 1901 a member of that next generation demonstrated just how little they knew and, in some cases, cared about the First Oregon Volunteer Cavalry Regiment's service. After the Portland *Oregonian* ran an editorial advocating for a memorial to local veterans of the Spanish–American War, former Company B sergeant John B. Dimick pointed out that there was no such memorial for the veterans of Oregon's Civil War commands. The editorial writer dismissed Dimick's call for a similar memorial for the veterans of the Oregon cavalry and infantry by sarcastically asking, "What bloody field did those heroes fall on?"[77] This attitude clearly irritated Dimick, as evidenced by his quick response. John Dimick, a state senator at the time he tried to enlighten the contemptuous editorial writer, suggested the editor educate himself before commenting on things he knew nothing about. The old trooper suggested a close read of the Oregon adjutant general's 1866 report. There he would learn "these regiments [Oregon Cavalry and First Oregon Infantry Regiment], by companies and detachments, had many battles with the Indians, and he will find out, too, that when battles were fought those days they got so close together that somebody got killed."

The Oregon soldiers had been "recruited by the Secretary of War and were as much a part of the 'grand army' as any regiments in the Army of the Potomac," he emphatically declared.[78] Dismissing Dimick's arguments and without looking into the reports, the editor mocked Dimick and all Oregon Cavalry or Infantry veterans who professed their service had been important. "On the whole," the writer proclaimed, their service "was not arduous—nothing like so arduous as that of the volunteers in the Indian hostilities of 1855–56, and preceding wars." Furthermore, Dimick's characterization "seemed an unnecessary and exaggerated glorification of the deeds of these two regiments."[79] It was a hopeless battle with someone who knew very little about the state's history and did not care to learn. The debate fizzled out after the last printed exchange on January 30.

Although State Senator Dimick would not live long enough to see the full consequence, it appears the exchange revived nostalgia about Oregon's Civil War regiments, at least among the Oregon veterans themselves. A year and a half after his letters were published in the *Oregonian*, and just a year before his death, Pacific Northwest historian Francis Fuller Victor wrote an article-length history of the First Oregon Volunteer Cavalry Regiment.[80] Then in February 1903, his surviving comrades formed the Association of the First Oregon Cavalry and First Oregon Infantry Volunteers. The organization, patterned after the national Union veterans' group, the Grand Army of the Republic (and similar to the United Confederate Veterans), gave the members the chance to reminisce about their contributions to the Union cause and the opening of the region during their service. The survivors, ranging in age from their late fifties to their eighties, had the benefit of more than thirty-five years of changes to influence how they put their service into perspective. After more than three decades, those who left a record of their thoughts echoed what some of their leaders said in the mid-1860s.

During and immediately after the war, the regiment's officers as well as the District of Oregon commander all described what the Oregon Cavalry had done as more arduous, dangerous, and important than the *Oregonian* writer acknowledged. In 1866 then colonel Currey applauded his men for enduring the long, brutal 1864 campaign, noting, "They bore the hardship with a spirit so commendable and soldier-like."[81] Captain Small, who spent two winters at Camp Watson, made it clear the Oregon troopers' (and their infantry counterparts) service was "one of the most dangerous and inglorious modes of warfare" as they served in "the mountains and desert plains of Oregon."[82] Lieutenant Waymire attested to the troopers' preparation to do more, explaining that the failure to be sent East "is the misfortune and not the fault of the Oregon volunteers."[83]

Not only was their service dangerous; with one important exception, it had been successful. They felt it was the unfortunate reality that the Oregon Cavalry had not crushed the Paiute, Bannock, and Shoshone (and to a lesser degree, Klamath and Modoc) resistance to white expansion. However, as the U.S. Regular forces found out starting in 1866, that was not an easy task. Despite the failure to eliminate attacks on white miners and emigrants, the Oregon Cavalry had achieved some success against those bands. Captain Drake and others found some solace in pushing Paiute bands south, out of Oregon. Even though it was not the full victory Drake and the Oregon cavalrymen desired, removing bands did help open the frontier regions for white development. According to former District of Oregon commander Brig. Gen. Benjamin Alvord, the Oregon troopers "have materially aided in developing the hidden treasures of the land," by which he meant Oregon east of the Cascades and western Idaho Territory. "The First Oregon Cavalry," he added, "have been devoted to the exploration and development of a part of Oregon heretofore marked on our maps as 'unexplored,' but which can no longer receive that designation."[84] Lt. Col. Charles Drew agreed, reporting his men had opened "a route from Northern California, Southern and Middle Oregon to the Owyhee and Boise regions." Their efforts had "opened a line for direct communication between Fort Klamath, Fort Boise and Fort Hall." Militarily, operations in southern Oregon had found "many of the haunts, strongholds, and hiding places of the most dangerous portions of the Snake and Piute [*sic*] Indians, that will be useful to the public and beneficial to the service in future operations."[85] Their officers knew their varied service in the 1860s would make further expansion possible.

There is only one extant record of any veteran of the Oregon Cavalry reflecting on or assessing their service to the nation or the region before Dimick stepped up to defend his service. Whether coincidence or not, most of the existing accounts did not appear in print or as speeches until after their service had been dismissed by the editorial writer at the *Oregonian* in 1901. One article by an anonymous veteran did, however, appear in 1875. In it the author echoed some of what the officers had written during their service and presaged what others said in the future. The veteran, writing in a somewhat florid style, declared, "I know the First Oregon Cavalry were the first to carry war into the very heart of their [Paiutes] country, and did service which they never received credit for. Many of our comrades fell and are now sleeping where no flowers are strewn upon their graves."[86]

John T. Apperson used a more reserved but no less heartfelt tone when he spoke at the fifth annual meeting of the Association of the First Oregon Cavalry and First Oregon Infantry Volunteers in 1908. As he wrapped up his presentation, the old lieutenant told his aged comrades, "I feel justly proud of my service. Comrades of the First Oregon Cavalry and Oregon Infantry your services entitles you to the same recognition, of having served your country during the period of the civil war, as is due and accorded to the comrades who volunteered from any other States of this Union."[87] Apperson echoed a sentiment written forty-four years earlier at the time of Lt. Stephen Watson's death in combat. In a letter to the *Oregonian*, a member of Drake's column wrote that the Oregon troopers who died in service, like Watson, were "just as deserving of praise to die here in the discharge of one's duty, as it would have been to fall at Chickamauga or Gettysburg."[88] The 1864 letter writer was correct; the thirty Oregon troopers who died during their service to the country (as well as those Washington and Oregon infantrymen who gave their lives in uniform) deserved the same recognition for their sacrifice as those who died on famous fields in the East, all as an extension of federal power from coast to coast.

The veterans were right; they had laid the groundwork for the transformation of the region from frontier, before the war, to an economic contributor to the national growth in the decades afterward. Their comrades who died in the nation's service did so as part of the Union's effort to use its massive military to subdue the rebellion from east of the Mississippi River and also in the trans-Mississippi region all the way to the Southwest. At the same time, the enhanced size of the military enabled federal and state authorities to force Indian tribes from Minnesota to California to submit to the power of the United States, which opened lands for white development at their expense. It did not always require bloody confrontations, although it often did, to force the treaties that slowly boxed the tribes into smaller parcels of land. The military also escorted white emigrants traveling to the West that was being opened for them. In the Pacific Northwest and in other places like Utah Territory, where district commander Col. Patrick Connor encouraged his men to prospect, the military was also used for exploration.[89]

The Pacific Northwest was another front of the transcontinental war effort. Service in the harsh environment between central Oregon and southern Idaho tempered some men like steel, giving them the ability to endure more than others, to appreciate opportunities wherever they found them, and for a substantial number of them, to assume leadership roles mostly (but not only) in the Pacific Northwest after their service. The Oregon troopers lamented not being sent east just as they were disappointed at not crushing the so-called Snakes. However, they participated in the early stages of the conflicts with bands of Bannocks, Northern Paiutes, and Northern Shoshones, which lasted into the late 1860s. Through exploration more than military confrontations, they helped open Klamath, Modoc, Paiute, and Bannock lands to white exploitations, regardless of their claims to the land. Oregon troopers were present and used as displays of federal strength at treaties with the Nez Perces, Klamaths, Modocs, and even the Paiute band led by the reviled and feared Chief Paulina—although with his people hungry and desperate, he later broke it. Even though their expeditions did not result in a major clash with any of the tribes they pursued, by spending six months riding the open frontier and trails for more than four successive years, they made those areas safer, though not entirely safe, for miners and frontier farmers and ranchers. They protected emigrant trains as they came into dangerous portions of the last stage of their journey. As many of them noted, they acquired and shared newfound knowledge about previously underexplored regions of eastern Oregon and southwestern Idaho Territory.

Writing in the *Oregon Adjutant General's Report* of 1865–66, Adjutant General Cyrus Reed summed it all up: The men who served in the First Oregon Volunteer Cavalry Regiment during the Civil War had "not been idle . . . a large scope of our country has been explored, which is now being settled. Under their protection, a large mining country has been developed, and millions of the precious metals brought into circulation and, I can say without fear of contradiction, that for long, and tedious marches, excessive privation and hardship, that our troops can produce as fair a record as any; still they have encountered a sufficient number of hostile Indians in every conceivable phase of attack to demonstrate how ready and willing they were to imperil their lives in their country's cause."[90]

Over the course of four years of active service, the Oregon Cavalry played a vital role in opening the interior Pacific Northwest. First as guardians against any potential (or rumored) insurgency by Confederate sympathizers, then increasingly as explorers and a military force to suppress the regional Native Americans, they served as agents of the federal government's exertion of power. That service impacted the men as profoundly as it did the region. Looking back at his years in the Oregon Cavalry, Lt. James Waymire remembered that through "the interesting experiences of that time, sometimes in conflict with the

Indians, often suffering from thirst and hunger in the desert," he formed friendships "that can never be broken."[91] Former captain William V. Rinehart agreed with his old friend, writing to Waymire's widow after his death, "Our service in the Oregon Cavalry brought us together in relations of closer friendship than falls to the lot of most men."[92]

NOTES

Introduction

1. Lt. J. W. Hopkins to Capt. John M. Drake, April 7, 1864, in U.S. War Office, *War of the Rebellion*, ser. 1, vol. 50, pt. 2, p. 808 (unless otherwise noted, all references are to series 1; hereafter cited as *OR*).

2. Special Order no. 70, May 6, 1864, *OR*, vol. 50, pt. 2, p. 841.

3. Drake, "Cavalry in the Indian Country," 25.

4. Lt. J. W. Hopkins to Capt. George B. Currey, April 11, 1864, *OR*, vol. 50, pt. 2, p. 815.

5. State of Oregon, *Report of the Adjutant General*, 32 (hereafter cited as *OAG*).

6. William Vance Rinehart, *Oregon Biographical and Other Card File*, Oregon Historical Society, Portland; George B. Currey and Jennie (Gaines) Currey, April 11, 1864, *OR*, vol. 50, pt. 2, p. 815.

7. Amanda (Gaines) Rinehart figures prominently in Rinehart's letters to Apperson. See W. V. Rinehart to John T. Apperson, January 10 and 23, 1865, John T. Apperson Papers, Northwest Room, Spokane Public Library, downtown branch, Spokane WA (hereafter cited as Apperson Papers, NWR); *Sunday Oregonian* (Portland), October 20, 1918.

8. Capt. George B. Currey to Gov. A. C. Gibbs, August 1863, Addison Crandall Gibbs Papers, Oregon Historical Society, Portland (hereafter cited as Gibbs Papers).

9. J. W. Perit Huntington report, September 12, 1863, in U.S. Government, *Annual Report*, 49.

10. Ruby and Brown, *Guide to the Indian Tribes*, 7–8; Madsen, *Bannock of Idaho*, 122–29.

11. Quoted in Madsen, *Northern Shoshoni*, 38.

12. Ruby and Brown, *Guide to the Indian Tribes*, 156.

13. Crum, "Paddy Cap Band," 184.

14. Voegelin, "Northern Paiute of Central Oregon," 97.

15. Ruby and Brown, *Guide to the Indian Tribes*, 156.

16. Chief Paulina was not the only one of the antagonists to have geographic places and waterways named after him. Currey's, Alvord's, and even Maury's names were also given to several places and bodies of water.

17. For devastating floods around Albany, which "[rendered] prospects exceedingly gloomy for our farmers," see the *Oregon Democrat* (Albany), January 28, 1862. For destructive snowfall totals, estimated at up to four feet, near The Dalles during the spring, see *Weekly Oregon Statesman* (Salem), March 17, 1862.

18. Kittell, *Bear Bravely On*, D-17.

19. See Masich, *Civil War in Arizona*, for a review of California volunteers doing similar work in Arizona Territory.

1. Divisions and Dangers

1. Ore. const., art. XVIII, § 2. See "Transcribed 1857 Oregon Constitution," Oregon State Archives, accessed November 2, 2020, https://sos.oregon.gov/archives/exhibits/constitution/Documents/transcribed-1857-oregon-constitution.pdf.

2. Nokes, "Black Exclusion Laws"; Nokes, "Peter Burnett."

3. *Oregon Sentinel* (Jacksonville), January 29, 1859.

4. McBride, "Annual Address," 42.

5. Kingsnorth, "Paine Page Prim."

6. For reviews of Lincoln's friends in Oregon, see Etulain, *Lincoln and Oregon*, chaps. 2 and 3; and Jewell, "Thwarting Southern Schemes," chap. 1.

7. The *Weekly Oregonian*, under the guidance of publisher T. J. Dryer, likewise supported Lincoln. See June 30, 1860, issues of the *Weekly* for an example.

8. *Population of the United States in 1860*, 583.

9. McConaghy, "Deplorable State," 18, 20. McConaghy explores young Charles Mitchell's attempt to escape to freedom in Victoria in her book *Free Boy: The True Story of Slavery and Mastery*.

10. *Population of the United States in 1860*, 583, 584.

11. Johannsen, *Frontier Politics*, 149.

12. *Oregon Argus* (Oregon City), November 10, 1860.

13. *Washington Standard* (Olympia), November 18, 1860.

14. Stevens, *Life of Isaac Ingalls Stevens*, vol. 2, 314.

15. Joel Palmer, diary entry for March 3, 1861, TS 2, MSS 114, Joel Palmer Papers, Oregon Historical Society, Portland.

16. San Francisco, which received the news on April 24, was the first Pacific Coast city to learn of the attack. *Alta California* (San Francisco), April 25, 1861.

17. *Weekly Oregon Statesman* (Salem), May 6, 1861.

18. *Oregon Democrat* (Albany), May 7, 1861.

19. *Washington Standard* (Olympia), May 5, 1861.

20. *Puget Sound Herald* (Steilacoom, Washington Territory), May 3, 1861; *Pioneer and Democrat* (Port Angeles, Washington Territory), May 2, 1861. The details from a South Carolina newspaper appeared in the May 17 edition of the *Pioneer and Democrat*.

21. Coverage can be found beginning in late April in papers throughout the populated parts of the state, including the *Daily Oregonian*, the *Oregon Argus*, the *Oregon Sentinel*, and the *Oregon Statesman*.

22. *Weekly Oregonian* (Portland), May 25, 1861.

23. Examples of reporting on the Pacific Republic scheme include *New York Daily Herald*, February 8, 1861; and *Chicago Tribune*, April 3, 1861.

24. After arriving at his new post in San Francisco, Gen. Edwin Sumner let the War Department know he felt there were serious efforts to draw California into a Pacific Republic. Brig. Gen. E. V. Sumner to Lieut. Col. E. D. Townsend, April 28, 1861, OR, vol. 50, pt. 1, p. 472.

25. Gov. John Weller's farewell address, quoted in Kibby, "Union Loyalty," 313.

26. Latham and Gwin's remarks were widely reported in California newspapers and less so in Oregon. See *Placer Herald* (Auburn CA), May 26, 1860; *Daily National Democrat* (Marysville CA), May 11, 1860; *Weekly Oregonian* (Portland), May 5, 1860; *Congressional Globe: The Official Proceedings of Congress* (Washington DC), 37th Congress, 1st Session, April 16, 1860, 1724–28. At the end of Latham's speech, Gwin concurs that a Pacific Republic is the course California should follow if war breaks out (1728).

27. Prosch, *Reminiscences of Washington Territory*, 51.

28. Brig. Gen. Edwin V. Sumner to Lt. Col. E. D. Townsend, April 28, 1861, OR, vol. 50, pt. 1, p. 472.

29. Prosch, *Reminiscences of Washington Territory*, 51.

30. *Washington Standard* (Steilacoom, Washington Territory), February 9, 1861.

31. Charges against Latham appeared not long after the presidential election. For a recent treatment of Gwin's various schemes, including his time as a proslavery senator from California, see St. John, "Unpredictable America," 56–84.

32. Keehn, *Knights of the Golden Circle*, 129; *Weekly Oregonian* (Portland), April 27, 1861.

33. Keehn, *Knights of the Golden Circle*, 6–13; Crenshaw, "Knights of the Golden Circle," 23–27. The Crenshaw article is often incorrect and must only be used with considerable caution.

34. Johannsen, *Frontier Politics*, 198–99.

35. *Oregon Statesman* (Salem), September 2, 1861.

36. *San Joaquin Republican* (California), January 16, 1861; OR, vol. 50, pt. 1, p. 433.

37. Maj. William W. Mackall to Col. George Wright, April 25, 1861, OR, vol. 50, pt. 1, p. 469; Maj. William W. Mackall, Special Order no. 60, 470; Maj. William W. Mackall, Special Order no. 76, Department of the Pacific, May 7, 1861; Maj. William W. Mackall, Special Order no. 76, OR, vol. 50, pt. 1, p. 479.

38. The best examination of Wright's particularly brutal campaign of revenge is Cutler's *"Hang Them All."*

2. Recruiting

1. Col. G. Wright to Maj. D. C. Buel, assistant adjutant general, Headquarters, Department of the Pacific, June 14, 1861, OR, vol. 50, pt. 1, p. 515.

2. Abstract from return of the Department of the Pacific, June 30, 1861, OR, vol. 50, pt. 1, p. 525.

3. John Whiteaker to Col. G. Wright, Department of the Pacific, September 1, 1861, OR, vol. 50, pt. 1, p. 599.

4. Col. George Wright to Capt. R. C. Drum, assistant adjutant general, Department of the Pacific, September 12, 1861, OR, vol. 50, pt. 1, p. 618.

5. Johannsen, *Frontier Politics*, 147.

6. *Oregon Sentinel* (Jacksonville), June 16, 1861.

7. *Weekly Oregonian* (Portland), September 28, 1861.

8. *Weekly Oregon Statesman* (Salem), October 21, 1861.

9. *Weekly Oregon Statesman* (Salem), November 4, 1861; Edwards, "Oregon Regiments," 19.

10. Kibby, "Union Loyalty," 317.

11. The secretary of war asked Downey to raise additional regiments in August, adding to the regiment of infantry and five cavalry companies requested on July 24. Simon Cameron, secretary of war, to John G. Downey, governor of California, August 14, 1861, OR, vol. 50, pt. 1, p. 569.

12. Fenton, "Edward Dickinson Baker," 12.

13. *Congressional Globe: The Official Proceedings of Congress* (Washington DC), 37th Congress, 1st Session (August 2, 1861), 379.

14. Fenton, "Edward Dickinson Baker," 12.

15. Lorenzo Thomas, adjutant general, to Thomas Cornelius, B. F. Harding and R. F. Maury, September 24, 1861, OR, vol. 50, pt. 1, pp. 632, 633.

16. Leaders in every territory and state from Nebraska westward, except California and Washington Territory, realized the superiority of cavalry over infantry. For a review of the recruiting of one of the Colorado regiments, see Rein's *Second Colorado Cavalry*. For a personal perspective on the recruiting of the First Nebraska Territorial Infantry Regiment, see Scherneckau, *Marching with the First Nebraska*.

17. Thomas A. Scott, acting secretary of war, to Col. Justus Steinberger, October 12, 1861, OR, vol. 50, pt. 1, pp. 656–57.

18. Matthew Deady, quoted in Bancroft, *Pacific States*, 639.

19. Additional information on Harding can be found in State of Oregon, *Biennial Report*, 639.

20. Despite a number of assertions that Maury graduated from the U.S. Military Academy, including in the preface to an 1860 letter George Pickett sent him that was published in the *Oregon Historical Quarterly* in 1908 and in my previous book, there is no indication he attended West Point, as there is no mention of him in Cullum's USMA graduate directory. See Cullum, *Biographical Register*.

21. Heitman, *Historical Register and Dictionary*, 2:61.

22. Maury's biographical information is from *Portrait and Biographical Record of Western Oregon*, 719.

23. This entire paragraph is drawn from *Portrait and Biographical Record of Western Oregon*, 315–16.

24. *Oregon Sentinel* (Jacksonville), October 26, 1861.

25. Col. George Wright to Gov. John Whiteaker, October 23, 1861, OR, vol. 50, pt. 1, p. 674.

26. Lt. Col. Albemarle Cady to Gov. John Whiteaker, November 1, 1861, OR, vol. 50, pt. 1, pp. 695–97.

27. Lt. Col. Albemarle Cady to Maj. R. C. Drum, November 9, 1861, OR, vol. 50, pt. 1, p. 716.

28. Jewell, *On Duty*, 17, 18.

29. Jewell, *On Duty*, 17, 18.

30. General Order no. 12, Department of the Pacific, June 4, 1861, OR, vol. 50, pt. 1, p. 498; Drake, "Oregon Cavalry," 398.

31. The determination of where the new officers were recruited is based on mustering officers listed in OAG; Jewell, *On Duty*, 167–244; and Edwards, "Oregon Regiments," 29–31.

32. A June 1862 gold strike not far from Canyon City temporarily ballooned its population well beyond that of Portland, but it was a transitory populace that dwindled over the next couple of years.

33. See Currey's report in OAG, 11.

34. General Order no. 16, War Department, May 4, 1861, OR, ser. 3, vol. 1, pp. 155, 157. The regimental officers included a colonel, a lieutenant colonel, and two majors.

35. "Population of the United States in 1860: Oregon," census.gov, accessed November 1, 2020, https://www2.census.gov/library/publications/decennial/1860/population/1860a-29.pdf.

36. Jewell, *On Duty*, 38.

37. Tamarac [pseud.], "Experiences of Co. A, 2d Cal. Cav," *National Tribune*, March 26, 1896.

38. Gorley, "Loyal Californians of 1861," 201–2.

39. For the role the Californians played in the southwest borderlands, see Masich, *Civil War in Arizona* and *Civil War in the Southwest*.

40. William M. Colvig, quoted in Jewell, *On Duty*, 255.

41. *Eugene Guard* (Oregon), September 15, 1927. Myers, sometimes spelled Meyers, is not listed in U.S. Adjutant General's Office, *Compiled Service Records for the Oregon Regiments* (hereafter cited as CSR); however, OAG shows when he enlisted and left the service and the bounty money he received. OAG, 175.

42. James Waymire, quoted in Victor, "First Oregon Cavalry," 135.

43. Shelly, "Reminiscences of Service in Company A."

44. Oregon Infantry, file for James M. Shelley, CSR.

45. Jewell, *On Duty*, 15.

46. Jewell, *On Duty*, 14, 15.

47. Jewell, *On Duty*, 19. During the Civil War the terms *squadron* and *company* were used interchangeably when describing cavalry units. After the war, *squadron* became the equivalent to a battalion (several companies).

48. Capt. George B. Currey to Gov. (Addison) Gibbs, April 18, 1863, Gibbs Papers.

49. *La Grande Evening Observer* (Oregon), March 5, 1906; *Oregon Daily Journal* (Portland), November 27, 1902. The obituary in *La Grande Evening Observer* incorrectly states that Currey joined the Oregon volunteers in 1857, but that was the year after the Rogue War had ended. Currey stated in the *Oregon Daily Journal* that he served in 1856, which was during the last of the conflicts in the Rogue River region.

50. For the role money played as a motivator for Union volunteering, see Marvel, *Lincoln's Mercenaries*.

51. Victor, "First Oregon Cavalry," 132; U.S. War Department, *Revised United States Army Regulations*, 506. The revised regulations also laid out a reimbursement scale based on miles traveled if the troopers had to provide their own feed for their horses.

52. Glenn Thomas Edwards states that the promised pay rate never materialized and that promises of $19 pay for their service, plus $12 for their horse (combined $31), ended up being $13 pay, plus $12 for the use of their horse. Edwards, "Oregon Regiments," 208; *Oregon Statesman* (Salem), January 12, 1863.

53. The bounty was still $100 during the 1863 effort to recruit Company G. *Oregon Sentinel* (Jacksonville), March 4, 1863; Shelley, "Reminiscences of Service," 2.

54. Nelson and Onstad, *Webfoot Volunteer*, 34–35.

55. Gallagher, "Through Battle, Prison, and Disease"; *Oregon Sentinel* (Jacksonville), November 5, 1864.

56. Jewell, *On Duty*, 38; Charles Montague, quoted in Jewell, *On Duty*, 250.

57. Victor, "First Oregon Cavalry," 134.

58. Col. Thomas Cornelius to U.S. Army Adjutant General, February 20, 1862, OR, vol. 50, pt. 1, pp. 885–86.

59. Gen. George Wright to Col. Thomas Cornelius, February 24, 1862, OR, vol. 50, pt. 1, p. 890.

60. William J. Matthews to Dear Etta, April 22, 1862, William J. Matthews Papers, Penrose Library, Whitman College.

61. Lt. David P. Thompson to Col. Thomas Cornelius, February 14, 1862, David Thompson file, CSR.

62. R. A. Cowles, CSR; OAG, 11–12.

63. U.S. War Department, *Revised United States Army Regulations*, 313.

64. Larson, *Sergeant Larson*, 45–46.

65. Recruiters used the same fluid approach to overlooking some of the strict guidelines before the war as well.

3. Transitions

1. Since the federal government did not grant full citizenship to Native Americans until 1924, *citizens* here means "whites."

2. The Willamette River is a northward-flowing tributary of the Columbia River.

3. *Oregon Daily Journal* (Portland), May 9, 1915.

4. Jewell, *On Duty*, 187.

5. Maj. Richard C. Drum to Messrs. Pingree, Belden, and others, August 31, 1861, OR, vol. 50, pt. 1, p. 599. Col. George Wright had been transferred to command of the District of Southern California.

6. Maj. Richard C. Drum to Col. B. L. Beall, August 31, 1861, OR, pt. 1, p. 598

7. Drake, "Cavalry in the Indian Country," 396; George B. Currey to Addison Gibbs, April 16, 1863, Gibbs Papers.

8. Drake, "Cavalry in the Indian Country," 7; OAG, 121, 127, 132; John M. Drake file, CSR; California State Census of 1852 (microfilm, M/F 144).

9. Drake, "Oregon Cavalry," 398.

10. Badger, "'All in Fact,'" 19.

11. Brig. Gen. Benjamin Alvord to Brig. Gen. George Wright, August 8, 1863, Thomas S. Harris file, CSR.

12. Charges listed in Dr. C. C. Dumreicher file, CSR. Dr. Dumreicher submitted a countercomplaint against Drake in September 1864 for his "uncalled for and injurious interference" in the medical detachment during Drake's 1864 summer campaign. The outcome of his countercomplaint compared to Drake's call for a court-martial is stark: Dumreicher was dismissed and Drake promoted, twice. Dr. C. C. Dumreicher to Lt. J. W. Hopkins, assistant adjutant general, September 4, 1864, John M. Drake file, CSR.

13. Col. Justus Steinberger remarks in William Capps, CSR.

14. For information on Thompson, see Gaston, Portland, Oregon, 2:194–98. For Prather, see Timber Pioneer (Montana), January 21, 1904.

15. Jewell, On Duty, 161–62.

16. The Tribune (Webster City IA), February 12, 1892; Riley Barnes, CSR.

17. Comparisons of places of birth are based on a review of the company rosters in OAG.

18. William Lewis file, CSR.

19. James Langlois file, CSR; OAG, 139; Portrait and Biographical Record of Western Oregon, 480.

20. Oregon Daily Journal (Portland), July 7, 1922; Oregon Statesman (Salem), April 1, 1934.

21. Gaston, Portland, Oregon, 2:633–34; Oregon Daily Journal (Portland), May 13, 1915.

22. For places of birth, review OAG; for Harkinson specifically, see CSR.

23. Calculated from a review of rosters in OAG.

24. William Kelly's file while in the Oregon Cavalry, CSR; Thrapp, Encyclopedia of Frontier Biography, 2:769; Henry, Military Record, 1:163.

25. Utley, Frontiersmen in Blue, 40; Ball, Army Regulars, 57.

26. William Johnson, CSR.

27. OAG, 152.

28. Compiled from a review of OAG.

29. William Kelly and James Waymire files, CSR.

30. This number is calculated from the biographical information on the officers in their individual compiled service records. See OAG, 12–124; and Jewell, On Duty, xliii.

31. McPherson, *For Cause and Comrades*, viii.

32. Drake, "Cavalry in the Indian Country," 396.

33. Henry, *Military Record*, 1:163.

34. I tallied thirty-eight men who listed soldier as their occupation. The percentage of soldiers was undoubtedly higher, since there were numerous individuals whose demographic information was not recorded. Compiled from entries for all Oregon cavalrymen in OAG.

35. *Army and Navy Magazine*, 1887, 15, 411.

36. The sketch of Montague is based on OAG, 147; "Charles B. Montague," *Oregon Native Son* 2 (1902): 483; U.S. Census Bureau, Linn County, Oregon, *Twelfth (1880) Census of the United States*, Washington DC; and "A History of the Royal Scots Greys—Richard Hill," Royal Scots Grey, accessed September 22, 2022, http://royalscotsgrey.com/0/locos/the-royal-scots-greys/.

37. Compiled from a search of OAG.

38. The spelling of Dimick's middle name includes one *l* in some sources and two in others. I am opting to use the *ll* spelling.

39. Sources for information on J. Henry Brown include Brown, "Autobiography," 47–48; *Oregonian* (Portland), August 17, 1898; and Joseph Henry Brown file, CSR.

40. Gaston, *Portland, Oregon*, 3:411–13; *Oregonian* (Portland), May 27, 1905; *Morning Enterprise* (Oregon City), May 31, 1912.

41. Dimick, quoted in Jewell, *On Duty*, 246.

42. For Dimick's biography, see Jewell, *On Duty*, 245–46; OAG, 151; Kittell, *Bear Bravely On*; *Oregon Statesman* (Salem), July 31, 1903.

43. Capt. George B. Currey to Gov. Addison C. Gibbs, April 16, 1863, Gibbs Papers.

44. All preceding quotes from Drake, "Cavalry in the Indian Country," 396.

45. Jewell, "Doing nothing," 604.

46. Drake, "Cavalry in the Indian Country," 397.

47. John M. McCall, quoted in Jewell, *On Duty*, 115.

48. Drake, "Cavalry in the Indian Country," 118.

49. David Hobart Taylor file, CSR.

50. Lowe, *Five Years a Dragoon*, 7.

51. Kittell, *Bear Bravely On*, A-18.

52. J. Halloran to Lt. J. T. Apperson, September 14, 1864, Cornelius Papers, OHS.

53. Silas Pepoon, quoted in Jewell, *On Duty*, 241–42.

54. Drake, "Cavalry in the Indian Country," 93.

55. OAG, 28–29.

56. Brooks and Reeve, "James A. Bennett," 143.

57. *Weekly Oregon Statesman* (Salem), December 21, 1863, summarizing an article from the Portland *Oregonian*.

58. *Washington Statesman* (Walla Walla), April 12, 1862. Since none of the Oregon cavalrymen were killed in April 1862, the deceased soldier must have been a member of the First Washington Infantry Regiment.

59. Numbers based on a tally of company rosters in OAG. The true number is difficult to determine because there is no information given for a number of the men.

60. Ella Lonn estimates that roughly two hundred thousand men deserted the Union armies during the war. Lonn, *Desertion during the Civil War*, 154.

61. Oregon Cavalry, Almarin Nottingham file, CSR.

62. Francis Ely file, CSR.

63. Col. Reuben Maury, telegram to Brig. Gen. George Wright, February 25, 1864, Ely, CSR.

64. Charles Garland, CSR.

65. John McCrossin, CSR.

4. Learning on the Job

1. Jewell, "Doing nothing," 602; David H. Taylor file, CSR.

2. McArthur and McArthur, *Oregon Geographic Names*, 106.

3. Drake, "Oregon Cavalry," 395.

4. For the roles weather and the environment played in Civil War service, see Browning and Silver, *Environmental History*; and Noe, *Howling Storm*.

5. Jewell, "Doing nothing," 603.

6. Drake, "Oregon Cavalry," 395; Jewell, "Doing nothing," 603.

7. Jewell, "Doing nothing," 603.

8. Drake, "Oregon Cavalry," 396.

9. The Southern Battalion included Company F, which had yet to be filled to the minimum required number of troopers.

10. James Waymire, quoted in Jewell, *On Duty*, 250.

11. James Waymire file, CSR.

12. OAG, 14.

13. Colonel Cornelius to U.S. Army adjutant general, February 20, 1862, OR, 885.

14. Colonel Cornelius to U.S. Army adjutant general, February 20, 1862, OR, 885–86.

15. Pepoon, quoted in Jewell, *On Duty*, 200.

16. Colonel Cornelius to U.S. Army adjutant general, February 20, 1862, OR, 886.

17. Lt. Col. Reuben Maury to Col. George Wright, March 27, 1862, OR, vol. 50, pt. 1, pp. 1005–6.

18. Jewell, "Doing nothing," 610.

19. Lieutenant Colonel Maury to Colonel Wright, March 27, 1862, OR, 1005–6.

20. William H. Rector, superintendent of Indian Affairs for Oregon, to Brig. Gen. George Wright, May 7, 1862, OR, vol. 50, pt. 1, pp. 1057–58.

21. Brig. Gen. George Wright to William H. Rector, May 12, 1862, OR, vol. 50, pt. 1, pp. 1068–69.

22. Capt. R. W. Kirkham to Col. Justus Steinberger, May 12, 1862, OR, vol. 50, pt. 1, p. 1068.

23. Col. Justus Steinberger to assistant adjutant general, Department of the Pacific, June 6, 1862, OR, vol. 50, pt. 1, p. 1123.

24. Colonel Steinberger to assistant adjutant general, Department of the Pacific, June 10, 1862, OR, vol. 50, pt. 1, p. 1130.

25. Colonel Steinberger to William Rector, June 30, 1862, OR, vol. 50, pt. 2, p. 1168.

26. Special Order no. 28, Headquarters District of Oregon, June 30, 1862, OR, 1167; Special Order no. 34, Headquarters District of Oregon, July 8, 1862, OR, vol. 50, pt. 2, p. 8.

27. Jewell, "Doing nothing," 611.

28. Jewell, On Duty, 18.

29. Jewell, On Duty, 17.

30. Jewell, "Doing nothing," 612.

31. Jewell, On Duty, 18.

32. Jewell, "Doing nothing," 615.

33. Jewell, "Doing nothing," 616.

34. Jewell, On Duty, 18.

35. Waymire, quoted in Jewell, On Duty, 251; J. Henry Brown, quoted in Jewell, On Duty, 253.

36. Col. Justus Steinberger to Col. Thomas Cornelius, May 10, 1862; Col. Justus Steinberger to assistant adjutant general, Department of the Pacific, May 20, 1862, OR, vol. 50, pt. 1, pp. 1063, 1084.

37. Col. Justus Steinberger to assistant adjutant general, Department of the Pacific, May 14, 1862, OR, vol. 50, pt. 1, p. 1073.

38. Colonel Steinberger to Colonel Cornelius, May 20, 1862, OR, 1085.

39. Abstract of returns for Department of the Pacific commands, June 30, 1862, OR, vol. 50, pt. 2, p. 1168.

40. OAG, 14.

41. Col. Justus Steinberger to assistant adjutant general, Department of the Pacific, May 19, 1862, OR, vol. 50, pt. 1, p. 1082.

42. Brown, quoted in Jewell, On Duty, 253; OAG, 14; William A Clark file, CSR; James Robinson file, CSR.

43. OAG, 14.

44. Special Order no. 20, District of Oregon, June 23, 1862, OR, vol. 50, pt. 1, p. 1155.

45. Special Order no. 108, Department of the Pacific, June 23, 1862, OR, vol. 50, pt. 1, p. 1153; General Order no. 6, District of Oregon, July 7, 1862, OR, vol. 50, pt. 2, p. 7.

46. Maj. R. C. Drum to Brig. Gen. Benjamin Alvord, July 11, 1862, OR, vol. 50, pt. 2, p. 16; R. C. Drum, assistant adjutant general, to Brig. Gen. Benjamin Alvord, July 11, 1862, Thomas Cornelius file, CSR; Brig. Gen. Benjamin Alvord to assistant adjutant general, Department of the Pacific, November 2, 1862, Thomas Cornelius file, CSR.

47. See the Justus Steinberger files in U.S. Army, Letters Received.

48. Brig. Gen. George Wright to Brig. Gen. Lorenzo Thomas, adjutant general, U.S. Army, June 12, 1862, OR, vol. 50, pt. 1, p. 1133.

49. Thomas A. Scott, Acting Secretary of War, to Col. Justus Steinberger, October 12, 1861, OR, vol. 50, pt. 1, pp. 656–57; Col. Justus Steinberger to assistant adjutant general, Department of the Pacific, May 5, 1862, OR, vol. 50, pt. 1, p. 1053.

50. *Weekly Oregonian* (Portland), July 19, 1862.

51. Jewell, *On Duty*, 169.

52. Edwards, "Oregon Regiments," 48–49.

53. Thomas R. Cornelius to Lt. J. T. Apperson, August 22, 1862, John T. Apperson Papers, Special Collections, Holland Library, Washington State University (hereafter cited as Apperson Papers, HL). Had Dr. Edwards been aware of this letter when he wrote his thesis, he likely would have come to a different conclusion than the one he wrote.

54. Drake, "Oregon Cavalry," 398.

55. Lt. William B. Hughes to Lt. Col. R. F. Maury, July 12, 1862, OR, vol. 50, pt. 2, p. 20.

56. Jewell, *On Duty*, 27; Lt. Col. Reuben F. Maury to Lt. W. B. Hughes, acting assistant adjutant general, District of Oregon, July 28, 1862, OR, vol. 50, pt. 2, p. 44.

57. Crawford's report of his 1862 activities is reproduced in Alford, "Captain Medorem Crawford's 1862," 74.

58. Jewell, *On Duty*, 28–29.

59. Jewell, *On Duty*, 30.

60. Report of Lt. Col. Reuben Maury, September 22, 1862, OR, vol. 50, pt. 1, p. 167.

61. Martin, "Report of Captain Medorem Crawford," 34, 35.

62. Jewell, *On Duty*, 31.

63. Jewell, *On Duty*, 31.

64. Jewell, *On Duty*, 120.

65. Shannon, *Utter Disaster*, 115, 119.

66. This is the way Van Ornum spelled his name in several pension applications; however, other secondary writers have spelled it differently. Shannon, *Utter Disaster*, 11 (in an unnumbered footnote). Schlicke, "Massacre on the Oregon Trail," 33–43, spells both Van Ornum and Utter (Otter) differently.

67. Reuben's three sisters were named Eliza, Minerva, and Lucinda. Shannon, *Utter Disaster*, 120.

68. Col. Justus Steinberger to Lt. Col. R. F. Maury, August 11, 1862, OR, vol. 50, pt. 2, p. 62.

69. Report of Lt. Col. Reuben Maury, September 22, 1862, OR, vol. 50, pt. 1, p. 167.

70. Brig. Gen. Benjamin Alvord to Maj. R. C. Drum, July 19, 1862, OR, vol. 50, pt. 2, p. 32.

71. For a review of the treaty from the Nez Perce perspective, see Josephy, *Nez Perce Indians*, 311–32. The Palouse tribe's involvement is covered in Trafzer and Scheuerman, *Renegade Tribe*, 46–59. Coverage of the Cayuses' participation can be found in Ruby and Brown, *Cayuse Indians*, 192–204.

72. Brig. Gen. Benjamin Alvord to Honorable William Pickering, governor of Washington Territory, July 28, 1862, OR, vol. 50, pt. 2, p. 43.

73. Brig. Gen. Benjamin Alvord to Brig. Gen. George Wright, October 6, 1862, OR, vol. 50, pt. 2, p. 154.

74. George Geary to Col. George Wright, April 20, 1862, OR, vol. 50, pt. 1, p. 467.

75. Alvord arrived in San Francisco in mid-June. Brig. Gen. Benjamin Alvord to Maj. R. C. Drum, assistant adjutant general, Department of the Pacific, June 17, 1862, OR, vol. 50, pt. 2, p. 1145. Alvord explicitly states that the creation of a permanent post was discussed in his November 4 report. Brig. Gen. Benjamin Alvord to assistant adjutant general, Department of the Pacific, November 4, 1862, OR, vol. 50, pt. 2, p. 206.

76. Maj. J. S. Rinearson to Lt. Frederick Mears, August 8, 1862, OR, vol. 50, pt. 2, pp. 56–57.

77. Col. George Wright to Maj. D. C. Buel, August 9, 1861, OR, vol. 50, pt. 1, p. 561.

78. Lt. William B. Hughes to Maj. J. S. Rinearson, July 18, 1862, OR, vol. 50, pt. 2, p. 30; Brig. Gen. Benjamin Alvord to Maj. J. S. Rinearson, September 7, 1862, OR, vol. 50, pt. 2, pp. 103–4.

79. Brig. Gen. Benjamin Alvord to assistant adjutant general, Department of the Pacific, November 1, 1862, OR, vol. 50, pt. 2, pp. 206–9.

80. Brig. Gen. Benjamin Alvord to assistant adjutant general, November 1, 1862, OR, vol. 50, pt. 2, p. 208.

81. Brig. Gen. Benjamin Alvord, cited in Josephy, Nez Perce Indians, 413.

82. Alvord, cited in Josephy, Nez Perce Indians, 412.

83. Brig. Gen. Benjamin Alvord to assistant adjutant general, November 1, 1862, OR, vol. 50, pt. 2, p. 208.

84. Josephy discusses the impact additional ore strikes and emigrant trains along the periphery of the reservation had on relations with whites. Josephy, Nez Perce Indians, 414–15.

85. Weekly Oregonian (Portland), July 5, 1862.

86. Oregon Sentinel (Jacksonville), August 2, 1862.

87. Jewell, On Duty, 37.

88. OAG, 13.

89. Colonel Steinberger to Colonel Cornelius, May 20, 1862, OR, 1086–87.

90. OAG, 14.

91. OAG, 14.

92. The petition is attached to a letter from Col. Justus Steinberg to "Sir" (presumably Brig. Gen. Benjamin Alvord), August 17, 1862, OR, vol. 50, pt. 1, pp. 161–62.

93. William H. Barnhart to Col. Justus Steinberger, August 4, 1862, OR, vol. 50, pt. 1, p. 160.

94. OAG, 15.

95. OAG, 15.

96. There was a more prominent Cayuse leader named Smohalla who was also called the Dreamer. Ruby and Brown, Cayuse Indians, 266.

97. Capt. George B. Currey to Col. Justus Steinberger, August 23, 1862, OR, vol. 50, pt. 1, p. 165; OAG, 16.

98. Report of Brig. Gen. Benjamin Alvord, August 26, 1862, OR, vol. 50, pt. 1, p. 159.

99. Col. Justus Steinberger to "Sir" (presumably Brig. Gen. Benjamin Alvord), August 23, 1862, OR, vol. 50, pt. 1, p. 164.

100. Apperson, quoted in Jewell, On Duty, 190.

101. Barnhart to Colonel Steinberger, August 4, 1862, OR, vol. 50, pt. 1, 160.

102. Apperson, quoted in Jewell, *On Duty*, 191.

103. *Weekly Oregonian* (Portland), October 11, 1862; *State Republican* (Eugene City OR), October 25, 1862.

104. U.S. Government, *Report of the Commissioner*, 157–60.

105. *OAG*, 14.

106. *OAG*, 16.

107. Brig. Gen. Benjamin Alvord to assistant adjutant general, District of Oregon, November 28, 1862, OR, vol. 50, pt. 2, p. 235; *Washington Statesman* (Walla Walla), December 6, 1862.

108. Pepoon, quoted in Jewell, *On Duty*, 201.

109. *OAG*, 16.

110. Capt. George B. Currey to Gov. A. C. Gibbs, December 1862, Gibbs Papers.

111. Brig. Gen. George Wright to Capt. George B. Currey, September 1, 1862, OR, vol. 50, pt. 2, p. 95.

112. Brigadier General Alvord to Brigadier General Wright, October 6, 1863, OR, vol. 50, pt. 2, p. 157.

113. Brigadier General Alvord to assistant adjutant general, November 28, 1862, OR, vol. 50, pt. 2, p. 208.

114. Circular from Brig. Gen. Benjamin Alvord, April 14, 1863, OR, vol. 50, pt. 2, p. 398.

5. Fully Under Alvord's Control

1. *New York Daily Tribune*, October 18, 1884; *Evening Star* (Washington DC), August 8, 1885; Warner, *Generals in Blue*, 4–5. Slightly more than half of the original founders of the society were women, illustrating its progressive nature. Nicolay, *Sixty Years*, 6.

2. Brig. Gen. Benjamin Alvord to assistant adjutant general, Department of the Pacific, October 14, 1862, OR, vol. 50, pt. 2, pp. 172–73.

3. Brig. Gen. Benjamin Alvord to assistant adjutant general, Department of the Pacific, February 10, 1863, OR, vol. 50, pt. 2, p. 308.

4. Maj. R. C. Drum, assistant adjutant general, Department of the Pacific, to Brig. Gen. Benjamin Alvord, January 16, 1863, OR, vol. 50, pt. 2, p. 289.

5. Brig. Gen. Benjamin Alvord to assistant adjutant general, Department of the Pacific, February 26, 1863, OR, vol. 50, pt. 2, p. 328.

6. Brigadier General Alvord to assistant adjutant general, February 26, 1863, OR, vol. 50, pt. 2, 329.

7. Brigadier General Alvord to assistant adjutant general, February 10, 1863, OR, vol. 50, pt. 2, p. 309.

8. Josephy, *Nez Perce Indians*, 408–9.

9. Apperson, quoted in Jewell, *On Duty*, 193.

10. William V. Rinehart, quoted in Jewell, *On Duty*, 171.

11. *Washington Statesman* (Walla Walla), April 25, 1863.

12. Post returns for May 1863, CSR; *Washington Statesman* (Walla Walla), June 13, 1863.

13. Jewell, *On Duty*, 55.

14. Capt. George B. Currey to Gov. A. C. Gibbs, May 13, 1863, Gibbs Papers.

15. Kittell, *Bear Bravely On*, C-14.

16. Rinehart, quoted in Jewell, *On Duty*, 171. Historian Alvin Josephy Jr. also mentions Yakimas among the group. Josephy, *Nez Perce Indians*, 418.

17. See Currey's report in OAG, 20.

18. OAG, 19.

19. Josephy, *Nez Perce Indians*, 429.

20. Brig. Gen. Benjamin Alvord to Col. R. F. Maury, May 29, 1863, OR, vol. 50, pt. 2, p. 464.

21. Brigadier General Alvord to Colonel Maury, May 29, 1863, OR, vol. 50, pt. 2, p. 465.

22. Apperson, quoted in Jewell, *On Duty*, 59.

23. Apperson, quoted in Jewell, *On Duty*, 60.

24. Jewell, *On Duty*, 62. Traversing the high mountain passes required a great deal of ascending and descending.

25. Compiled from OAG, 127–34. The records indicate that men usually deserted in groups of two or three.

26. Apperson, quoted in Jewell, *On Duty*, 61.

27. Col. R. F. Maury to acting assistant adjutant general, July 4, 1863, OR, vol. 50, pt. 2, p. 216.

28. Colonel Maury to acting assistant adjutant general, July 4, 1863, OR, vol. 50, pt. 2, p. 216.

29. Jewell, *On Duty*, 63.

30. Jewell, *On Duty*, 64.

31. Special Order no. 40, District of Oregon, April 30, 1862, OR, vol. 50, pt. 2, p. 417.

32. See Currey report's in OAG, 22.

33. Thomas S. Harris, letter of resignation and accepting letters from superior officers, Thomas S. Harris file, CSR.

34. Apperson, quoted in Jewell, *On Duty*, 194.

35. John Apperson file, CSR.

36. Apperson, quoted in Jewell, *On Duty*, 59.

37. OAG, 22.

38. Col. R. F. Maury to acting assistant adjutant general, District of Oregon, August 8, 1863, OR, vol. 50, pt. 1, p. 218. Maury sent two communications to district headquarters that day, both related to Currey's patrol.

39. OAG, 23; Jewell, *On Duty*, 65–66.

40. OAG, 23.

41. Capt. George B. Currey to Governor Gibbs, August 1863, Gibbs Papers.

42. OAG, 24; Colonel Maury to acting assistant adjutant general, August 8, 1863, OR, vol. 50, pt. 2, p. 218.

43. Jewell, *On Duty*, 66.

44. Col. R. F. Maury to acting assistant adjutant general, District of Oregon, August 3, 1863, OR, vol. 50, pt. 1, p. 217. Currey, Maury, and the anonymous soldier correspondents all spelled the river *Malade*, with an *e*, unlike the modern spelling, which does not include the *e*.

45. Jewell, *On Duty*, 66.

46. Jewell, *On Duty*, 69.

47. Jewell, *On Duty*, 66.

48. Jewell, *On Duty*, 69.

49. OAG, 24.

50. Colonel Maury to acting assistant adjutant general, August 3, 1863, OR, 215; Jewell, *On Duty*, 69.

51. Col. R. F. Maury to Brig. Gen. Benjamin Alvord, August 24, 1863, OR, vol. 50, pt. 1, p. 220.

52. Rinehart, quoted in Jewell, *On Duty*, 175.

53. Jewell, *On Duty*, 70; Colonel Maury to Brigadier General Alvord, August 24, 1863, OR, 220.

54. For accounts of Colonel Connor and the Californians' actions at the Bear River Massacre, see Madsen, *Glory Hunter*, chap. 6; Maxwell, *Civil War Years in Utah*, 185–94; and Long, *Saints and the Union*, chap. 7.

55. Colonel Maury to Brigadier General Alvord, August 24, 1863, OR, vol. 50, pt. 2, p. 221.

56. Col. R. F. Maury to acting assistant adjutant general, District of Oregon, September 10, 1863, OR, vol. 50, pt. 1, p. 222.

57. Colonel Maury to Brigadier General Alvord, August 24, 1863, OR, 220–21.

58. Jewell, *On Duty*, 71.

59. Jewell, *On Duty*, 76.

60. Col. R. F. Maury to acting assistant general, District of Oregon, September 23, 1863, OR, vol. 50, pt. 1, p. 223.

61. OAG, 25.

62. Col. R. F. Maury to acting assistant adjutant general, October 5, 1863, OR, vol. 50, pt. 1, p. 224.

63. See Waymire's report in OAG, 65–66; Colonel Maury to acting assistant adjutant general, October 5, 1863, OR, vol. 50, pt. 2, p. 224.

64. Colonel Maury to acting assistant general, September 23, 1863, OR, 223.

65. Jewell, *On Duty*, 82.

66. Colonel Maury to acting assistant adjutant general, October 5, 1863, OR, 224.

67. *Washington Statesman* (Walla Walla), April 18, 1863; Sewell Truax, CSR.

68. Lt. J. W. Hopkins, acting assistant adjutant general, District of Oregon, to Maj. Sewell Truax, July 3, 1863, OR, vol. 50, pt. 2, p. 512; Brig. Gen. Benjamin Alvord to commanding officer at Fort Lapwai, July 22, 1863, OR, vol. 50, pt. 2, p. 540.

69. Maj. Sewell Truax to acting assistant adjutant general, Headquarters District of Oregon, July 31, 1863, OR, vol. 50, pt. 2, p. 548.

70. Brig. Gen. Benjamin Alvord to assistant adjutant general, Department of the Pacific, July 1, 1863, OR, vol. 50, pt. 2, p. 508.

71. Lt. J. W. Hopkins, acting assistant adjutant general, District of Oregon, to Capt. R. S. Caldwell, July 10, 1863, OR, vol. 50, pt. 2, pp. 517–18.

72. Brig. Gen. Benjamin Alvord to assistant adjutant general, Department of the Pacific, August 19, 1863, OR, pt. 2, pp. 581–82.

73. Brig. Gen. Benjamin Alvord to assistant adjutant general, February 26, 1863, OR, vol. 50, pt. 2, p. 328.

74. Charles S. Drew file, CSR.

75. Capt. James Van Voast to Capt. E. S. Purdy, assistant adjutant general, Department of the Pacific, November 7, 1863, OR, vol. 50, pt. 2, p. 665.

76. See Charles S. Drew, letter to Department of the Pacific headquarters, October 13, 1864, in Drew file, CSR.

77. *Oregon Sentinel* (Jacksonville), July 8, 1863.

78. *Oregon Sentinel* (Jacksonville), July 8, 1863.

79. *Oregon Sentinel* (Jacksonville), July 22, 1863.

80. Brig. Gen. George Wright to Brig. Gen. Lorenzo Thomas, adjutant general, U.S. Army, March 16, 1863, OR, vol. 50, pt. 2, pp. 354–55.

81. OAG, 8. The candor of Rinehart's comments is because they were made in a private letter to Oregon's adjutant general Cyrus Read after Rinehart had left the Oregon Cavalry.

82. Captain Van Voast to Captain Purdy, November 7, 1863, OR, vol. 50, pt. 2, p. 666.

83. R. C. Drum, assistant adjutant general, Department of the Pacific, to Lt. Col. Charles Drew, June 9, 1863, OR, vol. 50, pt. 2, p. 478.

84. Captain Van Voast to Captain Purdy, November 7, 1863, OR, vol. 50, pt. 2, p. 666.

85. Captain Van Voast to Captain Purdy, November 7, 1863, OR, vol. 50, pt. 2, p. 665.

86. Stearns, "Fort Klamath," 2.

87. William Colvig, quoted in Jewell, *On Duty*, 257.

88. Gaston, *Portland, Oregon*, 2:156–60.

89. "Proclamation from the Governor," *Morning Oregonian* (Portland), January 8, 1863.

90. Rinehart, quoted in Jewell, *On Duty*, 172.

91. *Oregon Sentinel* (Jacksonville), August 19, 1863.

92. Jewell, *On Duty*, 73.

93. Company C had the most desertions during its existence, twenty-four. Lists for each company compiled from OAG.

94. Recruiting for the First Oregon Volunteer Infantry Regiment did not begin until December 1864.

95. The charges, including being drunk on multiple occasions while on duty and others for separate conduct unbecoming an officer, can be found in his service record from November 1863 to February 1864. John F. Noble file, CSR.

96. A recruiting advertisement issued by Bond can be found in *Morning Oregonian* (Portland), September 26, 1863; Gov. Addison C. Gibbs to Brig. Gen. George Wright, July 2, 1863, OR, vol. 50, pt. 2, p. 510.

97. *Washington Statesman* (Walla Walla), January 31, 1863.

98. *State Republican* (Eugene OR), March 14, 1863.

99. *Morning Oregonian* (Portland), August 17, 1863.

100. *Weekly Oregon Statesman* (Salem), December 7, 1863.

101. Rinehart, quoted in Jewell, *On Duty*, 169.

102. W. V. Rinehart to "Lieut." (John T. Apperson), November 30, 1863, Apperson Papers, NWR.

103. Capt. George B. Currey to "Dear Lt." (John T. Apperson), April 18, 1864, Apperson Papers, NWR.

104. Brig. Gen. Benjamin Alvord to Gov. A. C. Gibbs, February 10, 1864, OR, vol. 50, pt. 2, p. 745.

105. Jewell, *On Duty*, 66.

106. Jewell, *On Duty*, 76.

107. Fort Boise remained in use until 1912; the last troops left Fort Klamath in 1890.

108. *Oregon Sentinel* (Jacksonville), September 23, 1863.

109. Brigadier General Alvord to Governor Gibbs, February 10, 1864, OR, vol. 50, pt. 2, p. 746.

6. Bold Plans

1. Brigadier General Alvord to Governor Gibbs, February 10, 1864, OR, vol. 50, pt. 2, pp. 744–45.

2. Brig. Gen. Benjamin Alvord to assistant adjutant general, Department of the Pacific, February 20, 1864, OR, vol. 50, pt. 2, p. 764.

3. Brig. Gen. Benjamin Alvord to assistant adjutant general, Department of the Pacific, March 18, 1864, OR, vol. 50, pt. 2, p. 796.

4. Brigadier General Alvord to Governor Gibbs, February 10, 1864, OR, vol. 50, pt. 2, p. 746.

5. Brigadier General Alvord to Governor Gibbs, February 10, 1864, OR, vol. 50, pt. 2, p. 745.

6. Brig. Gen. Benjamin Alvord to assistant adjutant general, Department of the Pacific, August 5, 1863, OR, vol. 50, pt. 2, pp. 556–57.

7. Capt. George B. Currey to 1st Lt. J. W. Hopkins, acting assistant adjutant general, District of Oregon, February 24, 1864, OR, vol. 50, pt. 1, pp. 307–8.

8. Captain Currey to First Lieutenant Hopkins, February 24, 1864, OR, vol. 50, pt. 2, p. 308.

9. Lt. Col. Thomas C. English to acting assistant adjutant general, District of Oregon, February 25, 1864, OR, vol. 50, pt. 2, p. 307.

10. See Brig. Gen. Benjamin Alvord's endorsement of Currey's report, March 9, 1865, in OR, vol. 50, pt. 1, p. 308.

11. Trafzer and Scheuerman, *Renegade Tribe*, 95.

12. Captain Currey to First Lieutenant Hopkins, February 24, 1864, OR, vol. 50, pt. 2, p. 308.

13. Col. R. F. Maury to 1st Lt. J. W. Hopkins, acting assistant adjutant general, District of Oregon, February 20, 1864, OR, vol. 50, pt. 2, p. 765.

14. Col. R. F. Maury to acting assistant adjutant general, District of Oregon, February 22, 1864, OR, vol. 50, pt. 2, p. 767.

15. 1st Lt. J. W. Hopkins to Lt. J. A. Waymire, February 24, 1864, OR, vol. 50, pt. 2, p. 769.

16. Ruby and Brown, *Guide to the Indian Tribes*, 55–57.

17. Drake, "Cavalry in the Indian Country," 58; Jewell, *On Duty*, 157–58.

18. Col. R. F. Maury to 1st Lt. J. W. Hopkins, acting assistant adjutant general, District of Oregon, March 2, 1864, OR, vol. 50, pt. 2, p. 775; Waymire's report in OAG, 67; Lesniak, *Let the Mountains Remember*, 34.

19. Colonel Maury to First Lieutenant Hopkins, March 2, 1864, OR, vol. 50, pt. 2, p. 775.

20. Jewell, *On Duty*, 104.

21. Col. R. F. Maury to 1st Lt. John W. Hopkins, acting assistant adjutant general, District of Oregon, March 27, 1864, OR, vol. 50, pt. 2, p. 800.

22. OAG, 67.

23. Jewell, *On Duty*, 104.

24. Jewell, *On Duty*, 68.

25. Report of Lt. James Waymire, April 17, 1864, OR, vol. 50, pt. 1, p. 311.

26. Report of Lieutenant Waymire, April 17, 1864, OR, vol. 50, pt. 1, p. 311.

27. Jewell, *On Duty*, 106.

28. Report of Lieutenant Waymire, April 17, 1864, OR, vol. 50, pt. 1, p. 312.

29. Report of Lieutenant Waymire, April 17, 1864, OR, vol. 50, pt. 1, p. 312.

30. Report of Lieutenant Waymire, April 17, 1864, OR, vol. 50, pt. 1, pp. 312–13; Jewell, *On Duty*, 106.

31. Report of Lieutenant Waymire, April 17, 1864, OR, vol. 50, pt. 1, pp. 312–13.

32. Report of Lieutenant Waymire, April 17, 1864, OR, vol. 50, pt. 1, p. 313.

33. Report of Lieutenant Waymire, April 17, 1864, OR, vol. 50, pt. 1, p. 314.

34. Report of Lieutenant Waymire, April 17, 1864, OR, vol. 50, pt. 1, p. 314.

35. Jewell, *On Duty*, 107.

36. Report of Lieutenant Waymire, April 17, 1864, OR, vol. 50, pt. 1, p. 314.

37. Jewell, *On Duty*, 107.

38. *Gold Hill Daily News* (Nevada), January 7, 1867.

39. *Gold Hill Daily News* (Nevada), January 7, 1867.

40. Report of Lieutenant Waymire, April 17, 1864, OR, vol. 50, pt. 1, p. 315.

41. 1st Lt. J. W. Hopkins, acting assistant adjutant general, to Capt. J. M. Drake, April 30, 1864, OR, vol. 50, pt. 2, p. 834; Brig. Gen. Benjamin Alvord to Headquarters, Department of the Pacific, April 29, 1864, OR, vol. 50, pt. 1, p. 310.

42. Drake, "Cavalry in the Indian Country," 14.

43. Capt. John Drake to acting assistant adjutant general, District of Oregon, November 6, 1864, OR, vol. 50, pt. 1, p. 336.

44. Special Order no. 33, District of Oregon, March 19, 1864, OR, vol. 50, pt. 2, p. 796.

45. Currey believed in using "friendly Indians as light mounted irregular troops." Capt. George B. Currey to Gov. A. C. Gibbs, January 25, 1864, Gibbs Papers.

46. There are discrepancies between what Drake included in his official report in 1864 and the notes he added to the journal he kept during the expedition. Capt. John Drake to acting assistant adjutant general, District of Oregon, November 6, 1864, OR, vol. 50, pt. 2, p. 335; Drake, "Cavalry in the Indian Country," 11.

47. Drake, "Cavalry in the Indian Country," 13.

48. Drake, "Cavalry in the Indian Country," 15–16.

49. Drake, "Cavalry in the Indian Country," 101.

50. Drake, "Cavalry in the Indian Country," 29, 89.

51. Dumreicher file, CSR.

52. Drake, "Cavalry in the Indian Country," 14.

53. Drake, "Cavalry in the Indian Country," 16.

54. John M. Drake, quoted in Jewell, On Duty, 112.

55. Drake, "Cavalry in the Indian Country," 58.

56. Drake, "Cavalry in the Indian Country," 16.

57. Drake, quoted in Jewell, On Duty, 112; Drake, "Cavalry in the Indian Country," 22.

58. Unless otherwise noted, information about Drake's movements in subsequent paragraphs is taken from Drake, "Cavalry in the Indian Country," 13–16.

59. Drake, "Cavalry in the Indian Country," 17.

60. Ruby and Brown, Guide to the Indian Tribes, 264.

61. Drake, "Cavalry in the Indian Country," 22.

62. Drake, "Cavalry in the Indian Country," 22.

63. Drake, "Cavalry in the Indian Country," 24.

64. Drake, "Cavalry in the Indian Country," 24. While the two camps cannot be determined exactly, since the first was near Madras (elevation 2,242 feet) and the command passed to the north of the base of Grizzly Mountain, which is roughly 3,200 feet, the trail gained some elevation.

65. Drake, "Cavalry in the Indian Country," 24.

66. Brig. Gen. Benjamin Alvord to assistant adjutant general, Department of the Pacific, June 1, 1864, OR, vol. 50, pt. 2, p. 316; Drake, "Cavalry in the Indian Country," 25.

67. Drake, "Cavalry in the Indian Country," 25.

68. Drake, "Cavalry in the Indian Country," 26.

69. Drake, "Cavalry in the Indian Country," 31.

70. John M. McCall, quoted in Jewell, On Duty, 113; Jewell, "'All Cut to Pieces,'" 82.

71. McCall, quoted in Jewell, On Duty, 114; Jewell, "'All Cut to Pieces,'" 82.

72. Jewell, "'All Cut to Pieces,'" 82.

73. Jewell, On Duty, 116.

74. Jewell, On Duty, 118.

75. Jewell, *On Duty*, 114.

76. Drake, "Cavalry in the Indian Country," 31.

77. Drake, "Cavalry in the Indian Country," 32.

78. Drake, "Cavalry in the Indian Country," 33. Drake was more detailed in his journal than he was in his official report.

79. Drake, quoted in Jewell, *On Duty*, 111.

80. Drake, "Cavalry in the Indian Country," 37.

81. Drake, "Cavalry in the Indian Country," 39; Jewell, *On Duty*, 116.

82. Drake, quoted in Jewell, *On Duty*, 112.

83. Jewell, *On Duty*, 117.

84. Unless otherwise noted, the entire paragraph is based on information from Drake's journal between May 19 and June 6, in Drake, "Oregon Cavalry," 38–49.

85. Drake, "Cavalry in the Indian Country," 45.

86. Drake, "Cavalry in the Indian Country," 38–49.

87. Drake, "Cavalry in the Indian Country," 49.

88. Jewell, *On Duty*, 118.

89. Drake, "Oregon Cavalry," 45.

90. Lt. Col. Thomas C. English to acting assistant adjutant general, District of Oregon, March 6, 1864, OR, vol. 50, pt. 2, p. 782.

91. See Currey's report in OAG, 30.

92. OAG, 31.

93. Lt. J. W. Hopkins to Lt. Col. Thomas C. English, March 23, 1864, OR, vol. 50, pt. 2, p. 798.

94. Lieutenant Hopkins to Captain Currey, April 11, 1864, OR, vol. 50, pt. 2, p. 815.

95. Jewell, *On Duty*, 129.

96. Report of Capt. George B. Currey, April 28, 1864, OR, vol. 50, pt. 1, p. 317; OAG, 29–30.

97. I am using the spelling as given by Ruby and Brown in their history of the Cayuse tribe. Ruby and Brown, *Cayuse Indians*.

98. OAG, 30.

99. OAG, 31.

100. Report of Capt. George B. Currey, April 28, 1864, OR, vol. 50, pt. 1, p. 317.

101. OAG, 32.

102. OAG, 34.

103. OAG, 36, 38; Michno, *Deadliest Indian War*, 31.

104. OAG, 36.

105. OAG, 38.

106. OAG, 39.

107. OAG, 38–39. The total number of Paiutes killed is not entirely clear, since Currey reported two different numbers: six in his official report on June 8, 1864, in OR, vol. 50, pt. 1, p. 319, and five in OAG, 38–39.

108. OAG, 39; Currey report, June 8, 1864, OR, vol. 50, pt. 1, p. 319.

109. McArthur and McArthur, *Oregon Geographic Names*, 106.

110. *OAG*, 40; Capt. George B. Currey to assistant adjutant general, District of Oregon, July 2, 1864, *OR*, vol. 50, pt. 1, p. 320.

111. Capt. George B. Currey to Gov. A. C. Gibbs, August 18, 1864, Gibbs Papers.

112. The early part of Drake's campaign is covered in Lesniak, *Let the Mountains Remember*, chap. 5.

113. Jewell, *On Duty*, 130.

114. Drake, "Oregon Cavalry," 52.

115. Drake does not mention what became of the woman, but the Warm Springs scouts divided up what they found in her encampment. Drake, "Oregon Cavalry," 52.

116. Drake, "Oregon Cavalry," 60.

117. *OAG*, 40.

118. *OAG*, 40–42. Michno says Cayuse George's last name was Rundell; however, there was more than one "Cayuse George" in the period prior to and through early statehood. Michno, *Deadliest Indian War*, 377 (index with lists of references to Rundell); Drake, "Cavalry in the Indian Country," 80.

119. Drake, "Cavalry in the Indian Country," 67–68; Michno, *Deadliest Indian War*, 41; Jewell, *On Duty*, 134.

7. Missed Opportunities

1. Drake, "Cavalry in the Indian Country," 25.

2. Drake, "Cavalry in the Indian Country," 67.

3. Jewell, *On Duty*, 134.

4. John F. Noble, diary entry for July 4, 1864, MS 577, Noble Papers.

5. Drake, "Cavalry in the Indian Country," 67.

6. See Currey report, in *OAG*, 43.

7. Drake, "Cavalry in the Indian Country," 68.

8. Drake, "Cavalry in the Indian Country," 69.

9. Pepoon, quoted in Jewell, *On Duty*, 221.

10. Drake, "Cavalry in the Indian Country," 171.

11. *OAG*, 43.

12. Pepoon, quoted in Jewell, *On Duty*, 223.

13. Drake, "Cavalry in the Indian Country," 72–73; *OAG*, 42–43; Pepoon, quoted in Jewell, *On Duty*, 223.

14. Drake, "Cavalry in the Indian Country," 73.

15. Pepoon, quoted in Jewell, *On Duty*, 224.

16. *OAG*, 43.

17. Drake, "Cavalry in the Indian Country," 73–74.

18. Pepoon, quoted in Jewell, *On Duty*, 224.

19. Drake, "Cavalry in the Indian Country," 75.

20. Drake, "Cavalry in the Indian Country," 76.

21. *OAG*, 43.

22. Drake, "Cavalry in the Indian Country," 79.

23. Drake, "Cavalry in the Indian Country," 74, 75.

24. Pepoon, quoted in Jewell, *On Duty*, 201, 219, 223.

25. Drake, "Cavalry in the Indian Country," 75. Dr. Thomas Condon was an active amateur paleontologist during the early Oregon years. "Dr. Thomas Condon," *The Oregon History Project*, last modified March 17, 2018, https://www.oregonhistoryproject .org/articles/historical-records/dr-thomas-condon/#.x44n-nbkg2w.

26. See John Drake's letter to Thomas Condon, July 19, 1864, in McCornack, *Thomas Condon*, 36–37.

27. *Weekly Oregon Statesman* (Salem), July 25, 1864.

28. OAG, 43.

29. Drake, "Cavalry in the Indian Country," 68.

30. Drake, "Cavalry in the Indian Country," 74.

31. Drake, "Cavalry in the Indian Country," 80.

32. See a letter published in the *Morning Oregonian* (Portland), July 4, 1864, as an example, but more appear to have been published in *The Dalles Mountaineer* from comments by both Drake and Currey. Jewell, *On Duty*, 108–9.

33. Drake, "Cavalry in the Indian Country," 81–82.

34. *Weekly Oregon Statesman* (Salem), June 27, 1864.

35. *Semi Weekly Sentinel* (Jacksonville OR), September 23, 1863.

36. R. C. Drum to Lt. Col. C. S. Drew, March 18, 1864, OR, vol. 50, pt. 2, p. 804.

37. C. S. Drew, "Official Report of the Owyhee Reconnaissance Made by Lieut. Colonel C. S. Drew, 1st Oregon Cavalry, in the Summer of 1864," *Ethnohistory* 2, no. 2 (1955): 151. The original report was published serially in the *Semi Weekly Sentinel* (Jacksonville OR) in December 1864 and January 1865.

38. Lt. Col. C. S. Drew to assistant adjutant general, Department of the Pacific, June 24, 1864, OR, vol. 50, pt. 2, p. 877.

39. *Semi Weekly Sentinel* (Jacksonville OR), March 19, 1864.

40. Examples of the many articles include ones written in the *Semi Weekly Sentinel* (Jacksonville OR) on March 19, May 28, and June 18, 1864.

41. *Semi Weekly Sentinel* (Jacksonville OR), June 18, 1864.

42. Captain Van Voast to Captain Purdy, November 7, 1863, OR, vol. 50, pt. 2, pp. 665–66.

43. For an overview of Drew's activities in 1862 and 1863, see Jewell, *On Duty*, 10, 46, 50.

44. Michno, *Deadliest Indian War*, 54.

45. Drew, "Official Report," 152.

46. Jewell, *On Duty*, 138.

47. Drew, "Official Report," 152.

48. Drew, "Official Report," 154.

49. A note on the monthly returns for July and August states that Kelly left the column on July 9. William Kelly file, CSR. Michno gives July 8, though the monthly return makes it clear it was a day later. Michno, *Deadliest Indian War*, 55.

50. See Kelly, CSR, for communication between the dates of August 1 and August 14, 1864. See also *Weekly Oregon Statesman* (Salem), July 25, 1864. The Salem paper quotes sources in Jacksonville, including the local newspaper.

51. *Weekly Oregon Statesman* (Salem), July 25, 1864.

52. Drew, "Official Report," 155–56. Author Gregory Michno states that the civilian's name was John Richardson. Michno, *Deadliest Indian War*, 54–55.

53. Drew, "Official Report," 157, 158.

54. Drew, "Official Report," 158, 159.

55. Drew, "Official Report," 160.

56. Michno, *Deadliest Indian War*, 61n4.

57. Drew misspells the city of Sevastopol, part of the Russian Empire besieged for almost a year during the Crimean War.

58. Drew, "Official Report," 163.

59. Michno states that Chief Paulina's band was about to attack until it saw the mountain howitzer. Michno, *Deadliest Indian War*, 56.

60. Drew, "Official Report," 164.

61. Drew, "Official Report," 165.

62. Drew, "Official Report," 167.

63. Drew, *Official Report*, 19.

64. Brig. Gen. George Wright to Lt. Col. R. C. Drum, assistant adjutant general, Department of the Pacific, August 12, 1864, OR, vol. 50, pt. 2, p. 943.

65. Drew, "Official Report," 169.

66. Drew, "Official Report," 170; *Oregon Sentinel* (Jacksonville), December 10, 1864.

67. *Semi Weekly Sentinel* (Jacksonville OR), December 19, 1864.

68. *Semi Weekly Sentinel* (Jacksonville OR), December 10, 1864.

69. Drake, "Cavalry in the Indian Country," 81, 82.

70. Ludington, "Newspapers of Oregon," 259–60; Turnbull, *History of Oregon Newspapers*, 283. Drake and some of the Oregon troopers commented about the editor's hostility toward them.

71. Drake, "Cavalry in the Indian Country," 86.

72. Drake, "Cavalry in the Indian Country," 91.

73. Drake, "Cavalry in the Indian Country," 85; Jewell, *On Duty*, 183.

74. Drake, "Cavalry in the Indian Country," 93.

75. Drake, "Cavalry in the Indian Country," 92.

76. J. A. Waymire to "Dear Apperson" (John T. Apperson), September 4, 1864, Apperson Papers, HL.

77. Drake, "Cavalry in the Indian Country," 107.

78. Drake, "Cavalry in the Indian Country," 89.

79. Drake, "Cavalry in the Indian Country," 107.

80. He reached the camp on August 26; Drake's last mention of his presence in camp was September 9. Drake, "Cavalry in the Indian Country," 88, 95.

81. Drake, "Cavalry in the Indian Country," 100.

82. Drake, "Cavalry in the Indian Country," 106.

83. Drake, "Cavalry in the Indian Country," 116.

84. Pepoon, quoted in Jewell, *On Duty*, 228.

85. Jewell, *On Duty*, 135.

86. *OAG*, 44.

87. *Semi Weekly Sentinel* (Jacksonville OR), December 10, 1864; *OAG*, 44.

88. Pepoon, quoted in Jewell, *On Duty*, 231.

89. *OAG*, 45.

90. Pepoon, quoted in Jewell, *On Duty*, 231.

91. *OAG*, 45.

92. *OAG*, 45; Pepoon, quoted in Jewell, *On Duty*, 233.

93. *OAG*, 46; Pepoon, quoted in Jewell, *On Duty*, 235–36.

94. *OAG*, 46.

95. Pepoon, quoted in Jewell, *On Duty*, 236.

96. *OAG*, 48–49.

97. Pepoon, quoted in Jewell, *On Duty*, 243.

98. Brig. Gen. Benjamin Alvord to Lt. Col. R. C. Drum, assistant adjutant general, Department of the Pacific, July 11, 1863, OR, vol. 50, pt. 2, p. 897.

99. Edwards, "Oregon Regiments," 177–78.

100. Lt. William M. Hand to Gov. Addison Gibbs, February 28, 1863, Gibbs Papers.

101. John T. Apperson file, CSR.

102. Kelly's orders and his communications covering this confusing episode can be found in Kelly file, CSR, between the dates of August 1 and August 14, 1864. Also see *Weekly Oregon Statesman* (Salem), July 25, 1864.

103. The entire paragraph is based on Gibbs's speech, the text of which was included in OR. Special message from Gov. Addison Gibbs, October 20, 1864, OR, vol. 50, pt. 2, p. 1021.

104. W. V. Rinehart to "Dear Apperson," January 10, 1863, Apperson Papers, NWR.

105. Special message from Governor Gibbs, October 20, 1864, OR, vol. 50, pt. 2, p. 1021. For context, see Edwards, "Oregon Regiments," 183.

106. Capt. George Currey to Gov. Addison Gibbs, April 3, 1864, Gibbs Papers.

107. Special message from Governor Gibbs, October 20, 1864, OR, vol. 50, pt. 2, p. 1021.

108. *Oregon Statesman* (Oregon City), November 28, 1864.

109. Lieutenant Hand to Governor Gibbs, February 28, 1863, Gibbs Papers.

110. Edwards, "Oregon Regiments," 184–87.

111. This number is based on a review of the rosters for each company in OAG.

112. These numbers are based on a review of the company schedules in OAG.

113. Drake, "Cavalry in the Indian Country," 117.

114. *OAG*, 49.

115. Drake is referencing what are now called the Strawberry Mountains. Drake, "Cavalry in the Indian Country," 117.

116. Drew, "Official Report," 177.

117. Currey wrote detailed descriptions of his travels in the many letters he sent to Governor Gibbs in 1863 and 1864. See George Currey to Addison C. Gibbs, Gibbs Papers.

118. Drew, "Official Report," 177.

8. Doing More with Less

1. R. C. Drum, assistant adjutant general, Department of the Pacific, to Gen. Benjamin Alvord, March 24, 1865 (9:00 a.m.), OR, vol. 50, pt. 2, p. 1170.

2. General Order no. 15, Department of the Pacific, March 7, 1862, OR, vol. 50, pt. 2, p. 1154.

3. Lt. Gen. U. S. Grant to Edwin M. Stanton, secretary of war, August 15, 1864, OR, vol. 50, pt. 2, p. 945.

4. Special Order no. 51, District of Oregon, March 3, 1865, OR, vol. 50, pt. 2, p. 1153.

5. Dates for the separation for all officers can be found in OAG, 120, 121. See also their files in CSR.

6. James Waymire file, CSR; Drake, "Cavalry in the Indian Country," 118.

7. Richard S. Caldwell file, CSR.

8. See entries for each officer in OAG, 120–24.

9. Col. R. F. Maury to Col. R. C. Drum, assistant adjutant general, Department of the Pacific, April 7, 1865, OR, vol. 50, pt. 2, pp. 1188, 1189.

10. Colonel Maury to Colonel Drum, April 7, 1865, OR, vol. 50, pt. 2, p. 1189.

11. By 1865, cavalry commands serving at a fraction of their original strength were not uncommon in the east either. In late February 1865, the famed Michigan Cavalry Brigade, serving in George Custer's division in the Shenandoah Valley, numbered less than one thousand men, or roughly three hundred men per regiment. At their formation, those regiments number over eight hundred men each. Longacre, *Custer and His Wolverines*, 265.

12. R. C. Drum, assistant adjutant general, Department of the Pacific, to Col. B. F. Maury, May 12, 1865, OR, vol. 50, pt. 2, p. 1229.

13. Edwards, "Oregon Regiments," 143, 144.

14. See Dr. David Walker's report in OAG, 60.

15. Small Capt. Henry C. Small report in OAG, 54; John F. Noble, diary entries for January 11 and 14, 1865, John F. Noble Papers, Oregon Historical Society, Portland (hereafter cited as Noble Papers).

16. John F. Noble, diary entries for January 18 and 27, 1865, Noble Papers.

17. Lt. William M. Hand to Capt. H. C. Small, March 17, 1865, OR, vol. 50, pt. 1, p. 399.

18. OAG, 54–56; John F. Noble, diary entries for March 1–April 14, 1865, Noble Papers.

19. OAG, 55.

20. The nature of the wounds is recorded in Lieutenant Noble's diary. He was not on the patrol but saw the wounded when they returned to Camp Watson. John F. Noble, diary entry for April 17, 1865, Noble Papers.

21. *OAG*, 56.

22. *OAG*, 56.

23. George W. McKinny, diary entry for April 17, 1865. Copy of original in possession of the author, courtesy of Christina Chenoweth.

24. *OAG*, 56.

25. *OAG*, 57.

26. *OAG*, 58; George W. McKinny, diary entry for April 21, 1865. Copy of original in possession of the author.

27. *OAG*, 58.

28. John F. Noble, diary entries for April 21 and 22, 1865, Noble Papers; *Oregonian* (Portland), April 17, 1865. Somewhat surprisingly, Corporal McKinny did not mention the news about the president's assassination in his diary.

29. The news that Lee had surrendered (and the false report that Jefferson Davis had been captured) was printed in the *Morning Oregonian* (Portland), April 12, 1865.

30. For examples of such short patrols, see John F. Noble, diary entries for May 2, 4, 8, and 14, 1865, Noble Papers. "Saw nothing, all quiet on the road" (May 14) is a typical entry.

31. John F. Noble, diary entry for May 21, 1865, Noble Papers; George W. McKinny diary, May 21, 1865.

32. John F. Noble, diary entry for May 23, 1865, Noble Papers; George W. McKinny diary, May 23, 1865. Corporal McKinny wrote that Captain Small took eighty-five cavalrymen with him rather than a combined force of eighty, as Lieutenant Noble recorded. I have deduced that one of the sergeants led the twelve Company G men to the camp near Cottonwood House because all three of the cavalry officers were already on assignment.

33. John F. Noble, diary entries for May 26, 27, 29, and 30 and June 2, 1865, Noble Papers.

34. George W. McKinny diary, May 31 and June 1, 1865.

35. See Matthew Fitzsimmons file, *CSR*.

36. George W. McKinny diary, May 30, 1865.

37. Order no. 27, January 30, 1865, in Charles W. Hobart file, *CSR*.

38. Hobart file, *CSR*.

39. Lt. Charles W. Hobart to Capt. William Spencer, May 27, 1864, in Hobart file, *CSR*.

40. Notes on Fort Boise returns for May 1865, in Hobart file, *CSR*.

41. Report of Lt. Charles Hobart, July 13, 1865, *OR*, vol. 50, pt. 1, p. 420.

42. Report of Lieutenant Hobart, July 13, 1865, *OR*, vol. 50, pt. 1, p. 420; Michno, *Deadliest Indian War*, 112.

43. Report of Lieutenant Hobart, July 13, 1865, *OR*, vol. 50, pt. 1, p. 420.

44. William R. Jones file, *CSR*.

45. James Walker file, *CSR*.

46. All quotes in this paragraph are from the report of Lieutenant Hobart, July 13, 1865, OR, vol. 50, pt. 1, p. 420.

47. Report of Lt. Charles Hobart, July 18, 1865, OR, vol. 50, pt. 1, p. 424; Michno, *Deadliest Indian War*, 112–14. Hobart repeatedly refers to "Sergeant" Phillips; however, Charles Phillips was a corporal at the time. He was not promoted to sergeant until August 1865.

48. George W. McKinny diary, entries for May 31 and June 9, 1865.

49. George W. McKinny diary, June 10, 1865.

50. George W. McKinny diary, June 13–16, 1865; John F. Noble, diary entries for June 13 and 16, 1865, Noble Papers.

51. George W. McKinny diary, June 16, 22, July 1 and 8; John F. Noble, diary entries for June 15 and 16, 1865, Noble Papers.

52. George W. McKinny diary, July 4, 1865.

53. The summary of Small's activities for the summer of 1865 does not mention any encounters with Indians, nor did Sergeant McKinny make note of it in his diary.

54. *Oregon Sentinel* (Jacksonville), February 18, 1865.

55. For information about the *Brother Jonathan* voyage and sinking, see Schlicke, *General George Wright*, 330–35; *Daily Mountaineer* (The Dalles OR), August 20, 1865 (quoting a report based on interviews with some survivors); Lomax, "Brother Jonathan," 243–49; and Powers, *Treasure Ship*, 3–20, 91–106.

56. Col. Reuben Maury to assistant adjutant general, Department of the Pacific, June 22, 1865, in Maury file, CSR.

57. Special Order no. 140, District of Oregon, July 13, 1865, William J. Matthews file, CSR. The tally is based on a review of Company F's roster in OAG, 198–201. One of the new recruits, George Minor, died in November. By this time, the remaining companies were no longer referred to as regiments.

58. Fort Lapwai returns for July and August 1865, John Bowen, CSR.

59. Summary of service and Special Order no. 3, Subdistrict of Boise, July 31, 1865, James L. Currey file, CSR.

60. Capt. William Kelly to E. D. Waite, acting assistant adjutant general, District of California, October 14, 1864, in Charles S. Drew file, CSR.

61. The entire paragraph is based on information in CSR. See Capt. William Kelly to E. D. White, acting assistant adjutant general, District of California, October 14, 1864, in Charles S. Drew file, CSR; Company returns, November 1864, William Kelly file, CSR.

62. Michno, *Deadliest Indian War*, 104; Captain Kelly to J. W. P. Huntington, superintendent of Indian Affairs, April 8, 1865, in William Kelly file, CSR.

63. John M. McCall mentions Chief Paulina agreeing to a treaty in August 1865 in his journal. McCall, "First Oregon Cavalry," 106.

64. July 1865 returns for Reuben F. Maury in Maury file, CSR.

65. Col. R. F. Maury to Capt. William Kelly, May 11, 1865, OR, vol. 50, pt. 2, p. 1227.

66. Lt. J. W. Hopkins, acting assistant adjutant general, to Capt. J. M. Drake or Capt. G. B. Currey, June 8, 1864, OR, vol. 50, pt. 2, p. 862.

67. Col. R. F. Maury to Capt. William Kelly, May 11, 1865, OR, vol. 50, pt. 2, 1227.

68. McCall, "First Oregon Cavalry," 89, 91; Williams, "Point Lookout," 419–20.

69. Brig. Gen. Benjamin Alvord to Lt. Col. R. C. Drum, February 24, 1865, OR, vol. 50, pt. 2, p. 1144.

70. Brigadier General Alvord to Lieutenant Colonel Drum, February 24, 1865, OR, vol. 50, no. 2, p. 1144.

71. Special Order no. 114, May 29, 1865, in John M. McCall file, CSR.

72. John M. McCall file, CSR; McCall, "First Oregon Cavalry," 98.

73. *Coos Bay Times* (Oregon), April 4, 1910; Alexander Stauff file, CSR.

74. Col. R. F. Maury to Lt. J. M. McCall, June 27, 1865, OR, vol. 50, pt. 2, pp. 1270, 1271.

75. McCall, "First Oregon Cavalry," 99, 100.

76. McCall, "First Oregon Cavalry," 101–6.

77. McCall, "First Oregon Cavalry," 106.

78. McCall never mentions his first name.

79. McCall, "First Oregon Cavalry," 108.

80. McCall, "First Oregon Cavalry," 109–22.

81. Capt. William Kelly to Capt. B. F. White, August 15, 1866, in Kelly file, CSR.

82. McCall, "First Oregon Cavalry," 122.

83. Doyle, "Auburn."

84. George W. McKinny diary, July 28 and August 20, 1865.

85. George W. McKinny diary, August 11 and 26, 1865.

86. George W. McKinny diary, July 16 and 31 and August 4, 1865.

87. Michno, *Deadliest Indian War*, 119. Michno says the captive killed one of Bowen's men in his escape attempt, but there is no mention of anyone being killed from Company G of the cavalry or Company H of the infantry; thus, I have left that out.

88. OAG, 61.

89. OAG, 62.

90. *Daily Mountaineer* (The Dalles OR), November 25, 1865; OAG, 62.

91. OAG, 62.

92. Lt. Col. John Drake to acting assistant adjutant general, District of Oregon, June 1, 1865, OR, vol. 50, pt. 2, p. 1253.

93. Jewell, *On Duty*, 267–68.

94. Jewell, *On Duty*, 268.

95. This entire paragraph is drawn from the anonymous account in Jewell, *On Duty*, 268.

96. Jewell, *On Duty*, 269–70.

97. Michno, *Deadliest Indian War*, 117–18; *Idaho World* (Idaho City), September 9, 1865.

98. Michno, *Deadliest Indian War*, 14–144.

99. War Department to Maj. Gen. Henry Halleck, October 9, 1865, *Letters from the Secretary of War*, 298.

100. Jewell, *On Duty*, 270.

101. Rinehart, quoted in Jewell, *On Duty*, 186. For an example of Currey lobbying for a winter campaign, see Capt. George Currey to Gov. A. C. Gibbs, November 7, 1864, Gibbs Papers.

102. Rinehart, quoted in Jewell, *On Duty*, 186.

103. John M. McCall and William Kelly files, CSR.

104. Jewell, *On Duty*, 271; Thomas E. Shea file, CSR.

105. Jewell, *On Duty*, 271; Perry McCord file, CSR.

106. First Oregon Infantry, John M. Drake file, CSR.

107. Michno, *Deadliest Indian War*, 149.

108. Michno, *Deadliest Indian War*, 150.

109. Michno, *Deadliest Indian War*, 151–53.

110. Michno, *Deadliest Indian War*, 154–55.

111. Jewell, *On Duty*, 271.

112. William B. Phillips, CSR.

113. OAG, 63.

114. OAG, 63.

115. OAG, 63.

116. Determined from a review of the enlistments for the members of the First Oregon Volunteer Cavalry Regiment in OAG, 120–211.

117. Drake, "Cavalry in the Indian Country," 116.

9. To the End of Their Days

1. William H. Byars, quoted in Jewell, *On Duty*, 265.

2. John B. Dimick, quoted in Jewell, *On Duty*, 248.

3. J. Henry Brown, quoted in Jewell, *On Duty*, 253–54.

4. Byars, quoted in Jewell, *On Duty*, 265.

5. *Oregon, Washington, and Idaho Gazetteer*, 310; *Weekly Oregonian* (Portland), December 21, 1870; *Morning Oregonian* (Portland), September 25, 1874.

6. Jewell, *On Duty*, 187–88.

7. *Statesman Journal* (Salem), March 5, 1920; *Weekly Oregon Statesman* (Salem), September 30, 1892.

8. Jewell, *On Duty*, 155.

9. For details on Roberts, including the fact that former captain R. A. Cowles served as acting guardian when the teenager enlisted in February 1865, see Oregon Cavalry, Jasper Roberts file, CSR; and OAG, 140.

10. Jewell, *On Duty*, 255; *Medford Mail* (Oregon), March 20, 1903.

11. *Albany Weekly Herald* (Oregon), October 1, 1896.

12. *East Oregonian* (Pendleton), July 10, 1905.

13. *Coos Bay Times* (Oregon), April 4, 1910.

14. Jewell, *On Duty*, 158.

15. Officers could resign their commissions and leave the military almost at their choosing. In some cases, the resignation was not accepted immediately, but that would only be a delay.

16. Thomas Cornelius file, CSR; Lang, *History of the Willamette Valley*, 634–35; Evans, *History of the Pacific Northwest*, 2:279–80, 285–86; Bischoff, *We Were Not Summer Soldiers*, 143.

17. Benjamin Harding file, CSR.

18. Evans, *History of the Pacific Northwest*, 2:30.

19. This portion of the sketch of David P. Thompson is based on Gaston, *Portland, Oregon*, 2:194–98.

20. David P. Thompson file, CSR.

21. Gaston, *Portland, Oregon*, 2:196–200.

22. Jewell, *On Duty*, 245–46.

23. *Capital Journal* (Salem), January 30, 1889, and February 24, 1890; Hodgkin and Galvin, *Pen Pictures*, 76; *Morning Oregonian* (Portland), April 19, 1904.

24. Peter P. Gates file, CSR; *Statesman Journal* (Salem), August 30, 1894.

25. Biographical information drawn from Jewell, *On Duty*, 261.

26. Gaston, *Portland, Oregon*, 3:411–13; *Oregonian* (Portland), May 27, 1905; *Oregon City Courier* (Oregon), June 2, 1905. In a demonstration of how the former comrades-in-arms remained in touch, when Maj. Jacob S. Rinearson died, Killin served as the executor of his estate.

27. *Statesman Journal* (Salem), June 1, 1912; *Oregon Daily Journal* (Portland), June 1, 1912.

28. John Apperson file, CSR.

29. The date of his term in the Oregon House is a correction to what I wrote in Jewell, *On Duty*, 186. Sources for the portion of the Apperson sketch are drawn from *Oregon City Courier* (Oregon), April 5, 1917; Anonymous, *Guide to the Board of Regents Records*; and Albright, "Building's Renaming Sparks Debate."

30. Lang, *History of the Willamette Valley*, 281.

31. Jewell, *On Duty*, 261.

32. Ellis, *Norwich University*, 2:535.

33. *Pittsburgh Press* (Pennsylvania), April 3, 1910; Jewell, *On Duty*, 255.

34. Jewell, *On Duty*, 199–200.

35. *Albany Democrat* (Oregon), March 16, 1888.

36. *Rogue River Courier* (Grants Pass OR), March 1, 1912.

37. Larsell, *Doctors in Oregon*, 171, 344, 353, 354; *Lebanon Express* (Oregon), February 10, 1888.

38. *Sacramento Bee*, December 5, 1910.

39. Larsell, *Doctors in Oregon*, 195; *Albany Democrat* (Oregon), March 16, 1888.

40. *Pittsburgh Press* (Kansas), April 3, 1910.

41. OAG, 137; *News-Review* (Roseburg OR), March 9 and 10, 1916; U.S. Census Office, *Compendium of the Tenth Census*, Lakeview, Oregon.

42. *Oregon Statesman* (Salem), April 14, 1862.

43. "Disbursements," in State of Oregon, *Commissioners of the State Penitentiary*, 17, 75; Penitentiary Report, in State of Oregon, *Legislative Assembly of Oregon*,

24, 30; *Weekly Oregon Statesman* (Salem), November 4, 1873; Hendricks, "Bits for Breakfast."

44. Hendricks, "Bits for Breakfast."

45. *Albany Register* (Oregon), February 5, 1875.

46. *Albany Weekly Herald* (Oregon), October 1, 1896.

47. *Helena Weekly Herald* (Montana), June 20, 1889; *Anaconda Standard* (Montana), March 31, 1905; *Independent Record* (Helena MT), July 8, 1916; entry for Adrian Nappy in U.S. Government, *Historical Register of National Homes*, 1921–22.

48. Zephaniah D. Bones, CSR; *Oregon Good Templar* (Portland), August 25, 1870.

49. Jewell, *On Duty*, 199; Pepoon, quoted in Jewell, *On Duty*, 244.

50. Jewell, *On Duty*, 199–200; *Lincoln State Journal*, August 31, 1921; *Pawnee Republican* (Nebraska), September 1, 1921.

51. George P. Ockington file, CSR; *Boston Evening Transcript*, January 5, 1888; *Boston Globe*, August 20, 1888, and June 19, 1895; *United States Civil War Pension Index: General Index to Pension Files, 1861–1934*, ser. T288, roll 353, entry for George P. Ockington, Microfilm, National Archives and Records Administration, Washington DC. Ockington served first in Company F, but as the regiment downsized, he transferred to Company C.

52. Candler and Evans, *Georgia*, 3:138.

53. Formwalt, "Camilla Massacre of 1868," 399–426.

54. *Lawrence Daily Journal World* (Lawrence KS), June 15, 1917; Almarin Nottingham file, CSR.

55. Richard S. Caldwell file, CSR; *Daily Evening News* (Fall River MA), March 19, 1869.

56. What is now the state of West Virginia seceded from Virginia after Fortney had left the state.

57. Newton Fortney, CSR; *Wheeling Daily Intelligencer* (West Virginia), April 9, 1867.

58. The Barnes biographical information is drawn from Riley C. Barnes, CSR; and *The Tribune* (Webster City IA), February 12, 1892.

59. Jewell, *On Duty*, 161–62.

60. Drake, "Cavalry in the Indian Country," 116.

61. U.S. Government, *Letters Received by the Commission Branch*, RG 94, roll 0185.

62. William Kelly file, CSR; Thrapp, *Encyclopedia of Frontier Biography*, 2:769; Henry, *Military Record*, 1:163. Kelly's active campaigning in Arizona is a correction to what is in Jewell, *On Duty*, 155–56.

63. Jacob, "Military Reminiscences," 9–36; Dines, "Scandal in the Tenth Cavalry," 125–40.

64. F. L Town, post surgeon, to surgeon general, U.S. Army, October 17, 1874, in Silas Pepoon, U.S. Government, *Letters Received by the Commission Branch*.

65. George B. Currey to "Dear Lt." (John T. Apperson), April 19, 1864, Apperson Papers, NWR.

66. Drake, "Cavalry in the Indian Country," 111.

67. A note explaining that Waymire was left behind in Oregon is included in post returns for Fort McDowell, Arizona Territory, for June 1869; Arizona, January 1866 to December 1874, U.S. War Department, *Returns from U.S. Military Posts, 1800–1916*, microfilm roll 668, National Archives and Records Administration.

68. Heitman, *Historical Register and Dictionary*, 1:1010; Shuck, *History of the Bench*, 955.

69. Shuck, *History of the Bench*, 955; *Alameda County*, 234.

70. Shuck, *History of the Bench*, 955; *Alameda County*, 234, 236; *San Francisco Call*, September 18, 1906, and April 17, 1910.

71. Rinehart, quoted in Jewell, *On Duty*, 186; Zanjani, *Sarah Winnemucca*, 137.

72. Chauncey M. Messenger, csr; *Elma Chronicle* (Washington), November 7, 1908.

73. Gilbert, *Historic Sketches*, 38–39; *Post-Intelligencer* (Seattle), February 21, 1894.

74. *St. Helens Mist* (Oregon), December 11, 1896.

75. Gilbert, *Historic Sketches*, 38–39; *Post-Intelligencer* (Seattle), February 21, 1894; *Elma Chronicle* (Washington), November 7, 1908; *St. Helens Mist* (Oregon), December 11, 1896; Grant, *History of Seattle, Washington*, 477–79; *Sunday Oregonian* (Portland), October 20, 1918.

76. Some newspaper editors did criticize the Oregon Cavalry for not being more aggressive in their dealings with the various Indian tribes. Most of that criticism was aimed at the officers. The presence of off-duty cavalrymen (and infantrymen as well) led to clashes with civilians in Walla Walla, so the community had mixed feelings toward the soldiers.

77. *Sunday Oregonian* (Portland), January 27, 1901.

78. *Morning Oregonian* (Portland), January 30, 1901.

79. *Morning Oregonian* (Portland), January 30, 1901.

80. Victor, "First Oregon Cavalry," 123–63.

81. See Currey's report in oag, 47.

82. Small's report in oag, 63.

83. Waymire's report in oag, 65.

84. General Order no. 22, District of Oregon, October 25, 1864, or, vol. 50, pt. 2, p. 1032.

85. Drew, "Official Report," 177.

86. Jewell, *On Duty*, 271.

87. Apperson, quoted in Jewell, *On Duty*, 197.

88. Jewell, *On Duty*, 118.

89. The best books on Connor's mining enterprises while serving as a district commander are Madsen, *Glory Hunter*; and Maxwell, *Civil War Years in Utah*.

90. oag, 6.

91. Waymire, "Annual Address," 48.

92. *Oakland Tribune*, June 16, 1910.

BIBLIOGRAPHY

Manuscript Collections and Archives

Anonymous. *Guide to the Board of Regents Records, 1886–1929* (Oregon Agricultural College). University Archives, Oregon State University.

Apperson, John T. Papers, 1862–1865. NWC 0328, Northwest Room, Spokane Public Library, Spokane WA.

———. Papers, 1862–1865. Cage 1631, Special Collections, Holland Library, Washington State University, Pullman WA.

Brown, J.(oseph) Henry. "The Autobiography of Joseph Henry Brown." H. H. Bancroft Collection, University of California at Berkeley.

Cornelius, Thomas R. Papers, microfilm. Oregon Historical Society, Portland.

Gibbs, Addison Crandall. Papers. Oregon Historical Society, Portland.

Matthews, William J. William J. Matthews to Dear Etta, April 22, 1862. William J. Matthews Papers. Penrose Library, Whitman College, Walla Walla WA.

McKinny, George. Diary. Typescript in possession of the author, original in possession of Ms. Christina Chenoweth, Spokane Valley, Washington.

Noble, John F. Papers. Oregon Historical Society, Portland.

Palmer, Joel. Diary, 1861. Joel Palmer Papers. MSS 114, Oregon Historical Society, Portland.

Rinehart, William Vance. *Oregon Biographical and Other Card File*. Oregon Historical Society, Portland.

Shelley, James M. "Reminiscences of Service in Company A, First Oregon Infantry, 1864–66." MSS 391, Oregon Historical Society, Portland.

Shelton, John. "Statement of John O. Shelton in regard to a secret organization in Oregon." MSS 468, Oregon Historical Society, Portland.

Walker, Cyrus H. "Why the First Oregon Volunteer Infantry Was Organized." Walker Papers, MSS 264, Oregon Historical Society, Portland.

Published Works

Abernethy, Alonzo. "Incidents of an Iowa Soldier's Life, or Four Years in Dixie." *Annals of Iowa* 12, no. 6 (1920): 402–28.

Albright, Mary Ann. "Building's Renaming Sparks Debate." *Corvallis Gazette-Times* (Oregon), January 14, 2006.

Alford, Kenneth L. "Captain Medorem Crawford's 1862 Military Escort Emigration Report." *Overland Journal* 36, no. 2 (2018): 73–76.

Anonymous. *Alameda County: The Eden of the Pacific; The Flower Garden of California*. Oakland: Press of the Oakland Tribune, 1898.

———. "Army Officer's Report on Indian War and Treaties." *Washington Historical Quarterly* 19, no. 2 (April 1928): 134–41.

———. *An Authentic Exposition of the "K.G.C." "Knights of the Golden Circle"; or, A History of Secession from 1834 to 1861*. Indianapolis: C. O. Perrine, 1861.

———. *Bay of San Francisco: The Metropolis of the Pacific Coast and Its Suburban Cities; A History*. 2 vols. Chicago: Lewis, 1892.

———. "Charles B. Montague." *Oregon Native Son* 2, no. 6 (1902): 483.

———. "Clearwater Gold Rush." *Idaho Yesterdays* 4, no. 1 (1960): 12–15, 18–26.

———. *Oregon: End of the Trail*. Portland: Binford & Mort, 1940.

———. *Oregon, Washington, and Idaho Gazetteer and Business Directory 1884–85*. Vol. 1. Chicago: R. L. Polk and A. C. Danser, 1884.

———. *Portrait and Biographical Album of Johnson and Pawnee Counties Nebraska*. Chicago: Chapman Brothers, 1889.

———. *Portrait and Biographical Record of Portland and Vicinity Oregon*. Chicago: Chapman, 1903.

———. *Portrait and Biographical Record of the Willamette Valley Oregon*. Chicago: Chapman, 1903.

———. *Portrait and Biographical Record of Western Oregon: Containing Original Sketches of Many Well Known Citizens of the Past and Present*. Chicago: Chapman, 1904.

Badger, Alexander Caldwell, Jr. "'All in Fact . . . Agree with Me': Letters from Fort Vancouver." Edited by Dennis R. Defa. *Idaho Yesterdays* 41, no. 2 (1997): 10–21.

Ball, Durwood. *Army Regulars on the Western Frontier, 1848–1861*. Norman: University of Oklahoma Press, 2001.

Bancroft, Hubert Howe. *The Pacific States*. Vol. 2. San Francisco: History Company, 1888.

Beall, Thomas B. "Pioneer Reminiscences." *Washington Historical Quarterly* 8, no. 2 (April 1917): 83–90.

Beckham, Stephen Dow. "Lonely Outpost: The Army's Fort Umpqua." *Oregon Historical Quarterly* 70, no. 3 (1969): 233–57.

Beckwith, Albert Clayton. *History of Walworth County Wisconsin*. 2 vols. Indianapolis: B. F. Bowen, 1912.

Bensell, Royal A. *All Quiet on the Yamhill: The Civil War in Oregon*. Edited by Gunther Barth. Eugene: University of Oregon Press, 1959.

Bischoff, William N., ed. *We Were Not Summer Soldiers: The Indian War Diary of Plympton J. Kelly, 1855–1856*. Tacoma: Washington State Historical Society, 1976.

Blackett, R. J. M. *Divided Hearts: Britain and the American Civil War*. Baton Rouge: Louisiana State University Press, 2001.

Britton, Jesse Duane. "Bureaucrats, Miners, and the Nez Perce Indians: Treaty-Making in Washington Territory during the Civil War." PhD diss., Washington State University, 1988.

Brooks, Clinton E., and Frank D. Reeve, eds. "James A. Bennett: A Dragoon in New Mexico, 1850–1856." *New Mexico Historical Quarterly* 22, no. 2 (1947): 140–76.

Brown, J. Henry. *Brown's Political History of Oregon*. Vol. 1. Portland: Wiley B. Allen, 1892.

Browning, Judkin, and Timothy Silver. *An Environmental History of the Civil War*. Chapel Hill: University of North Carolina Press, 2020.

Burns, Robert Ignatius. *The Jesuits and the Indian Wars of the Northwest*. New Haven CT: Yale University Press, 1966.

Candler, Allen D., and Clement A. Evans. *Georgia*. 3 vols. Atlanta: State Historical Association, 1906.

Carmony, Donald F., ed. "Jacob W. Bartmess Civil War Letters." *Iowa Magazine of History* 52, no. 1 (1956): 49–74.

Carroon, Robert Girard, and Dana B. Shoaf. *Union Blue: The History of the Military Order of the Loyal Legion of the United States*. Shippensburg PA: White Maine, 2001.

Clark, William S. "Pioneer Experiences in Walla Walla." *Washington Historical Quarterly* 24, no. 1 (January 1933): 9–24.

Colmer, Montagu, and Charles E. S. Wood. *History of the Bench and Bar of Oregon*. Portland: Historical Publishing, 1910.

Corning, Howard McKinley. *Dictionary of Oregon History*. Hillsboro OR: Binford & Mort, 1989.

Coulter, C. Brewster, ed. *The Pig War and Other Experiences of William Peck: Soldier 1858–1862*. Medford OR: Webb Research Group, 1993.

Crenshaw, Olinger. "The Knights of the Golden Circle: The Career of George Bickley." *American Historical Review* 47, no. 1 (1941): 23–50.

Crum, Steven. "The Paddy Cap Band of Northern Paiutes: From Southwestern Oregon to the Duck Valley Reservation." *Nevada Historical Quarterly* 51, no. 3 (2008): 183–99.

Cullum, George W. *Biographical Register of the Officers and Graduates of the U.S. Military Academy at West Point, N.Y.: From Its Establishment in 1802 to 1890*. Boston: Houghton-Mifflin, 1891.

Cutler, Donald. *"Hang Them All": George Wright and the Plateau Indian War*. Norman: University of Oklahoma Press, 2016.

———. "'You Nations Shall Be Exterminated.'" *Military History Quarterly* 22, no. 3 (2010): 46–53.

Davenport, T. W. "Recollections of an Indian Agent." *Oregon Historical Quarterly* 8, no. 1 (March 1907): 1–50.

Dennison, George T., Jr. *Modern Cavalry: Its Organization, Armament, and Employment in War.* London: Thomas Bosworth, 1868.

Dines, Bruce J. "Scandal in the Tenth Cavalry: A Fort Sill Case History, 1874." *Arizona and the West* 28, no. 2 (1986): 125–40.

Doyle, Susan Badger. "Auburn." Oregon Encyclopedia. Accessed February 25, 2022. https://www.oregonencyclopedia.org/articles/auburn/#.YugH13bMKUk.

Drake, John M. "Cavalry in the Indian Country, 1864." Edited by Priscilla Knuth. *Oregon Historical Quarterly* 65, no. 1 (1964): 4–119.

———. "The Oregon Cavalry." *Oregon Historical Society Quarterly* 65, no. 4 (1964): 392–400.

Drew, C. S. *Official Report of the Owyhee Reconnaissance.* Jacksonville: Oregon Sentinel, 1864.

———. "Official Report of the Owyhee Reconnaissance Made by Lieut. Colonel C. S. Drew, 1st Oregon Cavalry, in the Summer of 1864." *Ethnohistory* 2, no. 2 (1955): 146–82.

Dunn, J. P., Jr. *Massacres of the Mountains: A History of the Indian Wars of the Far West, 1815–1875.* New York: Archer House, 1958.

Dustin, Charles Mial. "The Knights of the Golden Circle: The Story of the Pacific Coast Secessionists." *Pacific Monthly* 16, no. 5 (1911): 495–504.

Edwards, Glenn Thomas, Jr. "Benjamin Stark, the U.S. Senate, and 1862 Membership Issues, Pt. I." *Oregon Historical Quarterly* 72, no. 4 (Winter 1971): 315–38.

———. "The Department of the Pacific in the Civil War." PhD diss., University of Oregon, 1963.

———. "Holding the Far West for the Union: The Army in 1861." *Civil War History* 14, no. 4 (1968): 307–24.

———. "Oregon Regiments in the Civil War Years: Duty on the Indian Frontier." Master's thesis, University of Oregon, 1960.

———. "Six Oregon Leaders and the Far-Reaching Impact of America's Civil War." *Oregon Historical Quarterly* 100, no. 1 (Spring 1999): 4–31.

Ellis, William Arba. *Norwich University, 1819–1911: Her History, Her Graduates, Her Honor Roll.* 3 vols. Montpelier VT: Capital City Press, 1911.

Ellison, Joseph. "Designs for a Pacific Republic, 1843–62." *Oregon Historical Quarterly* 31, no. 4 (1930): 321–42.

Etulain, Richard. *Lincoln and Oregon Country Politics in the Civil War Era.* Corvallis: Oregon State University Press, 2013.

Evans, Elwood. *History of the Pacific Northwest: Oregon and Washington.* 2 vols. Portland: North Pacific History Company, 1889.

Fendall, Lon W. "Medorem Crawford and the Protective Corps." *Oregon Historical Quarterly* 72, no. 1 (1973): 55–77.

Fenton, William D. "Edward Dickinson Baker." *Oregon Historical Quarterly* 9, no. 1 (1908): 1–23.

Ficken, Robert E. *Washington Territory.* Pullman: Washington State University Press, 2002.

Field, Virgil, comp. *The Official History of the Washington National Guard.* 7 vols. Tacoma: Headquarters Military Department of Washington Office of the Adjutant General, n.d.

Fischer, LeRoy H. "The Western States in the Civil War." *Journal of the West* 14, no. 1 (January 1975): 1–4.

Formwalt, Lee W. "The Camilla Massacre of 1868: Radical Violence as Political Propaganda." *Georgia Historical Quarterly* 71, no. 3 (1987): 399–426.

Forte, David George. "Civil War Activities in the Northwest." Master's thesis, Central Washington University, 1979.

Frazer, Robert W. *Forts of the West.* Norman: University of Oklahoma Press, 1972.

Frost, Robert. "Fraser River Gold Rush Adventures." *Washington Historical Quarterly* 22, no. 3 (July 1931): 203–10.

Gallagher, Patrick, ed. "Through Battle, Prison, and Disease: The Civil War Diaries of George Richardson Crosby." *Vermont History* 76, no. 1 (2008): 19–45.

Gamboa, Erasmo. "Supply Line to the New Frontier." *Columbia* 8, no. 4 (1994): 21–28.

Gaston, Joseph. *Centennial History of Oregon.* Chicago: S. J. Clarke, 1912.

———. *Portland, Oregon: Its History and Builders.* 3 vols. Chicago: S. J. Clarke, 1911.

Gibbs, Addison. "Oregon Grapeshot." *Oregon Historical Quarterly* 65, no. 3 (1964): 296.

Gibbs, George. "Beginnings of Militia in Washington." *Washington Historical Quarterly* 11, no. 3 (July 1920): 202.

Gilbert, Benjamin. "Rumours of Confederate Privateers Operating in Victoria, Vancouver Island." *British Columbia Historical Quarterly* 18, nos. 3–4 (1954): 239–54.

Gilbert, Frank T. *Historic Sketches of Walla Walla, Whitman, Columbia, and Garfield Counties, Washington and Umatilla County, Oregon.* Portland: Printing and Lithographing House of A. G. Walling, 1882.

Gilliss, Julia. *So Far from Home: An Army Bride on the Western Frontier, 1865–1869.* Edited by Priscilla Knuth. Portland: Oregon Historical Society Press, 1993.

Gorley, Hugh A. "The Loyal Californians of 1861." In *Civil War Papers of the California Commandery of the Military Order of the Loyal Legion of the United States,* 197–211. Wilmington NC: Broadfoot, 1995.

Goulder, W. A. *Reminiscences: Incidents in the Life of a Pioneer in Oregon and Idaho.* Boise: Timothy Regan, 1909.

Grant, Frederic James. *History of Seattle, Washington.* New York: American Publishing and Engraving, 1891.

Griffin, Dorsey. *Who Really Killed Chief Paulina? An Oregon Documentary.* Netarts OR: Self-published, 1991.

Hageman, Todd. "Lincoln and Oregon." Master's thesis, Eastern Illinois University, 1988.

Haller, Granville O. *The Dismissal of Major Granville O. Haller of the Regular Army of the United States by Order of the Secretary of War*. Paterson NJ: Daily Guardian, 1863.

———. *San Juan and Secession*. Seattle: Shorey Book Store, 1967.

Hamblett, E. T. "Sovereign Americans on San Juan Island." *Washington Historical Quarterly* 1, no. 1 (1906): 75–77.

Hansen, David Kimball. "Public Response to the Civil War in Washington Territory and Oregon, 1861–1865." Master's thesis, University of Washington, 1971.

Hawthorne, Julian, and George Douglas Brewerton. *History of Washington: The Evergreen State, from Early Dawn to Daylight*. New York: American Historical Publishing Company, 1893.

Heitman, Francis B. *Historical Register and Dictionary of the United States Army, from Its Organization, September 29, 1789, to March 2, 1903*. 2 vols. Washington DC: Government Printing Office, 1903.

Hendricks, R. J. "Bits for Breakfast." *Oregon Statesman* (Salem), March 30, 1934.

Henry, Guy Vernor. *Military Record of Civilian Appointments in the United States Army*. Vol. 1. New York: D. Van Nostrand, 1873.

Hickenlooper, Frank. *An Illustrated History of Monroe County, Iowa*. Kansas City MO: Hudson-Kimberly, 1896.

Hodgkin, Frank E., and J. J. Galvin. *Pen Pictures of Representative Men of Oregon*. Portland: Farmer and Dairyman, 1882.

Hoop, Oscar Winslow. "History of Fort Hoskins, 1856–65." *Oregon Historical Quarterly* 30, no. 4 (1929): 346–61.

Hopper, Sidney Glenn. *Indian Wars in the Old Pacific Northwest*. Burnaby, British Columbia: Artarmon, 1996.

Hull, Dorothy. "The Movement in Oregon for the Establishment of a Pacific Coast Republic." *Oregon Historical Quarterly* 15, no. 3 (1916): 177–200.

Hunt, Aurora. *The Army of the Pacific, 1860–1866*. Glendale CA: Arthur H. Clark, 1951.

Husby, Karla Jean, comp. *Under Custer's Command: The Civil War Journal of James Henry Avery*. Edited by Eric J. Wittenberg. Washington DC: Brassey's, 2000.

Jacob, Richard T. "Military Reminiscences of Captain Richard T. Jacob." *Chronicles of Oklahoma* 2, no. 1 (1924): 9–36.

Jacobs, Orange. *The Memoirs of Orange Jacobs*. Seattle: Lowman & Hanford, 1908.

Jewell, James Robbins. "'All Cut to Pieces': Lt. John McCall and the First Oregon Cavalry Regiment on the Crooked River." *Military History of the West* 45 (2016): 77–87.

———, ed. "'Dear Mrs. Wilmer': Trooper J.J. Rohn Describes the Steptoe Battlefield." *Military History of the West* 32, no. 2 (2002): 71–77.

———, ed. "'Doing nothing with a vengeance': The Diary of David Hobart Taylor, First Oregon Cavalry, January 1–May 30, 1862." *Oregon Historical Quarterly* 110, no. 4 (Winter 2009): 598–622.

———. "Fighting the Civil War in the Far West: Captain John Drake and the Firefight along Crooked River, Oregon." *Blue and Gray Magazine* 32, no. 5 (2016): 25–27.

———. "Left Arm of the Republic: The Department of the Pacific during the Civil War." PhD diss., West Virginia University, 2006.

———, ed. *On Duty in the Pacific Northwest during the Civil War: Correspondence and Reminiscences of the First Oregon Cavalry Regiment.* Knoxville: University of Tennessee Press, 2018.

———. "Thwarting Southern Schemes and British Bluster in the Pacific Northwest." In *Civil War West: Testing the Limits of the United States,* edited by Adam Arenson and Andy Graybill, 15–32. Berkeley: University of California Press, 2015.

Johannsen, Robert W., ed. "A Breckinridge Democrat on the Secession Crisis: Letters of Isaac I. Stevens, 1860–61." *Oregon Historical Quarterly* 55, no. 4 (1954): 283–310.

———. *Frontier Politics and the Sectional Conflict: The Pacific Northwest on the Eve of the Civil War.* Seattle: University of Washington Press, 1955.

———. "Spectators of Disunion: The Pacific Northwest and the Civil War." *Pacific Northwest Quarterly* 44, no. 3 (1953): 106–14.

Johnson, Sidona, comp. *A Short History of Oregon.* Chicago: A. C. McClurg, 1904.

Jolivette, Tristan Edward. "Continuing the Cause: Union Soldier Reenlistments of 1864." Master's thesis, California State University, 1999.

Josephy, Alvin, Jr. *The Civil War in the American West.* New York: Alfred A. Knopf, 1991.

———. *The Nez Perce Indians and the Opening of the Northwest.* Boston: Mariner, 1997.

Keehn, David C. *Knights of the Golden Circle: Secret Empire, Southern Secession, Civil War.* Baton Rouge: Louisiana State University Press, 2013.

Kenner, Charles L. *Buffalo Soldiers and Officers of the Ninth Cavalry, 1867–1898.* Norman: University of Oklahoma Press, 1999.

Kenny, Judith Keyes. "Founding of Camp Watson." *Oregon Historical Quarterly* 58, no. 1 (1957): 5–18.

Keyes, Erasmus D. *Fifty Years Observation of Men and Events.* New York: Charles Scribner's Sons, 1884.

Kibby, Leo P. "Union Loyalty of California's Civil War Governors." *California Historical Society Quarterly* 44, no. 4 (1965): 311–21.

Kincaid, Harrison Rittenhouse. *Political and Official History and Register of Oregon.* N.p.: 1899.

King, W. W. "Pacific Coast Soldiers." *National Tribune,* October 21, 1886.

Kingsnorth, Carolyn. "Paine Page Prim: Lawyer, Judge, Supreme Court Justice." *Jacksonville Review* (Oregon), November 30, 2016. https://jacksonvillereview.com/paine-page-prim-lawyer-judge-supreme-court-justice-carolyn-kingsnorth/.

Kip, Lawrence. *Indian War in the Pacific Northwest.* Lincoln: University of Nebraska Press, 1999.

Kittell, Allan, ed. *Bear Bravely On: Letters from Sergeant John Buel Dimick, First Oregon Volunteer Cavalry, to Almira Eberhard, 1862–1865.* Portland: Lewis and Clark College, 1983.

Kittredge, Frank A., comp. "Washington Territory in the War between the States." *Washington Historical Quarterly* 2, no. 1 (October 1907): 33–39.

Knox, Bonnie, and Larry D. Knox. *Pinkney Lugenbeel*. Wooster OH: Self-published, 1990.

Knuth, Priscilla. "'Picturesque' Frontier: The Army's Fort Dalles." *Oregon Historical Quarterly* 67, nos. 3–4 (1966): 5–53, 292–333.

Kuykendall, George B. "Reminiscences of Early Days at the Old Umpqua Academy." *Oregon Historical Quarterly* 19, no. 1 (1918): 34–36.

Lacy, Ruby, and Lida Childers. *Pioneer Peoples of Jackson County, Oregon*. Ashland OR: R. Lacy, 1990.

LaLande, Jeff. "'Dixie' of the Pacific Northwest: Southern Oregon's Civil War." *Oregon Historical Quarterly* 100, no. 1 (Spring 1999): 32–81.

Landes, Cheryl. "The San Juan Island Pig War." *Canadian West* 10, no. 2 (Summer 1994): 16–18.

Lang, H. O. *History of the Willamette Valley*. Portland: George H. Himes, 1885.

Larsell, O. *The Doctor in Oregon: A Medical History*. Portland: Oregon Historical Society, 1947.

Larson, James. *Sergeant Larson*. San Antonio TX: Southern Literary Institute, 1935.

Lesniak, D. J. *Let the Mountains Remember*. Bend OR: Maverick, 2014.

Lewis, William S. "The First Militia Companies in Eastern Washington Territory." *Washington Historical Quarterly* 11, no. 4 (October 1920): 243–49.

Lomax, Alfred L. "Brother Jonathan: Pioneer Steamship of the Pacific Coast." *Oregon Historical Quarterly* 60, no. 3 (1959): 243–49.

Long, E. B. *The Saints and the Union: Utah Territory during the Civil War*. Urbana: University of Illinois Press, 1981.

Longacre, Edward G. *Custer and His Wolverines: The Michigan Cavalry Brigade, 1861–1865*. Conshohocken PA: Combined, 1997.

Lonn, Ella. *Desertion during the Civil War*. Lincoln: University of Nebraska Press, 1998.

Lowe, Percival Green. *Five Years a Dragoon ('49 to '54): And Other Adventures on the Great Plains*. Kansas City MO: Franklin Hudson, 1906.

Ludington, Flora Belle. "The Newspapers of Oregon, 1846–1870." *Oregon Historical Quarterly* 26, no. 3 (1925): 229–62.

Lutz, John. "Inventing an Indian War: Canadian Indians and American Settlers in the Pacific Northwest, 1854–1864." *Journal of the West* 38, no. 3 (July 1998): 7–13.

Lyman, W. D. *Lyman's History of Old Walla Walla County*. Chicago: S. J. Clarke, 1918.

MacDonald, Benjamin. "Narrative." *Washington Historical Quarterly* 16, no. 3 (July 1925): 186–97.

Madsen, Brigham. *The Bannock of Idaho*. Moscow: University of Idaho Press, 1996.

———. *Glory Hunter: A Biography of Patrick Edward Hunter*. Salt Lake City: University of Utah Press, 1990.

———. *The Northern Shoshoni*. Caldwell ID: Caxton, 2000.

Manring, Benjamin. *Conquest of the Coeur D'Alenes, Spokanes, and Palouses*. Fairfield WA: Ye Galleon, 1975.

Martin, Charles W. "Report of Captain Medorem Crawford, Part II." *Overland Journal* 3, no. 1 (1985): 27–37.

Marvel, William. *Lincoln's Mercenaries: Economic Motivation among Union Soldiers during the Civil War*. Baton Rouge: Louisiana State University Press, 2018.

Masich, Andrew E. *The Civil War in Arizona: The Story of the California Volunteers, 1861–1865*. Norman: University of Oklahoma Press, 2006.

———. *Civil War in the Southwest Borderlands, 1861–1867*. Norman: University of Oklahoma Press, 2018.

Maxwell, John Gary. *The Civil War Years in Utah: The King of God and the Territory That Did Not Fight*. Norman: University of Oklahoma Press, 2016.

McArthur, Lewis A., with Lewis L. McArthur. *Oregon Geographic Names*. Portland: Oregon Historical Society, 1981.

McBride, John R. "Annual Address." In *Transactions of the Twenty-Fifth Annual Reunion of the Oregon Pioneer Association for 1897*, 31–55. Portland: George H. Himes, 1898.

McCabe, James O. *The San Juan Water Boundary Question*. Toronto: University of Toronto Press, 1964.

McCall, John Marshall. "The First Oregon Cavalry and the Oregon Central Military Road Survey of 1865." Edited by L.C. Merriam Jr. *Oregon Historical Quarterly* 60, no. 1 (1959): 89–124.

McConaghy, Lorraine. "The Deplorable State of Our National Affairs: The Civil War in Washington Territory." *Journal of the West* 51, no. 3 (2012): 16–26.

———. *Free Boy: The True Story of Slavery and Mastery*. Seattle: University of Washington Press, 2015.

McCornack, Ellen Condon. *Thomas Condon, Pioneer Geologist of Oregon*. Eugene: University of Oregon Press, 1928.

McGinnis, Ralph Y., and Calvin N. Smith, eds. *Abraham Lincoln and the Western Territories*. Chicago: Nelson-Hall, 1994.

McLarney, Donald F. "The American Civil War in Victoria, Vancouver Island Colony." Paper presented at the Highline Community College, Des Moines WA, 1972.

McPherson, James. *For Cause and Comrades: Why Men Fought in the Civil War*. New York: Oxford University Press, 1997.

———. *Ordeal by Fire*. New York: McGraw Hill, 1982.

Merrill, Irving R., ed. *Bound for Idaho: The 1864 Trail Journal of Julius Merrill*. Moscow: University of Idaho Press, 1988.

———. "The Civil War in the West: The 1864 Trail Season." *Overland Journal* 9, no. 4 (1991): 15–27.

Michno, Gregory. *The Deadliest Indian War in the West: The Snake Conflict, 1864–1868*. Caldwell ID: Caxton Press, 2007.

Miller, Henry. "Letters from the Upper Columbia." *Idaho Yesterdays* 4, no. 1 (1960–61): 14–22.

Moomaw, Juliana P. "Oregon: Patrolling the New Northwest." *Journal of the West* 14, no. 1 (January 1974): 5–24.

Morrison, Perry D. "Columbia College, 1856–60." *Oregon Historical Quarterly* 56, no. 4 (1955): 326–51.

Mott, Marguerite. "Activities in the Northwest, 1848–1861, under the Direction of the United States War Department." Master's thesis, Washington University, 1932.

Murphy, Lawrence R. "The Enemy among Us: Venereal Disease among Union Soldiers in the Far West, 1861–1865." *Civil War History* 31, no. 3 (1985): 257–69.

Murray, Keith A. *The Pig War*. Tacoma: Washington State Historical Society, 1968.

——. "Pig War Letters: A Romantic Account of the San Juan Crisis." *Columbia* 1, no. 3 (1987): 11–20.

Nash, Lee. "Harvey Scott (1838–1910)." Oregon Encyclopedia. Accessed January 21, 2021. https://www.oregonencyclopedia.org/articles/scott_harvey_1838_1910_/ #.X7L5JshKg2w.

Nelson, Herbert, and Preston Onstad, eds. *A Webfoot Volunteer: The Diary of William M. Hilleary, 1864–1866*. Corvallis: Oregon State University Press, 1965.

Nelson, Kurt R. *Fighting for Paradise*. Yardley PA: Westholme, 2007.

Nicolay, Helen. *Sixty Years of the Literary Society*. Washington DC: Privately printed, 1934.

Noe, Kenneth W. *The Howling Storm: Weather, Climate, and the American Civil War*. Baton Rouge: Louisiana State University Press, 2020.

Nokes, R. Gregory. "Black Exclusion Laws in Oregon." Oregon Encyclopedia. Accessed February 28, 2021. https://www.oregonencyclopedia.org/articles/exclusion_laws/ #.X-rvtNhKg2w.

——. *Breaking Chains: Slavery on the Trail in the Oregon Territory*. Corvallis: Oregon State University Press, 2013.

——. "Peter Burnett." Oregon Encyclopedia. Accessed February 10, 2021. https:// www.oregonencyclopedia.org/articles/burnett_peter/#.ymhXvKhKg2z.

O'Gorman, J. Tim. "The Pig War." Master's thesis, University of Idaho, 1980.

Onstad, Preston E. "Camp Henderson." *Oregon Historical Quarterly* 65, no. 3 (1964): 297–302.

——. "Fort on the Luckiamute: A Resurvey of Fort Hoskins." *Oregon Historical Quarterly* 65, no. 2 (1964): 173–96.

Ord, Edward O. C. *Ord's Diary in Curry County, Oregon, 1856*. Wedderburn OR: 1970.

Pambrun, Andrew Dominique. *Sixty Years on the Frontier in the Pacific Northwest*. Fairfield WA: Ye Galleon, 1978.

Partridge, Charles Addison. *History of the Ninety-Sixty Regiment: Illinois Volunteer Infantry*. Chicago: Brown, Pettibone, 1887.

Payne, William Kenneth. "How Oregonians Learned about the Civil War: The War between the States as Reported in the Oregon Press, 1861–1865." Master's thesis, University of Oregon, 1963.

Perko, Richard. "A Forgotten Passage to Puget Sound: The Fort Steilacoom–Walla Walla Road." *Montana: The Magazine of Western History* 35, no. 1 (1985): 38–47.

Pickering, William. "Washington's War Governor." *Washington Historical Quarterly* 8, no. 2 (April 1917): 91–95.

Pomeroy, Earl. *The Pacific Slope: A History of California, Oregon, Washington, Idaho, Utah, and Nevada*. 1965. Reprint, Lincoln: University of Nebraska Press, 1991.

Potter, David M. *The Impending Crisis 1848–1861*. New York: Harper Torchbooks, 1993.

Powers, Dennis M. *Treasure Ship: The Legend and Legacy of the S.S. Brother Jonathan*. New York: Citadel Press, 2006.

Pratt, Harry E. "22 Letters of David Logan, Pioneer Oregon Lawyer." *Oregon Historical Quarterly* 44, no. 3 (1943): 253–85.

Prosch, Charles. *Reminiscences of Washington Territory*. Fairfield WA: Ye Galleon, 1969.

Prosch, Thomas W. "The Indian War in Washington Territory." *Oregon Historical Quarterly* 16, no. 1 (March 1915): 1–23.

——. "Oregon in 1863." *Oregon Historical Quarterly* 14, no. 1 (1913): 61–64.

——. "The United States Army in Washington Territory." *Washington Historical Quarterly* 2, no. 1 (October 1907): 28–32.

——. "Washington Territory Fifty Years Ago." *Washington Historical Quarterly* 4, no. 2 (April 1913): 96–104.

Prucha, Francis P. *American Indian Treaties*. Berkeley: University of California Press, 1994.

Rein, Christopher M. *The Second Colorado Cavalry: A Civil War Regiment on the Great Plains*. Norman: University of Oklahoma Press, 2020.

Richter, William L. *Historical Dictionary of the Civil War and Reconstruction*. Lanham MD: Scarecrow Press, 2011.

Rickey, Don, Jr. *Forty Miles a Day on Beans and Hay*. Norman: University of Oklahoma Press, 1983.

Rinehart, William Vance. "War in the Great Northwest." *Washington Historical Quarterly* 22, no. 2 (1931): 83–98.

Rowen, Richard D., ed. "The Second Nebraska's Campaign against the Sioux." *Nebraska History* 44, no. 1 (1963): 3–53.

Ruby, Robert H., and John A. Brown. *The Cayuse Indians: Imperial Tribesmen of Old Oregon*. Norman: University of Oklahoma Press, 1972.

——. *A Guide to the Indian Tribes of the Pacific Northwest*. Norman: University of Oklahoma Press, 1992.

Scherneckau, August. *Marching with the First Nebraska: A Civil War Diary*. Edited by James E. Potter and Edith Robbins. Norman: University of Oklahoma Press, 2007.

Schlicke, Carl P. *General George Wright: Guardian of the Pacific Coast*. Norman: University of Oklahoma Press, 1988.

——. "Massacre on the Oregon Trail in the Year 1860." *Columbia* 1, no. 1 (1987): 33–44.

Schwantes, Carlos Arnaldo. *The Pacific Northwest: An Interpretive History*. Lincoln: University of Nebraska Press, 1996.

——. *The Utter Disaster on the Oregon Trail: The Utter and Van Ornum Massacres of 1860*. Caldwell ID: Snake Country, 1993.

Sheridan, Philip H. *Personal Memoirs of P.H. Sheridan*. 2 vols. New York: Charles L. Webster, 1888.

Shuck, Oscar T. *History of the Bench and Bar of California.* Los Angeles: Commercial Printing House, 1901.

Smith, John E. "A Pioneer of the Spokane Country." *Washington Historical Quarterly* 7, no. 4 (October 1916): 267–77.

Stacey, C. P. *Canada and the British Army, 1846–1871.* Toronto: University of Toronto Press, 1963.

Stanke, Jerry. "Camp Lyon." *Idaho State Historical Reference Series,* July 16, 1965.

Stanley, George F. *Mapping the Frontier: Charles Wilson's Diary of the Survey of the 49th Parallel, 1858–1862, while Secretary of the British Boundary Commission.* Seattle: University of Washington Press, 1970.

State of Oregon. *Biennial Report of the Secretary of State of the State of Oregon to the Legislative Assembly, Nineteenth Regular Session.* Salem: W. H. Leeds, 1897.

———. *Journal of the Senate Proceedings of the Legislative Assembly of Oregon for the Fourth Regular Session, 1866.* Salem OR: W. A. McPherson, State Printer, 1866.

———. *Report of the Adjutant General of the State of Oregon, for the Years 1865–6.* Salem: Henry L. Pittock, 1866.

———. *Report of the Superintendent and Commissioners of the State of Oregon, Accompanied by Reports by Physicians and Chaplin's, Fifth Regular Session.* Salem: W. A. McPherson, 1868.

———. *Report of the Superintendent and Commissioners of the State Penitentiary of the State of Oregon, Fifty Regular Session, September 1868.* Salem OR: W. A. McPherson, State Printer, 1868.

Stearns, Orson A. "Fort Klamath and 'The Bread Riot': A Near Tragedy of Early Days." *Journal of the Shaw Historical Library* 3, no. 2 (1989): 1–9.

Stevens, Hazard. *The Life of Isaac Ingalls Stevens.* 2 vols. Boston: Houghton, Mifflin, 1900.

St. John, Rachel. "The Unpredictable America of William Gwin: Expansion, Secession, and the Unstable Borders of Nineteenth-Century North America." *Journal of the Civil War Era* 6, no. 1 (2016): 56–84.

Tamarac [pseud.]. "A Lost History: Experiences of Co. A, 2d Cal. Cav., Not Recorded Officially." *National Tribune,* March 26, 1896.

Tanasoca, Steven, and Susan Sudduth, eds. "A Journal Kept by George A. Harding." *Oregon Historical Quarterly* 79, no. 2 (Summer 1978): 172–202.

Tate, Michael L. *The Frontier Army in the Settlement of the West.* Norman: University of Oklahoma Press, 1999.

Thrapp, Dan L. *Encyclopedia of Frontier Biography.* 3 vols. Spokane WA: Arthur H. Clark, 1988–91.

Trafzer, Clifford E., and Richard D. Scheuerman. *Renegade Tribe: The Palouse Indians and the Invasion of the Inland Pacific Northwest.* Pullman: Washington State University Press, 1986.

Trimble, Will J. "A Soldier of the Oregon Frontier." *Oregon Historical Quarterly* 8, no. 1 (1907): 42–50.

Turnbull, George S. *History of Oregon Newspapers*. Portland: Binford & Mort, 1939.

U.S. Adjutant General's Office. *Compiled Service Records of Volunteer Union Soldiers Who Served in Organizations from the State of Oregon*. Microfilm, National Archives and Records Administration, Washington DC.

———. *Returns from U.S. Military Posts, 1800–1916*. Microfilm, National Archives and Records Administration, Washington DC.

U.S. Army. *Letters Received by the Office of the Adjutant General, 1861–1870*. M619. Microfilm, National Archives and Records Administration, Washington DC.

U.S. Census Office. *Compendium of the Tenth Census, June 1, 1880*. Washington DC, Government Printing Office, 1883–88.

U.S. Government. *Annual Report of the Office of Commissioner of Indian Affairs for the Year 1863*. Washington DC: Government Printing Office, 1863.

———. *Condition of the Indian Tribes: Report of the Joint Special Committee, Appointed under Joint Resolution of March 3, 1865; With an Appendix*. Millwood NY: Kraus Reprint, 1973.

———. *General Index to Pension Files, 1861–1934*. Ser. T288. Roll 107. Microfilm, National Archives and Records Administration, Washington DC.

———. *Historical Register of National Homes for Disabled Volunteer Soldiers, 1866–1938*. Ser. M1749. Microfilm, National Archives and Records Administration, Washington DC.

———. *Letters from the Secretary of War*, in *Executive Documents of the Senate of the United States Documents 50th Congress, Second Session*. Washington DC: Government Printing Office, 1890.

———. *Letters Received by the Commission Branch of the Adjutant General's Office*. Washington DC: National Archives and Records Administration, RG 94, roll 0185.

———. *Population of the United States in 1860: Compiled from the Original Returns of the Eighth Census Under the Direction of the Secretary of the Interior*. Washington DC: Government Printing Office, 1864.

———. *Preliminary Report on the Eighth Census, 1860*. Washington DC: Government Printing Office, 1862.

———. *Report of the Commissioner of Indian Affairs, Made to the Secretary of the Interior, for the Year 1869*. Washington DC: Office of the Commissioner of Indian Affairs, 1869.

U.S. War Department. *Returns from U.S. Military Posts, 1800–1916*; Microfilm Publication M617, 1550 rolls; roll 668. https://www.ancestry.com/search/collections/1571/.

———. *Revised United States Army Regulations of 1861 with an Appendix*. Washington DC: Government Printing Office, 1863.

U.S. War Office. *The War of the Rebellion: A Compilation of Official Records of the Union and Confederate Armies*, Ser. 1 and 3. Washington DC: Government Printing Office, 1897 and 1899.

Utley, Robert M. *Frontier Regulars: The United States Army and the Indian, 1860–1891*. New York: Macmillan, 1973.

———. *Frontiersmen in Blue: The United States Army and the Indian, 1848–1865*. New York: Macmillan, 1967.

———. *The Indian Frontier of the American West, 1846–1890*. Albuquerque: University of New Mexico Press, 1987.

Van Winkle, Roger A. "A Crisis in Obscurity: A Study of Pro-Southern Activities in Oregon, 1854–1865." Master's thesis, Western Washington University, 1968.

Victor, Francis Fuller. "The First Oregon Cavalry." *Oregon Historical Quarterly* 3, no. 1 (1902): 123–63.

Voegelin, Ermine Wheeler. "The Northern Paiute of Central Oregon: A Chapter in Treaty-Making, Part 1." *Ethnohistory* 2, no. 2 (1953): 95–132.

Vouri, Michael. *The Pig War: Standoff at Griffin Bay*. Friday Harbor WA: Griffin Bay Bookstore, 1999.

Walling, Albert G. *Illustrated History of Lane County*. Portland: A. G. Walling, 1884.

Ware, Eugene F. *The Indian War of 1864*. Lincoln: University of Nebraska Press, 1994.

Warner, Ezra J. *Generals in Blue: Lives of the Union Commanders*. Baton Rouge: Louisiana State University Press, 1964.

———. *Generals in Gray: Lives of the Confederate Commanders*. Baton Rouge: Louisiana State University Press, 1959.

Waymire, James A. "Annual Address." In *Transactions of the Twenty-Seventh Annual Reunion of the Oregon Pioneer Association for 1899*, 33–49. Portland: Himes and Pratt, 1900.

Wells, Edward Lansing. "Notes on the Winter of 1861–1862 in the Pacific Northwest." *Northwest Science* 21, no. 2 (1947): 2.

West, Elliot. *The Contested Plains: Indians, Goldseekers, and the Rush to Colorado*. Lawrence: University of Kansas Press, 1998.

Wetteman, Robert P., Jr. "A Virginia Soldier in the Frontier Army: The Letters of Sergeant John R. Whaley, Second U.S. Artillery, 1854–1859." *Military History of the West* 29, no. 1 (1999): 63–88.

Whitworth, George, F. "Retrospective of Half a Century." *Washington Historical Quarterly* 1, no. 4 (July 1907): 197–208.

Wiel, Samuel C. *Lincoln's Crisis in the Far West*. San Francisco: Privately printed, 1949.

Wight, Willard, ed. "Civil War Letters of John Young Lind." *Journal of the Presbyterian Historical Society* 39, no. 2 (1961): 76–87.

Williams, Jerold. "Point Lookout, the Natron Cut-Off, and the Changing Face of Lane County." *Oregon Historical Quarterly* 93, no. 4 (1992): 418–35.

Winans, W. P. "Fort Colville, 1859–1869." *Washington Historical Quarterly* 3, no. 1 (October 1908): 78–82.

Winks, Robin W. "The British North American West and the Civil War." *North Dakota History* 24, no. 3 (1957): 139–52.

———. *Canada and the United States: The Civil War Years*. Baltimore: Johns Hopkins University Press, 1960.

Woodward, Daniel H. "The Civil War of a Pennsylvania Trooper." *Pennsylvania Magazine of History and Biography* 87, no. 1 (1963): 39–62.

Woodward, Walter Carleton. *The Rise and Early History of Political Parties in Oregon, 1843–1868*. Portland: J. K. Gill, 1913.

Zanjani, Sally. *Sarah Winnemucca*. Lincoln: University of Nebraska Press, 2001.

INDEX

- - - - - - - - - -

Page numbers in italics refer to figures.

CPSIA information can be obtained
at www.ICGtesting.com
Printed in the USA
LVHW041549090523
746513LV00002B/87